Introduction to
THEATRE ARTS

VOLUME ONE / SECOND EDITION

TEACHER'S GUIDE

Suzi Zimmerman

MERIWETHER PUBLISHING
A division of Pioneer Drama Service, Inc.
Denver, Colorado

Meriwether Publishing
A division of Pioneer Drama Service, Inc.
PO Box 4267
Englewood, CO 80155

www.pioneerdrama.com

Editor: Debra Fendrich
Project Manager and Text design: Lori Conary
Cover design: Melissa Nethery

© Copyright 2020 Meriwether Publishing
Printed in the United States of America
Second Edition

ISBN 978-1-56608-263-1

"Though this be madness, yet there is method in't."
(Hamlet II. ii.)

SPECIAL THANKS
to those who took the time to share their thoughts about theatre education, their memories, their expertise, and their love of the arts. I appreciate each and every one of you! Thank you to Kailee Graves, Carissa Thompson, Tanya Glover, Samantha Mitchell, Alicia Hooper, Molly Grogan, Amanda Lynn, Will Johnson, Devin Dusek, Rosemary Frederickson, Meg Schramm, Patty Harrison, and Darin Baker.

A very special thank you to former colleague Greg Arp* for your modern and insightful additions to our technical theatre chapter. You are a force in theatre, and I am honored to have your assistance and your expertise!

And another huge thank you to former student Rachel DeRouen. You were a star when you were in seventh and eighth grades, and you continue to make me proud today. This is why I teach!

---

* Greg Arp is the Coordinator for Speech and Theatre for Plano ISD and the 2012 PISD Secondary Teacher of the Year. He serves as an adjudicator for the University Interscholastic Leagues One Act Play Contest.

A DOZEN YEARS AGO,
there was a student who always came to my room after the 3:30 bell to tell me goodbye. My room was at the end of a long hall, nowhere near the student exit. She went out of her way to visit every day, spreading her joy, ensuring her teachers had smiles at the end of each day.

She participated in every play and every special event. If a set piece needed to be constructed at home, she was always part of the team volunteering to do it. She was also extremely energetic and sometimes needed to be reminded that it was time to listen, not talk. But those times were rare, and she was quick to smile an apologetic, sweet smile. And it is that smile—tinged with a hint of mischievousness—that I will always remember.

Brenna lost her ten-year battle with cancer long before she was able to see all the shows and build all the props and smell all the wonderfully musty old theatres. But did she try! She was just 26 and had fought the disease her entire adult life, but despite it, she continued to live, explore, and shine.

While cleaning out some old keepsakes, I found a card from Brenna thanking me for being her teacher and director. It was signed, "I love you, Ms. Z." It reminded me of how she would say goodbye at the end of each long, difficult day. She was the little voice that continued to whisper, "This is why you teach. This is why nothing is ever impossible."

I love you, too, Brenna. Rest peacefully.

Ms. Z

PREFACE

I taught drama for years, but I was not like most ordinary drama teachers. Like my colleagues, I used exciting and energetic lessons, but I craved extreme organization, and I wanted to use handouts. My teachers from high school and college had a gift for being able to teach off the cuff, discussing theatre history or acting without ever using a worksheet. I was different. From the beginning, I kept saying to myself, "There has to be an easier way." I was a firm believer that the drama classroom must be fun, but I knew there had to be a standard for learning and evaluating. I searched the teacher supply stores for anything to help me find this balance, but there was very little for the secondary theatre arts teacher. I found myself spending hours preparing, trying to add order to my lessons, and trying to make my classes the best they could be.

After several years, I had the opportunity to share my accumulation of self-created curriculum with some colleagues, and they encouraged me to compile it into a workbook so that others could benefit. With about 300 individual documents to choose from, I found it difficult to narrow down the field. I remembered my first couple of years teaching middle school. I recalled how most of the middle school drama teachers in my area were actually English teachers or others who taught drama because the certified drama teachers were at the high schools. The textbooks we were given were really for high school students—probably hand-me-downs. The requirements of the class were a mixture of drama and speech, but there was a tendency toward social skills and problem-solving, too.

The students had a hard time handling the lack of structure. Fresh out of elementary schools, they were still used to sitting in desks, completing handouts with cute pictures. When given time to work on scenes, many would drift into mischievous groups, and soon there would be a recess-like chaos. I had to become very creative and organized in order to keep my classes running smoothly.

Little changed when I started teaching high school. This age group knew that they needed so many credits to graduate, and my class—to some—was just another credit. I had non-readers mixed in with gifted students, and because my class was an elective (and very fun), the number of students far exceeded the number of desks. Rather than kicking out kids, we kicked out the desks—and magic began. I soon learned that minor changes had terrific impact, and that just because something "had always been" did not mean it was right. Suddenly, I had a book to write!

Hopefully, the book you hold before you will be a guide, not an end-all resource. For beginning teachers, it may be a daily tool used to introduce their own curiosity-building lessons. For the experienced teacher, it may be a way to prime students for the tried-and-true instruction to come. Look at each activity, but only use those that you feel will help you to teach to the best of your ability.

Furthermore, this is by no means the last word. Every vibrant teacher has their own ideas. Ideas are too wonderful to let hibernate. Please share them with me so that I may share them with others.

Years after my hesitant beginnings as a teacher, my former students are making their marks onstage, in film, on television. One sixth-grade actor was so special that I told my mother to watch out for her. "Someday she will be famous." And she is! She is two-time Grammy winner, singer, and occasional actor Leanne Rimes. Another student just landed a national commercial for Toyota. And many others have found their success behind the scenes, as writers, directors, costumers, makeup artists, and the whole spectrum. There are those who, like me, make their major paychecks doing something steady, but they are still tip-toeing through the world of film, stage, and TV. And, of course, there are those who never went into theatre but who tell me they still use the skills they learned in my class as a vital part of their careers.

My favorite success story is my own son, Nicholas Zimmerman, who is working his way up the corporate ladder at a prestigious Hollywood film finishing house. He got his start when he was recruited to be a walk-on while at one of my rehearsals, and he's been creating film ever since. Today, nineteen years later, he's a Hollywood producer at a prestigious finishing house and mentors young film students on their career options.

CONTENTS

SECTION 3 – PRODUCTION TOOLS

SECTION 4 – TESTS AND MAJOR PROJECTS

STUDENT WORKBOOK
with Additional Notes for Teachers in bold

CHAPTER 1 – GETTING STARTED

CHAPTER 2 – EVALUATION

CHAPTER 3 – SCENE WORK

CHAPTER 4 – ACTING

CHAPTER 5 – CHARACTERIZATION

CHAPTER 6 – PUBLICITY AND OTHER PRODUCTION BUSINESS

CHAPTER 7 – PLAY PRODUCTION

CHAPTER 8 – THEATRE HISTORY

CHAPTER 9 – GAMES AND IMPROVISATION

CHAPTER 10 – PLANNING FOR THE FUTURE

SECTION 1
TEACHER TOOLS

HOW TO USE THIS BOOK

GETTING ORGANIZED

Preparing Your Lessons

Practicing Good Time Management

Preparing for a Substitute

    Theatre Arts Lesson Plan

    Weekly Calendar

    Substitute Survival Guide

    Substitute Schedule

Designing the Ideal Drama Classroom

CREATING STRUCTURE FOR YOUR CLASS

Using Bell Work and Theatre Journals

Applying Class Policies

Developing Policies on Makeup Work and Extra Credit

Using a Point System

    Rehearsal and Performance Expectations

    Extra Credit Policy and Request

    The Point System

    Point Graph

    Points Tally

THE DRAMA PROGRAM

Recruiting for Your Drama Program

Keeping Your Program Visible

Building a Parent Booster Club

Publicizing Your Shows

Avoiding Burnout

Planning the Drama Banquet

Using Awards

    Banquet Details

    Banquet Committee Responsibilities

    Awards Ballot

    Certificates of Excellence

Starting a Drama Club

Fundraising

HOW TO USE THIS BOOK

Your students have a workbook very similar to this one, except that theirs is in a three-ring binder so they can turn in individual pages, then put them back in place once you've graded them.

The other difference is that this Teacher's Guide has additional material intended for your eyes only, such as suggestions about developing your drama program, tests, instructional aids, and worksheet answers. These additional materials are located in the front of your book in Sections 1-4.

The second half of this Teacher's Guide has all the pages from the Student Workbook supplemented with notes to the teacher. In these pages, you will find helpful hints and additional activities, suggestions for using activities in your lessons, discussion starters, scenarios, keys for all worksheets, tests, and more.

Actually, your students do have some of the forms from your "teachers only" sections. These are mainly performance and activity evaluation forms so that your students will know exactly what your expectations are for them.

There are plenty of pages in Sections 1-4 of this Teacher's Guide that are designed to distribute to your students, such as the evaluations and the award certificates. These pages clearly state that you have permission to reproduce them. However, you may not copy any Student Workbook pages, either from this Teacher's Guide or from a copy of the Student Workbook. That would constitute copyright infringement, which is both against the law and an extremely poor example to set for your students.

GETTING ORGANIZED

This book is easy to use, but the trick to being a great drama teacher involves so much more than just having a good text. I hope you take a few minutes to read through this section before diving into the curriculum material in the rest of the book.

PREPARING YOUR LESSONS

You must get your students out of their seats and onto their feet. Prepare your lessons in advance, and try to keep students busy at all times. Format your classes so that each one follows a simple but effective pattern:

- First, start with a sponge activity such as bell work or a journal entry. This gets your students' minds focused on your lesson. It also keeps them quiet and still long enough for you to take attendance, pass out papers, and any other administrative tasks that do not require their attention. How much valuable class time is wasted each year while students watch their teachers do things that do not involve them?

- Next, present your lesson either by lecture, reading, demonstration, presentation, or by engaging your students in discussion. Limit this to only a small part of your class time when possible. Like art, music, dance, choir, and other arts, drama is only 15 to 25 percent theory. The rest is application, which means students must be applying the lesson in some sort of skill test each day.

- Once the material is presented, test students' understanding by having a demonstration and discussion or assigning a short, monitored, practice session.

- Evaluate their understanding and re-teach when necessary. Re-teaching may include presenting the lesson over again, stating it a new way, or assigning student mentors to assist those who have not yet grasped the skill or idea.

- Assign an activity for practice (a performance, test, or project) to further assess understanding but also to reinforce the learning. Specifically state the standards by which students will be graded.

- Make final evaluations of the students' understanding of the lesson.

- Assign homework or another activity to connect the current lesson to the next.

The following lesson plan for teaching the lesson on *The Actor's Voice* from Chapter 4 will help you to understand how to apply the above lesson cycle.

Use the *Theatre Arts Lesson Plan* to organize your unique lessons. Many schools require plans to be turned in weekly, and some even require teachers to use their particular format. Regardless of the format and frequency, it is very important to plan ahead, even if your school is one of the few that does not require lesson plans. Lesson plans are like road maps; it is easy to get lost in a lesson without one. The syllabus included in Chapter 1 will help to get you started.

Make several copies of the *Theatre Arts Lesson Plan* before you begin. The two columns to the right can be used for making notes about the success of a lesson or to differentiate between Drama I and Drama II.

You can also use them to keep up with different classes' progress, or if you find you do not need them, omit the columns altogether.

Sample lesson plan:

Date: 9/13	Bell Work: #7 Write a tongue twister using the first letter of your name.	Drama 1 ✓	Drama 2 ✓
Objective:	Today students will... learn about the actor's voice including vocabulary and basic speech skills		
Lesson:	*The Actor's Voice*, tongue twisters, 1-3 of *Articulation Activities*	✓	✓
Activity:	Voiced/Unvoiced table on page 90. Each student must present one tongue twister perfectly from page 93 either alone or in a group (3 students maximum); group will be given 15 minutes practice time. Must be memorized, clear, audible, and delivered with confidence. Extra points given for creativity.	✓	Did not finish with 2nd or 4th periods.
Assessment:	Presentation using *Evaluation I* form.	✓	"
Homework:	Complete the final exercise of the *Articulation Activities* for homework.	7th grade	✓

Rather than dating the lesson plan, use week numbers such as "week 1" and "week 2." This will allow you to recycle plans each year. If you are on block scheduling (classes every other day), one plan will cover two weeks.

PRACTICING GOOD TIME MANAGEMENT

Practice and demonstrate good time management. The calendar provided in this section is a blank *Weekly Calendar*. Make enough copies for the year and hole-punch them. You can keep them with your lesson plans or in your grade book. There is also a yearly calendar located at the back of the book.

Middle school and high school students have busy schedules, especially if they are involved in extracurricular activities such as drama. It can become overwhelming, but by keeping a planner and making a habit of using it daily, a busy life becomes more manageable. The same goes for the busy teacher. If you have ever missed a meeting or forgotten an assembly, you know how stressful and complex the rest of the day can become. We take for granted that our students know how to practice time management, but many do not. Become a good planner yourself, then show your students how you do it.

PREPARING FOR A SUBSTITUTE

One of the most challenging obstacles you'll face as a drama teacher is getting a substitute to take your place during absences, especially if they are unplanned. Substitutes have a tough job. Students are notorious for taking advantage of them. Consequently, these "filler teachers" like quiet rooms where they can take roll, assign class work, and keep students in control.

Having substituted for a drama teacher one day, a sub left her teacher a note saying, "I tried to get the kids to work on their scenes, but they wouldn't be quiet. They kept moving around and talking. I've subbed for years. This is the worst class I have ever been in. Please do not request me again!" When the teacher spoke with the sub, she was told she had been in hundreds of classrooms but never had she seen one in which the students were so rowdy. Upon questioning the sub further, the teacher learned that the retired librarian wanted an orderly room, and despite the regular teacher's instructions, she insisted that the students "whisper" their scenes to one another while staying in their seats.

The *Substitute Survival Guide* might help you avoid a similar situation. Think about your lessons carefully before leaving them with a sub. Remember, they probably will have neither your training nor tolerance. Your absence might be a good time to leave a quiet assignment or a movie. However, do not lose the opportunity to make it a learning experience! Include the *Movie and Play Evaluation*, or assign a script to read and include the *Script Report*. Both can be found in Section 2.

Leave an emergency substitute plan for those days when you do not have the convenience of planning your absence. Include generic plans that you do not intend to use in class (a movie star crossword puzzle or a simple art project) and all necessary copies and supplies. Put everything in a box and write "Emergency Substitute Plan" in large letters on it. When you call for your substitute, you can let them know where to find the plan.

THEATRE ARTS LESSON PLAN

CLASS/PERIOD:_____ WEEK(S) OF: _____

Date:	Bell Work:
Objective:	Students will...
Lesson:	
Activity:	
Assessment:	
Homework:	

Date:	Bell Work:
Objective:	Students will...
Lesson:	
Activity:	
Assessment:	
Homework:	

Date:	Bell Work:
Objective:	Students will...
Lesson:	
Activity:	
Assessment:	
Homework:	

Date:	Bell Work:
Objective:	Students will...
Lesson:	
Activity:	
Assessment:	
Homework:	

Date:	Bell Work:
Objective:	Students will...
Lesson:	
Activity:	
Assessment:	
Homework:	

WEEKLY CALENDAR

Week of:	AM	√	PM	√
Monday / / Remember:				
Tuesday / / Remember:				
Wednesday / / Remember:				
Thursday / / Remember:				
Friday / / Remember:				
Saturday / / Remember:				
Sunday / / Remember:				

SUBSTITUTE SURVIVAL GUIDE

Date: _____ Teacher's Name: _____ Room#_____

RULES:

GENERAL INFORMATION

Duties:

Teacher restrooms:

Refreshments:

Security:

Assistance:

PROCEDURES

If a student is tardy:

If a student is absent:

If a student is not working:

If a student is ill or if there is an emergency:

SUBSTITUTE SCHEDULE

PERIOD	TIMES	CLASS	ASSIGNMENT	NOTES

DESIGNING THE IDEAL DRAMA CLASSROOM

The ideal drama classroom allows the teacher and students to explore the world of theatre fully without concern that noise, lighting, and movement will bother any surrounding classes. Many theatre teachers have rooms alongside English and math teachers, which forces them to conform to the environment of the core curriculum classroom—one of quiet and structure. In these areas of the school, the rooms have plenty of desks and fluorescent lighting, a teacher's desk, a window allowing passersby to peer in, constant announcement interruptions, and more. For teachers who intend to teach theatre "theory" with few or no performances, this classroom will work just fine. However, for the hands-on teacher who hopes to lead by example and allow students the victory of self-discovery, and who will guide their students to a multi-sensory, full-energy theatrical experience, there is a better design.

Because our intent is to teach about the stage and to allow students to express themselves in front of others with confidence, it is important that the classroom have some type of performance area. A raised wooden platform, some portable lights and curtains, and a simple sound system can turn any room into a performance area. If these items are out of the question, use masking tape to block off an area resembling the floor plan of a stage on your classroom floor.

Chairs are stackable and mobile, and unlike desks, they can be rearranged with little difficulty. Omit desks from your classroom and invest in clipboards instead. This way, you will have the freedom to have any size and type of performance space, and your students can sit in small groups or in a large circle.

If at all possible, request a classroom in the area of the school nearest the band and choir. These rooms are usually more private, remote, and have extra soundproofing, as well as likely being close to the auditorium.

Ask your maintenance crew to install an on/off switch for your announcements so that they can be turned off on performance days. Another option is to replace the speaker with a light. When the light blinks, you know the office is trying to reach you. A final option is to teach students to freeze or stop in a neutral stance if interrupted by announcements and then to continue without missing a beat as soon as the interruption is over. This last one actually has great real-life applications, teaching students to be prepared and flexible.

Storage is very important, as is security. Props, costumes, and set pieces require plenty of cabinets and shelves, preferably with locks.

Keep the posters and decorations to a minimum, especially if your classroom doubles as a performance area. Decorate your scene shop, office, and practice rooms instead.

Ideally, you should have quick and easy access to your thermostat. The lights used in theatre are extremely hot. They will instantly begin raising the temperature in your classroom, and if it is not well-ventilated, the heat may ignite dust, curtains, or other flammable material. Even if fire is not a danger, the comfort of your audience and students is important.

If you teach technical theatre, you will need a shop or an area for building sets. If possible, invest in a shop sink (a large tub-like basin and faucet) for washing up after painting. Because of safety concerns, you may want to hire a theatre consultant to assist you in setting up your shop, purchasing the right tools, and so on.

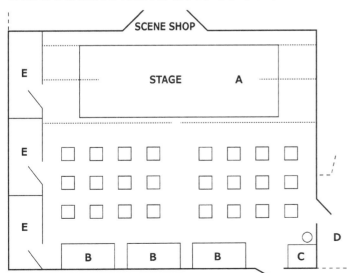

The ideal drama classroom would have a stage (A) made of movable sections that could be rearranged for a variety of sizes and performance styles. Mobile curtains on steel frames (dotted lines) are optional. Tables (B) could be a study area or could hold computers. The teacher would have a station (C) near the door and her office (D) for taking roll and watching performances. Students rehearse in quiet practice rooms (E) with windows or cameras. A scene shop located near the stage would allow for scenery storage, too.

CREATING STRUCTURE FOR YOUR CLASS

Even though students expect your class to be more fun and participatory than their core classes, you still need a structure to keep control and maintain good classroom management.

USING BELL WORK AND THEATRE JOURNALS

Many theatre teachers use a writing prompt as bell work during the first five minutes of the period so they have time to take roll and get ready for the lesson.

- Requiring this time to be absolutely quiet sets a calm tone for the upcoming class. You may even choose to play soothing music in the background.

- Plan each day's bell work when creating your lesson plans. If you tie the bell work to the day's lesson, the students' minds will be focused on the subject, which will make learning easier and will create more of an impact.

- Post what the bell work is each day on your bulletin board or classroom door. When students are absent, they can check to see what they missed, or students who know they will be absent can complete the assignment as homework.

- Grade bell work often and make comments in the margins. Students will be encouraged to write more if they feel that their hard work is being appreciated.

- If your class seems really affected by a particular bell work prompt, do not be afraid to redirect your lesson to accommodate their desire to learn and explore. For example, if they become absorbed in an activity that requires them to write a monologue, then they are probably ready for more. Consider assigning a monologue-writing activity for the day or keep it in mind for the near future.

- Use bell work journal prompts later as essay questions on tests and quizzes or as prompts for extra credit essays. You can grade these on insightfulness, imagination, and creativity, as well as including valuable information from class discussions.

- Teachers can call on students at random to discuss their bell work responses. This will encourage each one to complete the activity, enhance their understanding of a subject, and pave the way for the lesson to come. You may want to encourage discussion by giving one or two bonus points to each student who shares their response.

- Come up with your own unique questions that may be more applicable to your particular group of students or lessons than those included with this book. Spaces are provided for your ideas. Encourage students to come up with their own insightful ideas. Offer extra credit or other incentives for great ideas and record them in your book for years to come. Always remember to give students credit for their ideas even if they are no longer in your class, such as: "This question comes from Rainy, a sophomore student in my Spring 2020 Theatre II class. She asks..." That recognition will inspire future efforts from your present group.

Journals are a wonderful tool in your classroom for writing exercises beyond bell work. Have students write their thoughts about particular activities, scene work, or notes from the day's lessons. As a homework assignment, sometimes teachers tell students what the writing subject is, and other times they simply tell the students to write what they feel.

Journals are generally inspired by the lesson but can also help with an unexpected situation. For example, if you have a visitor who needs to speak with you right away but you are in the middle of explaining about the poster design project, then tell the class to begin designing a rough draft of their poster in their journals while you attend to your visitor. This gives them a quiet activity, allowing you a moment to do business. Then return to the journal as a point of return to the lesson. This will give it importance and students will see the need to complete it. Grade journals weekly or biweekly. Make notes to yourself about what you assigned each day in each class.

APPLYING CLASS POLICIES

The following pages are posters. Your students also have a poster with similar wording for both rehearsals and performances combined in their handbooks. You may wish to print several copies on colored paper and laminate them. Hang them in prominent places throughout your classroom and in your practice rooms. With the last performance expectation, "No one should enter or leave the classroom during a performance," teach this to students AND to adults who are not in your classes. It is very appropriate to place a sign on your door explaining that guests may enter but should stop and be as quiet as possible if a performance is in progress. If they can hear that a performance is in progress prior to entering, ask them to wait for the applause or teacher's voice before opening the door.

Some additional rehearsal and performance ideas are:

- If students use clipboards, have them tie a pencil onto a string and attach it to their clipboard so that they always have it.

- If students are writing out their scripts, have them make a second copy for you. Keep this on file in your office for days when they forget

AN ACTIVITY TO TEACH ABOUT DISTRACTIONS

Load a tray with about twenty small items, such as a key ring, paper clip, photograph, and so on. Tell your students you have a prize for anyone who can later recall all of the items from memory. Present the tray and give them thirty seconds to see everything without touching it. Remove the tray and give them one minute to get out their writing supplies. Warn them that their time is about to start and that they must have their supplies out before then. Start the time and tell them to begin.

While they are trying to concentrate, distract them by unwrapping candy, digging in your bag, coughing, checking your phone, smiling suspiciously at them, yawning loudly, and more. In other words, do things that they might realistically do without thinking during performances. Get up and leave and re-enter loudly. Act as though you are unaware of your distractions.

At the end of the three minutes, check their accuracy. Discuss what role the distractions may have played in the outcome. How might this relate to performances? Is it fair to those trying to focus? Is it fair to the audience? What kind of support is most appropriate for performances?

theirs. You may wish to apply a small penalty for chronic cases.

- Never allow students to use criticism that is inappropriately phrased. For example, if you hear a student say, "That's stupid," find a more positive way to phrase the comment while still allowing the student their opinion.

DEVELOPING POLICIES ON MAKEUP WORK AND EXTRA CREDIT

Do you have a student who has missed a lot of school? Perhaps they came into your class at mid-semester and getting fully caught up seems impossible. Or perhaps some unexpected illness or emergency kept them from school. Rather than urging this student to do all of the work they missed, negotiate. For each two grades missed, have them make up one assignment. Perhaps an essay can encompass many assignments, or consider giving credit for attending a theatre production at another school or in the community. Remember that students experience stress like adults, and if a student has missed work in your class, imagine the impending assignments in all of their classes combined.

Now consider this incident: Connor is a hardworking senior with a good GPA, which will

allow him to go to most any college he chooses. Your class will assist him with his speaking skills, another important step in reaching his goals of being a lawyer. On the day students choose partners for duets, he is out with the flu. He returns to school, and Caden, who was also out, is his only choice; he is smart but does not try. Connor becomes very frustrated when, on the first day of performances, his partner still has not memorized his lines. Neither can get through the scene, but you know that the fault does not lie with both of them. What do you do?

Is this a circumstance for extra credit? Sometimes the situation is not within the student's control and other times it is. What is your policy? I generally reserve extra credit for students who have completed all of their required class work but wish to improve their averages. It may also be used as makeup work for group activities a student has missed due to a legitimate absence. I do not like to use extra credit as a way for students to make up for poor effort. In any case, I strongly advice that you require each student to request permission to complete extra credit using the *Extra Credit Policy and Request* form prior to doing the assignment. It will be up to you whether or not to grant the request.

USING A POINT SYSTEM

There are some wonderful societies that students can join that will assist them in furthering their theatrical involvements. If your school does not participate in any of these, you can still incorporate these groups' ideas into your program. For example, the International Thespian Society rewards points each time a student participates in theatre. After so many points, they are invited to become members, and as they continue to accumulate points, they are promoted in rank. You can use a similar point system with your classes or your club. Reward students for getting involved, even on a small level. More importantly, reinforce the importance of academics. Points are awarded for auditioning whether the student is cast or not, for participating in crews, for all roles, for attending club meetings and live performances, for holding an office, and for grades and attendance in their other classes as well as in yours.

Use a point system to encourage participation and achievement. Chart points to identify student progress. It is very simple and can be tied to a variety of incentives. The point system supplied in this book uses stars to identify rank. A student with ten points is awarded a star on the *Points Graph*. Twenty points equals two stars, thirty equals three stars, and so on. Points can also be deducted for negative behavior, missing required meetings or rehearsals, and so on.

Use these ideas for rewarding students for achievements under the point system:

- Use the *Points Graph* to indicate progress where everyone can see it. You can use star stickers, color in the line, or draw a simple star in each space. The *Points Tally* chart can also be used to track progress by week or by club meeting.

- Purchase star pins and reward students with one for each twenty-five or fifty points. They can wear these on their jackets, backpacks, or club shirts.

- Recognize point achievements regularly.

- You may want to award certificates, small trophies, plaques, and even gift certificates for higher point achievements.

- Make announcements over your school's public address system congratulating promotions. Make small posters to place around your classroom.

- Tally points often, and make students responsible for returning forms.

- Requiring a parent's signature on *The Point System* form makes accountability easier on you.

- Consider awarding two free show tickets to each student who achieves a certain rank. They can pass these on to friends or family if they can't use them.

- Proudly display a Wall of Fame for those with the five or six highest accumulated points, and then elevate each year's top points to a more permanent status—similar to the Hollywood Walk of Fame. Consider giving those students two free tickets to each show for "eternity" (for as long as they like or as long as you are around to ensure it).

- Create other point earning events such as fundraisers, gathering props, and planning events. Be creative!

Unlike the *Points Graph*, which is used to visually track each student's progress, the *Points Tally* allows the teacher or a club officer to calculate points weekly or at each meeting. This is the official record. It may be a wise idea to keep each student's signed request on file in a large notebook with the tally sheet as the cover page. Points can be added to the tally each time (note that the columns are for dates) and then filed alphabetically within the notebook. Afterward, the totals can be added to the *Points Graph*.

Point systems work best within clubs where students have a personal stake in the final product, but they can work well in classes, too.

REHEARSAL EXPECTATIONS

Bring your script and a pencil every day.

•

Stay on task.

•

Work only in your group unless
otherwise instructed.

•

Keep criticism respectful and constructive.

PERFORMANCE EXPECTATIONS

Be quiet and still.

•

Have supplies ready in advance.

•

Do not try to distract performers.

•

Be supportive before, during,
and after performances.

•

Keep criticism constructive and offer
it only when appropriate.

•

No one should enter or leave the
classroom during a performance.

EXTRA CREDIT POLICY AND REQUEST

Extra credit is generally reserved for students who have completed all of their required class work but wish to improve their averages. It may also be used as make-up work for group activities a student has missed due to a legitimate absence. In any case, you must request permission to complete extra credit prior to doing the assignment. The teacher will inform you as to whether or not your request is granted.

Name:_____ Today's Date:_____

Reason for request:

Was an assignment missed? _____ If so, what was it? _____

To your knowledge, have you completed all other assignments in this class?

_____

Have you already completed extra credit during this grading period?

_____

Describe in detail the assignment you wish to complete:

_____   _____
Student Signature   Parent Signature/Phone

Do not write below this line

_____ Permission Denied
_____ Permission Granted
_____ Permission Granted after missing assignments are completed

Missing assignments:

If granted, extra credit due no later than_____. *This form must be attached.*

THE POINT SYSTEM

You can earn points by being involved in shows at school, at a community theatre, or through your church or temple. If you have several jobs in a show, you can get points for one acting job and one tech job. Circle the points you would like added to your total. Provide a copy of your report card when applicable and proof of attendance or participation for events taking place outside of school. Include show titles and dates in the "Comments" section.

ACTING (PER SHOW)

Auditioning for any part	1
Walk-on or non-speaking part	2
Supporting role, chorus, dancer	4
Lead role	5
Volunteer for a show	2

TECHNICAL (PER SHOW)

Crew chief	5
Crew member	4
Volunteer for a show	2

ATTENDANCE

Each meeting attended	1
Each club event attended	1

OTHER

Contest participant	4
Attending live performances	2

OFFICERS (PER YEAR)*

President	20
Vice president	15
Secretary	15
Treasurer	15
Committee chair	10
Committee member	5

REPORT CARD (PER CARD)

All A's	10
All B's	7
Passed all classes	3
Perfect attendance	5
TOTAL	

COMMENTS:

Officers will be awarded "office" points at the last meeting of the year. A point will be subtracted for each meeting missed. Points should never be requested before the end of a show or other event.

_____
Name

_____
Today's Date

_____
Student Signature

_____
Parent Signature

POINT GRAPH

NAMES	10	20	30	40	50	60	70	80	90	100

POINTS TALLY

DATES

NAMES										

Permission to photocopy this page granted with purchase of book. Non-transferable.

17

THE DRAMA PROGRAM

Ideally, the drama program at your school consists of both classes and productions, and possibly even a drama club or Thespian troupe. If you are not there yet, hopefully you are working towards this goal. Even if you don't have all three components, the thoughts and ideas shared in this section should help give you some ideas on how to expand or develop your drama program. Let's start by assessing what you already have:

- List all of the classes taught in your drama department.

- Name the teachers in the drama department.

- List all shows and events your department will produce this year.

- What performance facilities do you use?

- Where do you take your students in the course of a typical school year?

- What outreach do you promote (scholarships, drives, contests, volunteerism)?

- How are your past students using what they learned in your program to advance their educations or careers?

No doubt the first three prompts above were easy to fill out, but how about the rest? All of these things— and probably a whole lot more—make up your program. If you had a hard time answering any of these questions, then your program probably has some room for growth or, at least, exploration and clarification. To understand the scope of a strong school program, think of one you consider successful—the athletic program, for example. How does your drama program compare? You may think this is not a fair comparison because of the difference in funding and community support. Is that really the reason your program is not more successful, or is that the excuse you use to not build a stronger program?

Long before there was organized football, drama was busy making its mark in the world. But the journey has never been an easy one. There were times when theatre was banned and actors were outcasts. Luckily, persistent lovers of the art through the ages have refused to let it die, but it always takes hard work and passion.

To have a dynamic drama program, throughout the year you need to show your students, the school, and the community that theatre is exciting, rewarding, and vital. Many of these ideas are embellished upon later in this section.

- Take advantage of technology and social media. Create videos of student performances to post on YouTube, Facebook, or any of the platforms popular among your students. (When posting students' work or images, consider their privacy as well as your district's rules. Always keep in mind parents' wishes, as well.)

- Create a buzz by rewarding students who are active within the department. Give trophies, hold banquets in their honor, and offer scholarships. In some schools, you can even letter in theatre, so you might explore this option with your principal.

- Make your program the most inclusive one in the school, with opportunities for students who are not actors. All should feel welcome, because the arts need writers, managers, technical minds, networkers, set builders, and so on. Even those with behavioral problems or physical limitations can find a niche in theatre!

- Advertise your program by hanging posters, making announcements, submitting press

Encore!

Central High School Drama

Staging Excellence

An example of a poster advertising a high school drama program. The same art could be used on club shirts, bumper stickers, yard art, and flyers.

releases, wearing club shirts, and inviting notable guest speakers. There are plenty of other ways, as well, to let people know your program exists and to increase their interest in it.

- Purchase a trophy case or adopt one within the school. Use this to display student work, costumes, and trophies, perhaps updated once a month by a student committee. Remember, trophy cases are not just for trophies! Display student work, such as costume designs and pieces, models of set designs, programs, photos, etc.

- Create a scrapbook for each year, or maybe even for each show. A student committee, a booster group, or a drama club may be able to help. With modern technology, there are numerous ways that you can make a scrapbook available to parents, visitors, or administrators.

  ◊ Make actual scrapbooks to have available in your class or displayed in the lobby at your productions.

  ◊ Set up a laptop with a projector to show rotating photos of rehearsals and past productions. Maybe have this available in the counseling office or at back-to-school night or any other occasion where advertising your program would be appropriate.

  ◊ Keep a chronology of your production on a Facebook page, making sure to follow your schools privacy and internet usage policies.

- Host functions and events beyond plays, such as talent shows, fashion shows, and competitions. Not only will you be advertising your department, but you can also turn many of these events into fantastic fundraisers.

- Recruit younger students. One way is to hold auditions. Another is to provide incentives to older students when they bring younger ones to drama club meetings. Consider small-denomination gift cards, club gear, snacks, or the like as rewards. Older students make up your program's leadership; younger ones are the future and keep your program dynamic!

- Start a grandparents' club, where grandmas and grandpas can volunteer to run lines with students, make costumes, build set pieces. Or start a multi-generational book club, except that they read scripts instead of books. If any of your students have reading challenges—perhaps to the point that they are afraid to audition—a book club will generate volunteers to help instill confidence in your reading-challenged actors.

Note from the author: When I started teaching at Terrell High School, there was a well-established drama club. They were eager to meet the new teacher, and we hit it off from the start. They began the meeting by telling me that they wanted to replace the lights and the sound system in the auditorium.

They called the lighting system the Elephant. It was a huge piece of grey machinery with three giant switches. The handles to the switches, which required both hands and 180 degrees of clearance to maneuver, had broken off years earlier, and maintenance had replaced them with broomsticks. There was a note on the unit warning users about sparks and to keep the curtains away from the device.

The sound system was not a sound system at all. It was a speaker that didn't work. The only way to use the speaker was to have an interface, which the students said had never existed in their years at the school. When there was an assembly in the 1,000-seat auditorium, the vice principal brought in a hand-held speaker and attached a microphone to it.

At our first meeting, we planned to raise funds to replace the Elephant first and then to purchase a new sound system. As a club, we worked with the school board to win grants and secure funding, and we completed several fundraisers. The Elephant was retired and replaced by the holidays that first year. The school board was surprised and a bit appalled that a relic of the 1950s, which had been labeled a sparking hazard, was still in use. And, by the end of my second year, we purchased a portable sound system so that we could perform in our auditorium or anywhere we wanted.

I left Terrell after three years to teach at a school closer to my new home. The year I left, the school board voted to build a new, state-of-the-art auditorium. I always felt like my students' success and leadership brought attention to the stage and to performing arts, a program that had previously coasted along with outdated and dangerous (or missing) equipment.

Don't be afraid to set lofty goals and to ask your school's leadership for the things that will take your drama program to the next level!

- Develop a booster club made up of the parents of your students who are in productions. Besides helping with fundraising, these boosters are great worker bees who can create show programs, buy and sell concessions, make the scrapbook, plan the banquet, and do so much more. In many cases, parents can get things done within the infrastructure of the school that you cannot.

- Conduct fundraisers to buy equipment that is missing or outdated. Write a proposal requesting matching funds from your district, or write a grant seeking contributions from large companies or foundations within your community. Ask if your district employs a full-time grant writer. Even if they cannot write yours, you may be able to glean valuable information and insight.

- Hold a contest for monologue writing or some other skill. Host a competition and invite other schools to join in. Or take your students to compete in a contest held at a different school. Be sure to publicize the winning results!

- Host a multicultural assembly and invite groups to sing, dance, read poetry, or even do a fashion show. Multicultural events are a wonderful way to diversify your department.

- Find short plays with a lot of characters and produce a show in each class. Hold a night of one-act plays and produce each one back-to-back. This sounds like a lot of work, but if students learn to do each part of the show on their own, including house management, technical work, trouble-shooting, and so on, you will be simply an observer. Charge a small admission to cover the royalty fees, and combine it with a canned food drive to stock the local food bank.

- Produce a dinner theatre murder mystery in the community. People love these, and there are plenty of shows with audience participation to add to the fun. Dinner (or dessert) theatre gives you far more outreach than standard productions and is also a wonderful fundraiser!

RECRUITING FOR YOUR DRAMA PROGRAM

Many consider quantity much less important than quality. You can imagine a teacher saying, "I would rather have two good kids who really want to act than thirty who just want the credit." In an ideal world, that would be a great philosophy. Who wouldn't rather have a small group of focused students? However, in nine out of ten schools, a class will not make it if it does not meet a minimum enrollment. Furthermore, even strong programs will be cut if they are not involving enough students to make them of value to the administration. And larger programs garner larger budgets. In other words, quantity is also important.

> **Recruit students who <u>want</u> to sign up for your class.**
>
> **There will then be less room for students who are enrolled in theatre just because you have an opening and they need a credit.**

The challenge for your drama program is that you really need to be think ahead to recruit in the spring for the next school year. Look at your existing department. How many students do you have in your drama classes? How many teachers? Do you like the ratio or is there room for growth? If you have room to add more students, where will you get them?

Start by looking at your feeder schools, Do you know the teachers? What steps are you currently taking to get these students into your classes next year? These tips will help:Create posters listing your classes and the registration numbers. Remind students of all the fun activities you do and invite them to enroll. Send several posters to each school prior to students making schedule selections.

- Invite the local newspaper to do a story on your program. Prepare an exciting day for them. Tell them that you are really wanting to recruit younger students and make sure they have all of the enrollment information.

- Hold free weekend workshops or camps for younger students to teach them some of the fun things you do in class, and get some of your older students to help.

- Host a drama competition at your school and invite the feeder schools. Offer ribbons or trophies. Don't forget to brag about the winners afterward!

- Tour a short, small cast show to all your feeder schools to showcase the drama program. Some students might never have seen a live performance before. A fun comedy is by far the best!

- Assign a TV commercial project to your current students. The product they are promoting is your drama program. Use the best completed commercials to actually advertise by sending them to feeder schools, tagging participants and their parents on social media, showing them during announcements (if your school has video announcements), and asking other teachers to share them.

Besides working with feeder schools, you want to recruit students from within your own school who have a strong desire to be in your class. Advocate for them by helping arrange their schedules or by arming them with the benefits of being involved in drama. Often, they are under pressure from friends to take a different class, or from parents who don't understand that theatre develops good communication skills and creativity.

Next, take a look at the students in your school who have skill and talent but for some reason are not taking your class. Find out why and see if the obstacle might be easily overcome. Perhaps they just need a little encouragement, or maybe they did not realize the department existed. Ask teachers to recommend students who show a penchant for entertaining. Send out invitations telling them they were nominated by a teacher for this honor.

Look at your class offerings. Do you have a technical theatre class for those who love drama but do not want to act? If you do not feel qualified to teach it, you might be able to get a retired construction worker or theatre major from a nearby college to assist you on a volunteer basis. This will also give you a block of time for building scenery, making costumes, and gathering props. What a time saver!

In this day of digital everything, consider a digital video class. Many schools already offer these; if your school does not, you might be in for a shock. This opens the doors to participants who are interested in television journalism, technology, directing, producing, lighting and sound, special effects, editing, writing, podcast production, social media, and more. These students can produce promotional videos for the entire school or district, instructional videos, promotional pieces, archival pieces, and more. But most importantly for you, they can become the heart of your program's marketing, archiving, and social media presence. Don't worry if you don't know a thing about video or technology. Your students do, and with your leadership, they will teach you!

Do you offer an advanced class by audition only? This will appeal to more serious actors, recruit those wanting it for their credentials, and create a buzz for your program. But be prepared for a logistical dilemma. When you try to put your very best students into one class, two negatives are possible. One, you lose the leadership in your regular classes because suddenly your best students are no longer there. And two, finding one period of the day when everyone can take a class is impossible. There will be students who cannot be in your exclusive group because of another commitment (band, for example) that they are not willing or able to sacrifice. But despite the conflicts, many experienced teachers are convinced that an audition-only class is worth the added effort.

KEEPING YOUR PROGRAM VISIBLE

Do you have each class performing a show, either during class time or in the evening (or both!)? Class shows are very educational, they make wonderful fundraisers, and they are another way to increase community support. If you are the only teacher in your department and you are already directing a full load of shows, you may not want to take on additional performances or you may want to reserve them for your more advanced classes. However, departments with several teachers should consider rotating directing duties so that each class gets the opportunity to produce a play every semester. There are many entertaining one-act plays under twenty minutes that are ideal for class productions. You could also experiment with producing a full-length play by casting Act 1 from one class, Act 2 from another, and Act 3 from still another. An alternative may be doing a night of one-acts or scenes and monologues instead.

Another option would be to select a few "opening acts" for your mainstage production from your in-class scene work. You still want to keep the bulk of the attention on the main event, but consider allowing a duet from one class or a few monologues from another. This will increase attendance and awareness of your program, and you can utilize those additional students as ushers or box office help for your main show.

There are many functions and events other than traditional plays that can be beneficial learning experiences for your students, too. Try producing a celebration of your district's diversity by hosting a multicultural assembly. Invite an area celebrity to serve as guest speaker for a forum on arts in your community. Choreograph a fashion show using clothes from area merchants and employ students, teachers, and parents as models. Host a talent show showcasing your school's most extraordinary students.

If not having a stage or wishing yours was better is keeping you from producing plays and other events, take advantage of what you have and host your show in an unusual setting. Try doing *A Midsummer Night's Dream* in a grove of trees and have the audience bring lawn chairs. The library is a wonderful place for a murder mystery!

Well-organized competitions can be a wonderful way to teach students about the rewards of hard work. Research drama competitions in your area. Some schools participate in one-act play contests while others prefer scene and other shorter competitions. If one is not available, work with schools in your area to create one. You can also host competitions at your school and invite others in the area to participate. Because a small fee is usually charged for each event, hosting could be a terrific fundraiser.

BUILDING A PARENT BOOSTER CLUB

If you do not already have the assistance and support of a parent booster club, you probably want to give the idea some serious thought. Parents have a vested interest in their children's success, so you will find that there are many who are willing and eager to help. Being involved has many benefits for the parents:

- They have a tangible way of showing their children they support them.

- They meet other parents and develop friendships that can last far beyond the school year.

- They get to be involved in their teens' lives and get to know their friends.

- They develop a relationship with the teacher and become involved in the school community.

For you, the benefits are limitless! There are some jobs within your department that parents can take over completely... or at least as completely as you want. The parents bring a rich offering of time, skills, experience, and resources that they can put to use to handle publicity, posters, social media, scrapbooks, programs, fundraising, and so much more. They are often the best to handle the box office and can provide meals for late-night rehearsals. You will find that they often volunteer skills you never imagined you would need or want. Even in a small group, you will probably have some builders, some who sew, an artist or two, and a few great cooks. They will do just what their name implies: boost your program to a new level.

PUBLICIZING YOUR SHOWS

You want your shows to be well-attended by both the school community and the community at large, so advertising is important. Hopefully you can create a committee to help you. You may want to choose a parent from your booster organization to oversee the project, or you may have several students who can work as a team.

If your town still has a newspaper, take advantage of it. In the digital age, papers are becoming rare, so those that still exist are eager for positive stories. And parents love the chance to send copies of these printed stories to relatives. Even though they may act indifferent, it is still a big deal for students to see their likeness in print! In larger towns, getting recognition by the papers will require more persistence, but it can still be done. Some of the larger papers even run a neighborhood section once a week. Invite your newspaper to do stories and take pictures, and make sending out news releases a habit. Any time your program is mentioned, make several copies of the article and send "autographed" copies to your

principals, department head, superintendent, or those from whom you are seeking grants. Don't forget to put a copy in your scrapbook!

In addition to local newspapers, research your school paper, neighborhood or PTA newsletters, and the newsletters of some of the town's prominent organizations, like The Women's Club and the Rotarians. Many businesses have newsletters, and if you find a creative way to link your story to them, they will publicize your show. For example, if you are performing the play *The Diary of Anne Frank*, let your local synagogue and Jewish Community Center know. Ask if they know anyone who might speak to your students about the Holocaust. Find out what news resources they have, and ask for a little exposure. Another option is to ask your students to enlist the help of their church, parents' businesses, and other organizations. Consider inviting the adults in those organizations to your performances and enlisting them as volunteers for your community boosters or adopt them as grandparents for your grandparent boosters. Not every opportunity will be obvious; sometimes getting creative exposes opportunities that are win-win for your students and the community.

Another way to advertise your show is by creating colorful posters. It is difficult to have dinner in most towns without seeing posters of the school's track team, choirs, football team, and more. If you are not taking advantage of the trend, you are missing out on some serious exposure! Print them in bright colors and post them everywhere you are allowed, both in the school and around town. Increase your posters' value by including a promo code for a dollar off admission.

Did you get show shirts in advance for your cast and crew? Assign a day for everyone to wear them and your group will become walking billboards!

Remember to take advantage of the school's most immediate resources. If your school has a public address system, write commercials advertising your shows. Find out how to post events on the marquee outside, or perhaps your school has a scrolling message board in the lobby or cafeteria. Ask teachers to discuss upcoming performances in their classes. Does your school have an extra credit policy to encourage attendance at performance events? Offer to trade advertisements in the programs with a school sport team.

See Section 3 for more details about publicizing your show.

AVOIDING BURNOUT

Even the best teachers will run into obstacles and suffer from burnout due to the long hours, large classes, and seemingly constant struggles. You may find that for each few steps you take forward, someone, whether they know it or not, pushes you back a step. Speaking of steps, you will probably step on a few toes, and yours will be stepped on again and again. You will wish there were three of you and that each of you had two pairs of hands and an extra hour each day.

Overcoming obstacles is a part of every job, but for teachers, and especially fine arts teachers, this part of the job can easily be overwhelming... if you let it. You have to be in control of your job and your environment, not the other way around.

In the past month, what are some obstacles you have run into at school? What was your role? What could you have done differently to avoid the issue in the first place?

For example, say you discovered that both your group and the drill team thought they had the stage reserved on a particular rainy afternoon. Did you have the stage "formally" reserved? Could you rehearse elsewhere without any real consequence to your show? Would your insistence on having the stage be based on a real need or on stubbornness

> ## Top Ten Tips for Maintaining Positive School Relationships
>
> 10. Avoid being possessive.
> 9. Learn co-workers' names.
> 8. Volunteer when you can.
> 7. Treat office staff with appreciation.
> 6. Approach difficulties with logic rather than emotion.
> 5. Remember birthdays.
> 4. Be patient.
> 3. Practice the Golden Rule.
> 2. Always remember to say please and thank you.
> 1. Never gossip.

and selfishness? What could be gained by insisting that your group have the stage? What could be gained by allowing the drill team to have it and by checking on calendar discrepancies prior to the next rehearsal? Remember, you can only change that which you can control. Do not focus on the part of the problem you cannot change, just the parts you can.

If your obstacle was with a person, was it based on emotions or facts? Because theatre can be very intense, emotions tend to drive its troubles. Consequently, you should never rush into a situation angrily. Step back, get a cup of coffee, and write down the most logical solutions. Once your anger has subsided, share your ideas with the others involved and invite them to share theirs. Limit any debate about the topic to three minutes. If you cannot come to an agreement, state calmly that you are deadlocked on the issue, and perhaps you can come back to it after some thought.

Select one or two people who can and will advocate for you. They should be willing to stand up for your organization. If not, ask yourself what you can do to win their support. Productive networking within any organization is good business practice. Having negative working relationships has no business value. If you look at those around you whom you consider successful, you will probably find that they maintain positive relationships and avoid negativity. That does not mean that you succumb easily to the wishes of others and always say yes when asked for a favor. It means you learn to say no with tact and without feeling guilty. You assert yourself without being pushy. You tell someone you are not comfortable with their decision without becoming emotional.

Growth is another area on which to focus when finding your footing within your school and department. Where do you want to go? Do you see yourself staying in the same position or growing within the ranks? Many believe that the best way to strengthen job security is to become indispensable. If no one else can do what you do, you are less likely to be dismissed in budget cuts. On the other hand, some feel that becoming indispensable can anchor them in a lower-paying job because they become too difficult to replace.

PLANNING THE DRAMA BANQUET

Drama programs generally wrap up their year with a banquet. You worked hard all year long to produce quality shows, raise money, and develop a strong program. A banquet is one way that teachers, students, and parents can celebrate and share their appreciation with everyone. After all, it's been a year of victories and overcoming challenges. You will also be saying goodbye to those students who are moving on to new phases in their lives.

Unfortunately, the banquet tends to fall after the last show and right before finals, leaving you very little time and energy to plan it. If at all possible, assign the planning to your parent booster club. Not only does it relieve you of the work, parents take special pride in planning this event, because it is the culmination of all their children's long hours of work. It is a way they can show their young actors that they truly support their involvement in the theatre. If you don't have a parent booster club, perhaps your drama club officers could do much of the planning.

Regardless of who is responsible for planning the banquet, make copies of the two forms in this section to document ideas, assignments, dates, and prices. Not only will it help this year, it will also save the planning committee valuable time in future years. Set a meeting to "pass the torch," inviting those who will be doing the planning. However, if you feel very strongly about certain items, document your decisions prior to passing on the *Banquet Committee Responsibilities* and *Banquet Details* forms to whomever will be in charge. Let them know that you are available for consultation but that the bulk of the responsibility is theirs.

But wait! Before you can completely turn over the planning to others, there are three items over which you'll need to maintain control, or at least input:

• What will be the date of the banquet? Clear it with both the school's central calendar and your own to make sure there are no conflicts. Once the date

is determined, the planning committee can start working out the details. If your banquet is on a school night, it could possibly be at a restaurant or banquet hall. If it falls on a weekend or a holiday, the school might be a better option. Will it be casual, semi-formal, formal, or thematic? If using someone else's facilities, find out the limitations in advance. For example, a restaurant may not allow decorations for a theme party on their premises, whereas a school will probably not have those restrictions.

• What will be the format of the banquet? You will need to decide on speakers, the order of presentation, and the way you want each portion of the event styled. For example, will the awards be teacher's choice awards or will the students vote? Some schools even have their audiences vote throughout the year, such as Best Actor for each show.

• What is the budget amount dedicated to the banquet from either the club funds or the program account? Anything additional will need to be covered by selling tickets for the banquet. For example, if you have zero dollars set aside for the banquet, then each ticket will need to cover a share of the meal, entertainment, awards, decorations, and anything else to be included in the event. However, if you've designated $300 and the evening will cost $1200 including all of the above expenses, then divide the difference by the estimated number of attendees and that is your ticket price. If you start planning early enough, there might still be good ways to come up with funds. Could you set aside a certain percentage of the upcoming show's ticket sales or designate all proceeds from concessions for the banquet?

After these three pieces are determined, the planning committee can take over. Instruct them to break the overall evening into smaller, more manageable elements. It is important to put responsible people in charge of each item, set solid deadlines, and follow up with meetings, emails, or phone calls. There are so many details to consider when planning the banquet that sometimes the most important parts are forgotten or neglected. Remind everyone that the ultimate goal should be celebrating your program's and your students' accomplishments. Some who have attended other banquets might have some wonderful ideas. At the same time, you should not feel pressured to make your banquet like everyone else's. In the end, the event should be a reflection of your program, club, students, and year.

USING AWARDS

Just as Hollywood has its Oscars and Broadway its Tonys, your students need to feel recognized and appreciated. That is why one of the banquet events the students anticipate most is the awards ceremony. Best Actor and Best Actress are the two most common, but there can be any number of other awards, as well, and should include the crew and maybe even parents, drama club members, and so on. Just make sure to avoid awards that are based on appearance, popularity, or controversial subjects. You'll also need to decide what kinds of awards will be given. Will you give certificates, ribbons, trophies, plaques, or something unique like scene slates or masks?

How the winners are determined is up to you. Is it teacher's choice, voting, or some combination of the two? If voting is part of the process, you must decide who can vote—cast, crew, club members, and/or audiences—and when the voting will take place before the banquet. One suggestion is to have the students or the audiences vote, but have the teacher break any ties. Another possibility would be for teachers to name the nominees, and then the students vote. Or vice versa. Whether you're choosing yourself or having the students vote, you might want to use the *Awards Ballot*.

Your school may have rules in place for student voting. If not, you must decide how voting is to be handled. These suggestions may help:

- Make sure you provide a list of all students nominated or eligible for each award so it's not just a popularity contest.

- If having students or audiences vote, maintain control of the ballots at all times.

- If having your audience vote, the ballot should be a loose sheet of paper, not part of the program to tear out. Parents might not want to ruin their memento and will choose instead not to vote. Provide tables, pens, and ballot boxes.

- Do not let any students tally the votes, and retain all ballots for your records.

If using voting, consider using social media to post your award categories and nominees' performances. For example, with student and parent permission, post the three best monologues from your various performances and encourage viewers to share them. The ones with the most "likes" will be the winners of your People's Choice awards. But, as is always the case with social media and students, stay very close to your public posts! Students are not adults, and posts can very quickly become negative or harmful if someone decides to make a hurtful comment.

There are three pages of certificates included in this section ready to copy onto pretty paper. These can be used for the awards ceremony at the banquet, as well as at any other time.

Even months before the banquet, use awards in your class to honor those who have done well, made great improvements, or gone above and beyond what is expected of them. For instance, awarding your beginning actors is a wonderful way to encourage participation, and it also tells the students that their efforts are being noticed. If you have a hard time thinking of reasons to give out certificates, get clues from your grade book. Any time a student makes above 95 percent for a six-week period, honor them. If a student goes from failing a six-week period to passing, honor them. Here are some other ideas:

Best Memorization Skills	Best Characterization
Best Actor	Best Energy
Most Creative Ideas	Best Actress
Best Monologue	Best Duet
Best Improvisation	Best Blooper
Best Dialect	Best Test Score
Super Researcher	Best Project
Funniest Scene	Most Improved Actor

And remember to thank parents, fellow teachers, your custodial staff, and whoever else goes above and beyond to drive your program in the right direction.

BANQUET DETAILS

Now that you have worked out the general idea of your banquet, you will want to start working out the details.

STARTING
FUNDS:$_____

Date:_____ Day of Week:_____ Time:_____

Location: _____

Address: _____

Contact Name:_____ Phone:_____

Dress Code: _____

Describe the meal and its courses (Restaurant? Catered? Other?):_____

_____

_____

Location Fee:_____ Meal Costs (total):_____

Location Fee (per student):_____ Meal Costs (per student, including tip): _____

Is the fee based on the number of students attending?   ☐ YES   ☐ NO

If yes, how many must attend to get this price? _____

What if fewer come? _____

What if more come?_____

Describe the entertainment for the evening, including times, costs, names of contacts, and telephone numbers:_____

_____

List the events of the evening in order, including who will perform each task and about how long the task will take. This will help to plan your overall schedule.

1. _____

2. _____

3. _____

4. _____

5. _____

6. _____

7. _____

8. _____

9. _____

10. _____

How and when will you pay for the evening? _____

Has this been handled?   ☐ YES   ☐ NO

Who will be attending the banquet? Drama club, cast and crew members, drama classes?

_____

_____

BANQUET COMMITTEE RESPONSIBILITIES

There are so many details to consider when planning your banquet that sometimes the most important parts are forgotten or neglected. Ask friends and teachers who attend other banquets what they do. You may find that they have some wonderful ideas. At the same time, you should not feel pressured to make your banquet like everyone else's. In the end, your event should be a reflection of your program, club, teacher, students, and year.

Who is on the banquet committee? _____

_____

_____

Who is in charge of the location? _____ Deadline: _____
Research prices, negotiate the cost, and work out details of making payments

Who is in charge of the meal? _____ Deadline: _____
Finalize the price, tip, the different courses, and make payment arrangements

Who is in charge of the entertainment?_____ Deadline: _____
Research, finalize the price and the selection, and make payment arrangements

Who is in charge of the awards?_____ Deadline: _____
List the titles of the awards you wish to give (Best Actor, Best Techie, etc.):

_____

_____

_____

Will award winners receive certificates, trophies, etc.? _____

Where will you purchase these?_____

How will you pay for them? _____

How will awards be decided? Student vote? Teacher's choice?_____

Who will pay for the evening? Will the cost be covered by profits from shows, will you sell tickets, or will you do a fundraiser?_____

If you sell tickets, will the price cover the meal, the location, the entertainment, the awards, or all of these?_____

Will parents and administrators be invited? _____
(Many clubs pay for an administrator to attend their banquet. Awarding them with a certificate of appreciation for their support may encourage continued support.)

Plan a meeting of the banquet committee, the officers, and the teacher about a week before your banquet to discuss final details. Your meeting will be on: _____

AWARDS BALLOT
Please vote only once for each category.

COMEDY

Best Actor_____

Best Actress _____

Best Crew Member_____

Best Supporting Actor _____

Best Supporting Actress _____

Best Actor
in a Minor Role _____

Best Actress
in a Minor Role _____

DRAMA

Best Actor_____

Best Actress _____

Best Crew Member_____

Best Supporting Actor _____

Best Supporting Actress _____

Best Actor
in a Minor Role _____

Best Actress
in a Minor Role _____

MUSICAL

Best Actor_____

Best Actress _____

Best Crew Member_____

Best Supporting Actor _____

Best Supporting Actress _____

Best Actor
in a Minor Role _____

Best Actress
in a Minor Role _____

Best Dancer_____

Best Singer_____

OVERALL

Best Actor_____

Best Actress _____

Best Light Crew
Member_____

Best Sound Crew
Member_____

Best Set Crew
Member_____

Best Stage Crew
Member_____

Best Costume
Crew Member _____

Best Makeup
Crew Member_____

Best Prop Crew
Member_____

Best Publicity
Crew Member _____

Best House
Crew Member_____

Best Attitude _____

Hardest Worker _____

Most Improved _____

Most Encouraging _____

Most Prepared _____

Most Likely to
Succeed in Theatre _____

COMMUNITY

Best Parent Volunteer_____

Most Supportive Faculty
(non-theatre member) _____

Most Supportive
Audience Member _____

Most Supportive
Business/Community
Member _____

Congratulations!

_____

for achievement in the area of

_____

On this _____ day of _____, _____

_____

SUPERJOB

Awarded to

_____

for outstanding improvement and success in

_____

_____   _____

Award of EXCELLENCE

Awarded this _____ day of _____ , _____

_____

has made outstanding contributions to theatre
for excellence in the field of

_____

_____   _____

CONGRATULATIONS!

has ascended to new heights by earning

_____ POINTS

You are a Superstar!

_____ Director

_____ President

STARTING A DRAMA CLUB

Having a strong drama club is a wonderful way to increase your program's profile in the school and community. As a matter of fact, there is no end to the number of benefits having a club can bring to your students, the school, and to you.

- Drama clubs increase awareness of your program.

- They are educational and promote leadership.

- Clubs allow those who cannot take your class to participate in the overall production process.

- They can be profitable to your program.

A well-run drama club has endless possibilities and can be a dynamic boost to your overall program. Even though a club takes time, it also can be a huge help. As you become comfortable with your club, new ideas will surface and you will discover that it is fun and helpful, giving you a team of workers to make your job easier.

Step One: Elect Officers

If you do not already have a drama club, start by calling a meeting or by inviting students individually. At this first gathering, inform them of your intentions and tell them that they can elect temporary officers from this first group. Once you have a more established club, you can hold permanent elections. Inform them in advance of each office's basic responsibilities.

President—Assists teacher in running each meeting; liaison between drama club and teacher. Takes leadership over certain areas alongside VP.

Nominations: _____

Vice President—Works with president, sharing all responsibilities and/or taking leadership over certain areas. Also can assist secretary.

Nominations: _____

Secretary—Takes notes, takes attendance, and does all filing and paperwork. Often the one to communicate with other students, request announcements, put ads in school publications, etc.

Nominations: _____

Treasurer—Assists teacher in collecting dues and keeps records of all finances.

Nominations: _____

Who are your new officers?

President: _____

Vice President: _____

Secretary: _____

Treasurer: _____

Others: _____

If your school has announcements, do not miss the opportunity to publicly congratulate these students. You may also want to make a large poster. Remember to set the date for the next meeting and include it in both the announcement and on the poster. It is best to set dates and post them well in advance.

Your next meeting is _____

Step Two: Decide on Meetings

Have your officers meet without the rest of the club to begin ironing out the details of your organization. For example, when will you meet? Many drama clubs meet weekly, but they quickly find that they run out of things to do. Others meet only when business needs to be done. These clubs fail to appeal to most students and membership suffers. Before making your final decision, consider your show schedule, the availability of the room, student activities, and even your mission.

- Meeting once or twice each month works for most groups.

- Try choosing a day that is easy to remember, such as the first and third Tuesday of each month; have an alternate plan for meeting days that fall on holidays.

- Check with the school's master calendar so that you can avoid conflicts well in advance, and add your dates to the calendar as soon as possible.

- Choose a time for meetings to start and end.

Have students decide on the kind of structure they want to use to run their meetings. Many use parliamentary procedure while others use a less rigid style. Your group will have its own ideas as to what will work and what will not. You may even wish to use a strict system for the business part of your meetings and then adjourn to a more relaxed format.

Now you will need to decide what to do in your meetings. There will always be a certain amount of business that needs to take place, such as discussing field trips, performances, workshops, contests, purchases, scholarships, club shirts, and attendance, just to name a few. Post a mailbox outside your room so that members can suggest topics as they think of them between meetings. Before your group gathers, the secretary should create an agenda.

Improvisations and theatre games are a super way to reward students for attending the meeting and getting the business done, so hopefully they can be the second part of every meeting. Try using the games listed in Chapter 9 and ask your students for suggestions. These types of activities in a casual setting are wonderful ways to involve reluctant students and to build your more experienced students' skills.

Step Three: Set Goals

Now that you have elected officers and decided on meetings, you are ready to begin building the rest of the club. At your second meeting, ask members to begin brainstorming club goals. Write down all of their ideas. You want to find a "common thread" in their train of thought.

As you progress, a mission statement will start to form. The mission statement you choose for your club should clearly define what it is you seek to accomplish and by what standard. It will stand to remind the members of the club what they are doing and why. A club without a mission will lack vision. An example of a mission statement is:

"The drama club of RJ Smith High School seeks to promote a higher level of interest in theatre and the production process by producing quality plays, encouraging higher attendance, and granting scholarships to its members."

Now, begin formatting your goals into a statement. If your school has a mission statement, it may be a good idea to incorporate its message into yours. This will increase your club's administrative and faculty support and make your club integral to the school's success. Draft your mission statement using these helpful phrases:

Who (the club)

Seeks to do what (the missions)

By doing what (the actions)

By what standard (adjectives like "quality" in the example above)

Use blank paper or a chalkboard to edit your statement. Is there a way to make your mission statement more concise by looking at your wording or summarizing several ideas into a single phrase? For example, plays, musicals, and assemblies can be summarized as productions. Your mission statement should be succinct.

Once you have chosen a final statement, record it here for safekeeping:

_____

_____

Step Four: Build Your Club's Identity

Now that you have your mission statement, assign committees to each goal and create a plan for accomplishing each one. Goals should remain on the agenda until completed.

An early goal in the formation of your club is deciding on rules and expectations. Your school may require you to submit these to be filed as the club's official charter. Regardless, it would be wise to agree on solid rules and expectations before making any further decisions. Consider addressing attendance, behavior (both at and away from meetings and functions), grades, participation, and anything else your students consider important. However, try to limit rules to five or six total and keep them positive ("members must attend every meeting" instead of "do not miss any meetings"). If the club feels the need to go into great detail, have them create a set of bylaws that support the general idea of each rule. These can be filed away and referred to when needed. Once your rules are solid, create a poster and place it in a prominent location. You may also want to include them in a club pamphlet.

Branding is a fun and important way to distinguish your club. Strong branding improves recognition, promotes pride, and gives purpose. Like any product, a club's brand gives it a personal connection to the consumer or, in your case, the members and the school community. Do not underestimate the importance! Entire careers are built on the concept of branding; you have students in your midst who may be considering a future in marketing who will be inspired to get involved with this aspect.

One of the most basic forms of branding is the motto, a short phrase or sentence that summarizes your club and that generally accompanies your logo. For example, a drama club with a pirate logo, complete with hook hand, chose as its motto: "The Pirate Players—get hooked on drama!" Unlike the

NAME THAT CLUB!

What's in a name? Think about it… The products we buy at the grocery store have descriptive names that try to make them more appealing. Cars have names that conjure images of speed and sophistication. What do you want your club's name to say about your program? *Choose wisely!*

mission statement, the motto should be just a few words and reflect your organization's personality.

You will want to design a logo to accompany your motto. A logo is a picture or symbol that will represent your club visually. Sometimes the logo and motto are combined to make a single "word picture." Remind your students of the popular logos that successful companies use; they are almost always very simple and can generally "speak for themselves." Many drama clubs use masks or clap boards, both of which are readily available in clip art packages. Often these are integrated with the school mascot.

Coming up with your logo and motto could be a fun task for one of your early meetings, or you could hold a contest. Allow members to submit ideas, perhaps on a homemade poster, and have them vote on their favorite. You might even involve the art club! Once your members decide on the club's logo and motto, display it proudly!

Will you be purchasing club shirts or jackets? Both are popular ways to promote an organization, but you may decide that having a club shirt and also having shirts for each show becomes expensive or redundant. If this is the case, consider some alternatives. For example, select a short-sleeved t-shirt for one show, a long-sleeved t-shirt for another, and perhaps a tote bag for your one-act. Maybe have your club gear be a zipper hoodie that can be worn with the other items. A more budget-friendly option might be to select a heavy-duty shirt that everyone likes, such as bowling shirts or mechanics' shirts. Put your logo and motto on the back and save the front for show patches and pins. Patches are an inexpensive way to display students' names, offices, achievements, and shows. They can also be used as incentives for selling a certain number of tickets for each show. Pins work great alongside patches and can be bought at trophy shops or in catalogs; they can be used to display rank, awards, honors, or to indicate number of years in the club. Another alternative to doing a club t-shirt is to have show caps. Your principal may give you special permission to wear caps on show days. Regardless of your decision, create a committee to explore the options, keeping in mind students' budgetary restrictions. Shirts and commemorative items are a fabulous way to earn additional money for your program, but placing too much burden on your participants might frighten away talented students who fear being ostracized.

Step Five: Create a Plan of Action

Now that you have the basic structure for your club—officers, goals, a mission statement, a club identity, and meetings—it is time to create a plan of action. Ask your students what is important to them. Maybe performing is their number one goal and fundraising is next. Ask yourself how one goal can be used to achieve another. For example, are you making money on your shows? Why or why not? Capitalize on the "whys" and find solutions for the "why nots." Put a student or group in charge of following through on each task, and set a deadline for them to present a solid plan to the club. Ask for a progress report at each meeting.

A club scrapbook, either paper or electronic, can be a fun on-going project and can also be a wonderful tool for promoting the organization. You will want a large committee to oversee this as it is very time-consuming. Request that students share copies of their club-related pictures, articles, and other items. Set aside a day once a month to meet. This could be done at meetings or after the meeting has adjourned, or committee members could meet on their own time. Then find creative ways of displaying your scrapbook. Ask the school secretary or counselors to display it on their office coffee tables.

Social media, if allowed by your school, is also a fitting responsibility for your drama club. It can be used in lieu of a scrapbook, and also for communication and announcements, as an advertising tool, or as a resource to find difficult props. For example, the Audrey props and dentist chair for *Little Shop of Horrors* are difficult and expensive to come by, but a quick search of the Facebook Marketplace brought up dozens of listings. If you are not an expert on social media, chances are your students are! Ask them to brainstorm other ways to use social media in your drama club and for your productions. However, use great caution with any online activity. Make sure only very trustworthy, mature students have access to the club's social media accounts, and do not let students make purchases on the Marketplace. That should be the job of an adult due to student safety.

Perhaps the most common goal of middle and high school drama clubs is to see students continue exploring theatre, either onstage or behind the scenes, after they graduate. It is the mark of a successful drama teacher! For that reason, giving scholarships should be at least one of the activities of every high school drama club. There are many benefits to doing this. For one, it gives your drama club a solid purpose. Students will know that the money they are raising will go to a good cause. They will also know that if they meet certain requirements, some of the scholarship money could be theirs. The community will also be more apt to respond to your needs if they know that the result will be an opportunity for higher education. Find out if other clubs in your school or district are giving scholarships. Get as much information as you can and then decide how you want to handle this issue in your organization. Your school may have strict rules about doling out scholarship money. They may also be able to help design the structure of the award. There are many things to work out in advance, such as:

- Who will be eligible for the award? Will it only be given to students in your club vs. the larger drama program?

- Might scholarships be used for non-college classes, such as acting classes at a local theatre?

- Will you choose one student or divide it among several?

- Might scholarships be used to cover application fees, which can be excessive?

- What criteria will you use to decide who will get the award? You may want to base it on grades, participation, attendance, and/or behavior. If you are giving out just one award, you will need to have very strict guidelines. However, if you want to give awards to all senior drama club members, your guidelines may be more relaxed.

- How will you give the reward? Will you write a check directly to the student or to the college or university?

- How much will you give? You may set aside a certain amount, or you may decide that all money made on concessions will go into a scholarship fund. Seek matching grants!

FUNDRAISING

Beyond funding scholarships, fundraising is a necessary evil to almost every drama program and your drama club or parent booster club should help. Find out your school or district's policy on the matter.

- The most obvious and educational way to raise money is by charging admission to their shows. Generally, the admission price for a school production is around the price of a movie ticket. You may also want to see what other organizations in your area are charging and price your shows accordingly.

- Consider having a silent or live auction after your show. Solicit parents or local business to donate items, services, and so on.

- If you are not doing concessions at your shows, you are missing out on an easy fundraiser. This is a wonderful job for either your parent boosters or your drama club, but if neither of them can do it, invite the choir or band. Swap events with them, so they can sell concessions at your shows if you can sell them at their concerts.

Fun Raising

Try one of these three fabulously fun ideas to raise money:

1. Host a karaoke contest. Have parents and businesses donate food and drinks, rent a karaoke machine, and have a great time. Invite the community, teachers, and students.

2. Have an all-community talent show featuring students, parents, and local talent.

3. Host a night of improvisation featuring your students, but also invite others to join in once in a while. You may even offer an award for the best community participant.

Your club or program can profit from each of these events by charging admission, selling concessions, and having a student, parent, or professional video company make copyright-free DVDs that you duplicate and sell.

SECTION 2
EVALUATION TOOLS

EVALUATIONS

Role Scoring
Teacher Evaluation
Rehearsal Evaluation
Performance Evaluation
Peer Evaluation
Self-Evaluation
Audience Behavior Evaluation
Movie and Play Evaluation
Game and Activity Evaluation

Role Scoring
Teacher Evaluation
Teacher Evaluation Tally
Teaching Strategy Improvement Plan
Activity/Rehearsal Grade
Performance Evaluation 1
Performance Evaluation 2
Peer Performance Evaluation
Self-Improvement Plan
Audience Behavior Grade
Movie/Play Evaluation
Script Report
Game/Activity Evaluation
Game/Activity Suggestion

EVALUATIONS

Evaluations are an important part of both school and theatre. This section will provide you with all the tools necessary to evaluate performances, to understand the reasons behind student and teacher evaluations, and to use the results to make improvements.

ROLE SCORING

When students are cast in various roles or as they practice scenes, they will need to study each character fully. Have them use the *Role Scoring* worksheet found here and in Chapter 5 of their workbooks to fully flesh out their characters. The worksheet is designed for students who are more book oriented.

For students who are more visually or tactually oriented, the *Role Scoring* worksheet may lack the level of stimulation they require. Instead, these students can accomplish the same results using art. Ask each student to bring two magazines, scissors, and glue to class. You will need to provide copy paper or cover stock large enough to cover their scripts, whatever size they may be, like an actual book cover. They can then find pictures, words, or phrases in their magazines to adhere to their new "cover" in collage fashion. When they are finished, they will insert their scripts. If allowed, have them tape or glue their covers to their scripts as a constant visual reminder of their characters. Allow them to present some of their questions and picture answers and then discuss them.

If students will get to keep their scripts after the production, they can collage pictures directly onto the covers, but remind them to keep the pages of the script clear of distractions. Those pages are for business only, for cues, blocking notes, etc.

Each character in a play (or scene) has a unique personality and a goal. Scoring characters lets the actors understand how they stand, why they reply the way they do, why they are so hard-headed, or why they use long, quiet pauses. Directing students to take certain actions without their commitment to

the whys and hows is empty. The result is "acting" and "directing." But by taking these actions from a deep understand of the character—of the character's place in the scene and the events, of the character's relationship with other characters—the result is more genuine. The audience doesn't have to try to believe it; they simply accept it because they become lost in the moment.

When a character interacts with another character often in a play, especially when there is a great deal of conflict, consider having the two actors score each other as well as themselves. And, when a situation in a play takes on the role of antagonist, consider having your students think of the situation as a character. Scoring the "situation character" can help young actors understand how their actions are being affected by the situation and how humans tend to form relationships with those situations.

As an example, take *The Diary of Anne Frank*. Anne has relationships with all of the characters in the play, but the real antagonist is her situation: the deportations conducted by the Third Reich, which forces her and her family into hiding in the attic. And that invisible situation character forms most of her decisions in the play. The characters each need to understand their relationship with that situation. To take it a step further, the situation could be replaced with Hitler. While he never makes an appearance onstage, it is clear that he has impacted the action before the opening, during the course of the play, and beyond the final curtain. A good director will encourage exploration of his character and his relationship to other characters, and a good actor will feel his presence in each scene.

TEACHER EVALUATION

Colleges have used teacher evaluations for years to help instructors improve their classroom strategies. Many teachers have their students critique their performance even if it is not required by the school or district. As theatre teachers, we do not just evaluate our students, we also teach them the importance of evaluating each other and themselves. What better way is there to reinforce the importance and effectiveness of the evaluation process than to allow students to evaluate you as an instructor?

Pass out copies of the *Teacher Evaluation* form later in this section along with the exam on the last day you will see your students. Ask them to complete the evaluation first and turn it in before they start the exam. You do not want them to evaluate you after becoming tired or frustrated if your exam proves challenging. Once you have collected the data, use the *Teacher Evaluation Tally* sheet that accompanies the form. Similar to how your students complete the *Self-Improvement Plan* form, you must create your own plan for becoming a more effective teacher.

Use the *Teacher Evaluation Tally* form to understand your students' perceptions of your teaching skills. Use one form for each class period and one form for an overall view.

Tally the rating each student gave you for each category in a single class. For example, if student A from first period gave you a 9 for demeanor, make a single hash mark under the number 9 above the diagonal for the first question. After you have completed this task for the entire class, count the marks for each number and multiply it by the number for that column. Write the result below the diagonal. For example, if you have five hash marks under the number 9, write 45 below the diagonal. Once this is done for each number, total the row and divide by the number of students who responded to the question (the hash marks) to find the average of how you ranked in the class.

When you have completed each class, use a fresh tally sheet to find the averages for all of your classes. Use the totals to complete the *Teaching Strategy Improvement Plan*. Afterward, look at your totals. Ask yourself if there is an area that is a serious red flag. For example, if you averaged high on most items but extremely low on a couple, you may need to change your strategies in those particular categories. Perhaps they are related, or maybe the comments students wrote will give you some insight into how you can improve. Seek advice from a trusted colleague or find classes in that area on the internet.

Remember to analyze the time of day, the subject matter, and the correlation between how you feel about a class and how they feel about you. If your two o'clock class scores you low every semester or year, perhaps the best solution is to have your planning period moved there. Save your findings from year to year and compare them. If you find that the same areas are scoring low each year, it is time to make some serious adjustments. Try to overcome your weaknesses by investing more deeply in your strengths.

REHEARSAL EVALUATION

Another challenge unique to the drama program is individual rehearsal time. Unlike band and choir where the group rehearses together, drama class usually requires students to polish their scenes individually or in pairs. This can be a recipe for disaster if the teacher is not well prepared.

First, before rehearsal time, state your expectations for the activity clearly: "Today you will block your scenes and write blocking in pencil using acceptable symbols and terminology." Next, define the grading process and consequences for failing to complete the task: "You will receive a daily grade for how well your scenes are blocked. You should be able to hand your script to a random classmate, and they should be able to use your blocking notes to perform your scene as you would. Staying on task will improve your grade." Pass out a copy of the *Activity/Rehearsal Grade* form to each pair or group working together. (You will want to have filled in the top part prior to making copies.) Have students fill in their names in the chart and keep it near their rehearsal areas.

Circulate amongst the groups as they rehearse or complete the activity. There are spaces for four rounds (or four times around the class), but ideally you should continue to make the rounds for the entire period. Mark the chart each time you pass. A student doing what you asked them to do and not wasting time will receive a four. Being completely off task and making it difficult for others to do their work garners a zero. At the end of the period, retrieve the *Activity/ Rehearsal Grade* forms and figure the scores using the chart provided. A student who received a four each time will have sixteen points, which is 100% for the day. Students will soon realize that rehearsal time is graded just as worksheets are. They will begin to approach the activity with greater seriousness.

While circulating, encourage positive behavior. Say, "This group is setting a great example of how to stay on task." Or try, "I know it's not easy memorizing that many lines. You're doing a wonderful job, and I hope the other groups are encouraged by your commitment." If a group needs to be directed, try redirecting them but also complimenting them:

"You have good energy. Don't let it cause you to become disruptive. Instead, focus that energy into your scene work." Or try, "You're making some really courageous choices with volume, but remember that in life and in fiction, characters don't always want to be loud. Sometimes they get better results by trying to be quiet. It could be creepy, or it could be a way to remain undetected. Explore that as an option so that your audience notices the peaks and valleys." When students know they are being monitored but that they are also appreciated and improving, they have greater respect for rehearsal time.

PERFORMANCE EVALUATION

There are two performance evaluations in this book. Both are found here as well as in Chapter 2. They are very similar, but the first covers broader categories (like voice) and the second addresses details within the categories (like articulation, projection, and confidence). Because *Performance Evaluation 2* is more detailed, you will find you will need to write fewer comments. For example, if a student needs work on articulation, the teacher simply circles the appropriate number for that area. On *Performance Evaluation 1*, the teacher would score the student appropriately on voice, but then would have to comment that the articulation needs work.

Because some teachers feel more comfortable writing the comments, you have your choice of forms. Introduce students to the one you will use. You may also want both. In a class with 30 students, a ten-minute duet and oral evaluation could take 20 minutes with setup, strike, and so on. In those cases, consider the tool you can complete in that time. But in a smaller class, you may choose more written comments and a shorter oral evaluation. The students have samples of these two forms in Chapter 2 of their workbooks, where there are also additional details for you in this Teacher's Guide.

PEER EVALUATION

One of the most important and meaningful assignments performers have is to evaluate their peers. When we attend a performance, whether we mean to do it or not, we mentally evaluate the talent. If it stops there, it is still a learning experience, but a passive one. A good teacher will take it a step further by having class members analyze what they like and what they feel could use some additional work.

By doing this, students are improving their judgment, and they begin mentally filing away important data that will enhance their own performances. If Marcy sees Mikey continually upstaging himself, she will remember his mistake. When she is polishing her own scene, she will use more caution when blocking so that she does not repeat her classmate's mistake. Likewise, when Mikey sees how Marcy stays open to the audience, he will take note and it will positively influence his scene the next time.

SELF-EVALUATION

This process of evaluation is even more meaningful when it comes to critiquing one's self. From early in our lives, we are told that saying good things about ourselves is not nice; we should reserve our praise for others. Consequently, many young people grow up unable to see the positive in their appearances, accomplishments, and social skills. If someone compliments a young woman on her complexion, she is likely to list all the bad things about it. It is much healthier to teach children to simply say, "Thank you."

Children become attracted to the arts because they are enjoyable; many stay because they discover

that there is a high level of satisfaction in performing or in making props or in stage management. Help those in your care to find the good in their work. When having students fill out the *Peer Performance Evaluation* (found here and in Chapter 2), tell them that they must also evaluate themselves. You will find that this is much harder for them than evaluating their peers. Then, once everyone in class has performed, have students complete the *Self-Improvement Plan* form, using the comments from their teacher evaluation and those given by their peers on the *Peer Performance Evaluation* forms. It will not be long before you begin to see the benefits.

AUDIENCE BEHAVIOR EVALUATION

During performances, grade students based on their audience etiquette. Decide on a value for each mark (five or ten points). Instruct your class on the expectations and consequences. Use the *Audience Grade* form included in this section during scenes and make a mark each time a student does not meet expectations.

- Quiet and still: Students are in their seats making no distracting sounds or movements both during and between scenes.

- Attentive: Students are sitting up, watching performances, and not reading, looking at their phones, or doing homework.

- Appreciative: Students are clapping appropriately after each performance, regardless of the quality; they are giving appropriate responses such as laughter at humorous parts.

- Supportive: Students are not attempting to distract performers; their behavior and comments before, during, and after peers' performances are encouraging.

- Evaluation: Students are using the time between performances to evaluate their peers.

MOVIE AND PLAY EVALUATION

Movies are wonderful teaching tools, especially when students are taught to analyze the plot, action, characters, theme, and more. All too often, teachers use movies to fill time when a regular lesson is not feasible. The movie itself is not a bad choice; failing to incorporate it into a lesson is.

Invest in some good movies, especially those that have been made from plays you will use in your lectures. Some good examples include:

Antigone, starring Irene Papas, directed by Yiorgos Tzavellas, English subtitles

Romeo and Juliet, starring Leonard Whiting and Olivia Hussey, directed by Franco Zeffirelli

William Shakespeare's Romeo + Juliet, starring Leonardo DiCaprio and Claire Danes, directed by Baz Luhrmann

Doctor Faustus, starring Richard Burton and Elizabeth Taylor, directed by Nevill Coghill and Richard Burton

A Raisin in the Sun, starring Sidney Poitier and Claudia McNeil, directed by Daniel Petrie

Pride and Prejudice, starring Colin Firth and Jennifer Ehle, directed by Simon Langton

Hamlet, starring Mel Gibson and Glenn Close, directed by Franco Zeffirelli

Glengarry Glen Ross, starring Al Pacino, Jack Lemmon, Alan Arkin, Ed Harris, Kevin Spacey, and Alec Baldwin, directed by James Foley

Of course, play scripts are also valuable classroom resources. You should have a class library of scripts spanning many genres from a variety of play publishers. Reading scripts can also be an ideal makeup or extra credit assignment.

The *Movie and Play Evaluation* form here and in Chapter 2 is a helpful tool for students to use when evaluating either movies or live performances. You can also use the *Script Report* form like a book report to encourage students to read and analyze a script for some of the most basic theatrical elements, such as plot, characters, and setting. The second page of this form is optional and intended for advanced theatre students.

GAME AND ACTIVITY EVALUATION

Games can also have great educational value. If students are not aware that they are learning and they just think a game is fun, then great, you were able to take them from point A to point B painlessly. On the other hand, if students feel that they are being asked to do something for no reason, an enjoyable learning experience may be going to waste.

After playing a game in class, have students discuss what they think they learned and how it can be applied to acting or another drama skill. Take notes for future use. Have students complete the *Game/Activity Evaluation* form and use them to gauge student responsiveness. Allow students to teach you their games too. Even if they do not know how the game applies to acting, you might! New games will keep the class lively and fresh, and by allowing students to teach you, you have created an educational partnership.

ROLE SCORING

Answer the following questions in detail. Use any means available to find the answer. When you have exhausted all resources to find the answer, make one up. Explain any answer that you make up.

1. What play is your scene from?

2. Is it a monologue, duet, or a scene containing three or more characters?

3. What is the scene about?

4. What is your character's name? What are they like?

5. To whom is your character talking?

6. What happened just before the start of this scene?

7. What do you think will happen in the play after this scene?

8. When and where does the scene take place?

9. How old is your character? Are they mature or immature for their age? Explain.

CONTINUED ON NEXT PAGE

ROLE SCORING, CONT.

10. What do they do for a living?

11. What are their hobbies?

12. How does the title of the play relate to your character?

13. What does your character want in this scene?

14. If your character repeatedly made a gesture in this scene, what would it be and why?

15. What color do you associate with your character and why?

16. What object do you associate with your character and why?

17. What animal do you associate with your character and why?

18. In real life, would you be your character's friend? Why or why not?

CONTINUED ON NEXT PAGE

ROLE SCORING, CONT.

19. How is your character like you?

20. How is your character different from you?

21. What is your character's most positive trait?

22. What is your character's status in the world? Do they have money or power?

23. What does your character want from life?

24. What does your character fear and why?

25. Who does your character admire and why?

26. What are/were your character's parents like?

27. If your character had one wish, what would it be and why?

TEACHER EVALUATION

DATE: _____

TEACHER NAME:_____ CLASS: _____

Do not put your name or any identifying information on this form!
Rate this teacher on a scale of 1 to 10 with 1 being lowest and 10 being highest.
Use the space below each question or the back of the form for making comments.

1. **Demeanor:** How would you rate this teacher's overall demeanor or personality?

   1 2 3 4 5 6 7 8 9 10

2. **Discipline:** Did the teacher handle discipline fairly, thoroughly, and effectively?

   1 2 3 4 5 6 7 8 9 10

3. **Grading:** How would you rate this teacher's fairness in regard to grades?

   1 2 3 4 5 6 7 8 9 10

4. **Lessons:** How well was information presented in the lessons?

   1 2 3 4 5 6 7 8 9 10

5. **Re-teaching:** If a student or group of students did not understand a lesson, how effective was this teacher at clarifying the information?

   1 2 3 4 5 6 7 8 9 10

6. **Testing & Evaluation:** How effective were the teacher's testing or evaluation methods?

   1 2 3 4 5 6 7 8 9 10

7. **Tutoring:** Was the teacher available and willing to work with students outside the classroom?

   1 2 3 4 5 6 7 8 9 10

8. **Organization:** Was the teacher organized, on time, and well-prepared?

   1 2 3 4 5 6 7 8 9 10

9. **Appearance:** How would you rate the appearance of the classroom?

   1 2 3 4 5 6 7 8 9 10

10. **Classroom Environment:** How would you rate the room itself in regard to comfort, décor, lighting, etc.?

   1 2 3 4 5 6 7 8 9 10

TEACHER EVALUATION TALLY

YEAR/SEMESTER: _____ CLASS/PERIOD: _____ CLASS AVERAGE: _____

	1	2	3	4	5	6	7	8	9	10	TOT.	AVG.
1. **Demeanor**: How would you rate this teacher's overall demeanor or personality?												
2. **Discipline**: Did the teacher handle discipline fairly, thoroughly, and effectively?												
3. **Grading**: How would you rate this teacher's fairness in regard to grades?												
4. **Lessons**: How well was information presented in the lessons?												
5. **Re-teaching**: If a student or group of students did not understand a lesson, how effective was this teacher at clarifying the information?												
6. **Testing & Evaluation**: How effective were the teacher's testing or evaluation methods?												
7. **Tutoring**: Was the teacher available and willing to work with students outside the classroom?												
8. **Organization**: Was the teacher organized, on time, and well-prepared?												
9. **Appearance**: How would you rate the appearance of the classroom?												
10. **Classroom Environment**: How would you rate the room itself in regard to comfort, décor, lighting, etc.?												

TEACHING STRATEGY IMPROVEMENT PLAN

SEMESTER/YEAR: _____

1.   How many classes do you teach? _____

2.   Are they all the same class or do they vary? _____ If they vary, write the classes in order, their scores, and their approximate times. Is there a pattern or connection between the time and the score?

3.   Which class is your favorite? _____ What was your average score for this class? _____ Why do you like this class best?

4.   Which is your least favorite? _____ What was your average score for this class? _____ What do you like least about this class?

5.   In which specific area did you score the highest? _____

6.   How can you use this strength to enhance your teaching?

7.   In which specific area did you score the lowest? _____

8.   What specific things can you do to improve this for next semester or next year?

9.   Record your scores for each section and explain how you intend to increase your effectiveness in that area next year or utilize your strengths to improve your overall performance in the classroom.

a.   Demeanor   _____
b.   Discipline   _____
c.   Grading   _____
d.   Lessons   _____
e.   Re-teaching   _____
f.   Testing/Eval.   _____
g.   Tutoring   _____
h.   Organization   _____
i.   Appearance   _____
j.   Environment   _____

NAME _____ PERIOD _____ DATE _____

ACTIVITY/REHEARSAL GRADE

During the activity or rehearsal, keep this form with you. It is the only one you will receive, so please be responsible for it. Remember to turn it in at the end of the activity for a grade.

ACTIVITY: _____

TODAY'S GOAL:

As the teacher visits your group, they will mark your sheet. Please keep it handy. Other than the names of the members of your group, do not mark within the grid.

0 = Completely off task, away from group
1 = With group but off task
2 = Occasionally working toward goal, but often off task
3 = Working toward goal, but sometimes off task
4 = Working hard to achieve final goal

Names:	Round 1	Round 2	Round 3	Round 4	Total	Grade
	0 1 2 3 4	0 1 2 3 4	0 1 2 3 4	0 1 2 3 4		
	0 1 2 3 4	0 1 2 3 4	0 1 2 3 4	0 1 2 3 4		
	0 1 2 3 4	0 1 2 3 4	0 1 2 3 4	0 1 2 3 4		
	0 1 2 3 4	0 1 2 3 4	0 1 2 3 4	0 1 2 3 4		
	0 1 2 3 4	0 1 2 3 4	0 1 2 3 4	0 1 2 3 4		
	0 1 2 3 4	0 1 2 3 4	0 1 2 3 4	0 1 2 3 4		

Grading Scale

| 1=6% | 1=13% | 3=19% | 4=25% | 5=31% | 6=38% | 7=44% | 8=50% |
| 9=56% | 10=63% | 11=69% | 12=75% | 13=81% | 14=88% | 15=94% | 16=100% |

Who is absent from your group today?

Teacher's Comments:

NAME _____ PERIOD _____ DATE _____

PERFORMER #_____ CHARACTER _____

PLAY/PLAYWRIGHT _____

PERFORMANCE EVALUATION I

1. Introduction: Student states their name and the character, play, and playwright with confidence. Groups may do a group introduction or designate an individual to introduce the members.
   1 2 3 4 5 6 7 8 9 10

2. Energy: Performance is enthusiastic, has appropriate movement and emotional levels, and holds the audience's attention.
   1 2 3 4 5 6 7 8 9 10

3. Voice: Performance includes mastery of projection, articulation, pronunciation, confidence, and intensity. May also include a variety of levels of projection and/or dialect.
   1 2 3 4 5 6 7 8 9 10

4. Movement: The use of posture, body language, gestures, blocking, props, and business supports the goal of the scene. May include some pantomime.
   1 2 3 4 5 6 7 8 9 10

5. Facials: The scene includes appropriate facial expressions; the actor refrains from "making faces" when they become distracted.
   1 2 3 4 5 6 7 8 9 10

6. Pacing: The scene progresses at a rate that keeps it interesting and shows confident memorization; it meets the time limitations set by the teacher.
   1 2 3 4 5 6 7 8 9 10

7. Characterization: The character is fully defined and focused, has a unique personality, and uses emotions, body language, and vocal expressions that support the goal of the scene.
   1 2 3 4 5 6 7 8 9 10

8. Focus: Student remains focused on the scene and is not distracted by peers, visitors, sounds, mistakes, or calls for lines.
   1 2 3 4 5 6 7 8 9 10

9. Closing: Student finishes scene and returns to their seat without commenting on the performance or "making faces."
   1 2 3 4 5 6 7 8 9 10

10. Lines and memorization: The scene is memorized, but the student is prepared and has given the script to someone who will call lines out clearly. If lines are needed, they are requested quickly and there is little disruption to the flow of the scene. Lines are worth _____ points each.
    1 2 3 4 5 6 7 8 9 10

BONUS POINTS FOR VOLUNTEERING:	Performer	Score	Minus Lines Missed	Plus Bonus	Final Score
5 points for the first volunteer,					
4 points for the second,					
3 points for the third, and					
2 points for all other volunteers.					

NAME _____ PERIOD _____ DATE _____

PERFORMER #_____ CHARACTER _____

PLAY/PLAYWRIGHT _____

PERFORMANCE EVALUATION 2

1. **APPROACH AND SET UP**
   Timely   0 1 2 3 4 5
   Confident   0 1 2 3 4 5

2. **INTRODUCTION**   0 1 2 3 4 5

3. **ENERGY**
   Vocal   0 1 2 3 4 5
   Physical   0 1 2 3 4 5
   Emotional   0 1 2 3 4 5

4. **VOICE**
   Projection / Intensity   0 1 2 3 4 5
   Articulation and Diction   0 1 2 3 4 5
   Confidence   0 1 2 3 4 5

5. **BODY**
   Body Language   0 1 2 3 4 5
   Gestures   0 1 2 3 4 5
   Blocking   0 1 2 3 4 5
   Movement   0 1 2 3 4 5

6. **FACIAL EXPRESSIONS**   0 1 2 3 4 5

7. **PACING AND TIMING**
   Variation / Flow   0 1 2 3 4 5

8. **CHARACTERIZATION AND EMOTION**
   Defined Character   0 1 2 3 4 5
   Focused / Consistent   0 1 2 3 4 5
   Believable   0 1 2 3 4 5

9. **LINES CALLED CORRECTLY**   0 1 2 3 4 5

10. **CLOSING**   0 1 2 3 4 5

BONUS POINTS FOR VOLUNTEERING:	Performer	Score	Minus Lines Missed	Plus Bonus	Final Score
5 points for the first volunteer, 4 points for the second, 3 points for the third, and 2 points for all other volunteers.					

NAME _____ PERIOD _____ DATE _____

PEER PERFORMANCE EVALUATION

Give specific information about each performance. You will be graded on completion as well as your ability to phrase comments constructively. Be thorough. *Include a critique of your own performance.*

Performer	This performer was great at...	But could use a little more work on...
1.		
2.		
3.		
4.		
5.		
6.		
7.		
8.		
9.		
10.		
11.		
12.		
13.		
14.		
15.		
16.		
17.		
18.		
19.		
20.		
21.		
22.		
23.		
24.		
25.		
26.		
27.		
28.		
29.		
30.		

NAME _____ PERIOD _____ DATE _____

SELF-IMPROVEMENT PLAN

Answer each question honestly. Any honest answer will be given credit. This worksheet is intended to help you and your teacher analyze the success of the scene you performed in this class and to create a strategy for the next performance.

1. Character, play title, playwright:

_____

2. *How* and *where* did you practice (both in class and outside of class)?

3. Did anyone in particular help you? Who was it and how did they help?

4. How much time did you practice outside of class?

5. Did you use all of the class time the teacher gave you? If not, what were you doing instead of practicing?

6. In what areas did you score highest from the teacher and what were some of the comments?

7. In what areas did you score lowest from the teacher and what were some of the comments?

8. According to your peers, what were some of your strengths?

9. According to your peers, where do you need to focus your efforts to improve?

10. In your opinion, what areas of your performance need the most attention?

11. What exercises or activities will you use to sharpen the skills that need improvement?

12. What can the teacher do to help you achieve success for the next performance? Is there anything you would like to have explained or taught again?

NAME _____ PERIOD _____ DATE _____

AUDIENCE BEHAVIOR GRADE

NAME	Not Quiet & Still	Not Attentive	Not Appreciative	Not Supportive	Inconsistent Evaluation	Total

NAME _____ PERIOD _____ DATE _____

MOVIE/PLAY EVALUATION

Answer each question completely. Use a separate sheet if more space is needed.

Which did you see? *(Circle one)*   MOVIE   PLAY

Title: _____

Director: _____   Playwright: _____

(if applicable)

Main Characters: Actors:

_____   _____

_____   _____

_____   _____

1. What was the plot *(the storyline)*?

2. Most stories attempt to teach a lesson *(the moral)*. What lesson do you think this story was trying to teach?

3. What was the setting *(specifically when and where did it take place)*?

4. How did the set *(the buildings and scenery)* add to the play or movie?

5. What was your favorite costume and why?

6. What was your favorite special effect, sound effect, or lighting effect? Explain.

7. How did music add to the play or movie? Explain.

8. Was stage combat used? How?

9. What colors were used repeatedly? Why do you think the director chose these colors?

10. Who was your favorite character? Explain.

11. Did you like the movie or play? Explain.

NAME _____ PERIOD _____ DATE _____

SCRIPT REPORT

After you have read the play, answer the questions on this report thoroughly.
You may have to do some research to find some of the answers.

Title: _____

Playwright: _____

Date published: _____ Publisher: _____

Other plays written by this playwright: _____

_____

What type of play is this? (Circle all that apply.)

Comedy   Tragedy   Historical   Classic   Full-length   One-act   Musical

Other: _____

1.   Where does the play take place?

2.   What is the time period for the play?

3.   List the main characters and tell a little about each of them:

4.   What is the play about?

5.   What is the climax of the play?

NAME _____ PERIOD _____ DATE _____

SCRIPT REPORT - CONT.

6.   How is the conflict resolved?

7.   What did you think of the play?

8.   If you were in this play, which character would you be and why?

9.   What is the theme or message of the play?

10. Find a line that you think supports the general theme of the play and write it here. Indicate the speaker, the act, and the scene.

11. Choose a character who undergoes a great change from the beginning of the play to the end. Describe the change and the impact it has on the course of the story.

12. What events led to the beginning of the play?

13. What do you think might have happened after the conclusion of the play?

14. Find several examples of symbolism and explain them.

NAME _____ PERIOD _____ DATE _____

GAME/ACTIVITY EVALUATION

Title of activity: _____

Date played: _____

Who else was in your group? _____

How fun was this activity?   ☐ Very fun   ☐ Pretty fun   ☐ Somewhat fun   ☐ Not at all

In what areas did playing this game strengthen your theatre skills? *(Circle all that apply.)*

Movement	Acting	Voice	Creativity
Quick Thinking	Teamwork	Plot Development	Writing Skills
Non-Verbal Skills	Concentration	Timing	Other: _____

What was one specific thing you learned from this activity? _____

_____

How does this apply to your acting or another drama skill? _____

_____

GAME/ACTIVITY SUGGESTION

Title of activity: _____

Where did you play or learn about this activity? _____

How many people can play at a time?_____ How much space is needed?_____

Are there any other requirements?
_____

Explain in detail how to play: _____

_____

_____

_____

_____

How would playing this game benefit theatre students? *(Circle all that apply.)*

Movement	Acting	Voice	Creativity
Quick Thinking	Teamwork	Plot Development	Writing Skills
Non-Verbal Skills	Concentration	Timing	Other: _____

SECTION 3
PRODUCTION TOOLS

PRODUCTION TOOLBOX

Auditions
Rehearsals
Props
The Program (Playbill)
Costumes
    Audition Application
    Audition Scorecard
    Production Contract
    Rehearsal Attendance
    Production Needs List
    Local Media
    News Release Form
    Publicity Checklist
    Designing Your Poster
    Biography Worksheet
    Costume Measurements

PRODUCTION TOOLBOX

AUDITIONS

Auditions can be as strenuous as opening night. Decide in advance if you will do open or closed auditions. Most schools conduct open auditions, where everyone watches all auditions, because they are a wonderful learning experience and they are faster. If you do not know all of the students, assign them numbers and make large number signs for their shirts. Have each student fill out the *Audition Application* in this section and submit it to you prior to the audition.

For your first level of auditions, choose one or two short scenes for each character and make sides, which are copies of the scenes for the purpose of auditions. If the publisher will not permit sides, mark the scripts with colored sticky notes. For musicals, first auditions normally include singing and a short cold reading.

Callbacks generally place actors where they would likely be cast so that directors can see and hear them in specific roles. Callbacks for musicals usually include more acting and some dancing. There will also be singing from the roles for which the actor is being considered. Those who will potentially work side- by-side are often paired up for a quick visual comparison. Certain plays include dialogue which requires the boy to be taller than the girl, or vice versa. Regardless, seeing how the actors look together can be revealing to a director.

As each student auditions, mark the *Audition Scorecard*. If actors will read only once before callbacks, then you might label the four columns "Voice," "Movement," "Overall Acting," and "Appearance" for a play or "Dance," "Song," "Monologue," and "Cold Reading" for a musical. If they will be reading more than once, you can use a single column for each time they take the stage. The card will help you narrow down your choices, but the final casting should be done by impressions, not numbers. Save the completed cards and file them for future reference. You may never need them, but they are an official record.

REHEARSALS

Requiring a *Production Contract* like the one in this section ensures that all students and parents are in agreement with your rehearsal schedule and any fees, and that the expected behavior has been noted. It also gives you pertinent contact information in case of an emergency. This is also a great opportunity to recruit parent volunteers. Some directors even require parents or other adult family members to volunteer for at least one job. This will make your job much easier.

Because teamwork is so important and attendance is a must, it is imperative to have every actor available when they are called. The director has enough to do without having to take roll and call missing students. Put the responsibility in their hands by requiring them to sign in each and every rehearsal on the *Rehearsal Attendance* form. A copy of this schedule can be posted on the callboard before rehearsals begin to serve as the official production schedule.

Your assistant director, not you, should be in charge of noting who is not present at the start of each rehearsal. While you are preparing for rehearsal, they can be locating missing students. It is wise, though, for only adults to issue demerits for tardiness.

Here is an idea for making your scheduling easier. Have you ever accidentally omitted a student from the rehearsal schedule because you were scanning the script for names? Instead, make a list of the page numbers (or scenes) from your play. Post these on the callboard and have students sign each page (or scene) in which they act. After you make your rehearsal schedule, your assistant can match names and pages/scenes quickly, noting each student who is called that day. It is a quick procedure that saves a great deal of time and worry.

PROPS

Have you ever needed an unusual prop but had no idea where to find it or how to go about making it? Every director and theatre teacher has had some crazy item that pushed their imaginations and their patience to the limit. You try to think "outside the box," but that means coming up with unique props and one-of-a-kind costume pieces that you will probably spend more time getting than the audience will even notice or appreciate. However, once the creative idea has struck, even if the audience could care less, you care, and nothing less will do. The following are some suggestions that the teachers, directors, club officers, parents, or any other patrons can use to feed their creative fancies.

- Host a scavenger hunt. Make a detailed list of everything you need on the *Production Needs List* and give every item a point value, possibly based on how difficult it might be to find or how expensive it would be to buy. Have parents, cast, crew, and other volunteers meet on a Saturday morning and break them into teams—each supervised by an adult. Give each a list and a deadline time, maybe about three hours. Send them out into the community with instructions to bring back as many items as possible. Tell them to get the donors' names for the program, and if items have to be returned, make sure they write down the addresses. Give the team with the most points free tickets or a pizza party. They are sure to be hungry after all their hard work. Give all the participants a reward, because without their efforts, your job would have been much harder.

- If you use the demerit system for tardiness or talking backstage, allow the students the opportunity to work off their demerits by finding props from your list. Again, by assigning point values to the items, you can have any number of points equal one demerit!

- Have a parent meeting or send a letter home itemizing needed props. Parents are super resources!

- Antique shops will often lend props in exchange for an ad in the program.

- Neighbors are usually happy to lend or donate unusual props.

- Make unique props using foam (spray/blocks), automobile headliner, tulle, soft wood, Plexiglas, plaster of paris, and recyclables.

- If you ask the art teacher, they may assign a prop to an advanced class as a project. The music teacher could have students brainstorm vocal or musical sound effects. The home economics teacher could have students make a costume or two. You may find that many teachers want to donate old items or help with the creation of needed props.

- If you are at the middle school level, consider requesting assistance from the drama department at the school your students will feed into. If you are at the high school level, contact your area community college theatre program for assistance with props. Often you can trade with them for their troubles. For example, after completing a production of *Alice in Wonderland*, you could barter with the director of another play, sending your large mushroom prop in exchange for one of the other school's props.

- If there are many theatre programs in your area, create a Facebook page for prop and costumes you no longer need or would like to use for bartering, and invite all the directors to participate.

- There are some wonderful supply houses that specialize in commonly used props. They are fairly reasonable, and you will have the props for future use too. When possible, it is better to buy than rent because the rent prices are often similar to the purchase prices, and afterward, you have nothing concrete to show for the money you spent.

- Some great items to hang on to when you come across them include any kind of foam or soft wood, large pieces of cardboard, corrugated aluminum, old wood paneling, any large amount of fabric (to use as wallpaper, drapes, or a backdrop), unused wallpaper, framed pictures (you can paint over large pictures when a specific painting is needed), rugs, Plexiglas, Halloween costumes and props, children's books and paper dolls (excellent costume ideas), partial cans of paint and any other art and craft supplies, and silk foliage and flowers.

- Search on the internet or on social media for schools or theatres that have performed your play recently. You can also ask the publisher for a list of those who have recently produced the play. Contact those directors to inquire about using their props or their resources.

- Search on eBay, Facebook Marketplace, or any other online resource for used props.

THE PROGRAM (PLAYBILL)

Start working on your program early. Unless you have a parent or reliable student who has volunteered to oversee ad sales, you may want to consider keeping the program simple. Still, even the simplest playbill should include the following:

- The exact play title and playwright(s) according to the script. The playwright's name should be no less than half the size of the title. If it is a musical, make sure you credit both the writer of the music and of the lyrics if not the same person.

- The required verbiage from the publisher stating that your performance of the play is legal: "Produced by special arrangement with Pioneer Drama Service, Inc., Englewood, Colorado." This line must be included on all your posters and printed advertisements and as well as on the printed playbill. The line suggests that permission has been obtained. Please read carefully the paragraphs below for additional information on the legality of obtaining permission.

- The cast and crew list, including the adult participants.

- Dates, times, and locations of the performances.

- A list of musical numbers and who sings in each song if your production is a musical.

- Optional items:

  ◇ Special thanks. Who has supported your program? Don't forget to thank your administration and the school janitor

  ◇ A synopsis (especially useful if your play is complex)

  ◇ Breakdown of acts and/or scenes with their locations and when they take place

◇ A letter from the director

◇ Student pictures and bios, created from having them fill out the *Biography Worksheet* (found on page 73 and in Chapter 6)

◇ Advertisements (especially if this is a fundraiser!)

Purchasing enough scripts for the entire cast, paying royalties for performing rights, and crediting the playwright and the publisher of the play are not only the director's responsibility as an artist but are also the law. Between the playwright, who spent a great deal of time creating the work, and the publisher, who makes it available for all of us, they own all the rights. When a director photocopies a script without permission and/or produces a play without paying the royalties, it is the same as stealing. They are taking something that belongs to somebody else without compensating them for it.

Producing a play illegally might seem like it would save you money, but it is illegal and the cost you pay will be far more than you think. If a teacher is caught infringing the copyright, the fines can be thousands of dollars, plus the teacher could be out of a job and subject to a lawsuit.

Even beyond the legalities, think of the lesson you are teaching your students if you choose to illegally make photocopies of the script or produce a play without paying the royalties. Do you really want to role model for them that it is okay to break the law and steal things just because you can't afford to pay for them?

COSTUMES

Your costumer will appreciate the *Costume Measurements* form included on page 74, and so will you. Because costumes for each show are unique, not all measurements are needed. Customize your form by including only what you need. This will save you valuable rehearsal time, and by filing it, you will have access to student sizes for future shows. You might need to update some measurements, so ask students if their sizes have changed.

Remember, just as you can keep stock set pieces, you might be able to have a stock costume supply. Many items can be slightly altered to create a period costume or accessory. Some helpful items to keep in stock include long, full skirts and petticoats, high-neck shirts (ruffles, lace, ties, plain, short or long sleeves) and tuxedo shirts, eyeglasses, hats, suspenders, belts, gloves, capes, shawls, jewelry, boas, ties, aprons, vests, and boots.

AUDITION APPLICATION

_____

SHOW TITLE

AUDITION DATES:_____AUDITION TIMES:_____

PLEASE PREPARE:_____REHEARSALS BEGIN:_____

NAME: _____ GRADE: _____ PHONE: _____

WHICH ROLES DO YOU SEEK?

| _____ | _____ | _____ |
| First Choice | Second Choice | Third Choice |

WHICH CREWS DO YOU SEEK?

| _____ | _____ | _____ |
| First Choice | Second Choice | Third Choice |

Previous acting experience:_____

_____

Acting classes:_____

_____

Stagecraft classes: _____

_____

Can you dance?   Very well   Good   Fair   Not at all   Will try to learn

  Circle all that apply: Tap   Jazz   Ballet   Modern   Couples   Line   Other:_____

Can you sing?   Very well   Good   Fair   Not at all   Will try to learn

Potential rehearsal conflicts (including dates):_____

_____

Explain why you should be selected for the cast: _____

_____

☐ _My child has permission to audition and attend all rehearsals._

Parent Signature _____ Date _____

AUDITION SCORECARD

PLAY:_____   1 = poor 3 = average 5 = excellent

JUDGE/DIRECTOR:_____   **MALES FEMALES BOTH**

#	NAME	AUDITION	AUDITION	AUDITION	AUDITION	AVG.
		1 2 3 4 5	1 2 3 4 5	1 2 3 4 5	1 2 3 4 5	
		1 2 3 4 5	1 2 3 4 5	1 2 3 4 5	1 2 3 4 5	
		1 2 3 4 5	1 2 3 4 5	1 2 3 4 5	1 2 3 4 5	
		1 2 3 4 5	1 2 3 4 5	1 2 3 4 5	1 2 3 4 5	
		1 2 3 4 5	1 2 3 4 5	1 2 3 4 5	1 2 3 4 5	
		1 2 3 4 5	1 2 3 4 5	1 2 3 4 5	1 2 3 4 5	
		1 2 3 4 5	1 2 3 4 5	1 2 3 4 5	1 2 3 4 5	
		1 2 3 4 5	1 2 3 4 5	1 2 3 4 5	1 2 3 4 5	
		1 2 3 4 5	1 2 3 4 5	1 2 3 4 5	1 2 3 4 5	
		1 2 3 4 5	1 2 3 4 5	1 2 3 4 5	1 2 3 4 5	
		1 2 3 4 5	1 2 3 4 5	1 2 3 4 5	1 2 3 4 5	
		1 2 3 4 5	1 2 3 4 5	1 2 3 4 5	1 2 3 4 5	
		1 2 3 4 5	1 2 3 4 5	1 2 3 4 5	1 2 3 4 5	
		1 2 3 4 5	1 2 3 4 5	1 2 3 4 5	1 2 3 4 5	
		1 2 3 4 5	1 2 3 4 5	1 2 3 4 5	1 2 3 4 5	
		1 2 3 4 5	1 2 3 4 5	1 2 3 4 5	1 2 3 4 5	
		1 2 3 4 5	1 2 3 4 5	1 2 3 4 5	1 2 3 4 5	
		1 2 3 4 5	1 2 3 4 5	1 2 3 4 5	1 2 3 4 5	
		1 2 3 4 5	1 2 3 4 5	1 2 3 4 5	1 2 3 4 5	
		1 2 3 4 5	1 2 3 4 5	1 2 3 4 5	1 2 3 4 5	
		1 2 3 4 5	1 2 3 4 5	1 2 3 4 5	1 2 3 4 5	

PRODUCTION CONTRACT

Student: _____ Show: _____

Position/Role:_____

There is a production fee of $_____ for this role. It is due by _____.

REHEARSALS

- Please mark rehearsals on your calendar as soon as the schedule is posted.
- Attendance and promptness are extremely important. ***Please, attend all scheduled rehearsals and be on time.***
- If you *must* be absent or tardy, call _____ at _____ and leave a detailed explanation.

Rehearsals you are expected to attend: Few   Several   Most   All

Rehearsals begin: _____ and end _____

Approximate rehearsal times: _____ through _____

Times _____ will _____ will not   run later during technical week and dress rehearsals.

The show runs: _____ through _____

OTHER REHEARSAL RESPONSIBILITIES

- Pay attention to the rehearsal schedule and make all deadlines.
- Be of assistance when and where possible.
- Keep the rehearsal facility neat.
- Respect others' property.
- Respect fellow cast and crew members, directors, parents, and any other participants.

COSTUMES

_____ Students will need to provide their own costumes.

_____ Students will need to pay for costume rentals.

_____ Students' costumes will be provided.

PARENT VOLUNTEERS ARE NEEDED

Parents, please circle all areas with which you're able to assist.

Transportation	Snacks	Set Construction	Ticket Sales	_____
Errands	Drinks	Box Office	Publicity	_____
Poster Design	Program Design	Props	Sewing	_____

PARENT INFORMATION

Name(s): _____ Email(s): _____

Phone(s): _____

I understand all that is expected of me and promise to abide by the above rules. My parents are aware of and support the rules of this contract.

_____   _____
Student   Date   Parent   Date

REHEARSAL ATTENDANCE

Show: _____ Week of: _____

NAME	CHARACTER	MON SCENES:	TUES SCENES:	WED SCENES:	THURS SCENES:	FRI SCENES:	SAT SCENES:	SUN SCENES:
		TIME IN: NOT CALLED	TIME IN: NOT CALLED	TIME IN: NOT CALLED	TIME IN: NOT CALLED	TIME IN: NOT CALLED	TIME IN: NOT CALLED	TIME IN: NOT CALLED
		TIME IN: NOT CALLED	TIME IN: NOT CALLED	TIME IN: NOT CALLED	TIME IN: NOT CALLED	TIME IN: NOT CALLED	TIME IN: NOT CALLED	TIME IN: NOT CALLED
		TIME IN: NOT CALLED	TIME IN: NOT CALLED	TIME IN: NOT CALLED	TIME IN: NOT CALLED	TIME IN: NOT CALLED	TIME IN: NOT CALLED	TIME IN: NOT CALLED
		TIME IN: NOT CALLED	TIME IN: NOT CALLED	TIME IN: NOT CALLED	TIME IN: NOT CALLED	TIME IN: NOT CALLED	TIME IN: NOT CALLED	TIME IN: NOT CALLED
		TIME IN: NOT CALLED	TIME IN: NOT CALLED	TIME IN: NOT CALLED	TIME IN: NOT CALLED	TIME IN: NOT CALLED	TIME IN: NOT CALLED	TIME IN: NOT CALLED
		TIME IN: NOT CALLED	TIME IN: NOT CALLED	TIME IN: NOT CALLED	TIME IN: NOT CALLED	TIME IN: NOT CALLED	TIME IN: NOT CALLED	TIME IN: NOT CALLED
		TIME IN: NOT CALLED	TIME IN: NOT CALLED	TIME IN: NOT CALLED	TIME IN: NOT CALLED	TIME IN: NOT CALLED	TIME IN: NOT CALLED	TIME IN: NOT CALLED
		TIME IN: NOT CALLED	TIME IN: NOT CALLED	TIME IN: NOT CALLED	TIME IN: NOT CALLED	TIME IN: NOT CALLED	TIME IN: NOT CALLED	TIME IN: NOT CALLED
		TIME IN: NOT CALLED	TIME IN: NOT CALLED	TIME IN: NOT CALLED	TIME IN: NOT CALLED	TIME IN: NOT CALLED	TIME IN: NOT CALLED	TIME IN: NOT CALLED
		TIME IN: NOT CALLED	TIME IN: NOT CALLED	TIME IN: NOT CALLED	TIME IN: NOT CALLED	TIME IN: NOT CALLED	TIME IN: NOT CALLED	TIME IN: NOT CALLED
		TIME IN: NOT CALLED	TIME IN: NOT CALLED	TIME IN: NOT CALLED	TIME IN: NOT CALLED	TIME IN: NOT CALLED	TIME IN: NOT CALLED	TIME IN: NOT CALLED
		TIME IN: NOT CALLED	TIME IN: NOT CALLED	TIME IN: NOT CALLED	TIME IN: NOT CALLED	TIME IN: NOT CALLED	TIME IN: NOT CALLED	TIME IN: NOT CALLED

PRODUCTION NEEDS LIST

Show: _____ Director(s): _____

Run Dates: _____ Props Mgr: _____ Costumes Mgr: _____

ITEM NEEDED/DESCRIPTION	SCENE	DIFFICULT TO FIND?	BORROWED FROM OR DONATED BY	DATE RETURNED
		HIGH MEDIUM LOW	Needs to be returned ☐	
		HIGH MEDIUM LOW	☐	
		HIGH MEDIUM LOW	☐	
		HIGH MEDIUM LOW	☐	
		HIGH MEDIUM LOW	☐	
		HIGH MEDIUM LOW	☐	
		HIGH MEDIUM LOW	☐	
		HIGH MEDIUM LOW	☐	
		HIGH MEDIUM LOW	☐	
		HIGH MEDIUM LOW	☐	
		HIGH MEDIUM LOW	☐	
		HIGH MEDIUM LOW	☐	
		HIGH MEDIUM LOW	☐	

LOCAL MEDIA

Of course you will publicize your upcoming show heavily on social media and your school and community's websites. But some people ignore all the advertisements they see online. That is why it is important to diversify your publicity to reach out to your community in a wide variety of ways. Consider these "old school" approaches in the chart below. They can still be very effective! Just make sure you leave yourself plenty of time as many of these will have deadlines several weeks in advance.

Name of Media	Contact	Phone Number	Email Address	Website
School Paper				
Local Paper				
School District Newsletter				
PTA Newsletter				
Local Radio Station				
Public Access TV				
Corporate Sponsors				
Other				

NEWS RELEASE FORM

Name of School: _____

Name of Director(s): _____

Title: _____

Playwright: _____

Presented By: _____

Dates and Times: _____

Location: _____

Reserved Tickets? Y   N   Phone: _____

Web Page: _____ Email: _____

Ticket Prices: Adult _____ Children _____ Students _____ Seniors _____

Synopsis or Description of Entertainment:

_____

_____

_____

_____

Event Sponsors:

_____

_____

_____

Other Information:

PUBLICITY CHECKLIST

Name of Show: _____ Dates: _____

Publicity Chairperson: _____

Publicity Committee: _____

DUTY	ASSIGNED TO	DEADLINE	COMPLETED?
Announce cast on school PA			
Submit news releases to school papers			
Design program			
Acquire student biographies for program			
Get ads for program			
Print program			
Design poster			
Print posters			
Distribute posters			
Design and print tickets			
Design flier			
Print fliers			
Distribute fliers			
Invite newspapers to rehearsal			
Submit news releases to papers			
Submit news releases to radio			
Make school PA announcement			
Make picture collage for lobby			
Invite administration/board			

DESIGNING YOUR POSTER

Designing your show poster can be a great deal of fun, and the finished products make excellent souvenirs for the cast and crew. This worksheet will help you to design and print your show's poster and can also be used for project posters in class.

Decide on a budget for the posters:

$_____

POSTER CONTENT

Show:_____

Playwright(s): _____

Presented by: _____

Dates: _____ Times:_____

Location:_____

Address:_____

Ticket Prices: Adults _____ Children _____ Students _____ Seniors _____

*How will you credit the publisher *(see script)*:_____

POSTER DESIGN

Who will design the posters?_____

What size will they be?_____

How many colors? Bleed or no bleed?_____

When is the deadline for completing the design?_____

COMPLETING THE PROJECT

How many posters will be printed?_____

Who will print them?_____

When is the deadline for getting them printed?_____

When does the printer need the art to meet the deadline?_____

Who will pick them up from the printer?_____

*Crediting the publisher is a legal and contractual requirement in most cases and is generally specified on the copyright page of the script.

BIOGRAPHY WORKSHEET

Complete this form and return it to _____

by _____ for your bio in the program.

Name *(as you want it to appear in the program)*:

_____

Character(s): _____

Crew(s): _____

Number of years in drama: _____ Drama club member: ☐ Yes ☐ No

Clubs and offices held: _____

_____

_____

Other activities: _____

_____

_____

Out of school activities: _____

_____

_____

Previous roles in plays: _____

Plans for the future: _____

_____

_____

Special thanks *(remember those who lent you props, etc.)*:

_____

_____

_____

_____

COSTUME MEASUREMENTS

SHOW: _____ COSTUMER: _____

	ACTOR	CHARACTER	SUIT SIZE	WEIGHT	HEIGHT	CHEST	WAIST	HIPS	OUT SEAM	INSEAM	THIGH	NECK	SLEEVE	HAT	SHOULDER TO SHOULDER	NAPE TO WAIST	NAPE TO FLOOR
M F																	
M F																	
M F																	
M F																	
M F																	
M F																	
M F																	
M F																	
M F																	
M F																	
M F																	
M F																	
M F																	
M F																	
M F																	
M F																	
M F																	
M F																	
M F																	
M F																	
M F																	
M F																	

SECTION 4
TESTS AND MAJOR PROJECTS

TESTS

Evaluation Test A (Difficult)
Evaluation Test B (Modified)
Recommended Essay Questions, Scoring, and Keys
Theatre History Test A (Difficult)
Theatre History Test B (Modified)
Recommended Essay Questions, Scoring, and Keys

MAJOR PROJECTS AND ADDITIONAL CREDIT

Major Project and Additional Credit Assignments
Major Project Questionnaire
Major Project Evaluation Tool

NAME _____ PERIOD _____ DATE _____

EVALUATION TEST A

1. **Evaluating talent is difficult, because it is based on:**

    A. Research   B. Opinion   C. Popularity   D. Mathematical Formulas

2. **A good actor uses their reviews:**

    A. To make improvements before his next performance.
    B. To get his firewood started.
    C. To show other actors how good he is.
    D. To get a raise.

3. **Knowing our strengths, using them well, and taking pride in them is a sign of:**

    A. Conceitedness   B. Trouble   C. Self-absorption   D. Confidence

4. **Whose evaluations should an actor consider when making an improvement plan?**

    A. Other students'   B. Their own   C. The teacher's   D. All of them

5. **Tyler is a young actor. Which of the following describes the preferred approach for his performance?**

    A. The teacher calls his name, so Tyler looks for his script. He can't find it, so he asks the teacher to make him a copy from her book. After several minutes, he takes the stage.
    B. The teacher calls his name, and Tyler takes his script to the stage saying that he's not ready and wishes he could go later.
    C. The teacher calls his name, Tyler gives his script to a prompter, and then he takes the stage and waits for the teacher to signal him to begin.
    D. The teacher calls his name, Tyler gives his script to a prompter, goes to get a drink of water, spits out his gum, and waits by the trash can talking to a friend until the teacher signals that she is ready.

6. **You can add energy to your scene with which of the following?**

    A. Action   B. Voice   C. Facial Expressions   D. All are correct

7. **In order for an actor's voice to be heard by everyone in the audience, the actor must:**

    A. Yell   B. Project   C. Stage Whisper   D. Use a microphone

8. **Actors must have very clear speech. Which of the following is not a factor in clear speech?**

    A. Gestures   B. Diction   C. Articulation   D. Projection

9. **You watch Zach, an actor, speak as though he wants to be heard. He projects, he is articulate and natural, and his voice is pleasant and fits the character. He does not appear to have stage fright. He is said to have vocal _____:**

    A. Confidence   B. Quality   C. Mastery   D. All are correct

10. **The way in which an actor holds their body to show age, health, confidence, and so on is called:**

    A. Gestures   B. Blocking   C. Business   D. Posture

11. **To plan out the stage movements characters will make in a play or scene is called:**

    A. Gesturing   B. Blocking   C. Business   D. Posturing

12. **The movements an actor makes with their hands to reinforce what they are saying are called:**

    A. Gestures   B. Blocking   C. Business   D. Postures

13. **The little things an actor does onstage to make their character appear "busy" are called:**

    A. Gestures   B. Blocking   C. Business   D. Postures

14. **Gestures, blocking, business, and posture are all a part of the actor's _____ or non-verbal communication.**

    A. Movement   B. Body Language   C. Pantomime   D. Mastery

15. **Every scene should include:**

    A. A Beginning   B. A Climax   C. An Ending   D. All are correct

16. **Which of the following best describes a "well-paced scene"?**

    A. It shows the audience that even though a scene is not memorized, it will be okay.

    B. It does not have to be interesting at all times or hold the audience's attention.

    C. It expresses the actor's understanding of the scene and their confidence in themself.

    D. It will exceed the teacher's time limit because that will show dedication.

17. **To make each scene and its characters unique and interesting, the actors need to:**

    A. Fully understand the play and its characters.

    B. Watch and copy the movie version, if there is one.

    C. Create a performance that will shock the audience into watching.

    D. Find a way to add stage combat and yell a lot.

18. **What is the most acceptable way to handle a distraction if you are onstage performing a scene?**

    A. If the announcements come on, speak louder than them and keep going.

    B. If someone is talking, shoot them a mean look each time they talk, but keep going.

    C. If a visitor walks in noisily, stay focused and in character, and keep going.

    D. If someone is making faces, stop, tell the teacher, and request their removal.

19. **What is the only acceptable thing to do after your performance?**

    A. Take your seat and evaluate yourself quietly.

    B. Roll your eyes because you forgot your lines.

    C. Ask for a re-do.

    D. Ask to see what your neighbor wrote about your performance.

20. **Memorizing your lines very well will help your scene in many ways. Which of the following statements about memorization is not true?**

    A. If you are unsure of your lines, you are more likely to have stage fright.

    B. Memorizing too well will take the freshness and spontaneity out of the scene.

    C. Forgetting lines early in rehearsals is normal, but as you get closer to performance, memorization should become second-nature.

    D. If you forget a line during rehearsal, stay focused and in character, and if the line still will not come, call out "line."

NAME _____ PERIOD _____ DATE _____

EVALUATION TEST B

1. **Evaluating talent is difficult because it is based on:**

    A. Opinion   B. Scientific Research

2. **A good actor uses reviews:**

    A. To make improvements before their next performance.

    B. To show other actors how good they are.

3. **Knowing our strengths, using them well, and taking pride in them is a sign of:**

    A. Conceitedness   B. Confidence

4. **Which evaluations should you consider when making an improvement plan?**

    A. Only the ones you like

    B. The teachers, other students, and your own

5. **Which of the following describes the preferred approach for you to take the stage?**

    A. The teacher calls your name, so you look for your script. You can't find it, so you ask the teacher to make a copy. After several minutes, you take the stage.

    B. The teacher calls your name, you give your script to a prompter, and then you take the stage and wait for the teacher to signal you to begin.

6. **You can introduce energy into your scene with which of the following?**

    A. Action, voice, and facial expressions

    B. By adding in a lot of stage combat that wasn't in the original script

7. **In order for your voice to be heard by everyone in the audience, you must learn to:**

    A. Yell   B. Project

8. **Actors must have very clear speech. Which of the following is not a factor in clear speech?**

    A. Gestures   B. Articulation

9. **You watch Zach, an actor, speak as though he wants to be heard. He projects, he is articulate and natural, and his voice is pleasant and fits the character. He does not appear to have stage fright. He is said to have vocal _____:**

    A. Confidence   B. Loudness

10. **The way in which an actor holds their body to show age, health, the character's confidence, and so on is called:**

    A. Business   B. Posture

11. **To plan out the stage movements characters will make in a play or scene is called:**

    A. Gesturing   B. Blocking

12. **The movements an actor makes with their hands to reinforce what they are saying are called:**

    A. Gestures   B. Blocking

13. **The little things an actor does onstage to make their character appear "busy" are called:**

    A. Business   B. Posture

14. **Gestures, blocking, business, and posture are all a part of the actor's _____ or non-verbal communication.**

    A. Movement   B. Body Language

15. **Every scene should include:**

    A. A beginning, climax, and ending.

    B. At least one good, loud argument.

16. **Which of the following best describes a "well-paced scene"?**

    A. It shows the audience that even though a scene is not memorized, it will be okay.

    B. It expresses the actor's understanding of the scene and their confidence in themself.

17. **To make each scene and its characters unique and interesting, the actors need to:**

    A. Fully understand the play and its characters.

    B. Watch and copy the movie version, if there is one.

18. **What is the most acceptable way to handle a distraction if you are performing a scene?**

    A. If the announcements come on, speak louder than them and keep going.

    B. If a visitor walks in noisily, stay focused and in character, and keep going.

19. **What is the only acceptable thing to do after your performance?**

    A. Take your seat and evaluate yourself quietly.

    B. Ask for a re-do.

20. **Memorizing your lines very well will help your scene in many ways. Which of the following statements about memorization is true?**

    A. If you are unsure of your lines, you are more likely to have stage fright.

    B. Memorizing too well will take the freshness and spontaneity out of the scene.

RECOMMENDED ESSAY QUESTIONS

1. **(Hard)** Acting is an art and a talent, like drawing and music. Some students feel uncomfortable being graded on their scenes or evaluating their peers because they consider talent something with which one is born and not something that can be taught. How would you convince a reluctant student that grading and evaluation are necessary and beneficial?

   (Easy) List five reasons why having your performance evaluated is necessary and beneficial.

2. **(Hard)** What would you like to be when you grow up? List the top five skills on the *Performance Evaluation* form that will most likely be a part of this chosen profession and explain how sharpening these skills will help you to succeed.

   (Easy) What would you like to be when you grow up? Think about the skills your teacher will critique during performances in this class. List three that you think will help you in your chosen profession and explain how improving them will help you in your future job.

3. **(Hard)** Confidence is a very important part of performing. Lacking confidence is one reason those with stage fright become nervous prior to taking the stage. They fear that those watching them will be critical of their performance. List four ways you think the class, teacher, and/or performer can alleviate this pre-performance stress.

   (Easy) Some students are afraid to perform in front of the class. They fear that their peers will make fun of them or judge them harshly. What could you say to them to help them feel more comfortable? Can you think of anything they could do to make themselves feel less nervous?

SCORING

The *Evaluation Tests*, both A and B, each have twenty questions. Without an essay question, each correct test answer is valued at five points using a 100-point grading scale. It is recommended that you include at least one essay question valued at 10 or 15. The following scale will make grading your tests easier.

At 5 points each, no essay question, find the number of questions missed and the percentage will follow:

-1 = 95	-5 = 75	-9 = 55	-13 = 35	-17 = 15
-2 = 90	-6 = 70	-10 = 50	-14 = 30	-18 = 10
-3 = 85	-7 = 65	-11 = 45	-15 = 25	-19 = 5
-4 = 80	-8 = 60	-12 = 40	-16 = 20	-20 = 0

If you include a 20-point essay question,
each correct answer will be worth 4 points instead of 5.

KEY: TEST A		KEY: TEST B	
1. B	11. B	1. A	11. B
2. A	12. A	2. A	12. A
3. D	13. C	3. B	13. A
4. D	14. B	4. B	14. B
5. C	15. D	5. B	15. A
6. D	16. C	6. A	16. B
7. B	17. A	7. B	17. A
8. A	18. C	8. A	18. B
9. A	19. A	9. A	19. A
10. D	20. B	10. B	20. A

NAME _____ PERIOD _____ DATE _____

THEATRE HISTORY TEST A

1. The first recorded theatrical performance was in _____ in about 2000 BC.
   A. Japan   B. Rome   C. Egypt   D. Spain

2. Despite the above recorded performance, the Greeks are credited with starting theatre to honor the god:
   A. Dionysis   B. Osiris   C. Zeus   D. Thespis

3. The Greek chorus originally danced around an altar singing the _____ or tragos.
   A. Wolf Song   B. Goat Song   C. Whale Song   D. God Song

4. The chorus member who stepped away from the chorus and engaged in dialogue was _____ , the first actor.
   A. Dionysis   B. Osiris   C. Zeus   D. Thespis

5. All of the acting in Greek plays was done by:
   A. Officials   B. Men   C. Women   D. Slaves

6. The writer of *Euminides* and the man who is often called the "Father of Tragedy" is:
   A. Euripides   B. Sophocles   C. Aeschylus   D. Aristophanes

7. _____ wrote *Oedipus the King* and *Antigone* and is often compared to Shakespeare as one of the greatest playwrights of all time.
   A. Euripides   B. Sophocles   C. Aeschylus   D. Aristophanes

8. _____ wrote about women, such as *Medea*, and he originated the prologue to summarize the plot for the audience prior to the action of the play.
   A. Euripides   B. Sophocles   C. Aeschylus   D. Aristophanes

9. The only writer of Greek comedy whose plays exist in whole today is _____ , who wrote *Birds* and *Frogs*.
   A. Euripides   B. Sophocles   C. Aeschylus   D. Aristophanes

10. Roman plays, which are not considered in the same class with Greek plays, consisted of:
    A. Dancing   B. Horseplay   C. Obscene mimes   D. All are correct

11. Which of the following was not a Roman writer?
    A. Plautus   B. Agamemnon   C. Terence   D. Seneca

12. In the medieval period, _____ plays were based on the lives of saints and stories from the Bible.
    A. Miracle   B. Passion   C. Morality   D. Masque

13. A play based on Christ's final week is called a _____ play.
    A. Miracle   B. Passion   C. Morality   D. Masque

14. Plays that were written to teach basic principles of right versus wrong are called _____ plays.
    A. Miracle   B. Passion   C. Morality   D. Masque

15. A spectacular play which used excess and extravagance to glorify the nobility was a:
    A. Miracle   B. Passion   C. Morality   D. Masque

16. Named after the queen who ruled for a great part of it, the _____ or Renaissance period saw a rebirth of great comedy and drama.
    A. Elizabethan   B. Victorian   C. Georgian   D. Italian

17. To finance their endeavors and to maintain their reputations, Renaissance actors sought the patronage of:
    A. Writers   B. Guilds   C. Gypsies   D. Noblemen

18. During the Renaissance period, _____ were prevented from acting for fear that it would cause immorality.
    A. Women   B. Criminals   C. Servants   D. Noblemen

19. The Elizabethan writer who is credited with introducing blank verse and who wrote *The Tragical History of Doctor Faustus* is:

    A. Ben Jonson   B. Christopher Marlowe   C. William Shakespeare

20. The bitter Elizabethan writer who got into trouble for writing whatever he felt was:

    A. Ben Jonson   B. Christopher Marlowe   C. William Shakespeare

21. Which of the following is not a Shakespearean play?

    A. *Volpone*   B. *Hamlet*   C. *Macbeth*   D. *Othello*

22. A poor man who wanted to attend a play by Marlowe, Jonson, or Shakespeare could stand in the "pit," the area in front of the stage. The people in this area were called:

    A. Penny Men   B. Groundlings   C. Standers   D. Pitters

23. Commedia dell'arte performances did not include which of the following:

    A. Scripts   B. Plots   C. Sub-Plots   D. Stock Characters

24. Commedia dell'arte plays were performed by traveling _____.

    A. Companies   B. Lazzi   C. Burle   D. Zanni

25. In commedia dell'arte, beautiful young lovers were called:

    A. Pantalone   B. Il Capitano   C. Innamorata   D. Fontesca

26. In commedia dell'arte, the flirtatious maidservant was the:

    A. Pantalone   B. Il Capitano   C. Innamorata   D. Fontesca

27. In commedia dell'arte, the heroine's father was named:

    A. Pantalone   B. Il Capitano   C. Innamorata   D. Fontesca

28. The English Royal Patent of 1662 did what?

    A. Made theatre illegal   B. Allowed women to act   C. "Legitimized" theatre   D. Both B and C

29. The comic trendsetter of the Restoration period who wrote *The Country Wife* was:

    A. William Congreve   B. George Farquhar   C. William Wycherly

30. The playwright who challenged audiences to think and who wrote *Arms and the Man* and *Saint Joan* was:

    A. Oscar Wilde   B. George Bernard Shaw   C. Oliver Goldsmith

31. The Japanese theatre style that uses dolls or puppets is called:

    A. Kabuki   B. Noh   C. Bunraku

32. The Japanese theatre style named after its three parts (singing, dancing, and acting) is:

    A. Kabuki   B. Noh   C. Bunraku

33. The American stage at first borrowed its early plots from the plays of _____.

    A. Japan   B. Italy   C. France   D. Britain

34. The eventual greatness of the American stage was almost overshadowed by the sudden impact of:

    A. Film   B. The Car   C. The Computer   D. The Telephone

35. _____ wrote *The Iceman Cometh* and *A Long Day's Journey into Night*.

    A. Eugene O'Neill   B. Thornton Wilder   C. Arthur Miller

36. The author of *Death of a Salesman* and *The Crucible* is:

    A. Eugene O'Neill   B. Thornton Wilder   C. Arthur Miller

37. _____ wrote *Cat on a Hot Tin Roof*, *A Streetcar Named Desire*, and *Night of the Iguana*.

    A. Thornton Wilder   B. Arthur Miller   C. Tennessee Williams

38. She wrote about a black family's struggles in *A Raisin in the Sun* and won a Pulitzer Prize for it.

    A. Lorraine Hansberry   B. Beth Henley   C. Lillian Hellman

NAME _____ PERIOD _____ DATE _____

THEATRE HISTORY TEST B

1. The first recorded theatrical performance was in _____ in about 2000 BC.
    A. Egypt   B. Rome

2. Despite the above recorded performance, the Greeks are credited with starting theatre to honor the god _____.
    A. Dionysis   B. Thespis

3. The Greek chorus originally danced around an altar singing the _____ or tragos.
    A. Wolf Song   B. Goat Song

4. The chorus member who stepped away from the chorus and engaged in dialogue with them was _____, the first actor.
    A. Dionysis   B. Thespis

5. All of the acting in Greek plays was done by _____.
    A. Officials   B. Men

6. The writer of *Euminides* and the man who is often called the "Father of Tragedy" is _____.
    A. Aeschylus   B. Sophocles

7. _____ wrote *Oedipus the King* and *Antigone* and is often compared to Shakespeare as one of the greatest playwrights of all time.
    A. Euripides   B. Sophocles

8. _____ wrote about women, such as *Medea*, and he originated the prologue to summarize the plot for the audience prior to the action of the play.
    A. Euripides   B. Aristophanes

9. The only writer of Greek comedy whose plays exist in whole today is _____, who wrote *Birds* and *Frogs*.
    A. Euripides   B. Aristophanes

10. Roman plays, which are not considered in the same class with Greek plays, consisted of:
    A. Horseplay   B. Complex plots and well-developed characters

11. Which of the following was not a Roman writer?
    A. Plautus   B. Agamemnon

12. In the medieval period, _____ plays were based on the lives of saints and stories from the Bible.
    A. Miracle   B. Passion

13. A play based on Christ's final week is called a _____ play.
    A. Miracle   B. Passion

14. Plays that were written to teach basic principles of right versus wrong are called _____ plays.
    A. Masque   B. Morality

15. A spectacular play which used excess and extravagance to glorify the nobility was a _____.
    A. Masque   B. Morality

16. Named after the queen who ruled for a great part of it, the _____ or Renaissance period saw a rebirth of great comedy and drama.
    A. Elizabethan   B. Victorian

17. To finance their endeavors and to maintain their reputations, actors sought the patronage of _____.
    A. Noblemen   B. Guilds

18. During this period, _____ were prevented from acting for fear that it would cause immorality.
    A. Women   B. Criminals

19. The Elizabethan writer who is credited with introducing blank verse and who wrote *The Tragical History of Doctor Faustus* is:

     A. Ben Jonson   B. Christopher Marlowe

20. The bitter Elizabethan writer who got into trouble for writing whatever he felt was:

     A. Ben Jonson   B. Christopher Marlowe

21. Which of the following is not a Shakespearean play?

     A. *Volpone*   B. *Hamlet*

22. A poor man who wanted to attend a play by Marlowe, Jonson, or Shakespeare could stand in the "pit," the area in front of the stage. The people in this area were called:

     A. Penny Men   B. Groundlings

23. Commedia dell'arte performances did not include which of the following:

     A. Scripts   B. Plots

24. Commedia dell'arte plays were performed by traveling _____.

     A. Companies   B. Lazzi

25. In commedia dell'arte, the beautiful young lovers were called:

     A. Innamorata   B. Il Capitano

26. In commedia dell'arte, the flirtatious maidservant was the:

     A. Pantalone   B. Fontesca

27. In commedia dell'arte, the heroine's father was named:

     A. Pantalone   B. Il Capitano

28. The English Royal Patent of 1662 did what?

     A. Allowed women to act   B. "Legitimized" theatre   C. Both A and B

29. The comic trendsetter of the Restoration period who wrote *The Country Wife* was:

     A. William Wycherly   B. George Farquhar

30. The playwright who challenged audiences to think and who wrote *Arms and the Man* and *Saint Joan* was:

     A. Oscar Wilde   B. George Bernard Shaw

31. The Japanese theatre style which uses dolls or puppets is called:

     A. Bunraku   B. Noh

32. The Japanese theatre style named after its three parts (singing, dancing, and acting) is:

     A. Kabuki   B. Bunraku

33. The American stage at first borrowed its early plots from the plays of _____.

     A. Italy   B. Britain

34. The eventual greatness of the American stage was almost overshadowed by the sudden impact of:

     A. Film   B. The Car

35. _____ wrote *The Iceman Cometh* and *A Long Day's Journey into Night*.

     A. Eugene O'Neill   B. Thornton Wilder

36. The author of *Death of a Salesman* and *The Crucible* is:

     A. Thornton Wilder   B. Arthur Miller

37. _____ wrote *Cat on a Hot Tin Roof*, *A Streetcar Named Desire*, and *Night of the Iguana*.

     A. Tennessee Williams   B. Arthur Miller

38. She wrote about a black family's struggles in *A Raisin in the Sun* and won a Pulitzer Prize for it.

     A. Lorraine Hansberry   B. Beth Henley

RECOMMENDED ESSAY QUESTIONS

1. **(Hard)** How did the events and politics of the various time periods affect the plays that came from each period? What clues can today's readers or audiences get from the plays to help them understand the time periods in which they were written? Will future audiences be able to do the same with movies and television shows? Explain.

   (Easy) Explain why scholars believe plays might tell us about the places, people, and times in which they were written.

2. **(Hard)** How have restrictions on free speech affected plays throughout history? Compare those restrictions with modern day "freedom of speech." Which plays are a more accurate depiction of the time in which they were written and why?

   (Easy) Why do you think rulers wanted such strict control of what playwrights could write?

3. **(Hard)** At many points throughout history, plays were used as religious tools. Explain why you think plays were used, and identify other uses for plays and movies.

   (Easy) At many points throughout history, plays were used to honor gods and to teach about religion. Explain why you think this is. Also, can you think of some other useful purposes for plays and movies?

4. **(Hard)** Identify and explain some obstacles playwrights throughout history might have faced, not just in writing their plays, but in producing them and preserving them throughout history.

   (Easy) How did politics and laws affect a writer's ability to write and produce a play? Do you think that transportation and communication might have affected their abilities? Can you think of some things that might have happened to the old manuscripts to keep them from making it to the twenty-first century?

SCORING

On a 100-point scale, each correct answer is worth 2.6 points. Use the scale below to figure grades. The number of questions answered incorrectly is on the left, and the percentage is to the right.

-1 = 97	-9 = 77	-17 = 56	-25 = 35	-33 = 14
-2 = 95	-10 = 74	-18 = 53	-26 = 32	-34 = 12
-3 = 92	-11 = 71	-19 = 51	-27 = 30	-35 = 9
-4 = 90	-12 = 69	-20 = 48	-28 = 27	-36 = 6
-5 = 87	-13 = 66	-21 = 45	-29 = 25	-37 = 3
-6 = 84	-14 = 64	-22 = 43	-30 = 22	-38 = 0
-7 = 82	-15 = 61	-23 = 40	-31 = 19	
-8 = 79	-16 = 58	-24 = 38	-32 = 17	

KEY: TEST A			
1. C	11. B	21. A	31. C
2. A	12. A	22. B	32. A
3. B	13. B	23. A	33. D
4. D	14. C	24. A	34. A
5. B	15. D	25. C	35. A
6. C	16. A	26. D	36. C
7. B	17. D	27. A	37. C
8. A	18. A	28. D	38. A
9. D	19. B	29. C	
10. D	20. A	30. B	

KEY: TEST B			
1. A	11. B	21. A	31. A
2. A	12. A	22. B	32. A
3. B	13. B	23. A	33. B
4. B	14. B	24. A	34. A
5. B	15. A	25. A	35. A
6. A	16. A	26. B	36. B
7. B	17. A	27. A	37. A
8. A	18. A	28. C	38. A
9. B	19. B	29. A	
10. A	20. A	30. B	

MAJOR PROJECTS AND ADDITIONAL CREDIT

You may not believe in extra credit, but in theatre, it is almost a necessity. Grades are, for the most part, subjective, and the work often depends on cooperation. For these two reasons, high-achieving students may have added anxiety in your class, because they feel that their final grade is out of their control. For these students, you may want to consider allowing extra credit.

The *Major Project and Additional Credit Assignments* worksheet is full of a variety of challenging tasks that, if done well, will be both educational and a well-deserved bonus. You will probably want to require that they complete the *Extra Credit Policy and Request* in Section 1 first.

Consider using assignments from the worksheet in place of six-week or nine-week tests or even instead of semester exams too. Each is designed to challenge all types of learners in some area of the industry. Some are for the creative and artistic mind and some are for the linear or analytical thinker. Regardless, students will find themselves exploring areas of theatre that would be difficult in a classroom setting.

Here are some ideas to make your projects more successful for both you and your students:

- Select a due date early and send a notice home to parents. Ask them to mark their calendars so that there will be no surprises. Require the letter to be signed and returned.

- Post reminders and reinforce the importance of the assignment and its grading weight.

- Assign the project two to three weeks before it is due; allow your students at least two weekends.

- Display projects at your next show, in your trophy case, in your school library, or even at your administration building. Invite the local paper to see the projects to write a story.

- Take pictures of some of the better projects to use as examples in the following years.

- When possible, save the best three-dimensional projects. Pictures will not capture their depth.

A week and a half before the projects are due, assign the *Major Project Questionnaire* included in this section. This reminds students that they have a major assignment due soon. They must then gather the information for their project, such as the due dates, the rules, and so on. Once this is assigned, completed, and returned, students will have no excuse for not knowing about the project or its requirements. Also, if students have not yet begun the project, this will give them the opportunity to do some last-minute preparation. There is a place for partners' phone numbers in case groups plan to get together over the weekend to complete the work. If students do not seem to be progressing sufficiently on their projects, you may want to follow up with a phone call to their parents.

The *Major Project Evaluation Tool* will assist you in grading your classes' major projects. The various areas specified in the project list have already been broken down for you and assigned point values. It is important, however, that students know exactly how they will be graded. Either post a copy of this form so that students may review it or pass it out to students with their *Major Projects and Additional Credit Assignments* worksheet or the *Major Project Questionnaire*. Save time later by having students write their names on it and return it to you, and you will be ready to grade their projects well in advance.

If you want to save time and paper, print fewer copies of the evaluation tool, cut along the lines, and pass them out to students to attach to their projects. This will also make grading a breeze!

MAJOR PROJECT AND
ADDITIONAL CREDIT ASSIGNMENTS

	CATEGORY	PROJECT	NUMBER OF PARTICIPANTS	LENGTH REQUIREMENTS	RULES Unless specified, each group will prepare a short oral presentation of its project.
1.	ACTING	MONOLOGUE	1	_____ MINUTES	Memorized, appropriate for school, from a play (no movies).
2.	ACTING	DUET	2	_____ MINUTES	Memorized, appropriate for school, from a play (no movies). Parts must be balanced.
3.	ACTING	SCENE	3 - 5	_____ MINUTES	Memorized, appropriate for school, from a play (no movies). Parts must be balanced.
4.	TECHNICAL/ COSTUMES	COSTUME DESIGN	1	_____ DESIGNS	Must be from a play with which the student is familiar. Use plain paper (no lines) and stick with the same medium throughout (all pencil or all paint–don't switch back and forth). Identify characters, scenes, and fabrics. Use fabric swatches.
5.	TECHNICAL/ COSTUMES	COSTUME CONSTRUCTION	1 - 2	1 COSTUME	Make a costume from scratch. You may use a pattern and/or seek assistance, but YOU must make the costume and wear it for the oral presentation.
6.	TECHNICAL/ SET	SET MODEL	1	1 SET	Create a three-dimensional set to scale. Include fabric and texture swatches. It must be from a play.
7.	TECHNICAL/ SET	SET DESIGN	1	_____ DESIGNS	Design scenes, all from the same play, using drawing paper and colored pencils, ink, or paint. Include fabric and texture swatches. Identify the play and the scenes.
8.	WRITING	ONE-ACT PLAY	1 - 2	_____ PAGES	Write a one-act play using stage directions, dialogue, character development, and story development. It must be typed and performed as readers theatre.
9.	MUSICAL	SONG AND DANCE	1 - 2	_____ SONGS	Perform songs and accompanying dances from musicals. Each participant must be in costume. No costume changes allowed. Numbers must be related by style, musician, or play.
10.	TECHNICAL/ PUBLICITY	PROGRAM AND POSTER DESIGN	1	1 EACH	Design a program and a poster for a play. The poster should include all of the information required by the script and should entice the audience to attend. The program should also contain important information; actors' names can be fictional.
11.	TECHNICAL/ PUBLICITY	ADVERTISING	1	SEE RULES	Create a chart of _____ (#) places in your town to which a news release could be sent about upcoming productions. Be sure to include the name of the contact, the name of the business, the address, phone number, and email address for each. Create a fictional news release sample for an upcoming play.

	CATEGORY	PROJECT	NUMBER OF PARTICIPANTS	LENGTH REQUIREMENTS	RULES *Unless specified, each group will prepare a short oral presentation of its project.*
12.	TECHNICAL/ MAKEUP	MAKEUP DESIGN	1	_____ DESIGNS	Study a makeup plot in a makeup design book. Create designs of your own including the colors you would use, how and where to apply lines, highlights, and shadows, special items like facial hair, and removal techniques. Identify the characters.
13.	VIDEO/ MAKEUP	MAKEUP VIDEO	2	1 APPLICATION	You and a friend create a video showing the steps for safely and correctly applying a particular character's stage makeup. Also include safe makeup removal and some hints on caring for stage makeup. It must include credits.
14.	VIDEO/ ACTING	MOVIE	1 - 4	_____ MINUTES	Make a video of one of the following TV genres: commercials, TV talkshows, soap operas, news, movies, or a combination of these. It must flow well, be creative, and include credits.
15.	VIDEO	ANIMATION	1 - 3	_____ MINUTES	Explore cartoons using your video camera and some toys or other props to make a stop animation video. Research the topic in books or figure it out on your own. It must have a plot and credits, and it must flow.
16.	TECHNICAL/ EDUCATION	POWERPOINT PRESENTATION	1	_____ SLIDES	Create a PowerPoint presentation on any single theatre topic and present a slide show teaching that topic to the class.
17.	THEATRE EDUCATION	ORAL REPORT	1	_____ PAGES	Write a research paper on any single theatre topic and present it to the class orally. It must be typed with works cited.
18.	THEATRE EDUCATION	BOARD GAME	1 - 2	20"X 20" OR GREATER, AT LEAST 50 QUESTIONS	Create a board game that will teach about a single theatre topic, such as Shakespeare, theatre history, or acting terminology.

NAME _____ PERIOD _____ DATE _____

MAJOR PROJECT QUESTIONNAIRE

Complete the following questions about your project. By completing this worksheet, you are indicating to your teacher that you fully understand the expectations of the assignment.

1.   Which project will you be doing? _____

        Are you allowed to change your mind? ☐ Yes ☐ No

        Do you have to fill out a new questionnaire if you change your mind? ☐ Yes ☐ No

2. Will you have any partners? ☐ Yes ☐ No

3. List your partners and their phone numbers:

a. _____   Phone #_____

b. _____   Phone #_____

c. _____   Phone #_____

d. _____   Phone #_____

4. What date is your project due? _____

5. Describe the type of project you will be doing:

_____

_____

6. How much time do you think you will put into your project?

_____

7. If you have partners, how, when, and where will you meet to work on your project?

_____

_____

8. What work have you completed on this project so far?

_____

_____

9. Why did you choose this project?

_____

_____

10. What do you hope to learn from this project?

_____

_____

_____

_____

_____   _____   _____
Student Signature   Parent Signature   Parent's Daytime Phone

NAME _____ PERIOD _____ DATE _____

MAJOR PROJECT EVALUATION TOOL

Acting/Musical #1, 2, 3, 9

The acting evaluation grade should count as 100% of the grade, including the presentation. The same evaluation is used for the musical song and dance project. You may wish to conduct a question and answer session afterward.

One-Act Play Writing #8

____ (0-20) Minimum length requirements met
____ (0-10) Neatly typed
____ (0-20) Well-developed story with beginning, climax, and ending
____ (0-20) Well-developed characters
____ (0-10) Stage directions
____ (0-10) Plot
____ (0-10) Oral presentation (performed as readers theatre)

____ Total

Makeup Video #13

____ (0-10) Steps clearly identified
____ (0-10) Steps correct
____ (0-10) Makeup safety addressed
____ (0-10) Makeup removal clearly explained
____ (0-10) Makeup care clearly explained
____ (0-15) Outcome of sample make-up application
____ (0-15) Video editing or flow
____ (0-10) Credits included
____ (0-10) Oral presentation quality

____ Total

Costume/Set Design #4, 7

____ (0-10) Minimum number of designs completed
____ (0-10) Designs fit the play
____ (0-20) Neatness, appropriate use of paper and other medium
____ (0-20) Creativity
____ (0-10) Design theory clearly explained/supported
____ (0-10) Characters/scenes clearly identified
____ (0-10) Fabric/texture swatches
____ (0-10) Oral presentation quality

____ Total

Program and Poster Design #10

____ (0-15) Poster information complete as required by publisher
____ (0-15) Program information complete as required by publisher
____ (0-25) Program design and appeal; creativity
____ (0-25) Poster design and appeal; creativity
____ (0-10) Is the poster "inviting"?
____ (0-10) Oral presentation quality

____ Total

Movie/Animation #14, 15

____ (0-10) Minimum length requirements met
____ (0-15) Plot
____ (0-15) Well-developed story with beginning, climax, and ending
____ (0-20) Flow
____ (0-20) Creativity
____ (0-10) Credits included
____ (0-10) Oral presentation quality

____ Total

Costume Construction #5

____ (0-10) Design fits the play
____ (0-50) Neatness
____ (0-10) Appropriateness of costume to character (including movement and line references)
____ (0-10) Costuming theory clearly explained in a paragraph
____ (0-10) Worn for presentation
____ (0-10) Oral presentation quality

____ Total

Advertising #11

____ (0-20) Minimum number of contacts included
____ (0-20) Contact name, business name, address, phone, and email address for each
____ (0-25) News release
____ (0-10) Neatness
____ (0-15) Creativity
____ (0-10) Oral presentation quality

____ Total

PowerPoint Oral Report #16, 17

____ (0-10) Minimum number of slides or pages
____ (0-10) Topic clearly identified
____ (0-20) Topic thoroughly researched and covered
____ (0-20) Creatively arranged or worded
____ (0-10) Grammatically correct
____ (0-20) Captivating
____ (0-10) Oral presentation quality

____ Total

Set Model #6

____ (0-20) Design fits the play
____ (0-50) Neat, solid construction
____ (0-10) Scale used and explained
____ (0-10) Design theory explained, supported by designer in a typed paragraph
____ (0-10) Oral presentation quality

____ Total

Makeup Design #12

____ (0-10) Neatness
____ (0-5) Characters/play identified
____ (0-10) Minimum number of designs
____ (0-15) Appropriate use of color
____ (0-15) Appropriate use of lines
____ (0-15) Appropriate highlights
____ (0-15) Appropriate use of shadows
____ (0-5) Removal techniques addressed
____ (0-10) Oral presentation quality

____ Total

Board Game #18

____ (0-10) Neatness, sturdiness
____ (0-10) Minimum number of questions
____ (0-10) Topic clearly identified
____ (0-20) Topic thoroughly researched and covered
____ (0-10) Creatively designed
____ (0-20) Captivating and fun
____ (0-20) Effective oral presentation

____ Total

Introduction to THEATRE ARTS

VOLUME ONE / SECOND EDITION

STUDENT WORKBOOK

WITH

ADDITIONAL NOTES FOR TEACHERS

CHAPTER 1
GETTING STARTED

THE THEATRE FAMILY

Are You Ready for the Stage?
Getting To Know You Bingo

EXPECTATIONS

Rehearsal and Performance Expectations

Rehearsal, Performance, and Classroom Expectations
Bell Work

ADDITIONAL NOTES

Lesson Plans
Drama Syllabus
    36-Week Drama Syllabus
    Student Information
Getting to Know Your Students
Expectations
Daily Bell Work

LESSON PLANS

Here are some important things to remember when planning your lessons:

It is better to plan too much than too little. Always include items or activities that will support the lesson if time allows, but if time runs out, these items can be carried into the next class or omitted altogether.

Use the two columns of the *Drama Syllabus* to keep classes organized or to differentiate between levels such as Drama 1 and Drama 2. You may divide the columns before copying if additional ones are needed.

Print enough copies of the blank *Theatre Arts Lesson Plan* for your whole semester and save the blank original. Always save completed lesson plans from year to year. Make notes about what worked and what did not.

Highlight worksheets that need to be copied; make those copies in advance.

DRAMA SYLLABUS

The *Drama Syllabus* is the suggested one for a full year course. If you follow this schedule, your students will experience every major activity in the book. Most school years are about thirty-eight weeks, and this covers only thirty-six. The last week of each semester is generally considered "dead week." Students are taking exams, and there is no time for new instruction.

There are several forms in the book that do not require students to answer questions, nor will they need to read them at great length. They are very important, though. Examples include the different evaluation instruments used. By reviewing the forms with your students, you are preparing them for the method you will use to grade their work. This gives students an edge—a chance to understand the rubric you'll be using to grade them. So take some time to analyze the forms with them, answer their questions, and clarify any misunderstandings.

Cindy is a high school theatre teacher. In her district, she is the newest of five lead teachers and four assistant teachers; she is the only lead teacher without an assistant. She and the other eight teachers were required to attend an improv workshop together for teacher in-service credit where everyone but her had a "built in" partner. She thought that surely teachers would go out of their way to include her, but they did not. In the four hours, she never had a partner for paired scenes and had to work with the improv coach, who often stopped mid-scene to discuss skills and opportunities. Cindy watched as the other eight teachers had more opportunity to act all the way through their scenes, even though she did not. She thought it odd that the coach never encouraged the nine to mix up their partners or to include her. And finally, when the other teachers were judgmental about her improvisation— because she was regularly held up as an example by her coach partner—she felt singled out. By the end of the workshop, she felt alone and defeated. She definitely felt like the other eight teachers had gone out of their way to exclude her. She immediately thought of Brayden, a young man in her class who always seemed to be the last one selected for partner work due to his learning disability. She took what she experienced back to her class and used it to become a better advocate for Brayden and other students who are often underestimated by their peers.

36-WEEK DRAMA SYLLABUS

Week 1 - Getting To Know You
Understanding *The Theatre Family*
Fill out *Student Information form*
Student introduction speeches
Are You Ready For the Stage?
Getting To Know You Bingo
Discuss Expectations
Expectations worksheet
Introduce bell work and procedures

Week 2 - Scene Work, Memorization
Understanding Scene Work
Read and discuss monologues
Select monologue to perform
Complete monologue questions
Learning to Memorize
Memorization practice
Memorization grade

Week 3 - Evaluation
Rehearse monologues
Understanding Evaluation
Evaluation Test Review
Evaluation Test
Scene Work Cut-n-Paste

Week 4 - Evaluation, Performances
Rehearse
Review evaluation
Review *Performance Expectations*
Perform monologues (first performances)
Audience Grade
Peer Performance Evaluation

Week 5 - Improvement, Improvisation Games
Self-Improvement Plan
Improvisation
Understanding Improvisation
Game (TBA)
Game Evaluation
Rehearse

Week 6 - Polishing and Performing Monologues
Creating an Introduction
Introduction Practice
Perform monologues (second performances, same monologues)
Audience Grade
Peer Performance Evaluation
Game (TBA)
Game Evaluation

Week 7 - Acting, Voice
Acting
The Actor's Voice
Understanding the Actor's Voice
Read and discuss duets
Select partners and a duet to perform
Rehearse

Week 8 - Acting, Breathing, and Warming Up
Articulation Activities for review
Breathing Activity
Warming Up
Warm-up activities and games
Complete duet questions
Rehearse

Week 9 - Acting, Movement
The Actor's Body
More warm-up activities
Review evaluation tool
Review *Performance Expectations*
Perform duets (first performances)
Audience Grade
Peer Performance Evaluation

Week 10 - Improvement, Terminology
Self-Improvement Plan
Basic Play Terminology
Rehearsal Terminology
Mock Audition
Rehearse

Week 11 - Terminology
Basic Acting Terminology
Acting Terminology Crossword Puzzle
The Art of Timing
Crazy Clock
Rehearse

Week 12 - The Stage and Script, Performances
Script Scoring
The Stage
Perform duets (second performances, same duets)
Audience Grade
Peer Performance Evaluation

Week 13 - Characterization
Characterization Study Projects
Choose monologue or duet from a play
A Well-Defined Character
You as a Cartoon Character
Characterization Study Activity
Present projects
Rehearse

Week 14 - Publicity and Promotion
Publicity Projects
Complete Role Scoring using the character
or characters from latest scene
Publicity
Local Media
Creative Publicity
Rehearse

Week 15 - Publicity and Promotion, Performances
Perform scenes (first performances)
Audience Grade
Peer Performance Evaluation
Game (TBA)
Game Evaluation

Week 16 - Promotion
Self-Improvement Plan
News Release Form
Publicity Checklist
Designing Your Poster
Rehearse

Week 17 - Promotion
Designing Your Program
Program Worksheet
Designing Flyers, Tickets, and More
Present projects
Rehearse

Week 18 - Review, Performances
    Review
    Perform scenes (second performances, same scenes)
    Audience Grade
    Peer Performance Evaluation
    Game (TBA)
    Game Evaluation

Week 19 - Major Projects
    Discuss benefits of good time management
    Select scene from play
    Role Score scene
    Rehearse
    Possibly work on project in class

Week 20 - Play Production, the Production Staff
    What Makes a Production?
    Creating Mood
    Creating Mood Practice
    Rehearse

Week 21 - Creating Mood, Stage Makeup
    How can mood be incorporated into scenes?
    Stage Makeup Basics
    Perform scenes (first performances)
    Audience Grade
    Peer Performance Evaluation
    Project Questionnaire

Week 22 - Props, Costuming, and the Set
    Self-Improvement Plan
    Finding, Making, and Buying Props
    Costuming
    The Set
    Rehearse

Week 23 - Lights, Sound, and Non-Traditional Settings
    Lights and Sound
    Possible tour of light and sound facilities
    How can lights/sound be included in scene work?
    Producing Plays in Non-Traditional Settings
    Rehearse

Week 24 - Present Projects
    Present projects
    Perform scenes (second performances, same scenes)
    Audience Grade
    Peer Performance Evaluation

For the Theatre History unit, students will perform "reader's theatre" scenes to fit each grouping of time periods. These do not have to be memorized but must be familiarized and well rehearsed. Groups may participate together; parts must be fairly equal in size. Each scene must be a minute for each graded participant. Please have scenes selected early in the week. Rehearsal and performances will immediately follow the last lesson in the era.

Week 25 - Egyptian, Greek, and Roman Theatre History
    Theatre History Projects
    The First Performances
    Ancient Greek Theatre
    Roman Theatre
    Rehearse
    Performances
    (Possible audience grade and peer evaluations)

Week 26 - Medieval, Renaissance, and Elizabethan Theatre History
    Early Theatre Review
    Medieval Theatre
    Renaissance Theatre
    The Characters of Commedia dell'arte
    Elizabethan Theatre

    Renaissance and Elizabethan Review
    Rehearse
    Performances
    (Possible audience grade and peer evaluations)

Week 27 - Late European, American, Eastern Theatre History
    The English Restoration and Later Theatre
    American Theatre
    Eastern Theatre
    Rehearse
    Performances
    (Possible audience grade and peer evaluations)

Week 28 - Theatre History Review
    Catch up on theatre history performances
    Theatre history review
    Game (TBA)
    Game Evaluation
    Possibly begin presenting projects

Week 29 - Theatre History Projects
    Present projects
    Game (TBA)
    Game Evaluation

Week 30 - Theatre History Test Review, Improvisation
    Theatre History Test Review
    Theatre History Test
    Advanced Improvisation Games (TBA)
    Game Evaluation
    Improvisation Projects (due in one week)

Week 31 - Improvisation Projects
    Select final scene of the year from a play
    Advanced Improvisation Games (TBA)
    Game Evaluation
    Present Projects
    Rehearse

Week 32 - Planning for the Future
    Career Projects
    Role Score scene
    Planning for the Future
    Theatre Jobs
    Rehearse

Week 33 - Planning for the Future
    Acting Opportunities
    Non-Theatre Jobs
    Working as an Actor
    Perform scenes (first performances)
    Audience Grade
    Peer Performance Evaluation

Week 34 - Planning for the Future
    Self-Improvement Plan
    Resumes and Headshots
    Resume Form
    Sample Resume
    Sample Headshot
    Rehearse

Week 35 - Planning for the Future
    Your Future in Theatre Crossword Puzzle
    Present Projects
    Rehearse

Week 36 - Planning for the Future
    Perform scenes (second performances, same scenes)
    Audience Grade
    Peer Performance Evaluation

STUDENT INFORMATION

PREFERRED NAME: _____ LAST NAME: _____

GRADE: _____ AGE: _____ ID#: _____

EMAIL: _____ PHONE: _____

ADDRESS: _____

CITY: _____ ZIP: _____

Have you ever acted or worked on a play?

_____

_____

Would you like to be in plays?

_____

_____

Are you interested in studying theatre in college?

_____

_____

What are some of your career choices?

_____

_____

What do you want out of this class?

_____

_____

I am good at...

_____

_____

I need to improve on...

_____

_____

THE THEATRE FAMILY

While it is truly impossible to pinpoint, it is likely that acting had its beginnings in the days of cavemen. Scholars believe that kills were re-enacted for the tribe by hunters in the light of campfires. What followed was likely a slow evolution in storytelling, the passing down of history, religious and fable sharing, and news broadcasting. Eventually, troupes of actors would travel from town to town performing on wagons converted into stages. They would live as families, but women would not act for many years. Still today, performing (and the arts, in general) tend to be a family affair. Sometimes performing parents bring their young children to the set because the hours are long, and this is one way they can spend time with each other. Thus, young family members' love of the arts are imprinted from a young age.

Even when they are not related, cast members spend an extraordinary amount of time together. They share emotions and act out situations that are generally reserved for their closest friends and family. Can you imagine the difficulty of acting like you are in love with someone you barely know? It would be equally difficult to realistically portray hatred if the actor standing opposite you is a complete stranger or your best friend.

Cast members also count on each other to deliver their cue lines, use proper stage combat methods, and to be prepared. In the event that one feels another is falling short of their duties, the two will need to resolve their problems. All of this is more effective when the cast knows and likes one another versus a group of strangers or a situation where there is hostility. When you do scenes in class, you and your partner or group are a cast, so this also applies to you as a theatre student.

For young actors who are just getting started, knowing their classmates who will one day be their audience is also vital. Acting is very personal, and a great deal of teamwork, trust, and support are needed. Student actors stand in front of their classmates, allowing them to watch and listen, judge, and critique their performance. The stories in scene work are interesting because they explore emotions and situations not found in everyday life. While this makes a scene entertaining for the audience, it can be intimidating to inexperienced actors. Why?

First, each of us has certain emotions we are comfortable sharing with anyone and others we find more private—sadness, for example. By exposing these private emotions in front of our peers, we are letting them see us as more vulnerable. Second, many fear criticism and failure.

There are a number of reasons why performing can be a frightening experience, but there is also a simple solution. Actors must become a team—almost like a family. To start, the teacher and class will learn as much as they can about one another. Ground rules for what is acceptable before, during, and after performances are clearly defined so everyone feels safe. Finally, trust and dependability are developed so that performances are approached with eager anticipation rather than nervousness. Once the teacher is confident that each student is ready to be a respectful audience member and a dependable partner, performances may begin.

3

- What role do trust and reliability play in the climate of a performance classroom?

- What will improve your feeling of safety onstage? What does intimidation look like when you are standing in front of the class?

- Performers often develop close relationships with their performance partners and peers. They equate it to family. Do you feel comfortable performing in front of family? Why or why not? And how can you use what you know about performing in front of family to improve your comfort level, or your peers' comfort level, in class?

- What do you think defines good audience etiquette?

GETTING TO KNOW YOUR STUDENTS

You are a drama teacher. That means your students are expected to perform. This can be very problematic to many young people who feel vulnerable standing in front of the class, performing, and having their peers pass judgment on them. Your top priority is to establish the climate of your classroom so that all of your students feel comfortable with what is expected of them.

Discussion Questions:

- How comfortable are you speaking in front of your peers? If you have discomfort, what causes it?

- What is the most comfortable climate for a performance classroom? What is the best learning climate, and how do learning and comfort complement or contradict each other?

- What are some of the responsibilities that students have to one another during performances?

The *Student Information* form will introduce you to your students and will assist you in maintaining communications with parents. Keep a folder on each student for samples of their work, their citizenship, and other important information and use this sheet as the inside cover. Leave the back blank to log communications with parents, incidents within the classroom, or other data.

Now that you know what your students' backgrounds and goals are, be sensitive to their individual abilities and be mindful of their goals. For example, when studying theatre history, recognize the student who wants to study archaeology or geography and draw a parallel between their interests and what they are learning in your class. Many of your students will fail to realize that they are learning communication skills in your class. Remind them daily how their relatives, coaches, and others are benefiting from their better communication skills and how improvements in these skills can positively affect their futures.

Try this fun activity: Have students complete the *Student Information* form, omitting names. Take them up and pass them out at random. Have each student write a half-page introduction on their "mystery person" in the style of a riddle and have the class guess who the student is.

NAME _____ PERIOD _____ DATE _____

ARE YOU READY FOR THE STAGE?

How would you feel acting out each emotion, characteristic, or action onstage as part of your scene?

0 = WOULD NOT DO
1 = VERY UNCOMFORTABLE
2 = SOMEWHAT UNCOMFORTABLE
3 = COMFORATABLE

_____ HYSTERICAL	_____ JOYOUS	_____ PARENTAL
_____ REVERENT	_____ DEPRESSED	_____ HANDICAPPED
_____ FRIGHTENED	_____ IN LOVE	_____ DYING
_____ CHILDISH	_____ HATEFUL	_____ MENTALLY ILL
_____ ANGRY	_____ CRYING	_____ DRUNK
_____ PAINED	_____ LONELY	_____ SHAKESPEAREAN
_____ EVIL	_____ ECSTATIC	_____ STAGE FIGHT
_____ DITZY	_____ HEARTBROKEN	_____ FOREIGN ACCENT

ADD UP ALL YOUR NUMBERS AND PUT THE TOTAL HERE: _____

62-72: You are ready to take on just about any role with confidence. You would probably make a good partner for those who score either high or low.

40-61: You are on your way to feeling comfortable in just about any role. With a little work, you will be a confident actor. The more comfortable you are with your classmates and stage partners, the easier difficult roles will seem.

18-39: You have a lot of reservations about acting, but you will be able to overcome this by becoming more familiar with the class. Start with a less challenging scene, and if you need a partner, choose one who will be supportive and whose comfort level is higher than yours.

0-17: Once you get to know the class and see others perform, your confidence level will rise. Choose simple scenes to start and talk to your teacher about tutoring. If possible, do not be one of the first to do your scene. Watch and learn from the other performers. You may be more ready than you think.

4

Have students complete the *Are You Ready for the Stage?* activity included with the Theatre Family lesson. They should consider each of the characteristics, actions, or emotions and how comfortable they would feel portraying them in scenes. The various situations will affect different students in unique, maybe unpredictable, ways. Once they have considered each item, have them add their scores and read and discuss the results.

GETTING TO KNOW YOU BINGO

Talk to your peers and find someone who fits each of the traits in the squares below. Each of your classmates may sign your card _____ times. There will be a winner for the first row completed, the first X completed (from the four corners in to the center), for the first outer frame (all of the spaces on the outer edge of the card), and for the first blackout. Don't forget to ask your teacher to sign some squares. The center space is free!

I love to read	I have been on a crew for a play	I am good at history	I have been to an audition	I like to go to sporting events	I have more than three pets	I have never flown in an airplane
I do not like heights	I like action movies	I love to play video games	I do not watch much TV	I have been in a play	I am bilingual	I like to surf the internet
I like to take long walks	I write poetry or stories	I am quiet	I do not like unusual food	I am good at math	I am good at English	I have seen a live play
I do not care for social media	I plan to study theatre in college	I am a funny person	FREE	I am athletic	I like to care for people	I love the indoors
I like to go to the museum	I am artistic	I know someone famous	I ride the bus to school	I like to sing	I like to travel	I like to dance
I plan to go to medical school	I ate breakfast this morning	I plan to become a teacher	I do not have any pets	I have bungee jumped	I like to clown around	I like to swim
I plan to study law	I never eat breakfast	I walk to school	I love the outdoors	I get to school in a car each day	I am good at science	I am a serious person

5

Getting to Know You Bingo is a super way to get students talking to one another and using interpersonal communication skills. Use prize incentives like fast-food freebies, new pencils or school supplies, bathroom passes, or candy to reward winners. You may participate too.

- Be flexible. You may have a class where everyone likes heights. In those cases, either change the wording ("I do not like spiders") or omit the square.

- Set limitations on how many squares each student can sign on a single form.

  ◇ Up to 10 in a class—students may sign a form six times

  ◇ 11 to 13 in a class—students may sign a form five times

  ◇ 14 to 16 in a class—students may sign a form four times

  ◇ 17 to 25 in a class—students may sign a form three times

  ◇ 26 and up—students may sign a form two times

- Discuss the activity. What did they learn about each other? Did they discover they had something in common with someone? Were they surprised at any of their findings?

EXPECTATIONS

In theatre, there are certain rules of conduct that arise from the fact that when we are acting, we are making ourselves very vulnerable. First, it takes a brave person to expose their emotions and to take risks onstage. Second, it takes a strong person to allow others to criticize their hard work. It takes trust among cast members to know that the people with whom one is working are reliable and will do the jobs to which they have committed.

The expectations discussed in this chapter are the basic rules of rehearsal and performance. Discuss them with your students. Be consistent in your expectations. Point out that these class expectations prepare them for adult life—every rule can be linked to the expectations adults have at their jobs. Finally, tell them that while rules are a part of every class, in theatre they are part of the job.

Many of the expectations we have for our classes are clear. However, some choices students make within the classroom fall into an area that is very gray, with no obvious right or wrong answer, especially when teachers' requirements vary from class to class. In a student's math class, the teacher may say, "Do not come to class without your math book. I prefer you to be late than to come without a book." In history, the teacher might prefer students to be on time and share books with another. The *Rehearsal, Performance, and Classroom Expectations* worksheet in this chapter allows students to make choices based on what they think is best or what they think their teacher expects. Whether they are right or wrong is not important. The important thing is that they can explain their choices. Once the class has answered the questions, discuss them and tell your students which solutions work best for you and explain your reasons. If there is an answer you find unacceptable,

---

EXPECTATIONS

Like any other instructor, your drama teacher has clearly defined rules and expectations and ensures they are followed in order to have a well-organized class. Even though theatre is very different from math, science, and social studies, the expectations are basically the same: complete the work when, where, and how the teacher instructs.

Likewise, rehearsals and performances have basic standards, starting with how to give feedback. While helping classmates iron out the wrinkles in a scene, find ways to improve the performance without being negative or hurtful. Rather than saying, "That looks stupid," you might say, "That's one way of doing it, but maybe you can try…" If you cannot think of a constructive way to give feedback, then it probably does not need to be said. You can avoid coming across as negative by following up with statements like "I like that much better," or "That's much more believable." Use tact when offering advice, and remember that there is more than one correct way of doing things.

While others are performing, be supportive and courteous. Do not make noises, faces, or quick movements that might be construed as an attempt to distract them. After their performances, if the teacher allows, clap heartily to show your appreciation.

Another standard for class performances is to be prepared *prior* to the first actor taking the stage. If you are performing, you will need your script (even though lines are memorized, it is traditional to have someone with the script offstage in case you need a line) and anything needed for the scene. If you are evaluating, you will need a pencil, evaluation forms, and anything else required in the audience (timers, recording devices, etc.). In a busy classroom, the sound of a backpack unzipping or a piece of paper crackling is hardly noticeable. However, when everyone is quiet and focused on an actor onstage, every little noise is magnified and can become a terrible distraction. Likewise, having everyone wait on you while you dig for your script can seem like an eternity. Do you want your audience to get impatient waiting for you before evaluating your performance?

Obviously, students should stay seated before, during, and after each performance to avoid distracting the actors and audience. Both you and the teacher should use the time between each group to fill out the evaluation sheet. The next group may use this time to set the stage for their scene.

The student sitting closest to the door will be designated as the one who needs to gesture to any visitors to wait until a scene ends before entering the room. It will also be helpful to have a sign laminated and ready to post on the door prior to each performance. However, there will be those—like a principal—who will ignore etiquette and enter anyway. Performers who are mid-performance should freeze and stay in character; they should not interact with visitors but should focus on where they are in their scene. As soon as the visitor is situated, the teacher will call "action" so that the performers may continue. This is actually a fantastic way to learn focus and concentration.

Having a positive and supportive performance environment is fundamental to any successful theatre arts classroom.

6

---

state your reasons and give them a better way to handle the situation.

Commit to your preferences and make them a part of your daily expectations. Let students know what you would prefer them to do if they come to class without the proper materials. Will you have spare copies? While it would be best if they were responsible for their own scripts, if you keep spares, you will be prepared for occasional bouts of forgetfulness.

REHEARSAL EXPECTATIONS

Bring your script and a pencil every day.

•

Stay on task.

•

Work only in your group unless
otherwise instructed.

•

Keep criticism respectful and constructive.

PERFORMANCE EXPECTATIONS

Be quiet and still.

•

Have supplies ready in advance.

•

Do not try to distract performers.

•

Be supportive before, during,
and after performances.

•

Keep criticism constructive and offer
it only when appropriate.

•

No one should enter or leave the
classroom during a performance.

7

Always give students—including those in the audience!—bonuses for handling interruptions tactfully.

Every teacher has their own rules; some encourage clapping, while others do not allow it. Some have students drop their heads or say "scene" at the beginning and end of each scene. There is no right or wrong way to conduct laboratory performances. In general, feeder schools follow the procedure of the advanced school.

NAME _____ PERIOD _____ DATE _____

REHEARSAL, PERFORMANCE, AND CLASSROOM EXPECTATIONS

Rank the following scenarios 1 to 4 with 1 being the best solution and 4 being the worst. There is no right or wrong answer. Your teacher will discuss your answers with you.

1=BEST   2=SECOND BEST   3=THIRD BEST   4=WORST

1. Melissa is at the classroom door before she realizes that she has left her script in her locker. What should she do?

_____ She should turn around and go back to her locker even if she will be late to class.

_____ She should ask the teacher to allow her to return to her locker with a hall pass.

_____ She should try to find the book from which her scene came and write her lines out before rehearsal begins.

_____ If she has a partner, she should share a script with them and remember to bring her script next time.

2. You are completing a peer evaluation worksheet for duets. One group is not taking the assignment seriously and often breaks character. How should you phrase your criticism?

_____ "You are wasting the class's time."

_____ "That was a really funny scene. You made me laugh."

_____ "You two need to find other partners."

_____ "Maybe each of you should find partners who will complement you better and help you to be less nervous."

3. A visitor approaches the door during performances but does not enter. Instead he waits quietly at the door.

_____ Stay focused on the performance in progress. When the scene is over, the teacher will attend to the visitor.

_____ Get up and go over to the visitor. Figure out what he needs quietly and assist him.

_____ Motion to the teacher that a visitor is at the door so that she can figure out what he needs.

_____ Tell Matt the office needs to see him so that he can exit quietly during the performance.

4. On one rehearsal day your duet partner is absent. What do you do?

_____ Work quietly on your lines and blocking without her. When she comes back, the two of you can get caught up.

_____ Work on homework for another class. You can study your lines later in that other class since you will be caught up.

_____ Assist another group with their scene. You can prompt them, help them with their blocking, and give them direction when they request it.

_____ Wander from group to group trying to distract them. This is good preparation for performances since you never know what might happen. This will teach them to stay focused, and it will keep you busy during the rehearsal time.

NOTES: _____

_____

_____

_____

_____

_____

_____

_____

_____

BELL WORK

Your teacher may want you to complete a bell work or journal activity each day. They will instruct you as to when and how this is to be done. You should record your teacher's instructions here so that you may refer to them when needed. Bell work is located at the beginning of each section of this workbook.

- When will you be required to do bell work activities? _____
  _____

- Remember that this is a time to work quietly.

- These "mini-lessons" are important. Each day's bell work is intended to introduce what your teacher will discuss in class on that day, or it will somehow connect with the planned activity.

- Remember, if you are absent, you must complete the bell work activity for that day along with any other missed assignments.

- The space provided should be just the right size to complete the bell work. However, if you need more space, you may wish to rewrite it in your journal, leaving a note reminding both your teacher and you of the whereabouts of the finished assignment.

- Your teacher may call on you to share your responses with the class.

- Make sure each entry is dated so that you can easily find each one and refer back to it when needed.

- Your teacher may use bell work questions as essay questions on tests or quizzes.

- Share your own unique ideas for bell work questions with your teacher. He or she may offer an incentive for your creativity. Spaces are provided on the last bell work page of each chapter for writing your suggestions.

- Write neatly, because these will be graded.

- When will your teacher require you to turn these in? _____

- What else do you need to remember about completing bell work? _____
  _____

- Because responses are opinionated or theoretical, most teachers grade for completion rather than correctness. What will your teacher look for?
  _____
  _____
  _____
  _____

DAILY BELL WORK

If you will be using the daily bell work activities (called "sponge activities" in some areas) at the beginning of each chapter, then you will want to review your standards with your classes. The page *Bell Work* explains what it is and how and when to do it. Be sure to review this with each class.

Have them fill in the blanks. The first one, "When will you be required to do bell work activities?" means when within each class period. The reason the activity is called bell work is that it is traditionally completed at the tardy bell. As your students enter the classroom, this activity will get their minds focused on the task to be completed. However, you may wish to have them do it at the end of each day's lesson instead.

NOTES: _____

_____

_____

_____

_____

_____

_____

_____

CHAPTER 2
EVALUATION

DAILY BELL WORK—EVALUATION

UNDERSTANDING EVALUATION

ADDITIONAL NOTES

Bell Work
Evaluation
Teacher Evaluations
Peer Evaluations
Other Performance Evaluations

NAME _____ PERIOD _____ DATE _____

DAILY BELL WORK - EVALUATION

Answer each question as your teacher assigns it, using the space provided. Be sure to include the date.

1. Date: _____
   Why is it important to be evaluated?

2. Date: _____
   Why is it important to evaluate your peers' performances?

3. Date: _____
   Why is it important to evaluate yourself?

4. Date: _____
   What do you predict will be the strongest areas of your performance? In which areas will you need improvement? On what do you base these predictions?

13

BELL WORK

You may not be familiar with bell work, but have you ever heard of bell ringers, sponge activities, or warm-ups? Bell work is simply a short lesson given to students at the bell that signals the beginning of class. It serves many functions. First, if you find bell work that correlates to your lesson for the day, then you are encouraging exploration of the topic before the formal lesson—a type of preview to the main event. You may then begin your lesson with discussion about the bell work and segue into your planned lesson. Also, most teachers start each class by taking roll, signing absence slips, and dealing with tasks that involve only a few students. If you have twenty students and eighteen of them must wait three minutes while two get their make-up work, then fifty-four minutes of learning are being wasted. However, assigning bell work, expecting it to be completed, and tying it to the lesson means that everyone's needs are being met, your classroom is quiet and organized, and you are setting the pace for learning and for the upcoming lesson.

Create a place in your classroom where the daily or weekly bell work assignments can be displayed. Instruct students to enter the classroom quietly and begin the assigned bell work. Each sheet has four questions or prompts. However, you may not always go in order. Therefore, after four classes,

NAME _____ PERIOD _____ DATE _____

DAILY BELL WORK - EVALUATION

Answer each question as your teacher assigns it, using the space provided. Be sure to include the date.

5. Date: _____
   What are some things the director will evaluate about the actors' performances in your class?

6. Date: _____
   Define criticism in your own words. Can criticism be good? Explain why some is constructive and some is not.

7. Date: _____
   When you see others' criticisms of your performance, what should you do?

8. Date: _____
   What benefits might an actor get from recording their performance or voice?

---

your students may have two questions answered on one page and two on another. Keep track of them and grade them regularly. If there are prompts you haven't used, you can assign them for homework or extra credit, or you can use them on upcoming tests or quizzes.

While the drama classroom is active and fun, there must still be structure and expectations. Believe it or not, most students appreciate your organization and discipline. Because bell work generally comes at the beginning of the period, it will set the tone for the rest of your class time. It is best to expect students to work quietly, to complete the assignment, and to be reviewing either their scripts or workbooks until you are finished with your administrative tasks.

The best way to ensure that they will use the time you are providing is to set guidelines and to stand by them. Expect the work to be completed in absolute quiet. When students are absent, they must complete missed bell work just as they must complete any other missed assignments. They should never have to ask you for it if you post it in a prominent place in your room. Once you set a due date or time, stick by it for all students except those who are out on that day.

You will want to address the bell work of the day at least briefly. This is another way to ensure that students are using the time you give them. Call on several students to read their responses. Ask others to comment on what the first students wrote. Find

CHAPTER 2 — EVALUATION

NAME _____ PERIOD _____ DATE _____

DAILY BELL WORK - EVALUATION

Answer each question as your teacher assigns it, using the space provided. Be sure to include the date.

9. Date: _____

    List some comments you might make about a performance if you did not care about the actor's feelings.

10. Date: _____

    Phrase the above comments as constructive criticism.

11. Date: _____

    If you knew your comments would be anonymous, how might they be different? Explain why this is.

12. Date: _____

    Why is it important to plan the steps to making improvements? Can you think of other situations in which "improvement plans" are created?

15

a way to link either the prompt or the responses to your lesson for the day.

If you are having a hard time getting students to volunteer their ideas, you may give one or two bonus points to each contributing student. For those who were present but said they did not do the bell work, you may either mark "no credit" directly on their papers under the day's prompt or record it in your grade book.

A creative way to promote bell work participation is to use a jar for each class period. Come up with a variety of ways or reasons to add names to the jar. For example, if a student has a birthday, give them a "gift" of their name in the jar. Or allow students to earn bonus points, bathroom passes, or even "first pick of partners" coupons by adding their name to the jar. Then select a name from the jar each day, and have that person present their bell work.

NAME _____ PERIOD _____ DATE _____

DAILY BELL WORK - EVALUATION

Answer each question as your teacher assigns it, using the space provided. Be sure to include the date.

13. Date: _____

Many professionals are evaluated yearly before they can become eligible for raises or promotions. How do you think the prospect of receiving a larger salary affects their job performance?

14. Date: _____

_____

_____

15. Date: _____

_____

_____

16. Date: _____

_____

_____

NOTES: _____

_____

_____

_____

_____

_____

_____

_____

UNDERSTANDING EVALUATION

Evaluation is the way people feel about the quality of something. Before you buy a pair of shoes, you evaluate them. Are they a good value for the quality? Are they attractive? Are they comfortable? When you watch a movie, you evaluate it. Is the plot compelling? Are the actors believable? Does it hold my attention or resonate an emotion? Adults are evaluated at their jobs. Often, it is a formal evaluation that determines whether or not a professional will get a raise or how much that raise will be. A good evaluation may result in a promotion. When an actor performs, they are also evaluated.

Actors are selling a product that is difficult to evaluate early in their careers because it is based on an opinion. Actors are selling their talents. Many people think that talent is what you are born with. However, with training, actors can sharpen their skills so that the final product is a presentation the audience will enjoy. After the show, many actors anxiously await the reviews in the local papers so that they can read what the critics had to say about the performance. If the review is bad, the actor may be disappointed or angry, especially if they have no faith in the critic's taste. At the same time, actors' desire to perform well and improve daily will inspire them to take note of their weaknesses. When the reviews are good, actors will also take note of their strengths so that they may capitalize on them in the future.

Actors in training use many types of evaluations to learn their craft. Your teacher will use prior training and experience to critique you from an educated, mature point of view. Your peers will evaluate you from a more youthful point of view. And you will evaluate both yourself and your peers. By evaluating one's peers, you put yourself in the place of the critic and have the opportunity to learn even more. Many believe that self-evaluation is the hardest to do. Because we have been taught not to be "conceited,"

we have the tendency to cut ourselves down. However, knowing and capitalizing on personal strengths builds confidence, and that is one thing most successful people have in common: confidence.

The evaluations used for performances in this series of lessons have broken down the actor's craft into several small, manageable sections. In order to present the best possible performance, you must first know what is expected of you. The following descriptions summarize the information your teacher will use to complete the evaluation of your performances.

FOOD FOR THOUGHT...

Imagine a football player who is a great runner but can't throw very far. His coach says, "If you can improve your throw, you might make the team this year." The football player realizes that he probably lacks strength. He plans a strategy that includes several different muscle-building exercises for his arms while maintaining the program that made him a good runner in the first place. Within a few weeks, he sees a big difference and so does his coach. His hard work pays off when he makes the team. The actor can do the same thing. He must take the information he receives from his teacher and peers and plan a strategy to improve.

---

1. **Approach**: Once your name is called, you should approach the stage or acting area quickly and with a quiet sense of enthusiasm to make a positive first impression. Many teachers will take points off for a student asking to go later for any reason, especially when their name has just been called. Furthermore, points may also be deducted for taking time to get out a script, getting a drink, talking to a friend, or having a negative attitude about the upcoming performance. Scene work is like being at an audition—behave like you want the job and are qualified.

17

EVALUATION

Evaluation may be the most debated topic of theatre. Not only do directors have different styles, but they also subscribe to a spectrum of philosophies. Some directors believe in teaching students how to make good choices onstage; then they allow the students to make those choices with very little direction. Others believe the best way to promote teamwork is to block every movement of every scene, leaving no room for flexibility. There is no right or wrong way. If students are learning in a safe and healthy environment, all styles of directing have merit. The focus should be on three things: safety, healthy, and continued learning.

Try to balance all criticism with equal positive reinforcement. Remember, theatre is an art form. In art, beauty is definitely in the eye of the beholder. Other than lines and pronunciation, there are few rights and wrongs; there are mainly personal preferences. This is hard for teachers to remember when

2. **Set-up**: If chairs or props are allowed for the scene, you should set up quickly and quietly, then find your starting place (the place where the first line will take place), and calmly wait for the audience's attention before starting. Your director will have their own standards for how this will occur. Some will require eyes to be closed briefly or heads to be bowed. Others simply request that the actor seize the moment and demand the audience's focus.

3. **Introduction**: Many scene projects will start with an introduction. There are several types. A simple introduction includes your name and the character you will be portraying, followed by the title of the play and the playwright. These are more common in auditions. A creative introduction will give some backstory on the scene without explaining it, followed by your name, the character, and the title and playwright. Creative introductions are more common in scene competitions and lab work. Regardless of the style, the introduction must be said clearly and with confidence. Groups may do a group introduction or designate an individual to introduce the members.

There are two types of introductions, informative and entertaining. An informative introduction is factual. State your name, the character you are playing, and the title and author of the play. An entertaining introduction gives some facts plus a little insight into the plot and is often creatively worked into the scene.

- *Informative*—"My name is Edward Kinney, and I will be portraying the character of Mortimer from *Arsenic and Old Lace* by Joseph Kesserling."

- *Entertaining*—"Aunt Abby and Aunt Martha were very sweet. What elderly gentleman wouldn't feel right at home boarding in their quaint old house and dining on their delicious home-cooked meals? So you can imagine their nephew Mortimer's surprise when he hears what became of kindly Mr. Midgely. *Arsenic and Old Lace* by Joseph Kesserling."

4. **Energy**: Don't confuse energy with action. Even a quiet or sad scene must have energy. It may be vocal, physical, facial, or emotional. It may even be done with very intense eye contact. When you are energetic, your performance will appear enthusiastic, have appropriate movement and emotional levels, and will captivate the audience's attention, even during pauses between lines.

5. **Voice:** The voice is one of an actor's most important tools. As a matter of fact, we may never see many actors' faces, because they are voice-over artists—actors who mainly do commercials, radio, and animation. There are many qualities to a well-trained voice, but the main thing a director will look for is a mastery of projection, articulation, pronunciation, confidence, quality, and intensity. Other qualities a director may look for include a variety of levels of projection and/or dialect. For most scene work, actors will use their natural voices. However, becoming a professional voice artist requires actors to be able to manipulate their voices into unique characters—tones that aren't natural, like many of the unique cartoon voices.

- *Projection* is the use of a voice that can easily be heard throughout the audience without seeming like shouting since the desired result is not always a voice that is loud. Try using a variety of levels of loudness while still projecting your voice across distance.

- *Intensity* is the stressed tone of urgency or insistence in a voice, not to be confused with volume.

- *Articulation* is to say the word and all of its sounds clearly.

- *Pronunciation* is to say the word correctly. Sometimes words are pronounced differently depending on location or time period. Ask your teacher for help if you are unsure how to say a word.

> **Mastery** is the ability to successfully perform all parts of a task consistently and with little or no effort.

critiquing young performers. The following comments may be useful when evaluating your students:

- You made an interesting choice with your blocking, but I think you can find movement that will better support the needs of your scene.

- Is that gesture really something your character would do or is that more your nature?

- Careful with your pauses. Some seem to suggest memorization trouble.

- You have a good basic dialect; now take it to the next level.

- Excellent projection! Now experiment with using varying levels of volume.

- Wonderful facial expressions. Now work on matching your vocal expressions.

- *Quality* is the pleasantness of one's voice. Often this is not in the actor's control. Many people have physical reasons for not sounding "typical." It isn't always a bad thing, either. How many famous voices do you recognize the second you hear them because they are unusual? However, sometimes an actor's voice sounds odd because they use improper breathing techniques, use a "stage voice," or have a medical condition. Regardless, continuing to use poor speaking habits over a period of time could result in damage to one's voice or vocal cords.

- *Vocal confidence* is a combination of the projection, articulation, quality, and pronunciation. When you speak with vocal confidence, it sounds like you want to be heard. There is a naturalness to your voice, and the words flow in the way the character would speak.

6. *Movement*: The use of posture, body language, gestures, blocking, props, business, and occasionally some pantomime that supports the goal of the scene is all part of what is collectively called movement. In college and in many acting schools, entire classes are dedicated to this. Have you ever seen a silent movie? Other than a few bits of written dialogue flashing up on the screen, the actors had to tell the entire story with just their hands, faces, and bodies. In modern theatre, the preferred style of acting is much more natural, but knowing what is natural for a particular character and being able to present that onstage may require some training.

- *Posture* is how you hold your body. There are many factors that can affect posture, such as age, health, the character's sense of self-confidence, and the character's relationship with others in the scene (or, in the case of a monologue, the unseen person to whom the monologue is directed). Social status, job, and the storyline may also play a part in the posture you adopt for your character.

- *Body language* is the message a character sends without speaking. It may include facial expressions, gestures, posture, movement, and even breathing. Think of a scary movie where the bad guy is chasing a young woman. The camera catches her hiding in a corner, pressed tightly into the small space, making her body as narrow as she can. She is practically holding her breath, tears streaming down her face, trying not to make a sound. Her eyes flicker back and forth, scanning the shadows for any sign of movement. Her entire body is racked with silent sobs, and her knuckles are white from the pressure of clutching the cinder block wall behind her. She hears footsteps. Her body tenses and her eyes widen. Her once-shallow breathing ceases. The footsteps approach even closer and stop just in front of her. We can't see who he is, but we can see her expressions give way instantly to the scrunched-up face of a sobbing child. She clutches her arms around her own body, sobbing uncontrollably, and allows herself—eyes closed—to slide down the cinder block wall behind her and onto the floor, curled up like a baby. Was the man the bad guy? Was he someone with whom she felt safe? No one ever said a word, but the body language told us exactly what was happening.

> **Food for Thought...**
>
> How do the blind learn body language if they cannot observe others using it? Is it an instinct with which people are born?
>
> In 1995, researchers in Denmark conducted an experiment in which four people born blind were taught to use body language.
>
> The project was such a success that now those born blind in Copenhagen, Denmark, are entitled to a free three-year course in communicating with body language.

Posture and body language are both very important in creating believable movement

19

TEACHER EVALUATIONS

Many teachers prefer to watch student performances, make written comments, and then give a fully subjective grade. While this works for some, there will inevitably be several students who will want to know why they scored the way they did, and your comment card will probably not address each detail. Using an itemized evaluation allows the director to watch the performance, write comments, and give a grade. However, because the form is broken down into specific areas, they will be able to circle numbers, make shorter comments, and supply immediate feedback to students on their specific strengths and weaknesses.

There are two objective evaluation forms from which to choose in this book. The first, *Performance Evaluation 1*, is basic. It is divided into ten categories and each can be rated on a scale of one to ten. By adding the circled numbers, the sum becomes a grade based on a 100-point system. It was designed for all levels of acting classes.

The second, *Performance Evaluation 2*, is more detailed. It is still broken down into ten categories, but some of those are divided even more. Rather than circling eight on voice and writing comments to explain, the teacher can address the specific areas needing attention. This enables you to have in your scene work. Equally important are gestures, blocking, props, business, and pantomime. While these are often considered inseparable, each is unique and will be factored into your evaluation. It is imperative that you understand what your evaluator will be seeking.

- *Gestures* are the movements you make with your hands to reinforce the message you are sending with your voice. For example, when your mother tells you to go clean your room, she may point in that direction to emphasize her point, even though you obviously know where your room is. Gesturing becomes more exaggerated when you are emotional.

- *Blocking* refers to the deliberate movements the actors make regarding where they are onstage and if they are sitting, standing, etc. Scenes need some movement to keep the presentation interesting. However, every movement must have a reason. Most scripts have the blocking written in parentheses or italics. Beginning actors generally follow these stage directions until they are comfortable blocking their own movements.

- *Business* is all of the little things an actor does onstage, in character, to appear naturally busy. It is intended to support the scene, not distract from it. The script will give clues as to which business would fit the character, but often the actor must read between the lines. For instance, when a girl brushes her hair during a monologue in which she is talking about her first love, the hair brushing is the stage business.

- *Props* are the things an actor uses onstage to carry out the requirements of the scene. For example, if the scene requires a character to take a drink from a cup, the cup would be a prop. Many teachers do not allow the use of props for scene work. Always ask the teacher or director before bringing props to class. Never bring toy weapons, fake cigarettes, or empty liquor containers to class for a scene.

- *Pantomime* is pretending to use props. Remember the girl brushing her hair above? Now imagine her brushing her hair, but without a prop brush. The action makes us think she is brushing her hair—the way she holds her hand as though there is a brush in it. Actors may also have to pantomime walking through doors, drinking from a cup, talking on a phone, or thousands of other things. They may still be delivering lines; it's just the stage business that is pantomimed without props.

> Mime is an art form characterized by men and women in white and black face paint, black pants, striped shirts, and bowler hats. While this is a stereotype, it should bring to mind a specific picture of this mime character "trapped in a box" or "climbing a ladder." Each movement is carefully and artistically per-formed in a slightly exaggerated fashion. On the other hand, pantomime is the act of pretending to do something without the benefit of props. Movements are mostly natural, as if the actor were really performing a task.

7. *Facial Expressions*: Have you heard the expression a picture paints a thousand words? A single facial expression can do the same. Everyone probably remembers the picture of a young boy accidentally left home alone without adult supervision, mouth and eyes wide open, hands pressed squarely to each cheek. Expressions that support the goal of the scene are a vital tool. On the other hand, accidental facial expressions that tell the audience the actor made a mistake or forgot a line can ruin a good scene. Young actors must learn to cover their mistakes and not draw attention to them. Never allow an expression onstage that belongs to you—the actor—but does not fit the character.

8. *Pacing*: Most stories follow a basic pattern. The beginning of the story, the exposition, starts slowly but at a steady pace and builds

discussion, write more comments, or even to have more performances in a shorter amount of time. The total is still a potential 100, so the sum of the circled numbers is an automatic grade based on a 100-point system. This form was designed to meet the needs of larger classes or advanced acting students.

Here's a time-saving tip: On either evaluation, instead of adding the circled scores, count the digits to the right of the circled ones and subtract from 100. The results are the same, but you might find this method faster to calculate.

Ideally, each student should get four grades for every performance: a performance grade (which may or may not be counted as a test grade), a peer evaluation grade, an audience grade, and an improvement plan grade. By doing each of these, students are engaging in learning most of the elements of theatre required by national core arts standards. Furthermore, it is recommended that students do the first performance of a scene (including the above four grades), spend a week or two implementing the ideas and suggestions for improvement, then perform a second time (again getting four grades). This second performance should be of much higher quality and the grading much tougher. If you took off two points for each missed line in the first performance, you may wish to count off five points the second time around. You

in intensity toward the climax, the point of greatest action. After the climax, the story wraps up rather quickly in the denouement as it works its way to the end. (See figure.) Class scenes should follow the same basic pattern. They must have a beginning, middle, and end, and should progress at a rate that keeps them interesting and shows confident understanding and memorization. If the teacher has set a time limit, the scene must meet the requirements.

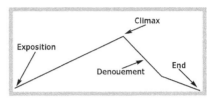

9. **Characterization**: When doing scene work, young people are often timid about trying anything new. They are afraid of being judged by their peers. The characters in their scenes are reflections of the actors themselves. To make each scene unique and interesting, actors need to fully understand what the play and the characters are all about. Many actors even study the playwright to learn more about the characters. Once the actor is armed with details about the play, character, and playwright, they can portray a character who is fully defined and focused, has a unique personality, and uses emotions, body language, and vocal expressions that support the goal of the scene.

10. **Focus**: A synonym for concentration, focus means to remain fully involved in the scene and to avoid being distracted by peers, visitors, sounds, mistakes, or calls for lines.

11. **Closing**: Once the scene is over, the actor sits back down without commenting on the performance or making faces in order to make a positive last impression. The teacher may require a particular scene ending, such as a bowed head or the words "scene" or "cut." Ask your teacher what they expect for a closing.

12. **Lines and memorization**: When performing, the scene should be memorized. However, occasionally forgetting a line early in the project is normal. To keep your performance smooth, give your script to someone who will prompt you loudly and clearly. When you forget a line stay focused and in character while trying to remember. If after a few seconds you still cannot remember, say "line," and your prompter will begin reading the line. Quickly pick up the cue and say the line from the beginning. Do not allow calls for lines to disrupt the flow of the scene. Ask your teacher if they count off when you call for lines and how many points each missed line is worth.

might even count the first performance as a daily grade and the second as a test grade.

Regardless of the form you use, and even if you choose to grade subjectively, discuss with your students the scores and comments upon returning their evaluations. This is a great opportunity to clear up any confusion, explain your professional opinions, and allow students to share their thoughts.

INTRODUCTION TO THEATRE ARTS I

NAME _____ PERIOD _____ DATE _____

PERFORMER #_____ CHARACTER _____

PLAY/PLAYWRIGHT _____

PERFORMANCE EVALUATION I

1. Introduction: Student states their name and the character, play, and playwright with confidence. Groups may do a group introduction or designate an individual to introduce the members.

   1 2 3 4 5 6 7 8 9 10

2. Energy: Performance is enthusiastic, has appropriate movement and emotional levels, and holds the audience's attention.

   1 2 3 4 5 6 7 8 9 10

3. Voice: Performance includes mastery of projection, articulation, pronunciation, confidence, and intensity. May also include a variety of levels of projection and/or dialect.

   1 2 3 4 5 6 7 8 9 10

4. Movement: The use of posture, body language, gestures, blocking, props, and business supports the goal of the scene. May include some pantomime.

   1 2 3 4 5 6 7 8 9 10

5. Facials: The scene includes appropriate facial expressions; the actor refrains from "making faces" when they become distracted.

   1 2 3 4 5 6 7 8 9 10

6. Pacing: The scene progresses at a rate that keeps it interesting and shows confident memorization; it meets the time limitations set by the teacher.

   1 2 3 4 5 6 7 8 9 10

7. Characterization: The character is fully defined and focused, has a unique personality, and uses emotions, body language, and vocal expressions that support the goal of the scene.

   1 2 3 4 5 6 7 8 9 10

8. Focus: Student remains focused on the scene and is not distracted by peers, visitors, sounds, mistakes, or call for lines.

   1 2 3 4 5 6 7 8 9 10

9. Closing: Student finishes scene and returns to their seat without commenting on the performance or "making faces."

   1 2 3 4 5 6 7 8 9 10

10. Lines and memorization: The scene is memorized, but the student is prepared and has given the script to someone who will call lines out clearly. If lines are needed, they are requested quickly and there is little disruption to the flow of the scene. Lines are worth _____ points each.

    1 2 3 4 5 6 7 8 9 10

BONUS POINTS FOR VOLUNTEERING:	Performer	Score	Minus Lines Missed	Plus Bonus	Final Score
5 points for the first volunteer, 4 points for the second, 3 points for the third, and 2 points for all other volunteers.					

PEER EVALUATIONS

It is vital that students evaluate each other and learn to respect the opinions of their peers. Teach students to phrase comments constructively, and never tolerate rudeness, even when it is directed at one's self. Do not allow students to argue when they disagree with criticism. Explain that they should listen to and respect each person's opinion. They do not have to incorporate others' ideas into their performances unless they are in agreement. As students begin analyzing their peers' performances, they also start mentally filing away ways to improve their own acting and performing skills. When they see their friends learning and having fun, they gain confidence, a necessary precursor to both creativity and skill expansion.

Some teachers give their student audience the same evaluation that they use. That's a lot of paper! Other teachers require each student to evaluate just two or three of their peers on the teacher form. This is still a great deal of paper, and students are only receiving feedback from a couple of people. And still others have the students evaluate peers in their journals or on notebook paper, but then there are no guidelines.

The *Peer Performance Evaluation* form is very simple, uses less paper, and has basic guidelines.

NAME _____ PERIOD _____ DATE _____

PERFORMER #_____ CHARACTER _____

PLAY/PLAYWRIGHT _____

PERFORMANCE EVALUATION 2

1. APPROACH AND SET UP

Timely	0 1 2 3 4 5
Confident	0 1 2 3 4 5

2. INTRODUCTION — 0 1 2 3 4 5

3. ENERGY

Vocal	0 1 2 3 4 5
Physical	0 1 2 3 4 5
Emotional	0 1 2 3 4 5

4. VOICE

Projection / Intensity	0 1 2 3 4 5
Articulation and Diction	0 1 2 3 4 5
Confidence	0 1 2 3 4 5

5. BODY

Body Language	0 1 2 3 4 5
Gestures	0 1 2 3 4 5
Blocking	0 1 2 3 4 5
Movement	0 1 2 3 4 5

6. FACIAL EXPRESSIONS — 0 1 2 3 4 5

7. PACING AND TIMING

Variation / Flow	0 1 2 3 4 5

8. CHARACTERIZATION AND EMOTION

Defined Character	0 1 2 3 4 5
Focused / Consistent	0 1 2 3 4 5
Believable	0 1 2 3 4 5

9. LINES CALLED CORRECTLY — 0 1 2 3 4 5

10. CLOSING — 0 1 2 3 4 5

BONUS POINTS FOR VOLUNTEERING:	Performer	Score	Minus Lines Missed	Plus Bonus	Final Score
5 points for the first volunteer, 4 points for the second, 3 points for the third, and 2 points for all other volunteers.					

Photocopying this page violates federal copyright law.   23

Have students write each performer's name or initials in the left column; when performing duets or group scenes, each performer goes on a separate line. After each scene, students will evaluate each participant. They will even make comments about themselves when they perform. There is only room for one or two comments, so they must analyze what they liked best and what they think needs the most attention. This leads to more thoughtful and targeted remarks.

Require the criticism to be specific. Consider making a poster of remarks that students have made that you find helpful—and possibly a separate poster of destructively phrased (unacceptable) remarks. Each comment should stand on its own and be easily interpreted without having to try to figure out what was meant. Good examples might include:

- Suspenseful introduction OR Introduction could use more suspense

- Energy perfect for the character OR Low energy came across as disinterest

- I understood every word OR Speech was a bit muddy

- Posture added to the character's distress OR Character needs to look physically defeated

INTRODUCTION TO THEATRE ARTS I

NAME _____ PERIOD _____ DATE _____

PEER PERFORMANCE EVALUATION

Give specific information about each performance. You will be graded on completion as well as your ability to phrase comments constructively. Be thorough. *Include a critique of your own performance.*

Performer	This performer was great at...	But could use a little more work on...
1.		
2.		
3.		
4.		
5.		
6.		
7.		
8.		
9.		
10.		
11.		
12.		
13.		
14.		
15.		
16.		
17.		
18.		
19.		
20.		
21.		
22.		
23.		
24.		
25.		
26.		
27.		
28.		
29.		
30.		

24   Photocopying this page violates federal copyright law.

- Your facial expressions spoke volumes OR Make sure your facial expressions remain true to the character when you aren't the one speaking

- Your dramatic pauses kept your scene interesting OR Your pauses seemed too intentional and didn't add to the scene

- Your characterization was so believable it frightened me OR This particular character shouldn't be just like you

- Good focus when partner dropped lines OR Stay in character when you experience line trouble

- It was obvious when your scene was over OR I was confused when you started talking right after your scene ended

- Excellent memorization OR Memorization is fundamental to a good performance

Even when a scene is perfect, something could be better; students do not benefit from a list of comments saying "perfect," so do not allow it even once. It will become a crutch; your audience evaluators will lean on that rather than looking critically at a good performance. When a scene is close to perfect, teach your audience to look at the more subtle components of a scene. In these cases, examples of constructive comments might include:

- Consider trying the scene from a totally different angle; what if your character knew a secret about the other character? Might that change her objective?

NAME _____ PERIOD _____ DATE _____

SELF-IMPROVEMENT PLAN

Answer each question honestly. Any honest answer will be given credit. This worksheet is intended to help you and your teacher analyze the success of the scene you performed in this class and to create a strategy for the next performance.

1. Character, play title, playwright:

2. *How* and *where* did you practice (both in class and outside of class)?

3. Did anyone in particular help you? Who was it and how did they help?

4. How much time did you practice outside of class?

5. Did you use all of the class time the teacher gave you? If not, what were you doing instead of practicing?

6. In what areas did you score highest from the teacher and what were some of the comments?

7. In what areas did you score lowest from the teacher and what were some of the comments?

8. According to your peers, what were some of your strengths?

9. According to your peers, where do you need to focus your efforts to improve?

10. In your opinion, what areas of your performance need the most attention?

11. What exercises or activities will you use to sharpen the skills that need improvement?

12. What can the teacher do to help you achieve success for the next performance? Is there anything you would like to have explained or taught again?

25

- What if your character were a bit more compassionate? I'm curious to see how her internal struggle would affect your timing.

- You do a great job with the anger in this scene, but what if your character tried hard NOT to be angry but grew more upset toward the end instead of throughout?

- Your scene was very well done but lacked a booming climax. Consider where that might be and how you could build up to it.

- I'm not sure your character's objective is clear. What are some ways you might make that clearer?

Obvious comments that should not be tolerated are those that are hurtful or not helpful. Also, vague comments are lazy. The evaluator might understand it at the time, but it does not translate to the actor. The evaluator must be specific. Unhelpful comments might include:

- Nothing
- Perfect
- Good
- Bad
- Diction
- Movement
- Try harder
- Boring

After all of the performances are completed, grade the *Peer Performance Evaluation* forms on completion and appropriateness of the comments,

NAME _____ PERIOD _____ DATE _____

MOVIE/PLAY EVALUATION

Answer each question completely. Use a separate sheet if more space is needed.

Which did you see? *(Circle one)*   MOVIE   PLAY

Title: _____

Director: _____   Playwright: _____
                                                                                  (if applicable)

Main Characters: | Actors:

_____ | _____

_____ | _____

_____ | _____

1. What was the plot *(the storyline)*?

2. Most stories attempt to teach a lesson *(the moral)*. What lesson do you think this story was trying to teach?

3. What was the setting *(specifically when and where did it take place)*?

4. How did the set *(the buildings and scenery)* add to the play or movie?

5. What was your favorite costume and why?

6. What was your favorite special effect, sound effect, or lighting effect? Explain.

7. How did music add to the play or movie? Explain.

8. Was stage combat used? How?

9. What colors were used repeatedly? Why do you think the director chose these colors?

10. Who was your favorite character? Explain.

11. Did you like the movie or play? Explain.

not on your opinion of their accuracy. Record the grade next to students' names and then remove the tops at the dotted line. This allows you to return the tiny name slip to them to see their score. It also allows the comments to remain anonymous, which will encourage honesty. Keep these until it is time to complete the *Self-Improvement Plan* forms.

Once the scenes have all been performed, it is time to complete the *Self-Improvement Plan* forms. Seat your class in a circle on the floor with their *Self-Improvement Plan* forms and a pencil.

1. First, return their evaluations. They can then begin filling out the improvement form using the comments from their teacher evaluation. Allow

them to talk during this time. You will be amazed by their comments and their enthusiasm.

2. Next, randomly return the graded *Peer Performance Evaluation* forms with the names removed.

   a. You need a way to control the forms, so you can either number them or have students put their initials on the first one they receive (which will not be theirs). This ensures they know when the first one they received gets back to them.

   b. They can record some of the criticisms onto their improvement worksheets (many will be repetitive). Then pass the form to their

CHAPTER 2 — EVALUATION

NAME _____ PERIOD _____ DATE _____

SCRIPT REPORT

After you have read the play, answer the questions on this report thoroughly.
You may have to do some research to find some of the answers.

Title: _____

Playwright: _____

Date published: _____ Publisher: _____

Other plays written by this playwright: _____

_____

What type of play is this? (Circle all that apply.)

Comedy   Tragedy   Historical   Classic   Full-length   One-act   Musical

Other: _____

1. Where does the play take place?

2. What is the time period for the play?

3. List the main characters and tell a little about each of them:

4. What is the play about?

5. What is the climax of the play?

27

right and continue with the next one. This will seem like chaos at first, but it is a great time for self-reflection and for sharing, so encourage conversation as long as it is about the performances or the forms.

c. When they get the *Peer Evaluation* they started with, they have seen all of them. Save them for any students who were absent.

Another way to control the flow of *Peer Evaluations* is to tape them to the walls and have students walk around to each one. If your room is set up for this, it might work better for you. Or you can lead a discussion about the comments on the forms and have students take notes.

INTRODUCTION TO THEATRE ARTS I

NAME _____ PERIOD _____ DATE _____

SCRIPT REPORT - CONT.

6. How is the conflict resolved?

7. What did you think of the play?

8. If you were in this play, which character would you be and why?

9. What is the theme or message of the play?

10. Find a line that you think supports the general theme of the play and write it here. Indicate the speaker, the act, and the scene.

11. Choose a character who undergoes a great change from the beginning of the play to the end. Describe the change and the impact it has on the course of the story.

12. What events led to the beginning of the play?

13. What do you think might have happened after the conclusion of the play?

14. Find several examples of symbolism and explain them.

28   Photocopying this page violates federal copyright law.

NOTES: _____

_____

_____

_____

_____

_____

_____

_____

_____

NAME _____ PERIOD _____ DATE _____

EVALUATION TEST REVIEW

Fill in the blanks in each of the following clues, then find the word hidden in the puzzle.
The number in parentheses indicates how many letters are in the answer.

1. Scenes should include a beginning, a _____, and a clear ending. (6)

2. Actors will spend time _____ their scene by carefully planning their movements. (8)

3. After a performance, actors should take their seat quietly and _____ their performance. (8)

4. Actors begin defining their character with their _____, or the way they situate their body. (7)

5. Articulation, diction, and projection are the main factors in clear _____. (6)

6. Actors should strive to make their characters _____, interesting, and believable. (6)

7. Actors must _____ their voices in order to be heard by everyone in the audience. (7)

8. Students should be _____ to take the stage with confidence and enthusiasm when their names are called. (8)

9. Knowing one's own strengths and being proud of them is _____, not conceitedness. (10)

10. Good memorization will alleviate stage fright and _____. (11)

11. Some actors mistake a lot of yelling and unnecessary movement for _____ when all they really need is well-planned action, a dynamic voice, and appropriate body language. (6)

12. In most cases, actors should ignore minor _____ from the audience and continue with their performances as normal. (12)

13. Body _____ is the non-verbal communication actors must use to make their characters appear real and natural. (8)

14. A well-paced scene will be memorized, within the teacher's time limits, and will hold the audience's _____. (9)

S	I	X	A	C	T	I	B	N	H	D	D	V	X	D
N	E	V	A	L	U	A	T	E	N	E	R	G	Y	I
O	W	L	P	O	S	T	U	R	E	R	A	E	P	S
I	P	R	O	J	E	C	T	V	G	A	E	S	E	T
N	A	T	T	E	N	T	I	O	N	P	H	T	C	R
I	F	V	E	U	Q	I	N	U	I	E	V	U	N	A
P	B	U	S	I	N	E	S	S	K	R	X	R	E	C
O	X	A	M	I	L	C	P	N	C	P	V	E	D	T
Q	W	E	E	X	N	E	V	E	O	M	O	S	I	I
S	H	T	G	N	E	R	T	S	L	A	I	D	F	O
P	A	R	V	C	T	O	X	S	B	N	C	N	N	N
E	X	O	H	L	A	N	G	U	A	G	E	A	O	S
I	M	P	R	O	V	E	M	E	N	T	S	H	C	X

15. Natural-looking _____ will help the actors to reinforce their lines with their hands. (8)

16. Actors with good vocal confidence speak as though they want to be _____. (5)

17. If good actors want to become even better, they will analyze their reviews to make _____ (12)

18. Evaluating actors is difficult because critics must use their _____. (8)

19. Hair brushing, writing, and hair twirling are all examples of stage _____. (8)

EVALUATION TEST REVIEW KEY:

1. climax
2. blocking
3. evaluate
4. posture
5. speech
6. unique
7. project
8. prepared
9. confidence
10. nervousness
11. energy
12. distractions
13. language
14. attention
15. gestures
16. heard
17. improvements
18. opinions
19. business

S	I	X	A	C	T	I	B	N	H	D	D	V	X	D
N	E	V	A	L	U	A	T	E	N	E	R	G	Y	I
O	W	L	P	O	S	T	U	R	E	R	A	E	P	S
I	P	R	O	J	E	C	T	V	G	A	E	S	E	T
N	A	T	T	E	N	T	I	O	N	P	H	T	C	R
I	F	V	E	U	Q	I	N	U	I	E	V	U	N	A
P	B	U	S	I	N	E	S	S	K	R	X	R	E	C
O	X	A	M	I	L	C	P	N	C	P	V	E	D	T
Q	W	E	E	X	N	E	V	E	O	M	O	S	I	I
S	H	T	G	N	E	R	T	S	L	A	I	D	F	O
P	A	R	V	C	T	O	X	S	B	N	C	N	N	N
E	X	O	H	L	A	N	G	U	A	G	E	A	O	S
I	M	P	R	O	V	E	M	E	N	T	S	H	C	X

OTHER PERFORMANCE EVALUATIONS

Another great tool for improving performances is to record them. Set up a camera at the back of the classroom and select one or two students to run it. When all the scenes have been recorded, watch and discuss them. If using a phone to record the scene, make sure the phone belongs to one of the performers so they have the recording to watch after the fact.

Many teachers like to hold discussions about the scenes after each performance. This is a great tool, especially when actors are allowed to try the suggestions on the spot.

Encourage your classes to attend live performances, both at school and away. Many theatre teachers require their students to attend school plays while some theatre teachers make attending non-school performances (or performances at other schools) a grade. Some request only a ticket stub or a note from a parent to prove their attendance, but most assign a written report of some sort. Having students write their observations is not only more educational, it is also better proof of their attendance.

Movies are another great way to demonstrate theatre elements and acting skills to your classes. It is also a smart way to occupy their time when you have a substitute teacher or other atypical class time. The *Movie and Play Evaluation* form ensures students pay attention and understand that there is a connection between what they are seeing on the screen and what they are studying in your class.

The *Script Report* form is used much like a book report. It allows students to read and analyze a script for some of the most basic theatrical elements such as plot, characters, and setting. The second page is optional and intended for advanced theatre students.

It is vital that students of all ages learn to read scripts from beginning to end, not just the part that they will perform. When only a section is read, the reader misses important information. Many times duets and monologues seem to tell a completely different story when read apart from the rest of the script. When possible, have students select pieces from actual scripts. You may even want to have your advanced students highlight potential scenes within full scripts so that younger students do not feel compelled to select performance pieces from monologue and duet books. This way your classroom will have full scripts to accompany each scene. You may then require a *Script Report* for each selected performance piece.

The second part of the *Script Report* is much more complex and might be best reserved for more advanced classes. It requires a deeper, more analytical level of thinking, whereas the first part requires more fact-finding. It is also a good option for extra credit, gifted students in average classrooms, or as part of a teacher-led classroom discussion.

Now that you have covered evaluation with your classes, it is time to test their knowledge. Make reviewing fun by playing "trashcan basketball." First divide your class into two teams. Then, using a wadded-up piece of paper and an empty wastebasket, ask a member from each team a question. If they answer correctly, allow them to take a shot. The first team to reach twenty points wins.

CHAPTER 3
SCENE WORK

DAILY BELL WORK—SCENE WORK

UNDERSTANDING SCENE WORK

LEARNING TO MEMORIZE

Whole-Part Memorization Practice
Part-Whole Memorization Practice

CREATING AN INTRODUCTION

Introduction Practice

REHEARSALS AND PERFORMANCES

Lab Scene #1 – Casey
Lab Scene #2 – Joey
Lab Scene #3 – Fatima
Lab Scene #4 – Nick
Lab Scene #5 – Pharrah
Lab Scene #6 – Jasper and Candy
Lab Scene #7 – Alix and Sam
Lab Scene #8 – Mira and Tam
Lab Scene #9 – Teacher and Taylor

ADDITIONAL NOTES

The Purpose of Scene Work

Introducing Scene Work

Selecting Scenes

Memorizing Scenes

Creating Introductions

*Scheduling Rehearsals
and Performances*

*Notes and Discussion
Questions for Lab Scenes*

Scene Work Cut-N-Paste

Scene Work Cut-N-Paste Key

NAME _____ PERIOD _____ DATE _____

DAILY BELL WORK - SCENE WORK

Answer each question as your teacher assigns it, using the space provided. Be sure to include the date.

1. Date: _____
    Explain the process by which you will memorize or have memorized your scene.

2. Date: _____
    Write out your scene in your own words.

3. Date: _____
    Summarize your scene.

4. Date: _____
    Why is good memorization important? Be specific.

33

NOTES: _____

_____

_____

_____

_____

_____

_____

_____

_____

NAME _____ PERIOD _____ DATE _____

DAILY BELL WORK - SCENE WORK

Answer each question as your teacher assigns it, using the space provided. Be sure to include the date.

5. Date: _____

    Role score your character. Identify and explain their favorite color, food, and type of music or song. Also discuss their greatest fear, accomplishment, and ability. Finally, explain what got them to this point at which you begin the scene and where they will likely go after it is finished?

6. Date: _____

    How are you like the character you portray in your scene? How are you different?

7. Date: _____

    If you were to perform your scene tomorrow, what would it be like?

8. Date: _____

    Why is trust an issue between duet partners? How might trust influence the cast of a play or musical?

THE PURPOSE OF SCENE WORK

Face it: students take your class because they think it's going to be fun or easy. Few take it because they want to learn all they can about theatre history or terminology.

As a teacher, scene work can be difficult. For younger students, finding scenes appropriate for their age is a challenge. Getting them to understand the scene can be even harder. Older students have an easier time finding scenes since they can believably play a wider range of ages. The appropriateness of what is available is still questionable, however.

The lab scenes in this book have been written for use in the secondary theatre classroom. They do not come from plays, so they are not recommended for long-term use. Rather, use them to introduce your students to scene work. Once they have tried one or two choices from this book, have them advance to scenes from plays so that they can study the storyline, the playwright, and the time period.

I call the scenes in this book lab scenes because they are like science experiments in a laboratory. Students are encouraged to explore, make choices, and try a variety of ideas. They are provided with several pages of probing questions to take their thinking to a higher level. Each scene is structured in a way so that certain skills such as timing, characterization, and varying volume are challenged.

CHAPTER 3 — SCENE WORK

NAME _____ PERIOD _____ DATE _____

DAILY BELL WORK - SCENE WORK

Answer each question as your teacher assigns it, using the space provided. Be sure to include the date.

9. Date: _____

    What are the things that need the most work before your performance?

10. Date: _____

    What do you like best about your scene? What do you like least? Explain.

11. Date: _____

    Attendance and behavior are vital in scene work and play production. Explain.

12. Date: _____

    What have you learned from your duet partner? What have you taught them?

35

INTRODUCING SCENE WORK

Prior to assigning scenes, start by introducing your students to the simplest principles. Understanding scene work using these lab scenes will teach them about the most basic expectations, even though scenes normally come from plays but these do not. Scene work is for the purpose of studying acting techniques, and it is important to review the evaluation forms afterwards. When first starting, you will need to inform them of your specific wishes. For example, will you insist on an introduction? If so, what format will the students need to use? When they finish their introduction, will they drop their heads before starting their scene? Will they say "scene"? After performing, what do you want them to do or say?

For beginners, the recommended method for starting a scene in class is with an introduction that includes the name of the student(s), the name of the character(s), the title of the play, and the playwright. Advanced students may use the competition introduction, which is much more creative and entertaining. It generally includes prose-like background on the scene, as well as the names of the characters, the play title, and the playwright.

The recommended closing for a scene when lights and sound are not being used is for the actors to drop their chins to their chests and wait for the audience to clap. This is not a bow, nor should it attempt to resemble one. It is more like the curtain being lowered or the scene slate being clacked.

NAME _____ PERIOD _____ DATE _____

DAILY BELL WORK - SCENE WORK

Answer each question as your teacher assigns it, using the space provided. Be sure to include the date.

13. Date: _____

Write a monologue from your character's point of view about a topic which has nothing to do with your scene.

14. Date: _____

Get with your duet partner and write a scene about being stranded on a deserted island. Each of you will write lines for the other actor to say. You must each have at least five separate lines.

15. Date: _____

Have you been happy with your performance so far? Why or why not?

16. Date: _____

Many teachers encourage students to attend acting competitions. How might this affect the way you rehearse your scene? Does competing appeal to you? Why or why not?

SELECTING SCENES

When students are ready to begin acting, you will want to either select a scene for them or allow them to select one for themselves. Some teachers start by narrowing down the choices to about four or six. Some can be male, some female, and some gender neutral. And if students choose to cross gender lines, know in advance how you will handle this. In theatre, there is a tradition of crossing gender lines. If students choose to explore a scene in a gender you did not expect, consider using this as an opportunity to discuss how plays were performed by all-male casts in Shakespeare's day or how it was once considered sinful for women to perform, leaving all characters to be portrayed by males. This has continued despite changes to laws and is now an excellent exercise in character exploration!

It is also recommended to begin with monologues rather than duets or group scenes. This allows students to work at their own pace. They will be independently responsible for their improvement, and they will not have to focus on anyone but themselves. They will also be able to learn more about acting prior to sharing the responsibility with a partner. Even when absent, actors will be able to progress and study.

Starting monologues are usually one to two minutes long. Starting duets can be quite a bit longer

UNDERSTANDING SCENE WORK

When preparing a scene for a class project, it is important to fully understand the context of the scene within the play from which it originated. For example, if you found Maggie the Cat's famous speech from Tennessee Williams's *Cat on a Hot Tin Roof* in a monologue book, you might think it is just an angry speech from a jealous wife to her husband. However, if you read the play in its entirety, you will discover a desperate woman clinging to a love and a way of life that were never really hers to begin with.

The monologues and scenes in this chapter, however, are not from plays. They are called lab scenes, which means they were written specifically for you to experiment with and learn from. Each contains elements of theatre or acting that will help introduce you to scene work, acting, and the stage without being too overwhelming. Once you are comfortable with doing basic scenes like these, you may then select a more challenging scene, such as one from a play.

As you study each scene, keep in mind the evaluation your teacher will use to grade your performance. What kinds of elements will your teacher seek? They will look for you to approach the performance area enthusiastically and confidently. Your introduction must be well-prepared, as must your performance. They will also look for your scene to have good energy; but remember that energy does not always mean big and loud. It will be difficult for your teacher to judge any of this, however, if they cannot hear or understand you, so remember to project, speak clearly, and be confident in your delivery. Use the appropriate non-verbal communication such as body language, gestures, and facial expressions to support your spoken lines.

Another element your teacher will seek is realistic, believable movements that reinforce the lines. Good timing is also important. You may want to increase your rate of delivery or use pauses to keep the scene energetic and interesting. And most importantly, your teacher will look for signs of a well-developed, consistent, and believable character.

When your scene is finished, make sure you employ the type of closing your teacher requested. For example, some teachers require students to "drop" their heads as a sign that the scene is over. Others require students to say "scene." If a performance is completely believable, it is difficult to tell when it is over without the assistance of lights or sound, so be sure to ask your teacher how they wish you to end your scene.

One of the most important things your teacher hopes they will not notice in your performance is memorization trouble. When a scene is memorized to perfection, the actor will be completely focused on the performance rather than on which line comes next. However, if you are not one hundred percent confident on your memorization, that will be the main thing on your mind. Excellent memorization is the key to clearing the path to a good performance.

EVALUATION AND SCENE WORK...

You just completed the chapter on Evaluation. Now it is time to put what you learned to work by practicing and performing lab scenes. Use these clues to complete the list of elements your teacher will seek in your performances.

- E _ _ _ u _ _ _ _ _ _ c, confident approach

- Well-prepared _ n _ _ _ d _ _ _ _ _ _

- _ n _ _ _ _—not always big and loud

- Speak _ l _ _ _ l and co _ _ _ d _ _ _ _ y

- Appropriate body language, gestures, and f _ _ _ _ _ _ _ _ _ _ _ _ _ s

- Realistic m _ _ _ m _ _ _

- Good t _ _ _ _ g

- Well-developed _ h _ _ _ c _ _ r

- The teacher's required _ _ _ _ _ _ g

- M _ _ _ _ _ _ _ _ to perfection

37

---

because they are much easier to memorize due to cue lines and teamwork. Duets should be at least four minutes long and may be as long as twelve or fourteen minutes. You may make allowances for students with reading or educational challenges. The length is not as important as the performance value. A short scene with a great structure is better than a long scene that never goes anywhere.

Start by having a student (or students) read one of the monologues aloud in class. Each is followed by a page of questions for discussion. These will help students to understand the scene and characters and to iron out potential misunderstandings. Do this with

each monologue. Do not be afraid to spend several days becoming familiar with them. Once each has been thoroughly explored, allow students to choose. When they have chosen their monologues, you may then move on to memorization.

LEARNING TO MEMORIZE

There are many ways to memorize. Many people have every song on their favorite radio station memorized. One reason is that songs are rhythmic and they often rhyme. These are two factors that make memorization easier. Have you ever had difficulty memorizing a series of items, but when the teacher put it to music, suddenly you were successful? Rhythm and rhyme are not normally a part of scene work; yet even if they were, most teachers and directors instruct actors not to rely on them.

Another reason why we memorize songs with little effort is that we hear them repeatedly. Repetition is often used in schools to assist students in memorizing a difficult series or long bit of information. Some actors can read a script a few times and have all of their lines memorized, even long monologues. This is the exception and not the rule.

Many songs are stories set to music. Knowing the events of the story is a third reason why songs are often easy to memorize. In acting and scene work, most experts will agree that knowing and understanding the events in a play is the best way to memorize it. This is called whole-part memorization. An actor using this process will need to know the entire plot and become especially familiar with what happens in the play just before and immediately after the scene to be memorized. They will also learn all they can about the characters involved. Often a character will have a hidden agenda in the scene, and if the actor is not aware of this, the scene will make little sense. It is extremely difficult to memorize a scene that you do not even understand. After an actor has completely researched the full play and characters involved, they may then need to read it aloud repeatedly until it is memorized. This requires a great deal of time even though much of the repetition is achieved in early rehearsals.

If repetition fails to work or if you cannot commit to the time-consuming process of whole-part memorization, you may wish to try a form of memorization less popular with professionals but often well practiced by students: part-whole memorization. In part-whole memorization, the actor breaks the scene down into smaller, more manageable chunks. These are memorized individually and then pieced back together bit by bit. While this is generally quicker, it is often used at the expense of fully comprehending the scene and its context within the play. As a result, performances may lack depth and characters may be shallow and lifeless, especially at first.

Discover which method or combination of methods works best for you. If the above methods do not produce positive results, try one of these suggestions:

- Record your lines and listen to them over and over again while going to and from school, when falling asleep, when you are getting ready for school, etc.

- Write your lines in a notebook. You may find that reading lines does little for memorization but that writing them helps with retention, especially if you say them aloud as you write them.

- Use creative devices for memorizing particularly challenging parts within a scene. For example, find a way to connect the last word of one line to the first word of the next line.

- If the scene is written in a difficult language or pattern, you may wish to try writing the scene in your own words and then converting it back into the language of the playwright.

- Once your scene is memorized, if you find yourself needing to peek at the same places repeatedly, you may wish to highlight those in a different color and spend more time working on just those spots.

MEMORIZING SCENES

Those who memorize well assume that everyone should be able to do the same. Those who struggle with memorization think that those who do it well have a magical power...or at least a gift. The truth is that memorization is a skill that can be learned, and once learned, it can be improved upon. Be patient with your students. Assist each in finding the memorization technique that works for each learning style.

The first technique discussed in this section, whole-part memorization, suggests that the best way to commit something to memory is to learn it in a large chunk or as a whole. This does not mean anyone expects students to read the scene and be able to recite it. Instead, whole-part theorizes that if a student understands the scene, knows the sequence of events, and has familiarized themself with the language by reading it several times, they will have it memorized. The benefits of this technique are numerous. Actors who use this method tend to have a fuller understanding of their characters and the play's theme, subtext, and symbolism.

Another way to memorize is to break the scene down into smaller pieces, memorize each section a line at a time, and then after all the lines within each portion are memorized, piece them back together. Students will not understand the scene as well, but they may make up for it as they begin the

WHOLE-PART MEMORIZATION PRACTICE

Write the exact time here: _____. Read the scene at the top of the page three times to yourself and then cover it. Write what you can remember on a separate piece of paper. Check yourself. How did you do? Now try reading it again out loud a couple of times. Again, cover the page and add what you can to your sheet of paper. Keep doing this until it is memorized. When you have the scene completely memorized and written out, put the exact time here: _____. How long did it take you to completely memorize this scene using whole-part memorization? Total time: _____.

1   **CASEY:** *(Brings MABEL a cup of hot tea.)* Careful. It's pretty hot. *(Starts to leave the room, but hesitates.)* Miss Mabel? I… Oh, never mind. Have you ever… *(Knocks over a broom.)* Oh, I'm so sorry. I am such a klutz! I'm just gonna go finish sorting the mail and then I'll leave. I'll see you tomorrow. *(Starts to leave.)* Miss Mabel… What's it
5   like? *(Uncomfortable, but curious.)* I mean, to be blind? You must get lonely. I mean, I can see pretty good, but sometimes I feel like I am completely in the dark, you know what I mean? I mean, I know you do, but do you really? I have this friend, Victoria, and she's pretty nice. She's just about the only person I know who's not old enough to have great-grandkids! Oh, sorry. I mean, she's the only friend I have my age.
10 Sometimes I don't even like her. Sometimes after we get together I promise myself I'm never gonna call her again or go to her house. But then, a few hours pass and I get so lonely, and I think that it's better to go to her house and sit around watching her smoke her dad's cigarettes and make prank calls than it is to be completely alone. I've never told anyone this, but… you won't tell, will you? One time she stole a CD
15 from the gas station. It was some old singer from a long time ago, and she doesn't even have a CD player. She did, but her stepdad sold it. I didn't know she'd taken it until we were halfway home. She thought it was so funny! I was just mad and scared. I kept looking over my shoulder thinking the cops were gonna come get us. I was afraid that if I told her how mad I was, she would think I was a baby. You
20 know, my momma may not be perfect, but she taught me right from wrong, and what Victoria did was wrong. It's not like she stole because she was hungry. She did it just for fun! That's the longest I ever went without calling her—a whole day! Miss Mabel… I… I never knew my grandma. My momma wouldn't have anything to do with her. She died about four years ago and my momma didn't even cry, wouldn't even
25 go to the funeral. And you know I never knew my daddy, much less his momma. I would be very proud if I could call you my grandma… Would that be okay with you?

rehearsal process. This method is called part-whole memorization because smaller parts are pieced together to make a whole.

If you find that your students are not taking memorization seriously, you may want to increase the stakes. Take a memorization grade at least a week before your first performances. Assign a point value to each line missed prior to taking the grades. Have students recite their scenes from memory, mark the missed lines and count them, and then subtract the total from 100. For example, if each line is worth five points and a student misses three lines, then the grade will be an 85.

One advantage to taking a memorization grade early in the rehearsal process is that students will be able to act without a script in their hands, allowing them to begin moving more freely. Furthermore, forgetting one's script will no longer be an excuse not to rehearse. Finally, students who tend to procrastinate will be forced to memorize prior to performances, allowing them to focus more on their art and less on their lines.

PART-WHOLE MEMORIZATION PRACTICE

Write the exact time here _____. Memorize the first line of the monologue and repeat it to yourself. Now memorize the second line. Once it is memorized, repeat the first two lines together. Continue to repeat this process until every line is memorized. Once the entire monologue is memorized, write it from memory on a separate sheet of paper and check yourself. How accurate was your memory? When you feel the scene is thoroughly memorized, write the exact time here _____. How long did it take you to memorize this scene using part-whole memorization? Total time _____.

1   **JOEY:** Darla's dad is this big writer guy. His name is Dwight—but that wasn't glamorous enough for the people that buy that stuff, so his pen name was Antonio Bishop. He wrote stories about this old guy who travels all over the world meeting beautiful women, but he never gets married because that would mean he'd have to settle down, you know?

5   So Darla, she says to me, "Do you think he wishes he'd never had me?" She took it real personal, you know? Her mom had died a few years back, and Darla figured her dad had become almost like the guy he wrote about... except for the part about having a kid. So he bought her a fast car.

     You know, my folks never went to college. My mom never even graduated from high
10   school. They got married right after my dad graduated, so she dropped out. I was born the night she should have graduated. After that, having babies was her hobby! The night of the accident, she told me number seven was on the way... and that I'd have to spend less time with "that girl"... and that she was fed up being up to her ears in babies and no help!

15   So I left. My mom was standing at the screen door holding a screaming kid yelling at me to come back, but I just kept going. Darla picked me up halfway, crying so hard she could barely see, so I drove. Her dad said he wanted her to get away from me for a while, so he was sending her to boarding school in New York starting in the fall. We both cried, and I just kept driving. Neither of us said it, but we were leaving.

20   We were on Highway 12 by Pearl Lake. For the first time since we left, we were quiet. I looked at Darla and she tried to smile, but then she suddenly looked scared, and I realized I was headed off the road right toward the lake. I swerved and the car started spinning. There was a lot of screeching and screaming, and then we hit something and everything went black.

25   When I woke up, we were wedged against the cliff. Her head was against my shoulder. She was having a real hard time breathing, but I couldn't move to help her. I could tell she was in a lot of pain. I wished it was me, but I didn't feel anything. I couldn't feel a thing... I saw the flashing red lights and heard the sirens. I couldn't hear Darla breathing anymore.

30   All we wanted was to be happy. We just wanted to be together... happy.

40   Photocopying this page violates federal copyright law.

NOTES: _____   _____

_____   _____

_____   _____

_____   _____

_____   _____

_____   _____

_____   _____

CREATING AN INTRODUCTION

When you do scene work in class, your teacher may or may not have you do an introduction. However, you will need to have one in most competitions, auditions, or public performances. An introduction or slate is a short piece at the beginning of your scene that tells the audience who you are, who you are portraying, the play from which your scene comes, and its playwright. There are basically two types: informative and entertaining.

Even though it is very basic, the informative introduction is generally considered the preferred type for most scene work in class and at auditions. It is succinct and simple: "My name is Clifford Redding, and I will be portraying the character John in *Last Wrongs* by James Calidon." In duets and scenes with three or more people, one person will usually introduce the others, or each actor may take part in the introduction. Prepare your introduction in advance so that it is fluid and sets the tone for a well-performed scene.

Alternatively, your teacher may require you to do an entertaining introduction. Like the informative approach, it contains the facts about the scene, but this one becomes a part of the entertainment and is also the preferred type for competition. Again, it must be as well-prepared as your scene. It will give some of the same basic information as the introduction above, but it will also offer some insight into the plot. Although it is not done in character, it is done in the mood and tone of the scene. In other words, if your scene is tragic, your introduction must not be funny or happy. At the same time, you should strive to create a defined transition from the "actor" speaking to the audience to the "character" in the play.

Another thing that sets the entertaining introduction apart from the informative one is that it does not necessarily have to come before the dialogue, although it does need to be placed toward the beginning. Actors will often begin their scene, stop and step out of character, give their introduction, and then continue with their scene. It may be that they feel the content of their introduction works best if first set up with some dialogue. The dialogue from the scene that precedes the introduction is called a teaser. It gets the audience interested in the scene, teasing them into believing they can settle in to enjoy, when suddenly the introduction is inserted. By then, they are hooked.

The entertaining introduction is also more flexible than the informative one. Rather than saying, "I will be portraying…" an actor might say, "John lives in a world where…" to indicate his character's name. He will probably not say his own name. There is an unlimited amount of room for creativity, and the rule of thumb is that almost anything goes. Sometimes actors give background on the playwright or the era in which the play is set. Other times they may tell what happened just before this particular scene in the play. They might even quote a poem, compare the scene to a modern-day headline, or act as though they are in counseling and the audience is their "therapist." Introductions should never exceed one minute.

The following example of an entertaining introduction is written as dialogue for better clarity.

41

CREATING INTRODUCTIONS

Different styles of introductions are used for different situations. For auditions, keep it simple: the actor's name, the character, the play, and the playwright are all you need. However, for competitions or performances with a live audience, get creative.

Read these sample introductions to your class. Point out the different parts as indicated. After you have read the introductions, identify which type you expect your students to use in class. Perhaps you will allow either to be used or you may offer bonus points to students who choose to create an entertaining introduction, which is the more difficult of the two. Regardless, be very specific about your expectations.

- Informative example: My name is Andy Withers, and I will be portraying the Cheshire Cat from *Alice in Wonderland* by Percy Glass.

- Entertaining example: Imagine a dream so disturbing, so frightening, yet so fascinating you aren't sure you want to wake up. Imagine a world so backward and odd that you are certain you must be dreaming. In Percy Glass's *Alice in Wonderland*, based on the story by Lewis Carroll, Alice finds herself in the world she had once playfully imagined. As in most cases, though, she discovers that the grass was really greener on the other side, and she cannot wait to get back—

SAMPLE INTRODUCTION

[Teaser]

JUAN: *(As KELLER.)* Katie, I will not have it! Now you did not see when that girl after supper tonight went to look for Helen in her room—

SARAH: *(As KATIE.)* No.

JUAN: *(As KELLER.)* The child practically climbed out of her window to escape from her! What kind of teacher is she?

[Introduction]

JUAN: *(Out of character, turning to face AUDIENCE.)* Captain Keller and his young wife, Kate, were blessed with a beautiful, happy baby.

SARAH: *(Out of character, turning to face AUDIENCE.)* But when illness robbed their child of her sight and hearing, they were left with a girl who could not communicate. She lived in darkness and total silence.

JUAN: *(Out of character.)* But her world was far from quiet. There was a voice screaming in her head, fighting to get out. The Kellers needed a miracle.

SARAH: *(Out of character.)* *The Miracle Worker*, by William Gibson.

[Scene]

(Both students return to their characters and the scene continues on through the end.)

JUAN: *(As KELLER.)* I thought I had seen her at her worst...

---

if she can! Perhaps the Cheshire Cat can help. *Alice in Wonderland* by Percy Glass.

In the second example, the playwright and character are identified, the story and author from which the play was derived are noted, and the introduction hints at the specific scene from which the monologue comes. There is a small amount of background on the storyline, and the listeners' interest is piqued both at the beginning and end. The only thing missing is the student's name, which is often the case with entertaining introductions.

Some great tricks to creating unique introductions include:

- A startling statistic that relates to your scene or play: "Six million men, women, and children were murdered for one reason and one reason only: their religion."

- A bit of background on the play or playwright: "Reginald Rose was on jury duty when he looked around the room and thought it would be a great setting for a play. From that fleeting thought, *Twelve Angry Men* was born!"

- A line from a poem, a line from the play or scene, a lyric: "The dandelions call to me and the white chestnut branches in the court. That butterfly was the last one. Butterflies don't live here anymore, in the ghetto."

NAME _____ PERIOD _____ DATE _____

INTRODUCTION PRACTICE

Create an introduction for three of the Lab Scenes at the end of this section. Remember, some are monologues and some are duets. Your format for your introduction will be different depending on the type of scene. Include at least one monologue and one duet. One of your introductions may be *informative* while the others are *entertaining*. Refer to *Creating an Introduction* on page 41 if you need assistance. Create fictional titles for your scenes and use Suzi Zimmerman, the author of this workbook, as the playwright.

Lab Scene # _____ Informative introduction

_____
_____
_____
_____
_____
_____
_____
_____
_____
_____

Lab Scene # _____ Entertaining introduction without teaser

_____
_____
_____
_____
_____
_____
_____
_____

Lab Scene # _____ Entertaining introduction with teaser

_____
_____
_____
_____
_____
_____
_____
_____
_____
_____

43

- Relate the scene to your audience: "Being thirteen is hard. Am I right? Imagine being thirteen and living your life in hiding, wary of every sound you make, fearing for your life."

- Most introductions are spoken out of character, but in most cases there are no hard-and-fast rules. The introduction works if it "hooks" the audience and contains the necessary information. However, if you are auditioning or taking your scene to a competition, there may actually be rules, so be sure to investigate that before preparing your intro.

- An entertaining introduction does not necessarily have to come before the dialogue, although it does need to be placed toward the beginning. Actors will often begin their scene, stop and step out of character, give their introduction, and then continue with their scene. The dialogue from the scene that precedes the introduction is called a "teaser."

Use the *Introduction Practice* worksheet to have students practice introductions.

REHEARSALS AND PERFORMANCES

Now it is time to get to work. You will begin rehearsing your scene, getting it ready for your first performance. Your teacher will give you details on their specific performance expectations.

Whatever time your teacher has allotted for you to prepare your scene, attendance is crucial. Ask your teacher in advance when they plan to conduct performances and write the date in your calendar. You will want to pace yourself accordingly. This guide assumes you will have five class sessions to prepare. Adjust it accordingly when planning your rehearsals.

Day 1—Rehearse your scene using your script. Mark ideas in the script using a pencil. Clarify any confusion early if you do not understand a word or a part of the script.

Day 2—Block your scene and write your blocking in your script in pencil. When will you sit? When will you stand and cross? Continue to work on memorization.

Day 3—Continue to rehearse using your script, but make it your goal to be doing the scene without the script by the end of this class period.

Day 4—Sit down and read your script again. Now that you have it basically worked out, it is important to make sure you did not miss anything, especially if you are working without a director. If you are required to use props, now is the time to work them in. Plan out your introduction and start practicing it each time you rehearse your scene.

Day 5—Have someone watch your scene and critique it, and do the same for them. Without arguing or defending your performance, thank them for their critique. You may now decide if you want to change anything based on their criticism. Spend the remainder of your rehearsal time polishing and perfecting your scene for performance.

How do you know when your scene is good enough for a performance? While the answer may seem straightforward, getting there and knowing when you are there may be more complex. Your scene will be ready for performance when it feels like second nature to you. In other words, when you feel like you could do it in your sleep, you are ready. It must be one hundred percent memorized, including lines and actions. If you are working with a partner, the two of you should be synchronized or almost instinctively paired in the scene. You also want to make sure that you are obeying the most basic rules of acting, such as projecting, remaining visible to the audience, and staying true to the script and the playwright's intent. Most importantly, the scene must have good energy throughout—even during silent pauses.

Now that you are ready, it's time to perform. Many teachers have their students perform scenes just once, while others prefer to see them twice, about two weeks apart. The benefits of doing each scene twice far outweigh doing them one time. For example, the audience and teacher will give the performers quite a bit of feedback after the first performance. Students should take that feedback to improve their scenes. Polishing scenes after a first performance is also similar to how actors polish a play after receiving feedback from the director. Finally, a perfected scene is great audition material, but few scenes are of that caliber after just one performance. Ask your teacher how many times you will perform your scene and record all the dates in your calendar.

SCHEDULING REHEARSALS AND PERFORMANCES

Post rehearsal and performance dates for scene work in a prominent place in your room. Try to plan to complete performances about a week before the end of the grading period. This way, unexpected delays will not be a problem. Also, try not to rehearse too many days back-to-back. Allow for some other activities that can be linked to the scene work, such as improvisation games, lessons, worksheets, and discussion. As with any other activity, occasional breaks are needed to keep scenes fresh. Generally, beginners need about five hours of in-class rehearsal for a one- to two-minute monologue whereas advanced students will only require about three.

After the first performances, allow two to three more hours for making improvements to their scenes before round two.

Prior to performances, remind students of your expectations, the grading policy, and so on. What is the ideal behavior for the audience? How much time will actors have to set the stage? Will students do an introduction, and if so, which type? What happens if they forget a line, if the announcements come on, or if a visitor interrupts? Everyone should be prepared for unexpected interruptions. The *Scene Work Cut-N-Paste* on page 179 will help your classes to understand how to handle common obstacles in performances.

LAB SCENE #1

CASEY, female, age 14

Casey has moved in with her great-aunt while her mother tries to get back on her feet after a third divorce. Her new neighborhood is on a quiet street with quiet, elderly people. Casey is the only one her age on the block. Sometimes she meets kids who are visiting their grandparents at the neighboring homes, but they do not stay long enough to become friends. Her only friend is a girl named Victoria, but Casey knows that it is only a matter of time before Victoria's bad choices get both of them into a lot of trouble. She has met Mabel, a kind, elderly blind lady who has asked Casey to spend an hour each day helping her around the house. The kitchen is tidy to a fault. She must be very careful not to rearrange anything, and she feels hopelessly clumsy.

1   **CASEY:** *(Brings MABEL a cup of hot tea.)* Careful. It's pretty hot. *(Starts to leave the room, but hesitates.)* Miss Mabel? I... Oh, never mind. Have you ever... *(Knocks over a broom.)* Oh, I'm so sorry. I am such a klutz! I'm just gonna go finish sorting the mail and then I'll leave. I'll see you tomorrow. *(Starts to leave.)* Miss Mabel... What's it like? *(Uncomfortable, but curious.)* I
5   mean, to be blind? You must get lonely. I mean, I can see pretty good, but sometimes I feel like I am completely in the dark, you know what I mean? I mean, I know you do, but do you really? I have this friend, Victoria, and she's pretty nice. She's just about the only person I know who's not old enough to have great-grandkids! Oh, sorry. I mean, she's the only friend I have my age. Sometimes I don't even like her. Sometimes after we get together I promise
10   myself I'm never gonna call her again or go to her house. But then, a few hours pass and I get so lonely, and I think that it's better to go to her house and sit around watching her smoke her dad's cigarettes and make prank calls than it is to be completely alone. I've never told anyone this, but... you won't tell, will you? One time she stole a CD from the gas station. It was some old singer from a long time ago, and she doesn't even have a CD player. She did,
15   but her stepdad sold it. I didn't know she'd taken it until we were halfway home. She thought it was so funny! I was just mad and scared. I kept looking over my shoulder thinking the cops were gonna come get us. I was afraid that if I told her how mad I was, she would think I was a baby. You know, my momma may not be perfect, but she taught me right from wrong, and what Victoria did was wrong. It's not like she stole because she was hungry. She did it just for
20   fun! That's the longest I ever went without calling her—a whole day! Miss Mabel... I... I never knew my grandma. My momma wouldn't have anything to do with her. She died about four years ago and my momma didn't even cry, wouldn't even go to the funeral. And you know I never knew my daddy, much less his momma. I would be very proud if I could call you my grandma... Would that be okay with you?

45

LAB SCENE #1

The first lab scene, Casey, is rated "easy" due to the character's simplistic emotions and easy-going nature. The most difficult part of the scene is the timing. Lead students in a discussion on timing using the *Art of Timing* lesson in Chapter 4. Identify the difference between cut-off and fade-off lines.

Also, remind them that their "listener" is blind. Have students bring blindfolds and lead them in a blind adventure around your school. Pair them and have each take turns being the "Casey" figure, assisting the "Miss Mabel" figure, even though she is not in the scene.

INTRODUCTION TO THEATRE ARTS I

NAME _____ PERIOD _____ DATE _____

CASEY

Answer the following questions about the character, Casey, from Lab Scene #1.

1. What do we know for certain about Casey?

2. What do we know for certain about Mabel?

3. What do we know for certain about the setting?

4. What year do you think it is? Why?

5. What is the scene about?

6. Is the scene comic, dramatic, or a combination of the two?

7. What happened just before the start of this scene?

8. What do you think might happen after the scene if the story continued?

9. If this scene was from a play, what do you think it would be called?

10. What does Casey want in this scene?

11. What do you think Casey's hobbies might be?

12. If Casey repeatedly made a gesture in this scene, what would it be and why?

13. What color do you associate with Casey and why?

LAB SCENE #1 FOR DISCUSSION...

- Casey is fourteen years old. How old are you? Do you think she is mature for her age or immature? How will that change the way you portray her?

- Do you know what it is like to be around a person who is blind person or a person with a disability? Do you think Casey is familiar with life around a disabled person? How will this affect the way you portray her character?

- Do you know what it is like to be in Casey's situation? She lives with her great-aunt in a senior community so that her mother can put her life back together. How will this affect the way you play her?

- Do you know anyone like Victoria? If so, how does this person's choices make you feel? How will that affect the way you portray Casey?

- Do you think Casey is nervous? Why or why not?

NAME _____ PERIOD _____ DATE _____

14. What object do you associate with Casey and why?

15. What animal do you associate with Casey and why?

16. In real life, would you be Casey's friend? Why or why not?

17. How is Casey like you?

18. How is Casey different from you?

19. What is Casey's most positive trait?

20. What is Casey's status in the world? Does she have money or power?

21. What does Casey fear and why?

22. Who does Casey admire and why?

23. What are Casey's parents like?

24. If Casey had one wish, what would it be and why?

25. What is your favorite line in the monologue and why?

26. Find ten words in Casey's monologue that you feel stand out as being the most descriptive of the overall purpose of the scene.

47

- Practice carrying a cup of hot tea carefully. Remember that the person to whom you are serving this hot beverage is blind. Then practice pantomiming this same action. Using pantomimed props can be very tricky, so keep practicing until you feel confident in your acting.

- There is quite a bit of timing written into this scene. Where will Casey pause? Where will she speed up? You may want to mark your script to help you.

/ = short pause (like a comma)

// = medium pause (like a period or a quick change of ideas)

/// = long pause (like a hesitation or a whole new subject)

- How would the scene change if Victoria stole a piece of taffy from the grocery store rather than a CD from the gas station?

LAB SCENE #2

JOEY, male, age 17

Joey is a rebellious teen in a small town. His girlfriend got a car for her sixteenth birthday from her writer father, but she feared the mountainous roads, so Joey did all the driving. When their parents feel they are spending too much time together and pressure them to back off from the relationship, Joey and Darla take one last cruise along Highway 12. Afterward, Joey recounts his story in group therapy.

1   **JOEY:** Darla's dad is this big writer guy. His name is Dwight—but that wasn't glamorous enough for the people that buy that stuff, so his pen name was Antonio Bishop. He wrote stories about this old guy who travels all over the world meeting beautiful women, but he never gets married because that would mean he'd have to settle down, you know? So Darla, she says to
5   me, "Do you think he wishes he'd never had me?" She took it real personal, you know? Her mom had died a few years back, and Darla figured her dad had become almost like the guy he wrote about… except for the part about having a kid. So he bought her a fast car.

You know, my folks never went to college. My mom never even graduated from high school. They got married right after my dad graduated, so she dropped out. I was born the night she
10   should have graduated. After that, having babies was her hobby! The night of the accident, she told me number seven was on the way… and that I'd have to spend less time with "that girl"… and that she was fed up being up to her ears in babies and no help!

So I left. My mom was standing at the screen door holding a screaming kid yelling at me to come back, but I just kept going. Darla picked me up halfway, crying so hard she could
15   barely see, so I drove. Her dad said he wanted her to get away from me for a while, so he was sending her to boarding school in New York starting in the fall. We both cried, and I just kept driving. Neither of us said it, but we were leaving.

We were on Highway 12 by Pearl Lake. For the first time since we left, we were quiet. I looked at Darla and she tried to smile, but then she suddenly looked scared, and I realized I was
20   headed off the road right toward the lake. I swerved and the car started spinning. There was a lot of screeching and screaming, and then we hit something and everything went black.

When I woke up, we were wedged against the cliff. Her head was against my shoulder. She was having a real hard time breathing, but I couldn't move to help her. I could tell she was in a lot of pain. I wished it was me, but I didn't feel anything. I couldn't feel a thing… I saw the
25   flashing red lights and heard the sirens. I couldn't hear Darla breathing anymore.

All we wanted was to be happy. We just wanted to be together… happy.

LAB SCENE #2

Joey's monologue is rated "challenging." He is recalling a terrifying event. Each actor has the ability to manipulate the scene in a way that will imply a different outcome.

Joey's audience, the other members of the group therapy session, is large. The actors may choose to use their actual audience—their fellow classmates—as the members of the group therapy session, or they may choose to speak to empty chairs.

There are no written stage directions in the scene. This does not mean actors should sit the entire time. On the contrary, encourage students to add their own blocking and to keep the scene energetic.

There is a great deal of room for character development, but the language and grammar should not be changed. Help students to identify a character type who would use the kind of grammar Joey uses. In what part of the country does his dialect suggest he lives?

NAME _____ PERIOD _____ DATE _____

JOEY

Answer the following questions about the character, Joey, from Lab Scene #2.

1. What do we know for certain about Joey?

2. What do we know for certain about Darla?

3. What do we know for certain about the setting?

4. What year do you think it is? Why?

5. What is the scene about?

6. Is the scene comic, dramatic, or a combination of the two?

7. What happened just before the start of this scene?

8. What do you think might happen after the scene if the story continued?

9. If this scene was from a play, what do you think it would be called?

10. What does Joey want in this scene?

11. If Joey repeatedly made a gesture in this scene, what would it be and why?

12. What color do you associate with Joey and why?

13. What object do you associate with Joey and why?

　　　　49

LAB SCENE #2 FOR DISCUSSION...

- Joey is seventeen years old. How old are you? Do you think he is mature for his age or immature? How will that change the way you portray him?

- Do you know what it is like to be the oldest of several children?

- Do you know what it is like to live in a small town? How will this affect the way you portray Joey?

- Do you know anyone in a situation similar to Darla's?

- How do you think it feels to have a girlfriend like Darla and have your parents pressure you to spend less time with her?

- Why do you think Joey is in group therapy?

- How long after the accident do you think this scene takes place?

INTRODUCTION TO THEATRE ARTS I

NAME _____ PERIOD _____ DATE _____

14. In real life, would you be Joey's friend? Why or why not?

15. How is Joey like you?

16. How is Joey different from you?

17. What is Joey's status in the world? Does he have money or power?

18. What does Joey fear and why?

19. Who does Joey admire and why?

20. What are Joey's parents like?

21. If Joey had one wish, what would it be and why?

22. What do you think happened to Darla?

23. What is Joey's future like now?

24. What is your favorite line in the monologue and why?

25. Find ten words in Joey's monologue that you feel stand out as being the most descriptive of the overall purpose of the scene.

- Identify some of the others in the therapy session with Joey. What are their names, their situations, and their personalities? How will those in therapy with Joey affect the way he speaks to each of them? Might he address them individually (without noting their names) and alter his tone accordingly?

- There are no stage directions written into this scene for a reason. You may choose to play Joey in a wheelchair, with an injury, or able-bodied. Regardless, you must remember to keep the dynamic and energetic, even if you choose to portray Joey as paralyzed. How will the scene stay energetic if he is unable to move?

- You may also choose Darla's fate. How do you think she came out of this and how will that affect your portrayal of Joey?

LAB SCENE #3

FATIMA, female, age 25

Fatima is the leader of the Sisterhood of Destiny, a club that preaches women's independence. She is having a hard time fighting off her urge to do the very thing she tells others not to do. She is getting ready for a rally and tries to practice her speech, pack boxes, and talk to her roommate all at the same time.

1   **FATIMA**: *(As though speaking at a rally.)* A woman is only independent when she is standing on her own two feet, paying her own way, and making her own decisions about education, career, and relation—oh! I almost forgot to tell you... I met the cutest guy! His name is Raul... He's Spanish. He's a buyer for a big Spanish department store, El Something-or-
5   Other. He was in town for a big market, and I ran into him on the subway—literally ran into him—tripped over some lady's briefcase and pushed him right on top of a man with flowers. Daisies everywhere! But this guy, Raul, he just looks up at me and says, "Are you, how you say, all right?" He looked like an angel! He has these big blue eyes and eyelashes that just kept waving to me! I almost kissed him right there on the spot! Have you seen my enrollment
10 forms? I had them right here on top of my *Live a Man's Life* book. Oh, look! Remember this? This is the Sisterhood at the first rally! Look, there's Alice and Breck and me and—ooh, gross! How'd she get in the picture? She married that writer who came to one of our meetings just so he could badmouth us in his column. The next day we had three members drop out, and we lost the support of the entire Lady Bikers Club! I heard she's already on her second baby,
15 and do you know she quit her job? A woman is only independent when she is standing on her own two feet, right? Can you imagine being a housewife, not working, just spending the whole day with kids, gardening, cooking, *(Starts liking the idea.)* cleaning, shopping, taking care of Raul—I mean, your husband? *(Shakes the thought off.)* You know, I don't think my speech is passionate enough. Maybe I should say something about the male conspiracy to glamorize
20 the... to disguise the role of the wife in a suburban setting as a desirable goal rather than the trap that it is. *(As a speech.)* Beware those who will shroud the position of the slave-wife in a veil of adorable little minivans, maternity clothes, and long walks in the park on sunny days, pushing the stroller, meeting other moms, not working. Not working. This speech is not working! *(Sits defeated, retrieving her clipboard from the seat.)* Enrollment forms! Found
25 them. *(Takes a piece of paper and a cell phone from her pocket and punches in the number.)* Raul? Hi, this is Fatima, remember? From the subway? Yeah. That one. Listen, I've had a cancellation today and thought maybe you'd like to have lunch?

51

LAB SCENE #3

The Fatima monologue is rated "challenging." The character is practicing giving a speech and becomes sidetracked, at which point her personality changes completely. The monologue also contains a great deal of required movement, some Spanish dialect, a wide range of emotions, some difficult timing, and several long lists. The listener, Fatima's roommate, adds little input to the storyline. There are also many subtle and some other obvious jokes. Students will probably need to research the women's liberation movement to grasp these fully. If time does not permit this research, help your actors to identify and understand the humorous parts of the monologue prior to the first performance.

Perhaps the most challenging part of the Fatima monologue, however, is the non-specific ending. Challenge students to find a gesture or facial expression they can use in reaction to Raul's response to the invitation that will give closure to the scene.

NAME _____ PERIOD _____ DATE _____

FATIMA

Answer the following questions about the character, Fatima, from Lab Scene #3.

1. What do we know for certain about Fatima?

2. What do we know for certain about the setting?

3. What year do you think it is? Why?

4. What is the scene about?

5. Is the scene comic, dramatic, or a combination of the two?

6. What happened just before the start of this scene?

7. What do you think might happen after the scene if the story continued?

8. If this scene was from a play, what do you think it would be called?

9. What does Fatima want in this scene?

10. If Fatima repeatedly made a gesture in this scene, what would it be and why?

11. What are some items Fatima might be packing for her rally?

12. What color do you associate with Fatima and why?

13. What object do you associate with Fatima and why?

LAB SCENE #3 FOR DISCUSSION...

- Fatima is twenty-five years old. How old are you? How will that affect the way you portray her? Why do you think Fatima is the leader of the Sisterhood of Destiny?

- This monologue may prove challenging because Fatima is doing several things at the same time and often throws herself off track. Try practicing this scene while getting ready for school in the morning, cleaning your room, or preparing a meal.

- There are several lines in Fatima's monologue that are purposefully written to sound a bit immature or feminine. Can you find them? Why do you think the playwright gave Fatima those lines?

- Do you know anyone like Fatima? How can you study this person or others to help you develop your characterization?

CHAPTER 3 — SCENE WORK

NAME _____ PERIOD _____ DATE _____

14. In real life, would you be Fatima's friend? Why or why not?

15. How is Fatima like you?

16. How is Fatima different from you?

17. What is Fatima's status in the world? Does she have money or power?

18. What does Fatima fear and why?

19. Who does Fatima admire and why?

20. What are Fatima's parents like?

21. If Fatima had one wish, what would it be and why?

22. What is Fatima's roommate doing while this monologue is taking place?

23. What is your favorite line in the monologue and why?

24. When Fatima speaks as Raul, will you use a Spanish accent? Why or why not?

25. Find ten words in Fatima's monologue that you feel stand out as being the most descriptive of the overall purpose of the scene.

53

- Do you know someone who makes you feel like Fatima felt when she met Raul? How can you use that in your portrayal of Fatima?

- What do you think her "cancellation" was?

- Insert Raul's responses to Fatima on the other end of the line using the ^ symbol.

- Remember Raul's responses to help you with timing and reaction when you perform. If acting is reacting, then imagining his responses will allow you to react.

LAB SCENE #4

NICK, male, age 27

Nick is a young, wealthy bachelor who owns a string of hair salons. He would love to meet a woman to become his wife. In this monologue, he is at his brother Jack's wedding and meets up with his cousin, whom he has not seen in a long time. They are on the balcony just off the dance floor.

1   **NICK:** Remember when we went swimming that year before Pops had cleaned the pool? It was so cold and nasty, but we didn't care! We just wanted to get summer started, and somehow swimming was the key. The next day the sun came out and Pops cleaned the pool—it was a perfect pool day! But we were all stuck inside with colds, and I ended up getting an ear
5   infection. *(Teasingly.)* You know, Pops told me not to tell you, but when he cleaned the pool, there were all sorts of creatures in it! I'm not kidding! *(Silence as a girl walks by.)* Whoa! Who's that? She's totally hot! She looks kind of like Kyle's wife—oh. She is. You know, that's been my luck. All through college, I would meet these pretty girls, and we would get along really well. We'd go out, and at the end of the night I'd be ready to make my move, and she'd
10   say, "Nick, you're really sweet, but I'm just not ready for a relationship." Next thing I knew, they'd be dating one of my friends and calling me for advice! Like I'd know the difference between a relationship and a hole in the ground! *(Slumps into a chair.)* It's all my mom's fault. She always made sure I was nice… polite. The girls would hear me say "Yes, ma'am" to a teacher and they would all say, "Oh, that's so sweet!" But, Kyle, man, he was a real jerk! He
15   never said more than two words in our geometry class. A pretty girl would walk in and the rest of us would just stare at her. Kyle would pretend not to notice—or maybe he really didn't. I don't know—but that girl would sit down right next to him. She'd act like she'd dropped her pencil, and he would ignore her. By the end of the first day, she was asking everyone who that cute, serious boy was. When he met Ginger, she totally snubbed him, and do you know what?
20   He ate it up! He acted like she was the last girl on Earth, and she acted like she didn't want anything to do with him. *(Pause.)* Guess what? When he decided to ask her to marry him, who do you think he called for advice? Yup. Me. The old Relationship Guru himself—Nicky-I-Just-Want-To-Be-Friends. That's me. *(Stands.)* You want to hear something funny? I bought these hair salons, so I'm around women all the time, right? You'd think I could meet someone
25   special? There's this one girl, Sasha, at one of the salons. I'm thinking of asking her out. But before I could get up the nerve, she says, "You're really nice, Nick. You got a good-looking friend you could set me up with?" *(Points.)* That's her—with Jack.

LAB SCENE #4

Nick's monologue is rated "easy" because his character is so clearly defined. He is one of those men who is so nice that women want to be his friend. He, however, is looking for a relationship. The challenge in the scene is to successfully play him as nice and not sappy or nerdy.

Students playing Nick may want to practice with a real girl walking by; the actor must time her passing and his eyes should follow her in a believable way. It seems easy, but it is not. After working with a real girl, he can then mimic those movements and the timing without her assistance.

Generally, it is more difficult to do a funny scene than a dramatic one because of the subtle timing. It is the timing more often than the lines that makes most moments humorous. Instruct students not to try too hard to make this scene funny.

NAME _____ PERIOD _____ DATE _____

NICK

Answer the following questions about the character, Nick, from Lab Scene #4.

1.   What do we know for certain about Nick?

2.   What do we know for certain about the setting?

3.   What year do you think it is? Why?

4.   What is the scene about?

5.   Is the scene comic, dramatic, or a combination of the two?

6.   What happened just before the start of this scene?

7.   What do you think might happen after the scene if the story continued?

8.   If this scene was from a play, what do you think it would be called?

9.   What does Nick want in this scene?

10.   If Nick repeatedly made a gesture in this scene, what would it be and why?

11.   What are Nick's hobbies?

12.   What object do you associate with Nick and why?

13.   What animal do you associate with Nick and why?

55

LAB SCENE #4 FOR DISCUSSION...

- Nick is twenty-seven years old. How old are you? How will that affect the way you portray him?

- Nick is young and wealthy. How do you think he got his money? Does he act rich?

- Nick is at his brother's wedding. How do you think weddings make him feel?

- Who is Nick's cousin to whom he is talking? Is the cousin male or female? How old are they? What is they like?

- In the second paragraph when the girl walks by, what do you think Nick does? Does he stop and stare? Does he smile or make eye contact?

- Do you know anyone like Nick? How can you study this person or others to help you to develop your characterization?

- Who are you more like, Nick or Kyle? Explain. How can you use this to assist you in portraying the character Nick?

- Does Nick resent his mother for teaching him to be polite? Explain. How will that affect the way you portray Nick?

- What is Kyle's relationship to Nick? How will this affect your characterization?

INTRODUCTION TO THEATRE ARTS I

NAME _____ PERIOD _____ DATE _____

14. In real life, would you be Nick's friend? Why or why not?

15. How is Nick like you?

16. How is Nick different from you?

17. What is Nick's most positive trait?

18. What is his status in the world? Does he have money or power?

19. What does Nick want from life?

20. What does he fear and why?

21. Who does Nick admire and why?

22. What are/were Nick's parents like?

23. If he had one wish, what would it be and why?

24. What advice would you give Nick if you were his cousin?

- How would Nick act if Jack was his brother and it was Jack and Sasha's wedding? How would this change if Jack was just a friend and this was his first date with Sasha?

- If this scene were from a play, at what point would Nick find the girl of his dreams? What do you think the outcome would be?

- Boys get labeled "nice but not datable" more than girls. Why is this?

- In the end, will Nick or Kyle be happier. Why?

LAB SCENE #5

PHARRAH, female

In this scene, Pharrah is talking to the women and the girls. It's casual. Because there is no context to the scene, imagine various situations in which a strong, educated woman might be telling this type of story. Create your own context for the monologue, and even try putting in into several different contexts to see what works best for you. (Pharrah is pronounced "Farah.")

1   **PHARRAH:** When I was 7, I wanted to be an architect. My favorite book was about a dinosaur whose best friend was a saber tooth tiger cub, and they explored prehistoric Earth together. My mom bought it for a quarter at a garage sale. It was brand new! She read it to me every night. I would be the dinosaur, and she would be the tiger. I got to where I knew it by heart,
5   but I also learned to recognize the words. And then the pages started falling out, so she put them into a scrapbook for me so that we didn't have to throw it away. She never got tired of doing things for me. Soon the scrapbook was filled with National Geographic articles, fossils, and fun things we found on our adventures. Every pre-pubescent wannabe archeologist should have such committed cheerleaders! Then, when I was in 7th grade, I had Mrs. Tucker's home
10   room. She was so old fashioned. One day she invited me to have lunch in her classroom, and that made me feel very special. She said I was her brightest student, even brighter than most of the boys. Did you hear me? Brighter than… most… of the boys? Can you believe it? She was trying to make me feel good, but that was the first time I realized that some people actually believed girls were less than boys or that they belonged in different categories. She asked
15   what I wanted to be when I grew up, and I told her: an archeologist. She made a sound. *(Makes sound of disgust.)* No. That wasn't quite it. It was more like this. *(Makes exaggerated sound of disgust.)* Yes. That's it. *(Badly imitating a woman's voice.)* "Pharrah, you might think you want to be a scientist now, because you're young. But when you become interested in boys, you'll change your ways! Boys like girls who are ladylike. There's nothing ladylike about
20   archeology." My mom had made me a turkey sandwich that day. The bread was kind of dry. I was glad. That dry bread was what stopped me from saying the first rude thing that came to mind. The aluminum foil in my fingers, pressed into my lap, tightened into a dense ball and was beginning to feel a bit dangerous. With a full mouth, I chewed and chewed and chewed, which gave me time to carefully plan out what I would say and to drop the foil to the floor
25   rather than hurtling it. I'd never even had a detention before, and I was pretty sure pinging the teacher with a foil ball would be, I don't know, at least out of school suspension. Finally, I swallowed. I leaned down to pick up the foil I'd dropped and saw the trashcan clear across the room. I aimed, heard Mrs. Tucker gasp, and shot anyway. Two points! No, that was at least a three pointer! Mrs. Tucker gave me a look, but it was lunchtime, and the rules were relaxed.
30   Plus, she liked to make a big deal out of her special lunches. I took a big swig of my milk. It was warm and not at all refreshing. I wanted to burp, but Mrs. Tucker wouldn't have tolerated that from a boy, even on special lunch day. And I'm pretty sure she wouldn't have thought it was "ladylike." I resisted the urge. I slowly pulled my heavy backpack onto my shoulder and looked at Mrs. Tucker and said, "Thank you for inviting me to lunch. It was very informative."
35   That was NOT what I was thinking, but it was safe. And then I made my way between the desks and headed for the door. But just as I was about to walk out, I turned to her and said, "Mrs. Tucker. Ladylike is overrated. And I am smarter than the boys. I'm ranked first in my class—all 112 of us, including every boy." She smiled. It wasn't a friendly smile. That was the smile of someone who wished a rule had been broken but knew it hadn't. I waved goodbye
40   and left. Just then that burp hit me, and it was out before I could stop it. Just loud enough to be heard but not so loud as to sound intentional. But just in case, I followed it with a just loud enough "excuses me" and headed to my next class. Ladylike is definitely overrated!

      57

LAB SCENE #5

Pharrah's monologue is rated "moderate." It's too long to be easy but lacks the complexity to be difficult. It combines a serious topic with a relaxed, comedic tone.

NAME _____ PERIOD _____ DATE _____

PHARRAH

Answer the following questions about the character, Pharrah, from Lab Scene #5.

1.   What do we know for certain about Pharrah?

2.   How old do you think Pharrah is?

3.   What year do you think it is? Why?

4.   What is the scene about?

5.   Is the scene comic, dramatic, or a combination of the two?

6.   What happened just before the start of this scene?

7.   What do you think might happen after the scene if the story continued?

8.   If this scene was from a play, what do you think it would be called?

9.   What does Pharrah want in this scene?

10. If Pharrah repeatedly made a gesture in this scene, what would it be and why?

11. What are Pharrah's hobbies?

12. What object do you associate with Pharrah and why?

13. What animal do you associate with Pharrah and why?

LAB SCENE #5 FOR DISCUSSION...

- We don't know Pharrah's age. What age do you feel is appropriate for her? How might the scene be different if played as a high school senior versus a 50-year-old woman?

- Do you think Pharrah became a paleontologist? Might you play the scene differently if you learned she became a young mother who had to drop out of school to raise her child?

- Who is Pharrah's listener in this scene? Could it be her boss? Might it be her spouse? Since it is not defined, find a listener whose presence in the scene is meaningful to you, the actor.

- What is Pharrah's purpose in telling this story?

- Why is the part of the story about the book and the scrapbook important to the rest of the scene?

CHAPTER 3 — SCENE WORK

NAME _____ PERIOD _____ DATE _____

14. In real life, would you be Pharrah's friend? Why or why not?

15. How is Pharrah like you?

16. How is Pharrah different from you?

17. What is Pharrah's most positive trait?

18. What is her status in the world? Does she have money or power?

19. What does Pharrah want from life?

20. What does she fear and why?

21. Who does Pharrah admire and why?

22. What are/were Pharrah's parents like?

23. If she had one wish, what would it be and why?

24. What advice would you give Pharrah if you were her cousin?

- What role do numbers play in this scene?

- What role do smells play in this scene? Can you use the mentions of smell to add interest to your performance? Can you relate to Pharrah's memories of smell? How?

- Is Pharrah's attitude a problem? How will you portray her so that the outcome is believable?

- What do you think happened to Pharrah's mother? Why were they broke, and do you think their financial situation turned around? What role does being broke play in a young person's formative years?

LAB SCENE #6

JASPER, male, 20 and **CANDY**, female, 20

Jasper is a fun-loving twenty-year-old college student. He makes good grades, but not good enough to get into law school—his original intention. His girlfriend, Candy, works very hard for her grades, which are not that much better than Jasper's. She has just finished taking an exam and is nervous about the outcome. She becomes frustrated when she finds Jasper playing video games with his friends instead of studying.

CANDY ENTERS JASPER'S dormitory TV room to find him playing video games with some of his buddies. She is carrying far too many books and hugs them close to her as if for comfort.

1   **CANDY:** Jasper. *(Louder this time.)* Jasper!

    JASPER: Oh! Hi, baby! *(Back to the game.)* I didn't see you—man! Got me! Didn't see you come in… Woo hoo! Got ya back! How'd you do on your anatomy exam? D'ya ace it?

    CANDY: I don't know. He hasn't posted the scores yet.

5   **JASPER:** *(Still playing.)* Well, how d'you think you did? *(CANDY shrugs.)* Huh, baby? I didn't hear ya. You think you passed, got a B, what?

    CANDY: Come on, Jasper! Can't you put that stupid game down for a minute and talk to me instead of the TV screen? *(The rest of the guys take this as their cue to EXIT, allowing the two some privacy.)* Bye, Andy. See ya, Vince.

10   **JASPER:** *(Slightly overlapping CANDY.)* See ya, guys. *(Turns to CANDY.)* Okay. Talk to me. What happened?

    CANDY: Nothing happened. I just took the test, that's all. Maxwell takes his time getting the grades up. It's like he's into this whole "torture" thing or something. He's such a jerk!

    JASPER: I thought you liked Maxwell…

15   **CANDY:** No, you're right. I do. I'm just anxious, that's all. This anatomy class has been a lot tougher than I thought it would be, and I'm having to work my butt off just to get a B. I haven't gotten less than that yet, and I don't want this class to be the first.

    JASPER: *(Pulls her toward him, almost paternally.)* Poor baby…

    CANDY: *(Pulls away, a bit too angrily.)* Stop it, Jasper! Don't patronize me!

20   **JASPER:** Baby, I'm not—

    CANDY: And stop calling me baby! I'm not a baby!

    JASPER: I just wanted—

    CANDY: You sit in here with your "boys" and play that stupid Night Fighter game—

    JASPER: Night Raider.

25   **CANDY:** Whatever! You sit in here like a little kid while I'm out working my butt off to make decent grades, and you get in there and ace tests in classes I can't even spell! Then you sit there so smug and act like it was not a big deal! *(Starts wiping away tears.)* And here I am all worked up and crying and yelling at you!

    JASPER: It's okay, ba— *(Stops abruptly, realizing what he was about to say.)*

30   **CANDY:** *(Calming down a little.)* No. It's not okay. This… *(Referring to her current state.)* …is not okay. I look around me, and everyone is having fun. I'm not having fun. I'm having a nervous breakdown.

LAB SCENE #6

The Jasper and Candy duet is rated "challenging." The scene begins with additional people, but the two actors will have to imagine them. There's really no need to allow stand-ins. Furthermore, Jasper has the added challenge of having to both "play the video game" and talk to Candy. Timing will be very important.

Candy must come across as being genuinely downtrodden without sounding self-pitying or whiny. Her dilemma is a real one that many people face, and at no time should the actor take it lightly or poke fun at the character.

The greatest obstacle will be for both actors to characterize their roles believably. Jasper must be laid-back in everything he does, and Candy should remain intense only until she is given good reason to relax. Even then her serious nature threatens to interfere.

1   **JASPER:** Look. Maybe I can help you. I mean, you're right. Stuff comes a lot easier for me than some people. But look at you! You can sing and act and draw and paint. You're an artist. I can't even draw a stick figure...

CANDY: Jasper, I appreciate what you are doing, but that's not the point. The point is—I don't
5   like college. I'm not even sure it's what I want to do anymore. Every time I'm having to miss a party to study or miss going out with you to go to the library, I think, "This wasn't what I got into this for. I want to paint."

JASPER: Maybe we could take a semester off to—

CANDY: I don't want you to do anything just because I'm losing it! This is my battle, not yours.

10   **JASPER:** Truth is, this isn't where I want to be anymore, either. I mean, my grades are okay, but they're not great. They're not good enough to get into law school, anyway.

CANDY: But that's all you ever wanted to—

JASPER: Not all I ever wanted. There's something else. *(He hesitates. CANDY gives him a look that says "go on.")* I'd like to be a teacher.

15   **CANDY:** A teacher. You? *(They both chuckle.)*

JASPER: Yeah. Me. A teacher. High school. Political science, maybe. Or geography. Maybe become a principal or something. What about you?

CANDY: What about me?

JASPER: I mean, if you leave here, what will you do?

20   **CANDY:** I don't know. For the first time in my life, I don't have a plan. Maybe I'll just paint. Who knows? Look. I'm really sorry.

JASPER: For what?

CANDY: For taking all this out on you. I guess I just got jealous that you can play games and have friends. I miss that.

25   **JASPER:** Hey! I have an idea. Let's stroll on over to Maxwell's office and see if the old guy is through with his torture of hardworking college students! I'll pin him down, and you can drip water on his forehead until he gives up the test scores!

CANDY: I have a better idea. Let's walk down to the Frosty Q and make ourselves sick on banana splits. Then we can come back here and play Night Fighter until our—

30   **JASPER:** Night Raider. The game's called Night Raider. If you're gonna—

CANDY: Whatever. You know, I think you get too stressed out over the little details. You need to loosen up, learn how to have fun! *(She pretend punches him on the arm. He returns the pretend punch. They start for the door. She reaches for her mammoth stack of books, and JASPER pulls her away with a stern look. He puts his arm around her and they start OUT.)*
35   Thanks. *(Almost to the door, CANDY looks longingly at her books one last time, then back to JASPER, who pretends not to notice.)*

LAB SCENE #6 FOR DISCUSSION...

- Jasper and Candy are both twenty years old. How old are you? How will that change the way you and your partner portray these characters?

- The scene starts with four people, but Eddie and Vince soon leave. When you perform, you will be onstage with only your partner. The departure of the two friends will be done in pantomime. You may want to practice a couple of times with "stand ins" playing the role of the two friends so that you can work out timing, reaction, and Jasper's first line after their "exit."

- The video game playing will be done in pantomime. Keep it energetic. You may want to practice your lines while playing a real video game so that you can work out timing and reaction.

- Have you ever known anyone like Jasper who did not have to study but still made good grades? How can you or your partner study this person or others to help you with characterization?

NAME _____ PERIOD _____ DATE _____

JASPER AND CANDY

Answer the following questions about the characters, Jasper and Candy, from Lab Scene #6.

JASPER

1. What do we know for certain about Jasper?

2. What does Jasper want in this scene?

3. If Jasper repeatedly made a gesture in this scene, what would it be and why?

4. What are his hobbies?

5. What object do you associate with Jasper and why?

6. What animal do you associate with Jasper and why?

7. In real life, would you be Jasper's friend? Why or why not?

8. How is Jasper different from you?

9. How is Jasper like you?

10. What is Jasper's most positive trait?

11. What is his status in the world? Does he have money or power?

12. What does Jasper want from life?

- Have you ever known anyone like Candy who worked very hard but still had a difficult time making the kind of grades they wanted? How can you or your partner study this person or others to help you with characterization?

- What do you think Candy's college major is?

- This is an energetic, but not a loud, yelling scene. The first time Candy gets angry, she should use restraint. By the time she finally begins crying, she should be at the peak of her anger.

- Timing is very important in this scene. There are a lot of cut-off lines in which one character interrupts another or a character abruptly stops speaking ("Baby, I'm not—"). There are fade-off lines where a character allows himself to be interrupted or lets his voice drift off ("I thought you liked Maxwell… "). There are also places where characters' lines could

CHAPTER 3 — SCENE WORK

NAME _____ PERIOD _____ DATE _____

13. What does he fear and why?

14. Who does Jasper admire and why?

15. What are Jasper's parents like?

16. If he had one wish, what would it be and why?

CANDY

1. What do we know for certain about Candy?

2. What does Candy want in this scene?

3. If Candy repeatedly made a gesture in this scene, what would it be and why?

4. What are her hobbies?

5. What object do you associate with Candy and why?

6. What animal do you associate with Candy and why?

7. In real life, would you be Candy's friend? Why or why not?

8. How is Candy different from you?

9. How is Candy like you?

10. What is Candy's most positive trait?

63

overlap for effect (CANDY: "Bye, Eddie. See ya, Vince. / JASPER: "See ya, guys."). These will all make the scene more challenging, but done properly, they will give the characters life and realism.

NAME _____ PERIOD _____ DATE _____

11. What is her status in the world? Does she have money or power?

12. What does Candy want from life?

13. What does she fear and why?

14. Who does Candy admire and why?

15. What are Candy's parents like?

16. If she had one wish, what would it be and why?

JASPER AND CANDY

17. What year do you think it is? Why?

18. What is the scene about?

19. What do we know for certain about the setting?

20. Is the scene comic, dramatic, or a combination of the two? Explain.

21. What happened just before the start of this scene?

22. What do you think might happen after the scene if the story continued?

23. If this scene was from a play, what do you think it would be called? Explain.

NOTES: _____

_____

_____

_____

_____

_____

_____

_____

_____

LAB SCENE #7

ALIX, male, 12 and **SAM**, male

Alix is a twelve-year-old boy and an only child. His father recently died in a car accident. His mother has gone into a deep depression, leaving Alix to get himself to school in the morning, cook his own meals, and take care of the housework. Sam is trying to help him cope with all the changes in his life.

SAM is sitting with his legs crossed on the table in the middle of the ingredients ALIX is using to cook.

1   **SAM:** So… so, so, so. Not talking to me today, huh? Whatsa matter? Cat got your tongue?

    ALIX: *(Shoots him a sideways glance.)* Shh! Mom's not feeling good. You're going to wake her up. And get down from there! What's the matter with you?

5   **SAM:** What's the matter with me? Hah! That's funny. *(Mockingly.)* "Get down! What's the matter with you?" What! You think you're grown up or something? *(ALIX ignores him.)* Whatcha making? Looks good. Wish I could have some, but I can't. Tried that once. Biggest mess you ever saw! It was a grilled cheese sandwich— you remember—right after your dad died. Your Aunt Paula came over to take care of you and your mom, and she made you a grilled cheese but you didn't want it, so I ate it. It tasted good, felt good going down. Trouble was, since I
10   don't have a stomach, it just landed on the floor. Plop! Chewed up grilled cheese goop all over your mom's rug.

    ALIX: Shut up!

    SAM: Your aunt didn't say anything, though. She just figured it was you, you know? Your dad dying like that, she didn't want to upset you.

15   **ALIX:** Sam, why are you here? I told you… I don't believe in ghosts, and you sure as heck aren't an angel! Why can't you just leave me alone? *(EXITS the room with a plate of food for his mom.)*

    SAM: *(Yells into the other room.)* You want me to leave? Say the word and I'm gone.

    ALIX: *(Returns with the food still in hand.)* Shh! I told you, Mom's not feeling good. If you wake
20   her up, she'll just start crying again. Just be quiet. And yes, I want you to leave! *(EXITS again.)*

    SAM: *(Not moving. Stage whisper.)* I keep telling you—you are the only one who can see me and hear me. I'll tell you why I'm here. Like I told you before, I'm here to help you. *(Silence.)* You act like you're not hurting and that you have to take care of everything. You think the second
25   your dad left this place you had to become instantly mature? *(Like an announcer.)* "Super Alix—never cries, even when he hurts real bad! Able to defeat sadness with a plate of sloppy joes!" *(ALIX returns empty-handed.)* I thought she was sleeping.

    ALIX: She is. I left it on her nightstand. She won't eat it. But if I don't leave something, she'll think I don't care.

30   **SAM:** You really think so? Alix… you really believe your mom would think you don't care? How long has it been? Two weeks? For two weeks you've been doing and doing and doing so that she can cry, cry, cry. When's it going to end? You going to let her cry herself to death?

    ALIX: *(Goes to push SAM, but his hands go right through him.)* Man, I said shut up! Just go away! Get out of here! I'm sick of you. I'm sick of everyone telling me that it'll get better. What do
35   you know? What do any of you know?

    65

LAB SCENE #7

The Alix and Sam duet is rated "challenging." The scene presents many emotions, especially for the character of Alix. The actor portraying him must be open to trying new things and to making himself vulnerable.

Sam is equally difficult, as he is an old man in a young boy's body. He should be wise without seeming old. He should be youthful without being childish. His true identity is a mystery, and even if the actors think they know who Sam is, they should continue to mystify their audience.

This scene is unique in that it deals with a very emotional subject using a combination of humor and seriousness. Both actors will need to clearly identify all of the specific emotional twists. They must then work hard to make these moments weighty or light, as this will be the best strategy to achieve the outcome they seek.

1   **SAM:** I know, Alix. I know. It sounds cliché, but we all die. Some of us live short lives, others live long lives, and in the end we all die. Life is the story and death is how it ends. Kind of.

ALIX: What do you mean, "Kind of"?

SAM: Take me, for instance. I'm dead, but my story isn't over. I am still waiting for the ending.
5   Once my story ends, then I can rest. Finally!

ALIX: You act like you're looking forward to it.

SAM: I lived a good life. I was happy. I had a wife and a child and a good—

ALIX: Wait a minute! You're just a kid! How could you…

SAM: That's just how you see me. You needed someone to talk to, and so you made me a kid—so
10   you would have someone to help get you through this.

ALIX: Sam. You know, my grandpa's name was Samuel Melvin McAlister.

SAM: *(Overlap.)* …Melvin McAlister. Yes, I know, Alix.

ALIX: *(Long silence.)* So. So you came to help me get through this. I made you?

SAM: Not really. I was "made" a long time ago. You kind of "conjured me up"!

15   **ALIX:** What's next?

SAM: I don't know, Alix. You tell me. It's all right there. You just have to find the strength to deal with what you already know is the truth. *(Pause.)* You okay?

ALIX: Yeah. I'm fine. *(Disbelieving look from SAM.)* No, really. I'm going to be okay. I, uh… thanks, Sam.

20   **SAM:** All right. Well, if you don't mind, I think I'll take one of these outside where they won't make such a mess. *(Grabs a plate of sloppy joes and starts off.)*

ALIX: Sam. Wait. My dad. He didn't suffer, did he? I mean, when he died, he wasn't in a lot of pain?

SAM: No, son. It was quick. *(Noise from the back room.)* Sounds like your momma's stirring.
25   Maybe she could use a napkin? You think? Well, go on…

ALIX: *(EXITS. From OFFSTAGE, as SAM pauses to make sure his job is done.)* Hi there, sleepy head. Made you a plate of sloppy joes! Here, let me help you sit up. Listen, I need some supplies for a project at school. After dinner, do you think… *(Trailing off and picking up SAM'S line.)* …you can run me down to the mall?

30   **SAM:** He's a good boy, son. A good boy. Everything's going to be all right. *(EXITS.)*

LAB SCENE #7 FOR DISCUSSION…

- Alix is twelve years old. How old are you? How will that change the way you portray him? Who do you think Sam is? What is his relationship to Alix?

- How will you portray his age? If this question confuses you, you may want to study the scene further.

- Do you know anyone like Alix? How can you study this person or others to help you to define your characterization?

- Do you know anyone who acts like Sam?

- Alix is cooking around Sam as though he is not there. Work this out so that the movement is fluid, almost as though Sam is invisible and Alix's movements go through him.

NAME _____ PERIOD _____ DATE _____

ALIX AND SAM

Answer the following questions about the characters, Alix and Sam, from Lab Scene #7.

ALIX

1. What do we know for certain about Alix?

2. What does Alix want in this scene?

3. If Alix repeatedly made a gesture in this scene, what would it be and why?

4. What are his hobbies?

5. What object do you associate with Alix and why?

6. What animal do you associate with Alix and why?

7. In real life, would you be Alix's friend? Why or why not?

8. How is Alix different from you?

9. How is Alix like you?

10. What is Alix's most positive trait?

11. What is his status in the world? Does he have money or power?

12. What does Alix want from life?

67

- At one point, Alix "pushes" Sam and his hands go "right through him." You will need to choreograph a special effect. Try facing each other with your sides to the audience. Alix will push through Sam's plane on the side away from the audience. That way you can achieve the optical illusion that Alix's hands are going through Sam when they are really going to his side. The most important part of this illusion, however, will be the timing and the two actors' reactions to the "magic trick." Alix may even continue to try to "touch" Sam in the moments after the special effect as if in wonderment.

- What might Alix's mother's reaction be if he told her about Sam?

- Is Sam real? Has he come to help Alix? Or has Alix conjured Sam's presence out of his own need for getting past his father's death?

- Why do children sometimes have imaginary friends?

13. What does he fear and why?

14. Who does Alix admire and why?

15. What are/were Alix's parents like?

16. If he had one wish, what would it be and why?

SAM

1. What do we know for certain about Sam?

2. What does Sam want in this scene?

3. If Sam repeatedly made a gesture in this scene, what would it be and why?

4. What are his hobbies?

5. What object do you associate with Sam and why?

6. What animal do you associate with Sam and why?

7. If Sam or someone like him came to you, how do you think you would respond?

8. How is Sam different from you?

9. How is Sam like you?

10. What is Sam's most positive trait?

NOTES: _____

_____

_____

_____

_____

_____

_____

_____

_____

_____

CHAPTER 3 — SCENE WORK

NAME _____ PERIOD _____ DATE _____

11. What is his status in the world? Does he have money or power?

12. What does Sam want long-term?

13. What does he fear and why?

14. Who does Sam admire and why?

15. What are/were Sam's parents like?

16. If he had one wish, what would it be and why?

ALIX AND SAM

17. What year do you think it is? Why?

18. What is the scene about?

19. What do we know for certain about the setting?

20. Is the scene comic, dramatic, or a combination of the two? Explain.

21. What happened just before the start of this scene?

22. What do you think might happen after the scene if the story continued?

23. If this scene was from a play, what do you think it would be called? Explain.

69

NOTES: _____

_____

_____

_____

_____

_____

_____

_____

_____

_____

LAB SCENE #8

MIRA, female, 29 and **TAM**, female, 17

Tam is a seventeen-year-old girl who is struggling to make sense of her life. Despite a loving and supportive home, she is unhappy. She is depressed and has decided to run from her sadness.

Mira is twenty-nine, but she appears much older. Like Tam, her life in her teens seemed like a huge burden. She chose to drink and do drugs to get through each chaotic day. Although she is clean now, each day is still a challenge. When she meets Tam, Mira feels an instant motherliness toward her and hopes to guide her away from a path of trouble.

The scene opens at the bus station. Mira has just arrived and she is resting before she starts the long walk to town. Tam ENTERS LEFT, waiting for her departure. She is a runaway, but chances are no one has discovered that she is missing yet.

1   **TAM:** Can I sit here? *(MIRA nods without looking to see who is talking.)* Thanks. *(Puts her backpack down so that it is between the two women when she sits. Takes a seat cautiously, not wanting to stare at the haggard woman next to her. MIRA stares at TAM'S shoes.)* I know. They don't really match. But, you know, I figured I'd be doing a lot of walking, so I put these

5   on. I have some better ones in the bag. *(Looks at MIRA'S shoes.)*

     MIRA: Yeah. It's a real fashion show out here. If you're not careful, the fashion police'll give y'a ticket. *(To an imaginary person OFF RIGHT.)* Hey, lady! *(Stands.)* Hey! Is that your kid? You better keep an eye on 'em. He almost got on that bus. Or are you sending him to Memphis alone? *(Responding to some OFFSTAGE gesture.)* Yeah, same to you. *(Sits.)* Some people

10   ought not to have babies. Her on the phone and her kid making like he's goin' to Graceland. *(Pause.)* Your shoes ar'lright. You won't get no ticket. I'as just yankin' your chain.

     TAM: I knew that. Fashion police.

     MIRA: *(MIRA looks up at her for the first time and becomes transfixed by an eerie familiarity. When TAM catches her staring, the older woman becomes a little embarrassed.)* Whatcher

15   name, kid?

     TAM: *(Suspicious.)* Why?

     MIRA: Why? Well, I dunno. Maybe I'm gonna go narc to that cop. *(Points.)*

     TAM: *(Nervous.)* Crap! Where? Where? What the… Forget you. I don't need this. *(Grabs her bag and begins to leave.)*

20 **MIRA:** Whoa! What's this? Hey, sit down. I'll leave you alone. Sorry. I didn't realize you were the sensitive type. I'as just making conversation. There ain't no cop, tennis shoe girl. *(TAM gives her a warning glance.)* Hey, you don't wanna give me your name. What else am I gonna call you? Tam? *(TAM is shocked.)* Don't be so surprised. It's on your keychain.

     TAM: It's short for Tamika.

25 **MIRA:** Tam's good. I'm Mira. It's short for Miracle. No, really, it is. My parents didn't think they were ever gonna have kids, and then just when my dad's about to retire, pow! My mom is pregnant at forty-seven! So they named me Miracle. It was pretty cool until the boys at school started calling me Miracle Whip. Before long I was Mayonnaise Girl, and you can just imagine where that went! So I shortened it to Mira. I hate mayonnaise.

30 **TAM:** Tamika is just Tamika. No history. We moved a bunch, so each year when school started and the teacher would call roll for the first time, she'd say, "Tamika Lang," and then everyone

LAB SCENE #8

The Mira and Tam scene is rated a strong "challenging." It is the longest of all of the scenes and it includes several monologues for both characters. The scene is also more mature than the others. However, while it deals with the serious and tragic topics of drugs and depression, it offers hope.

Like many teens, Tam is suffering from what appears to be depression. She is afraid to tell anyone for fear that she will be put on drugs. While she is slightly rebellious, her most outstanding characteristic is her quiet sadness. Mira, on the other hand, is a recovering drug addict and alcoholic. At one time she was homeless, and she even abandoned her child. We learn that she is sick, but we never discover the nature of her illness. Faced with an uncertain future, she is trying to find her daughter; along the way, she finds Tam. Having survived the very worst, Mira is hard, weathered, determined, and wise.

1   would turn to look at me like they wanted to see who the freak with the messed up name was. The teacher would raise her eyebrow at me like she expected me to say something. When I turned ten, I started going by Tam, but then people would see my name, "Tam Lang," and they would say, "Are you Chinese?" *(MIRA finds this humorous and laughs a strange laugh. At*
5   *first TAM is offended, then she begins to laugh. MIRA'S laughter turns to coughing.)* Are you okay? Here, let me get you a drink. *(She fishes into her pocket and pulls out a few loose bills and some change. It falls to the ground.)* Wait, wait. I'll get you a drink.

MIRA: No, really. I'm okay now. Save your money. Looks like you're gonna need it.

TAM: I don't mind. I mean, if you're sick or something, I'll get you a drink.

10   **MIRA:** No, honey. I ain't sick. *(Indicates the money that TAM is picking up.)* Is that all you got? *(TAM looks up, a little embarrassed but not really knowing what to say.)* You ain't gonna get too far on a burger's worth of change, not when the fashion police are hot on your heels. Where you headed? *(TAM shrugs, ignoring the question in a shy but polite way.)* You runnin' away?

15   **TAM:** Uh, yes, ma'am.

MIRA: Don't "yes, ma'am" me. I ain't that much older than you. I ain't thirty, you know. *(TAM is surprised.)* I know, I know. I'm not much to look at. I've had a rough life. I been on the streets since I was 'bout your age. What are ya? Sixteen?

TAM: *(Without missing a beat or looking up.)* Seventeen and a quarter.

20   **MIRA:** And a quarter, huh? Does that make you older than seventeen by a whole bunch? What grade're you in?

TAM: I'm not. I dropped out—unofficially—today. And I'm leaving. I'm going to Miami to work. Then I figure I'll join the Army or Navy or something and become an officer. I'm a really good leader. And you get to travel and stuff. And you don't have any nosey parents breathing down
25   your neck all the time or teachers looking at you like you're an alien or something. Or maybe I'll start my own business—an art gallery—or a tour guide business. I'll probably have to start off waiting tables, though, till I get something saved up or turn eighteen.

MIRA: And I'm gonna win the lottery, wake up beautiful, and get my daughter back and—oh, yeah, I'll be able to take cough syrup without thinking I'm gonna...

30   **TAM:** You have a daughter? *(She looks around half expecting to see a child but knowing she's not there.)*

MIRA: Had. State took her. She'd be about twelve. I'm going home to find her. That's where I'm headed. *(Points OFF LEFT.)* See those lights? That's where she is, and I'm heading there as soon as my feet start working again. *(Talking to her feet.)* Right, feet?

35   **TAM:** Why? Why'd they take her?

MIRA: I wasn't fit. I'd been on the streets a long time. I was an addict and a drunk. Her daddy was in the pen, and I was homeless. I'd go from shelter to shelter, and one morning I just got up and left. I got about three blocks away when I realized I had forgotten her, but I needed a fix real bad, so I figured I'd get hooked up and then go back and get her. But afterward,
40   I just kept walkin' the opposite direction of the shelter. I don't even remember how far I'd gone, but I started feeling really lonely. I kept seeing her waking up and me not there and her screaming for me. Then I imagined that they wouldn't take care of her or she'd wander out trying to find me. She was only two. I started running back toward the shelter and some cops saw me running. They told me to stop, but I honestly didn't hear them.

45   **TAM:** What happened? I mean, you don't have to tell me. I'm sorry, I'll stop...

     71

Mira and Tam's scene is much longer than the others in this chapter. This gives you the opportunity to teach your class how to cut a script. Often directors are faced with the dilemma of making a long script shorter. Sometimes play competitions require that entries be within a certain time limit. Other times, plays must be cut to exclude profanity, suggestiveness, or references to objectionable material.

Before cutting, consult with the publisher. Because published plays are protected under copyright laws, you must obtain written permission to make changes, including any cuts. However, that is not necessary with this scene, since you are being instructed to make cuts.

Next, read the play carefully several times. You may then start marking pages where potential cuts exist with colored paper or paperclips. Start by making large cuts; smaller cuts can be made later after you have an idea as to your time.

1   **MIRA:** They chased me down. I had a lot of crap on me, you know? Plus, I was higher'n a kite. I told 'em I lost my kid, but they just used that as another reason to lock me up.

TAM: So they took her.

MIRA: Nah, kid. That was just once. I screwed up a couple more times before they took her.
5   Enough for her to remember what a loser I'd become, I'm sure. You're not gonna get far on that *(Indicates TAM'S money.)*, and you might as well hear it from me—don't think you like me much anyhow. You might end up waiting tables for a while. But y'ain't joining no army and becoming no officer. An' don't think a kid is gonna make it big in Miami. You're just running. I don't know what from or who to, but it's a dead end.

10   **TAM:** No, I'm not like that, I'm gonna… You see, I figure I'll… Well, I know this family, you see *(Realizing how stupid she sounds.)*, and they live on this island where your fantasies come true. Okay. It's stupid, I know. It's funny—you're running to the town I'm running from. *(Indicates OFF LEFT.)* My dad's based there.

MIRA: What's the matter? He beat you?

15   **TAM:** No! No way! No, my dad's real cool. My mom's cool too. I mean, my whole family's pretty normal, I guess, except for me. I'm different. I've always been so sad, all my life. I can't ever remember being happy. I'm always tired, and nothing makes me excited anymore. The kids at school don't make fun of me or anything. They don't even know I'm there. You know, other than my name being on the attendance, I don't really exist at my school. At home I'm just so
20   lonely. I'm right there in the middle of that big house with my mom, dad, and my sister, but I'm not like them. I just want to close my door and stay in my room. I want to be left alone. I didn't think it was supposed to hurt this much. Being alive.

MIRA: Honey, it's really simple. You're depressed. You just need to get help. You seen a doctor?

TAM: Look who's talking!

25   **MIRA:** I'm clean, have been for a year, but it ain't easy. I made myself real sick when I was using. I ain't never gonna be in good health again. But, sweetie, it ain't too late for—

TAM: I don't want to talk to those Army doctors about this. They'd tell my parents I was crazy or put me on all sorts of drugs—sorry—and I'd end up loonier than I am now. *(Silence.)* Listen, I've got to go. I—I need to sort some things out. *(She starts OUT RIGHT, and MIRA quietly*
30   *looks down at her own shoes. TAM realizes that she's still running but she can stop before it's too late. She feels a bond with the woman who tried to help her, and now it's her turn to help.)* Well? You coming, Miracle Whip? *(MIRA looks up, confused.)* Come on. I haven't got all night. It's four miles back to town, and if I have my key *(Feels for a key in her pocket.)*—yes! No one will ever know I left. *(As they EXIT LEFT.)* You ever sleep in a bunk bed?

Always make cuts lightly in pencil so that changes are possible. For single lines, cross through the line. For large sections or pages, make an X over the section to be deleted and then draw two lines indicating specifically where the cut begins and ends.

Make sure that you do not cut anything that is referenced later in the play. Also, avoid cutting passages that identify or help to identify the theme. When possible, omit characters who will not be missed. Always make sure that changes make sense and maintain the playwright's original intent and the integrity of the storyline. Be prepared to continue making cuts long after you think you are done.

Alternatives to cutting include adjusting the pace or choosing a shorter play.

NAME _____ PERIOD _____ DATE _____

MIRA AND TAM

Answer the following questions about the characters, Mira and Tam, from Lab Scene #8.

MIRA

1. What do we know for certain about Mira?

2. What does Mira want in this scene?

3. If Mira repeatedly made a gesture in this scene, what would it be and why?

4. What are her hobbies?

5. What object do you associate with Mira and why?

6. What animal do you associate with Mira and why?

7. In real life, would you be Mira's friend? Why or why not?

8. How is Mira different from you?

9. How is Mira like you?

10. What is Mira's most positive trait?

11. What is her status in the world? Does she have money or power?

12. What does Mira want from life?

73

LAB SCENE #8 FOR DISCUSSION...

- Tam is seventeen. How old are you? How will that affect the way you portray her?

- Mira is twenty-nine, but she seems older in both appearance and personality. How will you portray her?

- Do you know anyone like Tam? How can you study this person or others to help you to define your characterization?

- Do you know anyone who acts like Mira?

- Mira speaks like someone who missed out on some school. As a matter of fact, we learn she has been on the streets since she was sixteen, and chances are she did not finish her education. Study her language closely.

- What posture, facial expressions, and body language should accompany the dialect Mira uses?

13. What does she fear and why?

14. Who does Mira admire and why?

15. What are/were her parents like?

16. If she had one wish, what would it be and why?

TAM

1. What do we know for certain about Tam?

2. What does Tam want in this scene?

3. If Tam repeatedly made a gesture in this scene, what would it be and why?

4. What are her hobbies?

5. What object do you associate with Tam and why?

6. What animal do you associate with Tam and why?

7. In real life, would you be Tam's friend? Why or why not?

8. How is Tam different from you?

9. How is Tam like you?

10. What is Tam's most positive trait?

- Imagine being so dependent on drugs that you would leave your own child in search of them. Remember, drug addiction is a disease. Was she sick? Was she out of control? Was she a bad person?

- Tam lacks self-confidence. She even dislikes her own name. Do you think her teachers and classmates really criticized her name or did Tam imagine it?

- Did Tam intend to run away when she went to the bus station, or did she go there in search of someone like Mira who would convince her to seek help? Explain.

- What do you think might happen once the two women get back to Tam's house? What will happen in the following weeks? What do you think will happen in the future for each of them?

NAME _____ PERIOD _____ DATE _____

11. What is her status in the world? Does she have money or power?

12. What does Tam want from life?

13. What does she fear and why?

14. Who does Tam admire and why?

15. What are her parents like?

16. If she had one wish, what would it be and why?

MIRA AND TAM

17. What year do you think it is? Why?

18. What is the scene about?

19. What do we know for certain about the setting?

20. Is the scene comic, dramatic, or a combination of the two? Explain.

21. What happened just before the start of this scene?

22. What do you think might happen after the scene if the story continued?

23. If this scene was from a play, what do you think it would be called? Explain.

NOTES: _____

_____

_____

_____

_____

_____

_____

_____

_____

_____

LAB SCENE #9

TEACHER and **TAYLOR**, student

1   **TEACHER:** Taylor, you're up.

    TAYLOR: *(Not expecting this; confused.)* What?

    TEACHER: You're up. *(Silence.)* Your monologue? You're next.

    TAYLOR: Now? Today? You mean, like, right now? *(TEACHER nods, not amused.)* Right now. Oh
5   boy. *(Stands. Pause. Sits.)* You know, I am not feeling well. I almost didn't come to school
      today.

    TEACHER: But you did.

    TAYLOR: *(Distracted.)* I did? *(Realizes.)* Oh. Of course. I did. *(Coughs.)* But I shouldn't have. I'm
      sick.

10 **TEACHER:** Taylor, do you have your monologue?

    TAYLOR: Do I have my monologue? Do I have my monologue! Of course I—this is the one from
      the script, right?

    TEACHER: The script? Taylor. The script? Really? They're all from scripts.

    TAYLOR: I knew that. I totally knew that. Uh, yeah, I've got it... here. *(Points to head.)* Memorized,
15   right? These are memorized? I'm doing the one about the... the b— ...no, the fa—

    TEACHER: The orphan, Taylor. You were doing the monologue about the orphan child. Here.
      (Hands Taylor a script.) Look familiar?

    TAYLOR: *(Looks at it.)* Of course! Yes. *(Looks some more.)* Oh, yeah, the orphan child. Man, this
      is good. This is sad. This is what I'm doing. Oh, my, this is so sad. *(Starts crying.)* Oh, my, god,
20   this is awful! This is terrible. I can't do this! This poor, poor child!

    TEACHER: Taylor, not that part. Turn the page. The yellow highlight. That's your monologue.

    TAYLOR: *(Reading.)* Yeah, whew. This actually looks familiar.

    TEACHER: Noted. Glad to know you've seen it before.

    TAYLOR: *(Reading.)* Much better. Much, much better. Yep. This is good. More me. Oh, yes, this
25   is funny. The kid's resilient! Wow. Love this. Whew!

    TEACHER: And that's the one you memorized?

    TAYLOR: Yeah. This is the one. But no. I did not memorize it.

    TEACHER: What were you doing when you were supposed to be memorizing the script?

    TAYLOR: When?

30 **TEACHER:** When everyone else in class was memorizing their monologues, what were you doing?

    TAYLOR: Who?

    TEACHER: Them. The class. Last week, when everyone was memorizing their two-minute
      monologue, what were you doing?

    TAYLOR: *(Mouths silently, but clearly shocked.)* Two minutes! *(Aloud.)* Studying. Yes. I was
35   studying. I think.

    TEACHER: What?

    TAYLOR: What what?

    TEACHER: What were you studying?

    TAYLOR: When?

LAB SCENE #9

This duet about a monologue is rated difficult due to its length and the lack of information on the character of Teacher. Also, there is an element of timing on Taylor's part that might be challenging for some actors.

This scene was written to be educational in many ways. Both characters are gender neutral, which can be both freeing and challenging. The scene mimics theatre teachers' daily challenges, so in many ways, it educates theatre students on many levels.

1 **TEACHER:** Last week, Taylor. What were you studying all last week when everyone else was memorizing their monologue?

TAYLOR: *(Tries to be polite.)* Let me break it down for you. I'll be honest. I didn't memorize the script because I was busy with more important stuff. I mean, this is important. Just not to me.

5 **TEACHER:** My class isn't important to you.

TAYLOR: Is that a question?

TEACHER: I don't know, Taylor. Is it?

TAYLOR: I'm confused.

TEACHER: Yes, you are. Look, I know you don't want to be an actor. You want to be a doctor,
10 right?

TAYLOR: Yes. Like my parents.

TEACHER: Don't think of it as an acting class. Think of it as a communication class. In this room, with my unimportant lessons, you will learn many important skills. Can you think of any?

TAYLOR: Memorization?

15 **TEACHER:** Yes. That's one. Any others?

TAYLOR: Time management?

TEACHER: Certainly. That's a great one too. Doctors must be able to do both of these. So let's say you are in medical school and you failed to memorize something because you were preoccupied with another "more important" class.

20 **TAYLOR:** I wouldn't do that. That's medical school. That's super important.

TEACHER: And if you can't do it here, in high school, then what makes you think you can do it later, in med school, when the workload is more challenging?

TAYLOR: Well, I—

TEACHER: Taylor, that wasn't a question, either. That was an opportunity for reflection.

25 **TAYLOR:** But it was a que—

TEACHER: No, Taylor. It wasn't. It may have sounded like a question, but a wise student, one who paid attention in theatre class, would recognize the subtext.

TAYLOR: Subtext?

TEACHER: Yes. The sentence did end in a question mark, but it was rhetorical. It was meant to
30 challenge your thinking… to take you beyond the obvious to a higher level of thinking. Higher level thinking exercises your brain, making it stronger, making you, a future doctor, better prepared for dealing with challenges. And you know, Taylor, not every kid who sets out to be a doctor makes it all the way. I'm not saying you're that kid. You're extremely bright and capable! But what are you going to do if you change your mind or don't make it into med
35 school?

TAYLOR: I've already thought about that. I've met a few of my parents' friends who started out in med school but changed their minds or…

TEACHER: …or were encouraged to take different paths…

TAYLOR: Yes. Because they weren't responsible. *(Long pause for self-reflection.)* I'm really sorry.
40 I'm sorry I didn't memorize the monologue. You have every right to be disappointed. And I had no right to say your class wasn't important. I'm sorry.

TEACHER: It takes a lot of character to apologize… even more to admit you're wrong, and even more to change and to come out on top. It shows a lot of resilience. You know what I mean?

NOTES: _____

_____

_____

_____

_____

_____

_____

_____

_____

1   **TAYLOR:** *(Looks at script.)* Yes.

     TEACHER: Taylor, do you need this class to graduate?

     TAYLOR: Yes. I need a fine arts credit.

     TEACHER: And I am assuming you will eventually need letters of recommendation from your
5   teachers for your college applications?

     TAYLOR: Yes.

     TEACHER: And would you like it if I wrote you a glowing letter?

     TAYLOR: I wouldn't expect you to do—

     TEACHER: I'm sorry, what was that? You were mumbling. But hey, don't worry. In theatre class,
10   I can also help you improve your diction and other communication skills. Because, you know,
     your patients will want to understand every word. They'll want to know they can count on
     you. Take a seat, Taylor. Sahid, you're up.

     TAYLOR: *(Sitting.)* Excuse me. Can I try again tomorrow?

     TEACHER: Take the script home, and this time read it. Memorize the highlighted part and
15   rehearse it. It won't be full credit, but I'll give you another chance to prove yourself. But
     honestly, Taylor, right now I wouldn't trust you to take my temperature. But this is the
     beginning of the semester. You've got time to convince me otherwise!

NOTES: _____

_____

_____

_____

_____

_____

_____

_____

_____

NAME _____ PERIOD _____ DATE _____

TEACHER AND TAYLOR

Answer the following questions about the characters, Taylor and Teacher, from Lab Scene #9.

TAYLOR

1. What do we know for certain about Taylor?

2. What does Taylor want in this scene?

3. If Taylor repeatedly made a gesture in this scene, what would it be and why?

4. What are Taylor's hobbies?

5. What object do you associate with Taylor and why?

6. What animal do you associate with Taylor and why?

7. In real life, would you be Taylor's friend? Why or why not?

8. How is Taylor different from you?

9. How is Taylor like you?

10. What is Taylor's most positive trait?

11. What is Taylor's status in the world? Does Taylor have money or power?

12. What does Taylor want from life?

79

LAB SCENE #9 FOR DISCUSSION...

- How old is Taylor? Is Taylor's gender important? Why or why not?

- How old is Teacher? Is Teacher experienced or fresh out of college? Might this make a difference in the portrayal?

- Is Teacher's gender relative? Explain.

NAME _____ PERIOD _____ DATE _____

11. What is Teacher's status in the world? Does Teacher have money or power?

12. What does Teacher want from life?

13. What does Teacher fear and why?

14. Who does Teacher admire and why?

15. What are/were Teacher's parents like?

16. If Teacher had one wish, what would it be and why?

TEACHER AND TAYLOR

17. What year do you think it is? Why?

18. What is the scene about?

19. What do we know for certain about the setting?

20. Is the scene comic, dramatic, or a combination of the two? Explain.

21. What happened just before the start of this scene?

22. What do you think might happen after the scene if the story continued?

23. If this scene was from a play, what do you think it would be called? Explain.

81

NOTES: _____

_____

_____

_____

_____

_____

_____

_____

_____

_____

SCENE WORK CUT-N-PASTE

Cut out each line below and rearrange them to create a true account of a successful performance. There are four lines which contain false information. *Do not include them.* When you are done, neatly tape or glue the story together on a clean sheet of paper with your name and turn it in for a grade.

Jamie and Farah are partners in a duet. Today they are doing a scene and they
then takes a seat and Farah stands to the right, quietly waiting for the teacher to
Jude from the play *Landscapes*, by Neil Dawson." The teacher has instructed
The prompter cues her, and Jamie remembers, so she picks up the line and keeps
sitting near them. They quickly arrange two chairs and a small table. Jamie
how they are going to introduce themselves. The teacher calls their names
announcements come on. The actors stop and patiently wait. When the
girls keep their energy up because they know that the class is also distracted. It
are not ready. They used the practice time to do homework. They don't know
like a couple of school girls who would rather not be onstage. The audience
Farah and this is my partner, Jamie. We are portraying the characters Molly and
interruption is over, Jamie asks, "Where would you like us to start?" The
is depressed. Jamie's facial expressions continually support the emotions her
returns to her backpack for gum, and fumbles around for a prop for her scene and
and they instantly get up and hand their script to a reliable girl with a clear voice
teacher gives them a line to go back to, and they do. Despite the interruption, the
say she is ready. She cues the students to start, and Farah says, "My name is
natural, and Farah's posture and body language are instant clues that her character
character is conveying. Their scene builds to a climax and the characters stay
are third. Both are ready. Each has memorized her lines, and they have decided
is their job to keep the audience tuned in. Jamie forgets a difficult line. She
start their scene, and they do. They begin their scene, speaking clearly, when the
pauses and stays in character. Still, she can't remember, so she says, "Line."
going, never losing her confidence. The movement the girls planned out looks
have a seat and write down their evaluations of themselves without saying a word.
them to bow their heads for a few seconds after their introduction and before they
announcements end, they start giggling and going on about the bad timing. The
realistic, even through an emotional argument. When the scene is over, they

Scene Work Cut-N-Paste Key:

Jamie and Farah are partners in a duet. Today they are doing a scene and they are third. Both are ready. Each has memorized her lines, and they have decided how they are going to introduce themselves. The teacher calls their names and they instantly get up and hand their script to a reliable girl with a clear voice sitting near them. They quickly arrange two chairs and a small table. Jamie then takes a seat and Farah stands to the right, quietly waiting for the teacher to say she is ready. She cues the students to start, and Farah says, "My name is Farah, and this is my partner, Jamie. We are portraying the characters Molly and Jude from the play Landscapes, by Neil Dawson." The teacher has instructed them to bow their heads for a few seconds after their introduction and before they start their scene, and they do. They begin their scene, speaking clearly, when the announcements come on. The actors stop and patiently wait. When the interruption is over, Jamie asks, "Where would you like us to start?" The teacher gives them a line to go back to, and they do. Despite the interruption, the girls keep their energy up because they know that the class is also distracted. It is their job to keep the audience tuned in. Jamie forgets a difficult line. She pauses and stays in character. Still she can't remember, so she says, "Line." The prompter cues her and Jamie remembers, so she picks up the line and keeps going, never losing her confidence. The movement the girls planned out looks natural, and Farah's posture and body language are instant clues that her character is depressed. Jamie's facial expressions continually support the emotions her character is conveying. Their scene builds to a climax and the characters stay realistic, even through an emotional argument. When the scene is over, they have a seat and write down their evaluations of themselves without saying a word.

CHAPTER 4
ACTING

DAILY BELL WORK—ACTING

ACTING

THE ACTOR'S VOICE

Understanding the Actor's Voice
Articulation Activities
Breathing Activity
The Actor's Body

WARMING UP

Basic Play Terminology

MOCK AUDITION

Rehearsal Terminology

BASIC ACTING TERMINOLOGY

Acting Terminology Crossword Puzzle

THE ART OF TIMING

Crazy Clock
Script Scoring

THE STAGE

Acting Review Game Board

ADDITIONAL NOTES

Bell Work
Voice Activities
   The Actor's Voice Key
   Understanding the Actor's Voice Key
Warm-Up Activities
Terminology Activity
Mock Auditions
In-Class Rehearsal
Teaching Technical Theatre
Production Activities
   Acting Terminology Crossword Puzzle Key
Non-Verbal Communication and Timing Activities
   Crazy Clock Key
   Script Scoring Key
Taping Off the Stage
Acting Review Board Game
   Acting Review Game Board
   Acting Review Game Cards

NAME _____ PERIOD _____ DATE _____

DAILY BELL WORK - ACTING

Answer each question as your teacher assigns it, using the space provided. Be sure to include the date.

1. Date: _____

   What do you think is meant by playwright's intent? Why is it important to actors?

2. Date: _____

   Why is it important to know the play before attempting to develop the character?

3. Date: _____

   List ways to establish mood in a scene. How would this affect the acting?

4. Date: _____

   Imagine listening to the radio in the 1930s. Because there was no picture, actors relied on their voices for 100 percent of their acting. How do you think this influenced their style?

85

BELL WORK

As in the other chapters, the bell work in this chapter attempts to introduce potential daily subjects. Some are discussed at length in the text of the book and others are not. Students and teachers will be responsible for answering these without assistance from the text. Record some of your best responses for future use.

BELL WORK 1

Playwright's intent is the goal the playwright had in mind for the piece at the time it was written. Intent is important because the playwright created it for a reason, which is part of the art. Reinterpreting a piece outside the boundaries of original intent is still art, but it is often an entirely different piece than its original.

BELL WORK 2

The only way to know the truth behind a character is to study the entire play. If you limit your reading to just one character's lines and the lines of those responding in a specific scene, you really don't know the entire context and which characters are right, wrong, intentionally misleading, misunderstanding, lying, or manipulating. This can lead you to come to erroneous conclusions about a character or their motivation. For example, reading only a few lines from *The Diary of Anne Frank*, you might think Anne has tragically poor self-esteem. However, after studying the entire play and her history, you realize she is bright and self-aware. She comes across as unsure because of her age, her circumstances, and her place in the family.

BELL WORK 3

You can establish mood in a number of ways: pacing/timing, pauses, tone, volume, posture, characterization, movement, costume, lighting, music, and even the location of your performance venue.

Color is one very obvious way to establish mood and one young people master early. Take a box of crayons, for example. If a teacher asked a group of third graders to choose three winter colors, they would likely pick cool shades such as blues, grays, and cool shades of green (evergreen is cool, lime is warm). Ask the same students to pick colors for a fall picture, and they will probably pull out the darker, warmer shades like orange, brown, and gold.

Like color, light can also help to set a mood. Bright, glaring light is fierce and energetic while dim, diffused light is relaxing. By adding colored gels to the lights, the two combine to create not only mood, but also depth and realism.

BELL WORK 4 AND 5

Radio and silent movies posed unique challenges to the actors, producers, directors, and technicians of the early part of the twentieth century. They were the mediums by which average people connected to the world of entertainment, but the technology was far from what it is today. Silent movies relied on music played on pianos at the movie theatre to help set the mood. To really know what was going on, audiences had to read the occasional updates flashed briefly on the screen. Many audience members could not read. There was no color, only black and white, and the timing was not believable; actors seemed to be moving in fast motion. However, few complained. It was the best thing going, and it was very advanced by the standards of the day.

Radio could at least hide the fact that things were not perfect, because no one could see what was happening behind the scenes. Foley artists created realistic-sounding effects to accompany the actors' voices and the plot. Wonderfully written scripts with dramatic cliffhangers ensured an audience eager for the next episode.

In both genres, artists relied on a wide range of talents that are taken for granted today. In silent films, plots were kept basic. The means did not exist by which a lot of details could be relayed. Actors were assigned the task of clarifying the storyline, using mainly their faces and bodies, so the style was exaggerated and forced. Those who wanted their voices heard went into radio, where the details were in the words and sounds, and appearances had little to do with the final product. Actors learned to use their voices in ways that brought characters to life, added dimension, and moved the audience. Foley artists filled in the gaps with realistic sound effects, and the "picture" was complete.

NAME _____ PERIOD _____ DATE _____

DAILY BELL WORK - ACTING

Answer each question as your teacher assigns it, using the space provided. Be sure to include the date.

5. Date: _____

    Imagine attending a silent film in the 1920s. Aside from occasional flashes of text, the entire story was portrayed through pantomime and music. How do you think this influenced the actors' styles?

6. Date: _____

    Many years ago, actors were encouraged to speak a certain, acceptable way. Accents were erased, and distinctive qualities considered to be harsh were toned down. Today, uniqueness is more marketable. Explain why you think this is.

7. Date: _____

    Write a tongue twister using the first letter of your name.

8. Date: _____

    List every step of brushing your teeth; include even the smallest detail. Explain why an actor might benefit from carefully observing this or any other activity.

CHAPTER 4 — ACTING

NAME _____ PERIOD _____ DATE _____

DAILY BELL WORK - ACTING

Answer each question as your teacher assigns it, using the space provided. Be sure to include the date.

9. Date: _____

   What habits might actors give characters to make them unique? List ten.

10. Date: _____

    Explain why posture is important in developing a character.

11. Date: _____

    Explain why actors should warm up their bodies, minds, and voices.

12. Date: _____

    Some actors let excuses like, "I'm having a bad day," get in the way of good character development or a good rehearsal. Why don't directors accept this as an excuse?

87

NOTES: _____

_____

_____

_____

_____

_____

_____

_____

_____

NAME _____ PERIOD _____ DATE _____

DAILY BELL WORK - ACTING

Answer each question as your teacher assigns it, using the space provided. Be sure to include the date.

13. Date: _____

Can anyone be taught to act? Why or why not?

14. Date: _____

What do you think about the link between actors, appearances, and success?

15. Date: _____

_____

_____

16. Date: _____

_____

_____

NOTES: _____

_____

_____

_____

_____

_____

_____

_____

_____

ACTING

Many people who have never acted think that acting is reciting with emotion. That is a part of it, but think of it as only the tip of the iceberg. There is a great deal more to acting than the audience ever realizes—that is, if it is done well.

Imagine going to a performance where a young actor is playing an elderly man. At times he is hunched over like a very old man whose spine is crooked. But perhaps he forgets to maintain this posture, and sometimes the audience sees a twenty-five-year-old "acting" like an older man. Perhaps the elderly gentleman character is from France, but the actor is not confident in his dialect, so the character sounds as though he is from some undiscovered country between France and England, maybe with a bit of German influence. When an actor is untrained, his performance becomes noticeable to the audience. They are continually reminded that this is a play. However, when an actor is polished and comfortable in his own performance, the audience forgets they are at a play and they become involved in the characters' lives.

Besides voice and movement, actors must also be fully aware of the play and how it is arranged. They must know and understand the difference between plot and setting, comedy and drama, and so on. It is also important that each actor who wishes to pursue a career in either theatre or film knows how to audition and then what will be expected of them at performances. However, in this class, think of each graded performance as an audition and each day that your teacher gives you to prepare for that performance as a rehearsal.

As you approach your first graded performance, if you have not already done so, you will want to understand the terminology used by those in the acting business. Furthermore, you should practice what is known as actor's etiquette or manners. Did you know that actors have a code of conduct for rehearsals? Timing is another important issue, an art that varies depending on whether you are doing comedy or tragedy, classic or modern, Eastern or Western theatre. With practice, you should feel comfortable with different pacing and tempo techniques.

By the time you finish this chapter, you will also understand how to mark or "score" your script. This helps rehearsals run more smoothly and allows actors to record action, pausing, and even breathing. There is also a whole new vocabulary associated with the stage itself. What do you do if the director tells you to take three steps left? Does he mean his left or yours? He means yours, and you will learn more about that at the end of this section. You will also learn what the different areas of the stage are called and where to stand to await your entrances.

Volumes upon volumes have been written on acting, so this is a very concise lesson. However, if you approach this as your basis and continue to build on it with additional classes and experience, you will soon have a solid understanding of the art of acting.

NOTES: _____

_____

_____

_____

_____

_____

_____

_____

_____

THE ACTOR'S VOICE KEY		
	VOICED	**UNVOICED**
<u>m</u>op	X	
<u>p</u>lay		X
<u>b</u>ear	X	
<u>q</u>uit	X	
<u>a</u>pe	X	
<u>ch</u>at		X
thi<u>ng</u>	X	
<u>y</u>es	X	
<u>e</u>dge	X	
<u>g</u>o	X	
<u>sh</u>op		X
<u>z</u>ap	X	
ba<u>ck</u>		X
<u>l</u>ight	X	
<u>t</u>oe		X
<u>f</u>ly		X

THE ACTOR'S VOICE

One of your greatest tools as an actor is your voice. With it you will add texture to the story, giving it a time and a place. You will also convey emotion and understanding, and your character will have an age and a history. However, in order to do this, you must sharpen your speaking skills. The voice with which one is born is rarely the voice one will take to the stage.

An actor's primary responsibility is to be heard, because unless the audience can hear the lines being spoken, they are getting only half the story. When onstage, each actor must project his or their voice to the farthest row in the auditorium. Even stage whispers must be loud enough to be heard while still sounding like a whisper. Besides volume, actors speak very clearly by articulating all of the sounds in a word. They must also learn to pronounce difficult words so that they can be understood.

Some of the parts that make up the actors' vocal "tool" are as follows:

1. **Soft Palate**—the soft tissue on the roof of the mouth towards the back
2. **Hard Palate**—the hard, bony part on the roof of the mouth
3. **Bony Ridge**—the bumpy, bony area behind the teeth
4. **Teeth**

The lips and tongue work with these parts, creating space, touching, or forming shapes. When the diaphragm pushes the air from the lungs and through the larynx and the parts above, sounds are made. Sometimes these sounds are voiced, meaning the vocal cords produce a sound that is carried with the breath. Other times the sounds are unvoiced. To understand voiced and unvoiced, try this activity. Hold out the "s" sound for five seconds. Now, do the same thing with a "z" sound. Your articulators are in basically the same position, but the "s" is unvoiced and the "z" is voiced. Do the same thing with "th" as in thing and then "th" as in those. Which is voiced? If you said the "th" as in those, you are right. What other sounds are voiced and unvoiced? Complete the chart to the left.

Vocal quality is also important. Can you recall an actor whose voice is "annoying" to you? How about one whose voice is soothing? Both of these are due to the quality of the actors' voices. Quality can be many things, but in general, it is the "pleasantness" of one's voice. It might have an unusual pitch (how high or low one's voice is) or it may be nasal (sounds like the speaker has a stuffed up nose). If a voice lacks inflection (a variance in tone), it is said to be monotone. A long time ago, actors worked hard to have a voice that was considered pleasant and normal, whatever that meant. However, as actors started to be recognized for their unusual voices, quality became less important, and uniqueness became the trend.

Say the words below. Check the appropriate column if the underlined part of the word is *voiced* or *unvoiced*.

	voiced	unvoiced
<u>m</u>op		
<u>p</u>lay		
<u>b</u>ear		
<u>q</u>uit		
<u>a</u>pe		
<u>ch</u>at		
thi<u>ng</u>		
<u>y</u>es		
<u>e</u>dge		
<u>g</u>o		
<u>sh</u>op		
<u>z</u>ap		
ba<u>ck</u>		
<u>l</u>ight		
<u>t</u>oe		
<u>f</u>ly		

VOICE ACTIVITIES

- Ask a local doctor's office to donate some tongue depressors or buy some craft sticks (similar to Popsicle sticks). Students can then use these to try some of the tongue twisters and other articulation activities included in this chapter, or come up with your own. By pressing down on the tongue depressors while speaking, students are forced to over-articulate and work their tongues around the obstacle. You can also have them place the stick between their top and bottom teeth to create about a half-inch gap between the jaws. These two exercises will help them to sharpen the clarity of their speech when there is no obstacle present.

- Write the sentence, "Can I help you?" on the board. Tell students to write ten different ways to say the sentence so that the meaning or interpretation varies. Urge them to consider inflection, tone, volume, posture, body language, subtext, emphasis on a single word, and so on. Have them take turns sharing one of their interpretations of the line. Encourage their imaginations by manipulating the situation. For example, what if this was a mother to a child? What if it was a child to a father? Perhaps the person asking the question does not really want to help. Maybe they resent having to ask the question.

Today, unusual voices and unique dialects have a place in the entertainment industry, especially in radio. Because the listener must rely solely on the sense of hearing, those who market products seek voice artists who will capture and maintain the audience's attention. Listen to commercials for the next few days. Take note of what you hear. Imitate the actors, and ask yourself, "Can I do that?" Bet you can!

What is imperative, though, is that actors learn to control their voices. When one has control, they can have many vocal styles, and that means more flexibility for roles. In order to have control, the actors should understand all of the aspects of their vocal tool. Try this activity: Exhale all of your breath and assume a bad posture. Without inhaling, recite the Pledge of Allegiance at a natural pace. Go on, try it. What happened? You started to run out of breath, so you tried to speed up. Then your voice became aspirate or breathy. Then you had to pause for a breath or risk passing out, right? Breathing control has often been considered the primary basis for a great voice. Consequently, breathing exercises are often the focus of many rehearsals and workshops. Experienced actors will spend years toning their diaphragm, the muscle that works the lungs, so that they can have a superior voice and so that their pauses sound naturally placed. Now, try the activity again, but this time, sit up and take a breath at the end of each sentence. Follow the breathing marks below that many actors use.

/ short breath (or pause)

// medium breath (or pause)

/// deep breath (or pause)

I pledge allegiance to the Flag of the United States of America, //

And to the Republic for which it stands, /

One nation under God, /

Indivisible, with liberty and justice for all. /

Hopefully, you had an easier time because you improved your posture and used the breath marks. Good posture and breath control are key to sharpening your acting skills. We will focus more on breathing later in the section.

Besides clarity, quality, and breathing, actors need to be able to use their voices to portray believable characters. For example, if a character is from a different region of the country or from a different country, the accent or dialect will need to be different from the actor's. Furthermore, the actor's voice will need to reflect the emotion the character is trying to convey based on the way the character would act, not the way the actor would. The actor may do this by changing the expression—the way a character stylizes their reactions to the events onstage—or they may change the level of energy, which is the power behind the voice. Some characters are loud; others have less volume while remaining very intense. This is the ability to emphasize without adding volume.

The students above stretch their facial and mouth muscles with "Big Face, Little Face." Start by opening your mouth and eyes as wide as possible. Hold for five seconds. Now scrunch your entire face so that it is small. Hold for five seconds. Repeat this several times. Next, when you make your face "big," stick your tongue out as far as you can and stretch your arms and legs so that your body takes up the greatest possible space. Hold for ten seconds. Then scrunch up your face and body, taking up as little space as possible while still on your feet and hold for ten seconds. Repeat the last two steps several times.

An extension on this activity will get your articulators ready for any tongue twister. The first is "Big Boat, Little Boat," and it works the lips. Start by making the sound of a motorboat with your lips, but keep them a bit loose. Now, tighten up the lips to make a faster, higher-sounding vibration. Repeat several times. Now exercise the tongue by trying "Big Drum, Little Drum." Start by making a big, loose sounding drum roll with the tip of your tongue, then try to speed up the air flow to create a tighter, faster sound. Again, repeat several times.

91

• Maybe these ideas will help to get your class started:

Loving mother to child

Priest to homeless man

Young man to beautiful girl

Librarian to book lover

Old man to another old man

Uninterested worker to customer

After completing the activity, discuss your findings. What other sentences could be used to do this activity?

• "The living voice is that which sways the soul." What does this quotation by Roman author and administrator Pliny the Younger mean? Take into consideration the dates during which he lived (61 - 113 AD). Might it have meant more at that time than today? What does he mean by "living voice" and "sways the soul"? What professions today might consider his saying their motto or credo? Write your interpretation of the saying in your own words.

• After trying the breathing activities suggested in this chapter, try to come up with your own. Be sure to record them for future use. Your singers might have some fun ideas from their music classes.

• *The Actor's Body* activity uses typecasting to help young actors identify characteristics that they may someday use to create a role. Typecasting

NAME _____ PERIOD _____ DATE _____

UNDERSTANDING THE ACTOR'S VOICE

Answer the questions about the actor's voice. Be sure to spell the answers correctly. Then put the numbered letters from the answers in the corresponding spaces below to decipher the mystery quotation.

1. A sound that does not use the vocal cords is called $\underline{}\ \underline{}\ \underline{}\ \underline{}_1\ \underline{}\ \underline{}_2\ \underline{}\ \underline{}\ \underline{}$.

2. An actor must $\underline{}\ \underline{}\ \underline{}\ \underline{}\ \underline{}_3\ \underline{}\ \underline{}_4$ to make sure their voice can be heard at the back of the auditorium.

3. If an actor is playing a character from a different area, they may have to use an $\underline{}\ \underline{}_5\ \underline{}\ \underline{}\ \underline{}_6\ \underline{}$.

4. $\underline{}\ \underline{}\ \underline{}_7\ \underline{}\ \underline{}\ \underline{}\ \underline{}_8$ control has often been considered the basis for a great voice.

5. $\underline{}\ \underline{}_9\ \underline{}\ \underline{}\ \underline{}_{10}$ is how high or low one's voice is.

6. If a voice lacks inflection, it is said to be $\underline{}\ \underline{}\ \underline{}\ \underline{}_{11}\ \underline{}\ \underline{}\ \underline{}$.

7. When air is pushed out of the lungs and through the larynx, the $\underline{}\ \underline{}\ \underline{}\ \underline{}_{12}$ work $\underline{}\ \underline{}\ \underline{}\ \underline{}\ \underline{}$ alongside the palates, the bony ridge, and the teeth to produce sound.

8. Even $\underline{}\ \underline{}\ \underline{}\ \underline{}\ \underline{}_{13}\ \underline{}\ \underline{}\ \underline{}\ \underline{}\ \underline{}\ \underline{}$ must be loud enough to be heard while still sounding like whispers.

9. A voice is labeled $\underline{}\ \underline{}\ \underline{}\ \underline{}_{14}$ if it sounds like the actor's nose is pinched.

10. Alter the power behind your voice, also called vocal $\underline{}\ \underline{}\ \underline{}\ \underline{}\ \underline{}_{15}$, to make the character's voice unique from your own.

Fill in the corresponding code to discover what
Pliny the Younger (61-113 AD) said about our topic.

$\overline{4}\ \overline{10}\ \overline{3}\ \ \overline{14}\ \overline{9}\ \overline{2}\ \overline{9}\ \overline{6}\ \overline{8}\ \ \overline{2}\ \overline{11}\ \overline{9}\ \overline{5}\ \overline{3}\ \ \overline{9}\ \overline{12}\ \ \overline{4}\ \overline{10}\ \overline{7}\ \overline{4}$

$\overline{13}\ \overline{10}\ \overline{9}\ \overline{5}\ \overline{10}\ \ \overline{12}\ \overline{13}\ \overline{7}\ \overline{15}\ \overline{12}\ \ \overline{4}\ \overline{10}\ \overline{3}\ \ \overline{12}\ \overline{11}\ \overline{1}\ \overline{14}.$

UNDERSTANDING THE ACTOR'S VOICE KEY

1. Unvoiced
2. Project
3. Accent
4. Breathing
5. Pitch
6. Monotone
7. Lips/Tongue
8. Stage whispers
9. Nasal
10. Energy

"The living voice is that which sways the soul."

---

is when a character is created in stereotypical fashion. While it is normally undesirable on legitimate stages, it is a great way to teach beginning acting skills and develop confidence onstage. Explain to your students that this is an activity and that within these two groups, the miners and the bankers, there exist many unique mannerisms. The miner may have many of the same traits as the banker and vice versa. The differences we seek in the two are caused by their environments, their social status, and their situations. By using twins, we can assume that had they pursued the same paths in life, they would have remained very similar. However, because they are living such different lives, they have each evolved in a different way. To liven the

discussion, talk about movies or books that deal with similar plot lines.

• Try this simple activity with your classes. First, do not plan any bell work activity for this day. As students enter your classroom before the bell, enlist the first three to five who arrive to be your spies. They will watch the others and write down their gestures and movements, large and small. They should try to remain inconspicuous, and they should not identify the students who make the movements. As the rest of the class enters, tell them that you are giving them five minutes of free time. After their five minutes are up, take the lists your "spies" made without letting the others in on your game. Now tell the class you

CHAPTER 4 — ACTING

NAME _____ PERIOD _____ DATE _____

ARTICULATION ACTIVITIES

Say each of the following articulation exercises several times. Listen to the way the letters sound. Take turns with your classmates so that you can hear each other. Sometimes we can learn best by listening to others.

1. Which witch watched which watch?

2. A big black bug bit a big black bear and made the big black bear bleed blue blood.

3. Unique New York

4. She sells sea shells by the sea shore.

5. Peter Piper picked a peck of pickled peppers; a peck of pickled peppers Peter Piper picked.

6. A cup of proper coffee in a copper coffee cup

7. Few free fruit flies fly from flames.

8. Lesser leather never weathered lesser wetter weather.

9. Rubber baby-buggy bumpers

10. Theopholus Thistle, the successful thistle sifter, successfully sifted some thistles.

> **Have you ever read Dr. Seuss's *ABC Book*?** It is a short book of tongue twisting fun for speakers of any age. It makes terrific practice for the actor's voice and characterization.
>
> Also try *Oh, the Places You'll Go!, The Cat in the Hat*, and many others.

TRY THESE FUN AND EFFECTIVE VARIATIONS:

- Say the tongue twisters with a mini-marshmallow on your tongue, but be careful not to choke!
- Try saying the tongue twisters while holding the tip of your tongue.
- Try putting the inflection in different places throughout the tongue twister to change the meaning.
- Try using a British or southern accent.
- How many times can you say each one in one breath?
- Practice doing a stage whisper using the tongue twisters.
- Can you say them using a musical scale? Start low and go up, then back down the scale on each one.
- Say each one backwards!

Now write tongue twisters of your own for each of the sounds D, H, X (or cks), and M. Remember, a tongue twister is easier to remember if it makes sense, even if it is silly sense. You can put the key sound anywhere in the word, but it will have more effect if it is at the beginning. Write your tongue twisters in your journals or on a clean sheet of paper.

93

want them to "act" for a play like students of their age in a classroom. Note the differences in their behavior from the first five minutes, and then tell them their time is up. You now have two examples of gestures and business, one real and one improvised. Take a few minutes to discuss them with the class before continuing with the lesson on gesture and business.

BREATHING ACTIVITY

Breathing is involuntary. Unlike many of life's other necessities, one can only live without breath for a few short minutes. A single simple breath supplies the blood with oxygen, which is then carried to the various organs. Even the skin benefits! By breathing fully and properly, the body works better, the organs are healthier, and the actor can be heard!

When we think of breathing, we often think of someone taking a deep breath while raising their shoulders and then lowering their shoulders as they release the breath. This is incorrect. The shoulders are not involved in the act of proper breathing. Try the activity below, repeating each bullet three times or until the activity has been mastered. By incorporating this into your daily warm-ups, you will experience proper breathing and an increased amount of energy. You will strengthen your diaphragmatic breathing and will find yourself projecting with greater ease.

THE HOT AIR BALLOON

- Stand and face your partner with your hands loosely hanging to your sides and your shoulders back (not stiff, just in good posture). Your knees should be directly under your shoulders, and your chin should be parallel to the ground. This will be referred to again as "perfect posture." Both of you take a slow, natural breath in through your nose and let it out naturally and slowly through your mouth. Did your partner's shoulders move? Probably a tiny bit, because when the lungs fill, the expansion of the chest cavity will cause some slight movement. If they appeared to move too much, as though the shoulder muscles were involved, let your partner know and try again until you are both satisfied with the results.

- Now place one hand on your diaphragm (the muscle that pushes air out of the lungs). It is between the stomach and the rib cage. Press in slightly and repeat the natural breath. Not much should happen except that you should be able to feel a little tightening of the muscle.

- With your hand over your diaphragm, take a slow, deep breath through your nose while counting to ten. Hold for five seconds and release through your mouth over the same ten count. This time you should have really felt some tightening of the diaphragm muscle. Find some space away from your partner and the others. With your feet shoulders' width apart, drop the top part of your body over so that you are bent at the hips—not the waist. Your arms and head should hang with no muscle control, and your knees should be slightly bent. Imagine you are a hot air balloon: your legs are the sturdy basket and from the waist up is the empty balloon, sagging to the ground. Now repeat the slow breathing activity above minus the hand on the diaphragm and, as your lungs fill with air, your body starts filling, too. Like a hot air balloon, you will fill from the base (your waist) up to the tips of your fingers—all in ten seconds. You will then reverse the process while exhaling. Keep the body thoroughly involved in the activity. (For variation, try the balloon activity for longer and/or shorter periods of time.)

- Assume the "perfect posture" described above. Moving only your mouth (and the muscles around your mouth), say "he \ he \ ha \ ha \ ho \ ho \ huh." Each syllable gets its own small breath (note the breath mark: \), and the entire line should be done in about three seconds. It's a bit like the deep breathing women do when they take childbirth classes. The last syllable, "huh," gets a thrust (like a punch in the stomach would sound). Start very shallow and unvoiced. Continue to "breathe" the line, getting deeper each time until you are as loud as you can be without voicing the syllables. Now add a quiet voice (a stage whisper), then a louder voice, and so on, until you are as loud as you can be without yelling.

NOTES: _____

_____

_____

_____

_____

_____

_____

_____

_____

NAME _____ PERIOD _____ DATE _____

THE ACTOR'S BODY

Aside from their voice, the actor's other great tool is their body. Using their body and voice, the experienced actor can be anyone they want to be, any age, any situation. Combining information, emotion, and their own personal style, the actor interprets the character. They analyze the character's posture based on age, health, social status, job, situation, and more. By adding the physical characterization to the vocal, a unique and interesting character emerges. By doing it well, the character is also believable.

Imagine a coal miner in his forties. He has six children and has just found out the mine is shutting down and he will lose his job. He has mined for over twenty years, and his health is suffering. Now imagine a banker in his forties, well-off, two children, fast sports car, tennis player. Can you see how they would stand, walk, gesture, and carry out everyday tasks? What if these two were twins? They started life the same, yet took different paths. If one actor had the job of playing both characters (which is often the case in "twin" shows), can you imagine how he might approach the characterization?

Compare and contrast the two brothers.

Imagine you are watching the miner drink a cup of coffee in a diner. Describe his posture, his hands, his movement, and maybe even the way he shifts his head.

Posture:_____

_____

_____

Hands:_____

_____

_____

Walk: _____

_____

_____

How might he react physically to a loud noise from outside the diner?

How might he react physically to the waitress dropping a tray of food?

Now describe the banker, who is having a cup of coffee down the street in an upscale hotel restaurant. How is he different from his miner brother?

Posture:_____

_____

_____

Hands:_____

_____

_____

Walk: _____

_____

_____

How might he react physically to a loud noise from outside the restaurant?

How might he react physically to the waitress dropping a tray of food?

95

NOTES: _____

_____

_____

_____

_____

_____

_____

_____

_____

THE ACTOR'S BODY CONT.

There are three basic types of stage movement:

- *Blocking* is the act of planning and carrying out stage directions. In some cases, the playwright gives the actors directions in the script. In others, the actors and director plan the movement. Remember that the audience will be "distracted" by movement, so be careful not to upstage other actors. Also, keep blocking natural and motivated. In other words, if there is not evident reason to cross from one area to another, then the movement will look unnatural to the audience.

- *Gestures* are the hand movements actors use to communicate or support communication. For example, a mother might shake her finger at her child as a way of reinforcing her line, "I told you not to go into the woods!" The same mother may use a gesture to send a message without supporting it with any dialogue. How might she gesture to the child to go to his room without speaking? How might she tell him to be quiet using only a gesture?

- *Business* is the little things an actor does onstage to appear naturally "busy," such as a painter cleaning her supplies, covering her paintings, and washing the paint from her hands in a wash basin. Remember the last time you had a long conversation with someone? You likely listened while doing other things, such as completing your homework, drawing pictures, or looking at your phone.

List some gestures and business actors might use in a scene about children at a playground.

GESTURES	BUSINESS

The above movements without the proper expression would be empty and hollow, lacking style. There are several different types of physical expression that actors can use to stylize their movements. They are:

- *Body language* — a type of non-verbal communication that includes posture, facial expressions, eye contact, and even gestures

- *Facial expressions* — non-verbal communication conveyed with the face

- *Posture* — the way one holds their body

- *Pace* — how fast or slow a character moves

- *Rhythm* — the beat to which a character moves (bouncy, strutting, slinky, with a limp, etc.)

- *Quirks and habits* — the little things characters do that make them unique and original (adjusting glasses, twirling hair, taking the steps two at a time, etc.)

NOTES: _____

_____

_____

_____

_____

_____

_____

_____

WARMING UP

Like athletes, actors must warm up their bodies before they start rehearsing or performing. Like singers, they must warm up their voices. Many even warm up their minds. Most high school and middle school directors require students to participate in warm-ups, and many professional directors host them as well. However, in some theatres, it is up to the actor to conduct their own warm-up routine. The following suggested warm-up routine is just that—a suggestion. Your teacher may have their own ideas. After you try the activities, discuss them. Decide what will and will not work for your group. After you are warmed up, have fun with the games and activities on the following pages.

Breathing—With your feet shoulder's width apart, hands hanging loosely by your sides, back straight, and chin parallel to the ground, do the fourth step of *The Hot Air Balloon* exercise described on page 94, saying "he / he / ha / ha / ho / ho / huh." Continue to "breathe" the line, getting deeper each time until you are as loud as you can be without voicing the syllables. Now add a stage whisper, then a louder voice, and so on, until you are as loud as you can be without yelling.

Articulating—Choose any of the tongue twisters from the *Articulation Activities* and repeat each one three to five times. Focus on over-articulating—emphasizing the sounds in an exaggerated way. When you have rehearsed for a few days, you may start noticing areas of concern, such as dropping ending sounds (saying "goin'" for "going") or substituting sounds (saying "bin" instead of "been"). Make a list of problem areas and create an articulation warm-up that specifically addresses those needs.

Before a physical rehearsal or show, the cast usually begins by warming up for about fifteen minutes, just as dancers, gymnasts, and athletes do. By stretching the muscles, the risk of injury is greatly reduced. Many shows require great strength and stamina, too, and the warm-up can help in both areas.

Stretching—Start in a standing position. Imagine something you really want dangling in the air above your head. With your feet glued to the ground, reach for it. After thirty seconds or so, it falls on the floor in front of you. Repeat this to the sides, and behind. You may then sit straight-legged on the floor and try the same activity imagining that the thing is stuck to your shoe but you cannot bend your legs.

Thinking—Imagine your character as an animal. Which animal would you be? Why? What characteristics of this animal does your character display? Imagine how the animal would move, what their voice would sound like, how this animal would get along with others, etc. Discuss the animals as a class and take note of how others in the group see your character. For variations on this activity, imagine your character as a color, an ice cream flavor, a household item, etc. You may even want to make a folder for your script on which you can create a collage incorporating these ideas for your character.

Besides being believable and unique, every actor wants to be uninhibited. An inhibition is that which keeps us from doing something because we're concerned how others may perceive us. We may think we look silly and that others will judge us, or we may fear seeming too enthusiastic. There are an infinite number of activities actors can do to help get rid of their inhibitions and to help them move better onstage. Try each of the following activities. Then respond to the activity on the lines provided.

The Mirror—In groups of two, stand facing your partner. Decide who will be "A" and who will be "B." "A" will start by slowly moving as though looking into a mirror while "B" duplicates

97

WARM-UP ACTIVITIES

- A suggested time for your warm-ups is five to seven minutes for those done in class and fifteen minutes for those done prior to longer rehearsals. In this time, try to include at least one or two activities for breathing, articulating, stretching, and thinking. There are many additional areas, however, that could be included depending on the day's needs. There are some fun activities for characterization, concentration, creating or increasing energy, and much more. Try some of the improvisation games in Chapter 9. You will find that students become more enthusiastic when they both understand and enjoy the warm-up activities.

- If you take notes during rehearsals and find that you are writing some of the same notes over and over, customize your warm-ups to address those recurring issues. For example, if the cast has trouble pronouncing a difficult name, turn it into a fun tongue twister.

the movement as if the mirror. After about a minute, switch. You can also try these variations on the game:

- Have one person lead while the entire class mirrors them.
- Plan a non-verbal scene using the mirror game based on waking up, getting ready for a date, or some other mirror situation. Perform it for the class.

What did you think of this activity?

_____

_____

How might an actor benefit from this activity?

_____

_____

Were you embarrassed about trying the activity? Why or why not?

_____

_____

Charades—Each student will write down the titles of five different movies on five little pieces of paper and fold them. Divide into two teams and put your movie titles still folded in front of the other team. Students will take turns picking one and acting out the movie title for their team to guess in a minute or less. There are standard gestures for charades, such as holding up a finger for each word in the title and tapping one's forearm once for each syllable in the word. Tugging your ear means "sounds like," and tapping your nose means "that's right." No talking is allowed.

What did you learn about movement by playing this game?

_____

_____

How might an actor benefit from this activity?

_____

_____

Were you embarrassed about trying the activity? Why or why not?

_____

_____

Picture Frame—Each student will write down a line from a poem, a saying, or a song lyric on a piece of scratch paper. You may do more than one. Fold it once and place it in the center of the room. Break into groups of three, four, or five and draw from the papers. Your team will have one minute to pose into a picture that could have this saying, lyric, or poem line as its heading. Then freeze and wait for the teacher. They will unfreeze you one group at a time so that you can look at the other groups' pictures. Try these variations on the activity:

- Bring in headlines to work from instead.
- Take pictures of the groups and create a wall with the saying, lyric, or poem line as its heading.

Why do you think this activity would help an actor with movement?

_____

_____

Even though the groups were frozen, how did they display energy?

_____

_____

Slo-Mo—Each student will select a simple activity, such as teeth brushing or making a pizza, and pantomime it in slow motion. You will only have about a minute. For variations try:

- Do the same activity while the teacher calls "slo-mo" or "fast forward."
- Have others guess the activity.

What did you learn from this activity?

_____

_____

Energy Circle—This is not as much a movement game as it is an energy game. However, in order to have movement, there should be energy. The entire class will stand in a circle. Decide who will start. They will clap at the person to their right, who will try to clap left at the exact same time. The second person will then turn to their right and "pass" the clap to the next person, who will again try to clap to the left at the exact same time. Start slowly.

- Play charades using movie titles. Students learn movement, acting, and creativity. To keep it more fun, use titles that students know. Ask students to write down movie titles and turn them in. Save these for another class, and use a different class's list for this group.

- Throughout this book, students are asked repeatedly for their opinions. The same goes for the warm-up activities included in this chapter. As teachers, we sometimes choose activities for our students based on what we, the educators, get from them. Because an activity is quiet, convenient, or fun for us, we assume that the students are also benefiting. However, this may not be the case. If students do not understand the validity of an exercise, they may grow to resent it, feeling like their time is being wasted. This may lead to a situation in which they no longer want to participate, do not take it seriously, or lose faith in its merits. Allow students to give feedback on the activities. You may discover that they simply did not understand how it related to the lesson. With a little clarification, the same student may appreciate the activity or at least participate more patiently.

Except for the first and last people, everyone will clap once to the left and once to the right. The primary objective is to clap at the exact same time as the person passing it to you. Once this is mastered, the objective changes to increasing the speed while maintaining the rhythm. Keep going around and around the circle until the teacher stops you.

What would be a situation in which this activity would prove most useful?

_____

_____

Energy Blast—This is a variation on the Energy Circle. Still in a circle, one person will start by making a one-syllable sound (or word) accompanied by a supporting movement. It should, like its name says, almost be a blast of energy. The person to their right will copy them, then the person to their right will go, and so on. When it gets back to the person who started the movement, they will again do the same movement and sound, but then the person to the right will start a new one, which will then be passed around the circle. Again, this must be kept in rhythm and the energy should remain high. The game will stop once everyone has started a sound and movement. There are some fun variations to this game including:

- Use facial expressions and movement but no sound (while keeping the energy high)

- Experiment with "intensity" rather than volume

- Use phrases and sentences

- Try different approaches to the same word each time around the circle. For example, one person might say "no" and everyone comes up with different ways to interpret the word. The next person may say "why," and so on.

Were you reluctant to participate in this game? Why or why not?

_____

_____

How might a rehearsal benefit from this game?

_____

_____

Styles Tag—In an open space, divide into groups of six to ten. For safety reasons, don't try this with groups any bigger than ten or with more than one group at a time. One person is "it." They will begin a character trait while trying to tag the others at the pace and style of that trait. For example, a monkey would chase the others quickly, while an old man would chase them more slowly. The others must take on this same style while trying not to get tagged. If you get tagged, you are "it" and must come up with a new style. For example, let's say the student who is "it" is a zombie, so everyone else must be zombies until someone is tagged. The next student is tagged and is a young girl on her cell phone, so all others become young girls on cell phones. That students tags someone, who becomes Winnie the Pooh, so all must become Winnie the Pooh.

What are some character styles or characterizations your class explored that might be useful in scene work?

_____

_____

Mime Race—Each student will list five common objects on five separate pieces of scratch paper. Collect them and set them aside. Select two teams of five. Each team will line up on opposite sides of the classroom facing the teacher, who will be in the middle. The last four players on each team will face away from their first players and the teacher. The teacher will draw a card and show it to the first players on each team, who will tap their team's second player on the shoulder so they can turn around. The first player will then act the word out. When the second player thinks they have it, they will turn to the third player and act it out. When one of the teams completes the race, the fifth player will whisper the word to the teacher, and if they are all correct, they win. If not, they must keep going, starting with the player who got it wrong.

What made this game difficult?

_____

_____

NOTES: _____

_____

_____

_____

_____

_____

_____

_____

BASIC PLAY TERMINOLOGY

Unscramble the words in parentheses using the context clues provided.

BASIC PLAY TERMINOLOGY KEY

Play
Playwright
Publisher
Script
Drama
Comedy
Tragedy
Farce
Melodrama
Beginning
Setting
Climax
Plot
Auditions
Monologues
Cold
Callbacks
Casting
Understudies

UNDERSTANDING THE PLAY AND ITS PARTS

A story acted out by actors on a stage is a _____ (ylap) written by a _____ (rywtphialg), also known as the author. Once the play is written, a _____ (pliusebhr) edits and prints the play, and then markets it to the public. The finished play book is called a _____ (tpcsri).

There are many different types of plays. A _____ (daram) is a serious play, while a _____ (cdyeom) is a funny one. A play with a sad ending is called a _____ (agteydr). Some plays are funny and sad at the same time. They are called tragicomedies. A play that makes fun of something is called a _____ (rafec), and a play that is overly dramatic is called a _____ (raodmeaml). There are plays with more than one act called full length and short plays called one acts. There are many other types of plays as well.

Plays, like stories, have several parts. The _____ (inenginbg) or the exposition, sets up the story. Often, this is where the _____ (titnegs), or location of the play, is introduced. The story then builds to a _____ (cximla). After this, there is falling action, also called the denouement (pronounced day-new-MAH), and then the end. Throughout the play, the storyline, or _____ (oltp), is developed.

GETTING THE PART

Actors attend _____ (unsiaitdo), or tryouts, to compete for parts. All auditions are different. Sometimes actors will perform several _____ (ogumolenos) they have memorized. Other times, the audition is a _____ (olcd) reading. That is where the director tells the actors to read parts from the script. The actor does not know in advance what parts they will read. If the director likes certain actors but needs to hear them read again, they will post _____ _____ (alcl bkcsa) and the actors will audition again. The director will then cast the play. There will be an actor for each role and maybe _____ (eeriunstddus) in case an actor is unable to perform for some reason. Often, these actors will have walk-on roles unless they are needed to fill in for the leads.

TERMINOLOGY ACTIVITY

On a day when you must be away from your classes, leave paper, art supplies, and a list of the terminology from either the *Basic Play Terminology* or the *Rehearsal Terminology* worksheet. Assign students, either individually or in teams, to create one of three projects using every word on the list: a board game, a poster, or a puzzle. Regardless of the type of project they choose, each must be challenging, educational, and attractive.

Afterward, you can choose the best to laminate and use both on your walls and in your lessons. If you laminate the puzzles, use dry erase markers to find or identify the answers. They can then be easily cleaned and reused. These are great for when you are testing and students finish early.

MOCK AUDITION

Divide into four groups:

The Producers (one to three students and the teacher): They have the final say because it is their money producing the show.

The Directors (one to three students): They are the artistic minds involved in the show. They make the decisions, but if the producers do not agree, the producers can override the directors.

The Assistant Directors (one to three students): They assist the directors. In auditions, they are mainly administrative, taking notes, running errands, and calling the actors up to the stage. They offer their opinions when asked.

The Actors (the rest of the class): They will be the ones auditioning for the parts.

Your class may approach this activity seriously as though it is a real audition, or you may make it improvisational, each building your own character and creating situations. Either way, here are the steps to follow:

1. Have the directors and producers pick a play or scene. You will need multiple copies, enough so that each actor onstage will have one each time the scene is read.

Ideally, the entire class should have one. You may want to use one of the lab scenes from Chapter 3 of this book.

2. Give the actors a couple of minutes to read over the scene while the producers, directors, and assistant directors have a short production meeting. They will discuss what they want out of each character.

3. Assemble your actors in a common area, and the production staff in another to start the auditions. Start by asking for volunteers. This is a good way to see who is enthusiastic. Have the students act out the scene in front of the class. Give every actor a chance to read once before anyone reads a second time.

4. Have another short production meeting. Discuss who fits certain roles and make a callback sheet to post on the door.

5. Conduct callbacks. By this time the students are more familiar with the script, and the characters should really be taking shape.

6. Have your final production meeting of the rehearsal process and cast your show. You may wish to cast understudies too. Make a cast list to put on the call board. Be sure to thank everyone who auditioned.

EXTENSION ACTIVITY

Once you have cast your mock show, complete the section on rehearsals, then have a day of mock rehearsals too. Assign those who did not get parts to do publicity and design posters for the mock show.

101

MOCK AUDITIONS

Holding a mock audition as explained on page 101 of the Student Workbook is an engaging way to teach your students auditioning techniques and terminology even if your school does not produce plays. For schools with a full year of shows, this activity will assist your actors in knowing exactly what will be expected of them during an audition.

Ideally, you will need a play or scene with enough copies for the entire class. It is illegal to duplicate any copyrighted play, so you may want to use one of the lab scenes from this book. This will be especially convenient, since all of your students will already have it.

To assign audition jobs, you may ask for volunteers, assign them based on what you know about each student, or draw them from a hat. The number of students in each class will determine how many you will have for each job. After the auditions, assign a short answer or essay about each student's experiences.

INTRODUCTION TO THEATRE ARTS I

NAME _____ PERIOD _____ DATE _____

REHEARSAL TERMINOLOGY

Unscramble the words in parentheses using the context clues provided.

Once the play has been cast, _____ (slhararsee) begin. The first is generally the read through. The actors sit in a circle to read and discuss the script. From this point forward, each rehearsal will strive to get the cast closer to opening night. Many directors like to start their rehearsals with warm-ups to exercise the actors' minds, bodies, and voices.

Both at rehearsals and away (but mostly away), the actors work hard to memorize their _____ (silen) so that they can have a smooth performance. They also spend many weeks learning about their _____ (hrcatsaerc), the roles in which they are cast. Each strives to unlock the mystery of their character's posture, movement, and body language and to use their hands to _____ (esrgute) naturally, as though the action was the character's and not the actor's. The actor will work to give their character a unique rhythm that aids in the progression of the scene. Eventually the play itself must develop a rhythm so that it stays energetic and entertaining. Some experienced actors feel very confident in their technique; however, even the best actors still take direction from the _____ (rteoidcr), the artistic head of the production.

Sometimes the script has _____ _____ (gaset ctiedisrno) written in with the lines, but often the director and actors decide when and where to move. This planning of the movement is also called blocking. Actors must memorize their blocking as well as their lines. Each _____ (rmsak) their script with a kind of "actors' code" called scoring.

LET'S GET TECHNICAL

About a week or two before opening night, the director and technical director will add the _____ (hilgts) and _____ (udson) to the rehearsal. These are called technical rehearsals. By this time, the set should be finished and in place and the actors should be using most of the _____ (sorpp) that they will need in the play, such as cups and glasses, food, hair brushes, and any other items their characters need to carry out the action of the play. The cast will continue to work with the technical crew (also called techies) throughout the remainder of the show. Several days before opening night, the costumer and makeup people will arrive for the _____ (edsrs) rehearsal. Many actors' performances change drastically at this point because, as one actor put it, "Getting into costume and makeup is like putting on the character's skin. You begin to look like them and feel like you think your character would look and feel, and with the lights and sound and the set, it's easy to start believing you are there!"

REHEARSAL TERMINOLOGY KEY

Rehearsals
Lines
Characters
Gesture
Director
Stage Directions
Marks
Lights
Sound
Props
Dress

IN-CLASS REHEARSAL

Remind your students often that the time you give them to work on their scenes in class is the same as rehearsal time for a play. Call the time "rehearsal" and use the same rules and standards you would if it were taking place after school. You may want to review the *Rehearsal and Performance Expectations* in Chapter 1 and use the *Activity/Rehearsal Grade* form in Section 2. When students know your specific expectations, they become more accountable.

TEACHING TECHNICAL THEATRE

Technical theatre is a broad subject—broad enough that it requires a full textbook on just that subject. The most basic terminology is included in this chapter mainly so that actors can know what is happening around them. You can find more information on technical theatre in Chapter 7 of this book.

If you do not have a technical theatre program at your school, contract a professional to come to your school to give a workshop or an overview. If you cannot afford the fee, appeal to your principal's sense of safety; perhaps they will fund the visit. If not, call a college in your area and ask if it has a theatre student who will teach your classes about basic technical theatre. Remember, safety must come first. If you are not adept at the technical side of the art, do not attempt to teach it. Students are injured every year by mishandling tools, fly systems, catwalks, and lights, and by not using caution around orchestra pits and hydraulic lifts.

BASIC ACTING TERMINOLOGY

Now that you better understand the voice and the process by which your teacher will evaluate you, you need to familiarize yourself with acting. Acting is a lot like pretending, but at a much more sophisticated level. When we pretend, we use our imaginations to improvise another life. In acting, the playwright has written the story, so there is much less improvisation. The actor is a messenger; it is their job to communicate the playwright's message to the audience.

Most plays today are written in a representational style: they are meant to represent real life, naturally and somewhat realistically. The actors and the audience do not interact. Actors perform as though there is a fourth wall between the stage and the house, the part of the auditorium where the audience sits. However, throughout history and even today, some plays are written in a presentational style in which the actors break the fourth wall. Unless you've seen a melodrama, where this is always the style, you might be most familiar with this type of presentation from TV shows like *The Office*. In a way, the audience becomes a character in the scene, and the characters speak to them. These are just two types, and within each of these, there are numerous others, which will be discussed in other sections.

Regardless of the play style, as an actor you will need to find a way to portray the character in a way that fits the playwright's intent and also is entertaining to the audience. It is always wise to research a character before you audition for the part. If you are trying out for several parts within the same play, be sure to make each character distinct and original so that the director will see your versatility.

The process of characterization can be quite intimidating for student actors, but it does not have to be. Let's say you're auditioning for the role of Anne Frank's mother. There are several basic places to look for information about this character:

- What she says about herself
- What others say about her
- What the playwright says about her, both in the preface and in the stage directions
- What one can deduce from the subtext (what the lines imply but never say)

CHARACTERS ARE LIKE ONIONS

Imagine a yellow onion straight from the market. The "outer skin" is papery, brown, and dry. If you peel that off, you will expose the next layer, still brown and papery, but a little less dry than the first one. The next layer may be dry at the top and bottom, but white and moist in the middle. If you want to eat the onion, you will have to peel off several layers.

Characters are like onions: they have many layers and getting to the part that the audience wants to see takes working through each layer carefully. The first is in the text of the play—what is said about the character, what they say about themselves, and what the playwright may have said in the character description at the beginning. The next layers come from the subtext—what is implied in the text but never said. If the character is non-fictional, the next layer will come from what was said about the person throughout history or in the media. And the final layer comes from the actor's and director's own personal interpretations.

Peel a character today and discover the delicious and nutritious parts hidden beneath the outer layers!

103

PRODUCTION ACTIVITIES

- Refer your students to the Actors' Etiquette list included in the basic acting terminology lesson on page 104 in their workbooks. Tell your students you are having a poster contest. For prizes, maybe you can even ask local restaurants if they would like to donate gift certificates, or ask your principal for shirts or mugs with the school logo. However, because you are also taking a grade, everybody must participate. Allow them to design and create posters that boldly display the rules of etiquette, putting their names on the backs. Choose your favorite three from each class, then send them to the art teacher, who can also pick a first-, second-, and third-place poster from each class, as well as overall. Ask the winners if you can keep their posters to place around the stage and classroom to remind actors of the rules of etiquette.Your students will love the competitiveness of the assignment, and you may reach a student or two who would otherwise rarely participate.

- Before each production opens, have your drama club, parents booster club, or Intro to Theatre classes decorate the dressing rooms, green room, and technical booth for the cast and crew. Your classes can make posters (remind them to say "break a leg" instead of "good luck"), blow up balloons, and so on. If your cast is divided

If the character is historical like this one is, you can also do research online and in books. If the character is from a classical play that has withstood the test of time, read what scholars have written over the years. And then, of course, the actor will role score the character to fill in any remaining blanks and gain deeper insight.

Once you have discovered all you can about your character, you can decide if you want to play them emotionally or technically. Emotional acting, also called method acting, requires the actor to experience all of the emotions that the character is experiencing. Developed by Konstantin Stanislavski, a Russian actor and director, the actor is urged to become the character. One of his key conditions, the "magic if," encourages the actor to imagine how he would respond if he was in this character's situation, if he felt this character's emotions, if he had the character's relationships.

Technical acting allows the actor to explore the character from a less emotionally-involved perspective. Actors analyze the conditions (the weather, time period, time of day, etc.), the obstacles (what is keeping them from their goal), and the objectives (what they want from the scene or the play). They observe people who fit the character type and act out their observations, adding their own special touches. One downfall to technical acting is that actors are not as involved in their characters, and in the event that something unexpected happens during a performance, the technical actor will be less likely to respond as the character would than as the emotional actor.

As you grow as an actor, you will form your own opinions and preferences. Most actors use a combination of these styles, but a few are very loyal to a single approach. Always be open to trying out an idea before opposing it, allowing you to expand your skills as an actor.

Like any other group project, a group of actors must develop a philosophy of teamwork. Because they are together in such a small space for so long, many casts become like a family. However, once in character, there is a certain protocol for working with others onstage.

As an actor, remember to pay attention to the production schedule and always meet deadlines. Be punctual, and always remember to bring your script and a pencil—you will be making changes! It is a good idea to have a notepad, too, for taking down notes. Be off book (having your lines memorized) by the director's deadline, to establish trust and professionalism with your fellow cast members. Be quiet backstage before entrances and after exits. When the director calls "places," get there quickly and quietly, and when they call "cut," stop and quietly await instruction.

ACTORS' ETIQUETTE

1. Be on time to auditions, rehearsals, performances, and all other events.

2. Be prepared. Bring all materials and have them where you can easily get to them.

3. Meet all deadlines.

4. Be focused. Concentrate on the job at hand. Do not allow distractions to interfere.

5. Be brave. If the director asks you to try something new, don't shy away because you are embarrassed. However, NEVER feel that you have to do something that compromises your beliefs.

6. Be helpful. Find out what you can do to help others and offer assistance.

7. Be courteous. Never offer advice to the others. That is the director's job.

8. Be aware that you are one of several. Do not use rehearsal time to try new things or memorize lines without asking the director first.

9. Be your absolute best every time.

into several different dressing rooms, they can even make nameplates for the doors.

- Have your drama club write inspirational quotes from famous writers or actors. Maybe members can attend some rehearsals and take pictures. These can be slid into the frames of mirrors, reminding the cast of some of their funnier moments. All embellishments should enhance the space but not crowd it.

- Parents can supply plates of healthy snacks like pretzels, fruits and vegetables, and bottled water. Remind them to avoid dairy, carbonated beverages, or caffeine.

One group at a time, have everyone resume their positions so the other groups can discuss their picture.

Teamwork is also required onstage. In a play, when someone who should not have the audience's attention does something to steal it from the actor who should have their attention, this is called "scene stealing" or" upstaging." Instead, actors whose presence onstage is not the center of attention must master the art of staying involved in the scene without stealing it. Still, these actors should not be invisible. They must place themselves so that they can be seen by the audience. They shouldn't be blocked by scenery or other actors, and when a different actor crosses from one area to another, they must counter-cross to where they can still be seen. Moving naturally is the key—everything an actor does onstage must be motivated. In other words, there must be a valid reason within the play for the character to perform each and every action.

Besides being upstaged by scenery and other actors, you can upstage yourself by turning away from the audience. Because it feels more natural, actors tend to face whomever is speaking, even if doing so turns them away from those who are watching the performance. The term "cheating out" refers to when an actor compromises, facing a point between the other actor and the audience. But you still have to make it look as though you are addressing the other actor.

The director always has to consider stage dressing, placing actors to create a specific stage picture, so they will assign very specific places for actors. However, sometimes, especially during long monologues, the director will tell the actor delivering the monologue to "take the stage." This means that actor is free to move anywhere on the stage. Because of the unpredictability of this actor's movements, teamwork becomes especially important so that the stage picture stays pleasant and balanced.

FREEZE FRAME

Learning to create a nice "stage picture" in which everyone is sharing the space and no one is being upstaged is both an art and a skill. There are also a variety of styles, each appealing in the appropriate context. For example, directors generally try to avoid putting actors in straight lines onstage, preferring instead to stagger them about naturally. However, in a play in which severity of order is exaggerated, a series of straight lines may have an artistic appeal.

Gather a bunch of "lines" from poems, plays, advertisements, greeting cards, headlines, instructions, recipes, internet memes, and anything else you can find. In this exercise, creativity and variety are part of the fun. Cut them into lines, sentences, words, fragments, phrases, or paragraphs. Put them in a hat, and break into groups of five to ten. Each group will then draw a slip of paper from the hat and create a "photograph" using every member of the group. Remember that every person is important to the final picture. Use two minutes to create the picture and freeze while someone takes a picture so everyone can remember their position before relaxing.

NOTES: _____

_____

_____

_____

_____

_____

_____

_____

_____

ACTING TERMINOLOGY
CROSSWORD PUZZLE CLUES

ACROSS

1. When the character has a valid reason for doing something, the action is _____.
3. Something that is implied but not spoken.
4. What the director says to get the actors ready to start the scene.
8. A play that has withstood the test of time.
11. What the director says to stop the action.
12. Something that keeps a character from their goal.
14. Each actor must develop a _____ character.
15. The process by which the actor seeks to make their role unique and entertaining.
17. An actor is _____ themself if they stand where the audience cannot see them.
18. During a long monologue, a director may tell an actor to _____ the stage, allowing them more freedom of movement.
19. A non-fictional character.
20. A play style that reflects real life.

DOWN

2. The style of acting that focuses on thinking more than feeling.
3. An actor is scene _____ or upstaging others if they distract the audience from the actor who should have their attention.
5. What the character wants from the scene or play.
6. The area behind the curtain where the actors cannot be seen.
7. To have one's lines memorized and not have to have the script in hand.
8. To move to another stage area.
9. The Russian actor/director who founded the Method style of acting.
10. A play style in which the actors address the audience.
13. To move because another actor has moved to block you.
15. When an actor compromises their body position so that the audience can see them, they are said to be _____ out.
16. Because the actors are so close for so long, they must develop a philosophy of _____.

ACTING TERMINOLOGY
CROSSWORD KEY

ACROSS	DOWN
1. Motivated	2. Technical
3. Subtext	3. Stealing
4. Places	5. Objective
8. Classical	6. Backstage
11. Cut	7. Offbook
12. Obstacle	8. Cross
14. Unique	9. Stanislavski
15. Characterization	10. Presentational
17. Upstaging	13. Countercross
18. Take	15. Cheating
19. Historical	16. Teamwork
20. Representational	

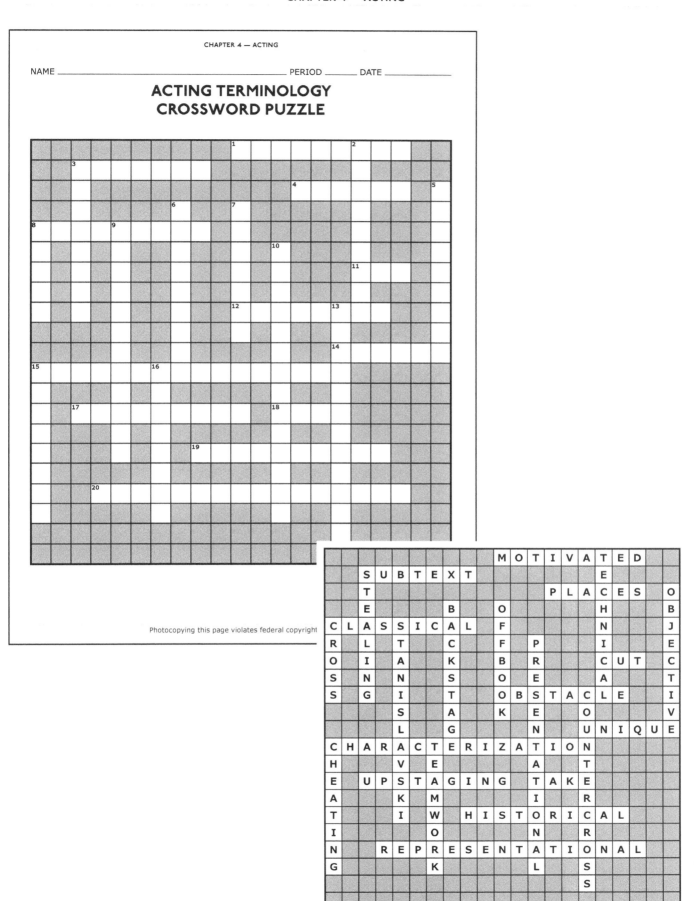

NAME _____ PERIOD _____ DATE _____

ACTING TERMINOLOGY
CROSSWORD PUZZLE

THE ART OF TIMING

Another important part of acting is timing, and different types of performances follow different rules. Think about the last time you heard someone tell a really funny joke. They set the joke up, then just before the punchline, there is a bit of a pause. The punchline is delivered, and then there is silence as the funny guy waits for his audience to laugh. Now, think about the last time you stumbled upon a soap opera. The timing is completely different, isn't it? Mysterious music that builds, lingering camera pans, long gazes, two people's hands that barely brush yet you can feel the electricity between them. Clearly, the pacing of building action in the joke-telling is very different from the building action of the soap opera.

Timing refers to the tempo and pace of line delivery, movement, and response. Actors must know how to keep their audience entertained, and they must be able to tell when they are falling short of this goal.

The art of timing cannot be taught. You must observe timing in real-life situations and bring those experiences to the stage. You must then experiment with what feels right, continue with what gets a good response from the audience, and learn from criticism. At the same time, you can use detective skills to get clues about line delivery from the script. The first step in doing this is to understand timing vocabulary and how the playwright uses punctuation in the script to convey their intentions. The terminology below and on the next page will help you get started.

ad-lib	To make up lines as the scene progresses.
beats	Sections of a scene. A scene is usually made up of several beats.
building a scene	The act of pacing the scene so that it keeps the audience eager for more. It has a beginning, a climax, an anti-climax (denouement), and an ending.
covering	The method actors use to hide mistakes in a scene. If a line is forgotten, another actor may say it or it might be fed to the one who forgot. Lines might even be made up. When done right, the audience never knows there was a problem.
cue	A line or other event on or offstage that tells actors to do or say something.
cut in	When a character interrupts another character's line with his own line.
cut-off lines	Lines that end abruptly without being completed. They are usually denoted with a dash after the last word.

NON-VERBAL COMMUNICATION AND TIMING ACTIVITIES

- A silent moment onstage can be a very uncomfortable experience for young actors. They suddenly feel vulnerable, like a mime whose hands are bound or a singer whose microphone will not work. However, a well-spent moment of silence can be a very powerful tool as long as the actors continues to act. They must keep the energy high with their hands, posture, face, eyes, and movement. This does not mean they must be active; it just means that the communication is non-verbal through the silence.

- Have your students break into pairs. Give them ten minutes to come up with a short scene of about three minutes in which speech is not used. Actors cannot attempt to communicate with any form of sign language. Instead, they must use subtle, realistic gestures, facial expressions, and

dead space	Uncomfortable silence that is attributed to poor timing, weak memorization, or bad breathing. This is different from an intended pause.
fade-off lines	Lines that drift off without being completed. They are usually denoted with an ellipsis, which looks like three periods in a row.
holding for laughs	The process by which an actor pauses after a funny line while the laughter from the audience lessens; all actors remain in character.
overlap	The method by which lines or parts of lines are said simultaneously by different characters.
pace	The speed at which a scene progresses.
pause	A period of silence that is intentional and used to convey deeper meaning than lines are capable of doing.
picking up cues	Refers to actors and technicians doing their jobs without pauses that could pull the energy down.
tempo	The "rhythm" of a scene.
top	When one actor starts the next line immediately after the cue line; no gap is left between the two lines.

Imagine being in the following situations. Rank them from 1 to 5, starting with which you think would have the slowest timing and ending with which you think would have the fastest.

_____ You woke up to realize you forgot to set your alarm clock. You have an exam in half an hour and you have to get ready.

_____ You work at a fast food restaurant and it's a very hectic lunch time. You have a large order to fill but you stayed up late doing a science project and are exhausted.

_____ You are in an elevator when your ex-best friend gets in. It's a long ride and you try to make polite conversation.

_____ You are in your sister's room reading her diary to your best friend on the phone when you hear the front door. Within seconds the doorknob begins to turn.

_____ You and your date just realized that you are running late for the movie, but you are having a great time just talking at dinner.

Discuss your rankings with the class.

109

EXTENSION ACTIVITY

Have students sit in a circle. One student starts a rhythm any way he or she wants. It can be vocal or physical, and props and words are allowed. Once the beat is established, another student will add a second beat. Each rhythm would support the others. Eventually, the "song" will grow to five or six sounds. Now have the students drop off one at a time until you are back at the original beat. The activity is best done without talking. Use eye contact to direct the students. Try some variations on the types of beats, such as hip-hop, country, or square dance, or allow students to use props for sound.

movement to convey a full scene with a beginning, a middle, and an end. Afterward, allow the audience to explain what they saw. If they are able to fully interpret the scene, the actors succeeded. If not, what might the actors have done differently?

- One of the hardest things to teach young actors is the subtle timing of a scene. The best way to help them understand the details, though, is to teach them about the chunks or beats of a scene. Tell them that acting a scene is a lot like driving a stick shift. You start out in first gear and gradually shift up as the "speed" or intensity increases. This can happen when actors change goals, a new character becomes active in the scene, or the conversation shifts directions. More often than not, scenes increase in urgency as they progress, so as actors go from beat to beat, they shift to higher gears. Like driving, though, it is sometimes necessary

CRAZY CLOCK KEY

1:00   building
2:00   top
3:00   cut-in
4:00   beats
5:00   dead space
6:00   ad-lib
7:00   tempo
8:00   covering
9:00   pause
10:00   pace
11:00   fade-off lines
12:00   cues

INTRODUCTION TO THEATRE ARTS I

NAME _____ PERIOD _____ DATE _____

CRAZY CLOCK

The Crazy Clock is confused. The timing terminology must go in the blanks, but where?
Use the clues to figure out where each term fits. Have fun and good luck!

- "A period of silence which is used to convey deeper meaning than lines are capable of doing" is directly in the middle of *cue* and *ad-lib* in the evening.

- "The speed at which the scene progresses" is two hours before midnight.

- "When an actor says his lines immediately after the end of his cue line" is after noon but before *ad-lib*.

- "Pacing the scene so that it keeps the audience eager for more" is after *pace* and before *top*.

- "A line or other event on- or off-stage that tells actors to do or say something" is at lunchtime.

- "To make up lines" is at the South Pole.

- "Lines that drift off without being completed" is after *pace* but before *cue*.

- "Uncomfortable silence that is attributed to bad timing" is two hours before "the rhythm of a scene."

- "Sections of a scene that stand apart from others" is before *ad-lib* and after *cut-in*.

- "The method actors use to hide mistakes in a scene" is before *pause* and after *tempo*.

- "No space left between the two lines" is two hours before "sections of a scene that stand apart from others."

- "Rhythm" is three hours earlier than "speed."

- "Uncomfortable silence" is between *ad-lib* and *cut-in* but after "sections of a scene which stand apart from others."

- *Top* is five hours before "rhythm" and an hour after "making sure each scene has a beginning, a climax, and an end."

- "When a character interrupts another character" is directly across from *pause*.

110

---

to downshift momentarily before again increasing the speed and shifting to a higher gear. The momentum becomes greatest as the scene reaches the climax, and like a driver who has reached the destination, the actors must begin the process of downshifting before stopping and turning off the engine.

- Another game that teaches actors the fine art of timing is called "Fast Forward." It can be done at play rehearsal using the lines from the play or in class using improvisation. Have students act out a scene. At some point in the scene call out "fast forward," "rewind," or "slow motion." The actors will immediately follow the command. When they rewind, they do not have to talk, but they have to try to retrace their movements backward and very quickly. Once they are allowed to go forward again, they must attempt to repeat the scene exactly as it happened before the rewind. Fast forward and slow motion require the actors to continue to talk, but

NAME _____ PERIOD _____ DATE _____

SCRIPT SCORING

For the first few weeks of rehearsal, most actors count on their scripts for lines, cues, and blocking. Many have their own, unique way of marking their scripts; due to the fast pace of the rehearsal, it may look like gibberish or chicken scratch to others, but the actor who wrote it will be able to read it.

It is a good idea to start by highlighting your lines in one color and stage directions in another. If you highlight your stage directions and the director has you do something different than what is in the script, draw a line through the highlighted movement and mark the new blocking in the outside margin. Next, choose a fine-tipped highlighter and begin marking character clues —anything the script or the characters in the play say about your character (including what they say about themself).

In rehearsal, always carry your script and pencil onstage until the director tells you not to. Even if it is in your back pocket, when you need it, it will be within reach. Other than the highlights, mark your script in pencil so that changes can be made quickly and neatly. Try to mark stage directions in the outside margin (away from the binding), because it is easier to see. The following is a suggested list of marks you may want to use when you mark your script.

X = CROSS	EN = ENTRANCE
D = DOWN	EX = EXIT
U = UP	/ = SHORT PAUSE
C = CENTER	// = MEDIUM PAUSE
R = RIGHT	/// = LONG PAUSE
L = LEFT	↑/↓ = STAND/SIT
⌣ = SPEED UP	__ = LIGHT STRESS (underlined once)
⌣ = SLOW DOWN	= HEAVY STRESS (underlined twice)

Unless your teacher has asked you to follow a certain protocol, there is no wrong way to score your script as long as you can recreate the scene during the next rehearsal. Also, your understudy may need your script if they understudy for more than one actor. In that case, make sure you keep your markings simple and always create a key in the front or back of the script so that others can interpret your marks.

Use the above key to interpret the following stage directions:

1. EN DL X C: _____

2. X UR ↓, read book: _____

3. EX DR: _____

Bonus: Using the diagram of a stage on the next page, can you figure out what shape the stage directions below are making? Can you make other shapes?

EN RC X UC X LC X DC EX RC

111

SCRIPT SCORING KEY

1. Enter downright, cross to center

2. Cross upright, sit and read book

3. Exit downright

---

they must alter the pace of their scene. The students are challenged to change their tempos and to stay focused on the scene. Afterward, discuss the activity with your students.

- Are students still confused about pacing? In pairs, have them write duets in which two actors may say only twenty words each. The rest of the duet must be nonverbal communication, which must be written into the stage directions. By writing the scene, those who are not comfortable with improvisation will get a better understanding of the power of silence. Have pairs act out their scenes.

TAPING OFF THE STAGE

Measure and record your stage's acting area. If you have balconies, measure those too. If you use the height of your stage (such as building sets with platforms), take that into consideration as well.

- If you will be conducting all rehearsals on the stage, it may help to tape it off. Determine the number of areas you will use and divide your stage accordingly. While most school stages are of the appropriate size for nine acting areas (like the diagram provided on page 112 of the Student Workbook), some are larger and require fifteen areas. Use masking or glow tape to mark them. If the tape will interfere, then mark only the "intersections" and draw a chalk line at the beginning of each rehearsal (it will be gone by the end of rehearsal).

- If you will be rehearsing in another facility, marking the practice stage with your performance stage's dimensions will assist your actors in knowing exactly where to move.

- For a musical or a show with intricate blocking, try dividing the apron of the stage into smaller sections and number them off. Actors can use these numbers to ensure that they are precisely where they need to be. Remove all (or most) tape prior to opening night.

THE STAGE

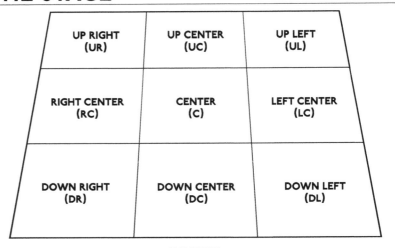

UP RIGHT (UR)	UP CENTER (UC)	UP LEFT (UL)
RIGHT CENTER (RC)	CENTER (C)	LEFT CENTER (LC)
DOWN RIGHT (DR)	DOWN CENTER (DC)	DOWN LEFT (DL)

AUDIENCE

BONUS KEY
The shape is a diamond

- There are many different types of stages, but most high schools and middle schools have what is called a proscenium stage. A proscenium stage is usually rectangular with one side open to the audience; the other three sides are backstage.

- Small and medium-sized stages are divided into nine areas. Some medium-sized and most larger stages have fifteen areas.

- The area closest to the audience is downstage and the area farthest away from the audience is upstage.

- The terms right and left refer to the actors' right and left, not the audience's.

- The acting area is the part of the stage set aside for acting.

- When the actors are not onstage, they are backstage. This refers to the area behind the curtain or the set that the audience cannot see.

- The wings are the areas to the left and right of the stage where the actors stand while waiting for their entrances. The wings are also considered backstage.

- The building where the play is performed is the theatre or the auditorium.

- The part of the auditorium where the audience gathers is the house.

- The narrow area between the audience and the stage is called the pit. In a musical play, this is the area generally set aside for the orchestra. Many directors use the pit as an additional acting area.

112   Photocopying this page violates federal copyright law.

ACTING REVIEW BOARD GAME

- Consider laminating several copies of the *Acting Review Game Board* on page 212 for future use. You may wish to enlarge them (very large copies can be made at some copy stores), copy them onto colored or heavy paper, or have students decorate them first. Regardless, making some additional sturdy boards will allow them to be used in other sections for varying topics.

- Make copies of the game cards for each student and have them cut them apart to use as vocabulary flash cards for learning terminology. Students can work alone or with others simply by reading the question on one side, then turning the card over to see if their answer was correct. They can then pile the cards they know in one

stack and those they do not know in another. Then they should continue to work with the stack of questions they don't know until all of the cards end up in the pile of correctly answered questions. Encourage students to make their own vocabulary cards and combine them with the laminated boards to play learning games throughout the year.

- Mark off your floor or a parking lot, classroom, or gym floor with tape, creating a giant version of the board game. Instead of game pieces, each student will move from square to square. Another student will read the cards for them. Only a few can play at a time, so this might be best used on days when large groups of students are out for testing or a field trip.

CHAPTER 4 — ACTING

ACTING REVIEW GAME BOARD

Use the 36 flash cards provided by your teacher to play the board game below. Up to four people can play. First cut the cards out and take a moment to study them. Then place them gray side down. You may use coins or other small objects for game pieces. Decide who will go first. Take the top card off the deck. Player One must define, answer, or complete the question. If they are correct, they may advance the number of spaces on the board game. If they are incorrect, they must go back the number of spaces on the flash card. Continue with Players Two, Three, and Four until one of the players reaches the end. Recycle used cards by placing them at the bottom of the deck. The first player to the end wins!

START Answer correctly to advance 3 spaces. →	Answer correctly to advance 2 spaces. →	Answer correctly to advance 3 spaces. ↓
Answer correctly to advance 2 spaces. ↓	Go to the space directly above this one before drawing your next card. ←	Answer correctly to advance 5 spaces. ←
Answer one question to move 3 spaces or answer two to move 6 spaces. If you answer two and miss either one, you must double the number of back spaces. →	Answer correctly to advance 2 spaces. →	Answer correctly to advance 2 spaces. ↓
Answer correctly to advance 1 space. ↓	Answer correctly to advance 4 spaces. ←	Go to the space directly above this one before drawing your next card. ←
Answer correctly to advance 2 spaces. →	Answer correctly to advance 2 spaces. →	Answer correctly to advance 3 spaces. ↓
Answer correctly to advance 1 space. ↓	Answer correctly to advance 2 spaces. ←	Answer one question to move 1 space or answer two to move 3 spaces. If you answer two and miss either one, you must double the number of back spaces. ←
Answer correctly to advance 2 spaces. →	Go to the space directly above this one before drawing your next card. →	**END**

You might even want to add some consequence cards like "You were caught trying to distract the actors. Move back 3 spaces," or "You forgot a line and no one could prompt you because you didn't have your script. Move back 1 space." The addition of some chance entertaining cards will add a bit of action to the game and extend the playing time.

- Call local fast-food restaurants and ask if they have any coupons for free french fries or drinks that you can use to reward the winners. You might also want to ask businesses for pencils or notepads with their company logo. Many places are happy to help teachers, especially when they think students will come to their stores or shops with their parents.

- Recycle old board games by using the game pieces, spinners, and, best of all, the boards. When an artistic student asks for extra credit, have them alter your game. Using a little paint, tape, or contact paper, the spaces can be changed to fit your needs (if they do not already). New cards can be made (another assignment for another student), and voila! You have a new learning tool for making lessons fun.

- If your classroom floor is concrete or tile, inquire into having it permanently painted with a generic board game. Many elementary schools use giant visual aids to teach the states and capitals, parts of the body, or anything else that can be painted. Students love the idea of being able to get up out of their seats, become human game pieces, and act as though they have somehow been magically reduced in size. If they are having fun, they forget they are learning, which is the best way to reach them!

- Is the board game too easy? Make a sheet of cards that look like those in the book. Include tasks like "Flap your arms like a chicken and move forward 1 space," or "Tell your teacher they're the greatest and move forward 2 spaces."

- Recycling board games benefits everyone. Your students will have a new theatre board game and the extra credit, you will have a great tool for your lessons, and the landfills will have a little less clutter. The game companies will be happy to know that their creation is in your classroom rather than in the trash.

ACTIVITY REVIEW GAME BOARD

START Answer correctly to advance 3 spaces. →	Answer correctly to advance 2 spaces. →	Answer correctly to advance 3 spaces. ↓
Answer correctly to advance 2 spaces. ↓	Go to the space directly above this one before drawing your next card. ←	Answer correctly to advance 5 spaces. ←
Answer one question to move 3 spaces or answer two to move 6 spaces. If you answer two and miss either one, you must double the number of back spaces. →	Answer correctly to advance 2 spaces. →	Answer correctly to advance 2 spaces. ↓
Answer correctly to advance 1 space. ↓	Answer correctly to advance 4 spaces. ←	Go to the space directly above this one before drawing your next card. ←
Answer correctly to advance 2 spaces. →	Answer correctly to advance 2 spaces. →	Answer correctly to advance 3 spaces. ↓
Answer correctly to advance 1 space. ↓	Answer correctly to advance 2 spaces. ←	Answer one question to move 1 space or answer two to move 3 spaces. If you answer two and miss either one, you must double the number of back spaces. ←
Answer correctly to advance 2 spaces. →	Go to the space directly above this one before drawing your next card. →	**END**

A variance in the tone of an actor's voice is called _____.

The actor's voice must reflect the _____ the lines and movements are trying to convey in the manner of the character, not the actor.

An actor's primary responsibility is to be _____.

When an actor's voice lacks inflection, it is said to be _____.

Combining information, emotion, and their own personal acting style, the actor is able to _____ the character.

A type of non-verbal communication in which messages are sent with posture, facial expressions, eye contact, and gestures.

The beat to which a character moves characterizes their _____.

Learning to properly control one's _____ will help each actor to strengthen their voice.

Vocal _____ includes many things but is generally the pleasantness of one's voice.

The author of a play is more traditionally known as a _____.

_____ is how fast or slow a character moves and speaks.

A _____ is a serious play while a _____ is a funny one.

An actor who speaks clearly, carefully pronouncing every sound without sounding fake, is said to have good _____.

A play with a terrible or sad ending is called a _____.

A _____ _____ must be loud enough to be heard by the audience while still sounding like a whisper.

The place where the action in a play happens is called the _____.

The story builds to a _____, or a high point in the action.

Actors must learn to _____, or speak loudly enough to be heard by every member of the audience.

HEARD Got it wrong? Go back 1 space.	**EMOTIONS** Got it wrong? Go back 2 spaces.	**INFLECTION** Got it wrong? Go back 3 spaces.
BODY LANGUAGE Got it wrong? Go back 1 space.	**INTERPRET** Got it wrong? Go back 2 spaces.	**MONOTONE** Got it wrong? Go back 3 spaces.
QUALITY Got it wrong? Go back 1 space.	**BREATHING** Got it wrong? Go back 2 spaces.	**RHYTHM** Got it wrong? Go back 3 spaces.
DRAMA/COMEDY Got it wrong? Go back 1 space.	**PACE** Got it wrong? Go back 2 spaces.	**PLAYWRIGHT** Got it wrong? Go back 3 spaces.
STAGE WHISPER Got it wrong? Go back 1 space.	**TRAGEDY** Got it wrong? Go back 2 spaces.	**ARTICULATION** Got it wrong? Go back 3 spaces.
PROJECT Got it wrong? Go back 1 space.	**CLIMAX** Got it wrong? Go back 2 spaces.	**SETTING** Got it wrong? Go back 3 spaces.

Define "cold reading."

What is the storyline of the play called?

Sometimes the script has _____ _____, or the actors' movements, written into it.

The section of the stage closest to the audience is _____ while the section farthest from the audience is _____.

A representational play is one in which life is represented _____.

A _____ play is one in which realism is not a major objective. Often the actors/characters talk directly to the audience.

Each actor must develop a _____ _____, one that fits the author's intent while remaining interesting to the audience.

Does stage left refer to the actor's left or the director's left?

Define "subtext."

_____ _____ one's character helps to answer questions remaining about the character after studying the play.

_____ _____ requires the actor to experience all of the emotions the character is feeling.

Who is the father of Method Acting and the "magic if"?

_____ _____ allows the actor to analyze the conditions and obstacles facing a character. The actor will also use observations and personal touches to create a unique character.

_____ _____ and _____ distracts the audience from what should be the focus of their attention.

Everything an actor does onstage must be _____, or have a valid and obvious reason for happening.

Define "stage picture."

_____ are sections of a scene that stand apart from others, creating "chunks" or "mini-scenes."

When one actor says his lines immediately after another actor's, leaving no space between the two, they are said to be _____.

STAGE DIRECTIONS Got it wrong? Go back 1 space.	**PLOT** Got it wrong? Go back 2 spaces.	**An audition for which actors are not told what to study or given scripts.** Got it wrong? Go back 3 spaces.
PRESENTATIONAL Got it wrong? Go back 1 space.	**REALISTICALLY** Got it wrong? Go back 2 spaces.	**DOWNSTAGE/ UPSTAGE** Got it wrong? Go back 3 spaces.
What is meant but is never said. Its meaning is implied in the lines; it is often referred to as the meaning "between the lines." Got it wrong? Go back 1 space.	**THE ACTOR'S** Got it wrong? Go back 2 spaces.	**UNIQUE CHARACTER** Got it wrong? Go back 3 spaces.
KONSTANTIN STANISLAVSKI Got it wrong? Go back 1 space.	**METHOD ACTING** Got it wrong? Go back 2 spaces.	**ROLE SCORING** Got it wrong? Go back 3 spaces.
MOTIVATED Got it wrong? Go back 1 space.	**SCENE STEALING & UPSTAGING** Got it wrong? Go back 2 spaces.	**TECHNICAL ACTING** Got it wrong? Go back 3 spaces.
TOPPING Got it wrong? Go back 1 space.	**BEATS** Got it wrong? Go back 2 spaces.	**The way the scene looks or is arranged at particular points throughout the play.** Got it wrong? Go back 3 spaces.

CHAPTER 5
CHARACTERIZATION

DAILY BELL WORK—CHARACTERIZATION

A WELL-DEFINED CHARACTER

ADDITIONAL NOTES

NAME _____ PERIOD _____ DATE _____

DAILY BELL WORK - CHARACTERIZATION

Answer each question as your teacher assigns it, using the space provided. Be sure to include the date.

1. Date: _____
   What are some ways you can research your character?

2. Date: _____
   Tell about someone you have observed away from school. Using only their appearance, actions, and environment, explain the "scene" as though they were a character in a play. Be specific and creative.

3. Date: _____
   What if your character from above met the character of the person sitting next to you? Read about each others' observed characters, and then describe the interaction between the two. Now add another neighbor's character and describe the scene.

4. Date: _____
   Regarding the above bell work, how might your character change as more characters are added? Why?

117

BELL WORK 1

There are a number of effective ways to research a character. Have students start with the scene they are performing. They should identify everything that is said about the character in the preface, stage directions, and dialogue. Many scenes lose their meaning when removed from the script, so when possible, they should read the entire play, taking notes on all characters and events relating to the scene. Literary criticism or other commentary on the play will provide them with additional information, and learning about the playwright can also help, since playwrights often "put themselves into their plays." If the character is historical, such as Anne Frank or Joan of Arc, students can research the real-life figure. Finally, they should fill in any gaps by role scoring the character.

Realistically speaking, students can get away with reading the script and role scoring, but professionals will need to delve even deeper to complete the process.

NOTES: _____

_____

_____

_____

_____

_____

_____

_____

_____

BELL WORK 5

Characters evolve as both the environment and the situation change. Imagine a character, self-confident and wealthy. She stands in her study, listening to classical music on an old-fashioned phonograph. Warm, comfortable candlelight flickers invitingly. Suddenly, the window flies open, knocking over the candles, splattering blood-red wax on her white satin gown. The room darkens. She fumbles nervously for matches, freezing in fear as the wind ceases abruptly. The needle is quietly, carefully lifted from the record. She hears breathing but is unsure if it is her own or an intruder's. From the dark corner by the phonograph, someone lights a match, briefly illuminating a hulking figure shrouded by a dirty cloak.

Discuss the changes in environment (comfort/fear, light/dark, wind, music) and the situation (the intrusion, the music stopping, the match lighting), and how each could potentially affect the woman. Although the scene is brief, the alteration is incredible.

NAME _____ PERIOD _____ DATE _____

DAILY BELL WORK - CHARACTERIZATION

Answer each question as your teacher assigns it, using the space provided. Be sure to include the date.

5. Date: _____
    How might one's character evolve as the environment or situation is altered?

6. Date: _____
    What role does the character's goal play in the development of their onstage personality?

7. Date: _____
    Why do you as an actor need to research your character? List the advantages.

8. Date: _____
    Role score a famous cartoon character. Identify and explain their favorite color, food, style of music (or song), thing about themselves. Also discuss their greatest fear, accomplishment, and ability. Finally, explain what got them to this point (the point at which a particular cartoon takes place) and where they will likely go after it is finished.

BELL WORK 6

A character's goal or objective is what they hope to achieve in a scene or a play. Goals are usually thwarted by the conflict of the play. For example, in *The Wizard of Oz*, Dorothy's short-term goals include getting to the Emerald City and seeing the wizard, but her long-term goal is to return home. Both affect the development of the character.

As Dorothy journeys towards the Emerald City, she meets many characters who help her to understand her fears, shortcomings, strengths, and desires. Obstacles get between her and her goal, and she calls upon her newfound strength and wisdom to get past them. By the end of the play, she has discovered confidence and happiness where it had always been. Her desire to achieve her goals helped her to find it within herself.

NAME _____ PERIOD _____ DATE _____

DAILY BELL WORK - CHARACTERIZATION

Answer each question as your teacher assigns it, using the space provided. Be sure to include the date.

9. Date: _____

    Role score a famous movie character. Identify and explain their favorite color, food, style of music (or song), thing about themselves. Also discuss their greatest fear, accomplishment, and ability. Finally, explain what got them to this point (the point at which the movie takes place) and where they will likely go after it is finished.

10. Date: _____

    What might you as an actor discover about your character by researching the playwright? Why?

11. Date: _____

    When a character is not clearly defined, why might the actor portraying the role need to know their favorite food, fears, or other unusual traits?

12. Date: _____

    Define "stereotype" in your own words. List character stereotypes used repeatedly in TV shows, movies, plays, and other media. Why do you think we see these character portrayals used so often?

119

NOTES: _____

_____

_____

_____

_____

_____

_____

_____

_____

INTRODUCTION TO THEATRE ARTS I

NAME _____ PERIOD _____ DATE _____

DAILY BELL WORK - CHARACTERIZATION

Answer each question as your teacher assigns it, using the space provided. Be sure to include the date.

13. Date: _____

_____

_____

14. Date: _____

_____

_____

15. Date: _____

_____

_____

16. Date: _____

_____

_____

NOTES: _____

_____

_____

_____

_____

_____

_____

_____

_____

A WELL-DEFINED CHARACTER

We all enjoy cartoons. With larger-than-life color and energy and characters who defy the norm, cartoons depict life beyond our wildest imaginations. We choose programming that takes us away from day-to-day life. These shows allow us to imagine life on a deserted island or to see what life as the richest kid in the world would be like.

Complete the chart at the bottom of the page. Then imagine the characters you selected, but instead of being like you described there, they are average or normal. Would you still remember them? Would you be likely to tune in each week? Probably not. In fact, many TV shows make an attempt to imitate life, but rarely do those shows stick around for long. Most successful programs depict characters that exist in unusual settings with exaggerated characteristics, or they may have a plot that is way out of the ordinary. That is why they stand out so much amidst all the characters from the wide range of other shows.

Like the most successful shows, plays are usually riddled with unique characters. Each has an individual personality, personal habits or quirks, or a speech pattern unlike any other. They may emphasize words differently, walk with a particular gait, or use an uncommon facial expression. Actors work hard to preserve each character's individuality while making them believable. The result should be a cast of believable characters who are unlike the actors portraying them. Even those characters with few lines or little stage time should be clearly defined. Any actor who thinks their character is too small to be defined is cheating both themself and their audience of an entertaining and believable play experience.

As you are cast in various roles or as you practice scenes, you will want to study each character fully. Use the *Role Scoring* worksheet later in this chapter to fully flesh out your character. Find out all you can about what the playwright says about them. What does the character say about themself and what can be learned from what other characters say about them? Do the other characters tell any lies or make misleading statements about your character? Why? And what does that say about each of them? There is probably a great deal of information about the character in the subtext, that which is implied but not said in the script. For example, an actor may assume that a quiet person is shy. Learn as much as you can about the playwright to gain valuable insight into the characters. After all, one can only write what one knows. Finally, use your imagination to fill in any remaining gaps while remaining true to what you already know.

Think of three of your favorite characters from cartoons and children's shows, then describe them each.

Character	Show	What makes this character interesting? What are they like?

121

NOTES: _____

_____

_____

_____

_____

_____

_____

_____

_____

_____

SAMPLE CHARACTER COMPARISON
using the characters from the cartoon *Scooby Doo*

CHARACTER	POSTURE/ WALK	APPEARANCE	HABITS/ QUIRKS	SPEECH	BEST QUALITIES
Shaggy	Hunched	Messy, baggy	Scared, hungry	Hippie	Friendly, funny
Scooby	Hunched	Dog collar	Scared, hungry	Rike a drog	Loyal, funny
Velma	Small steps	Frumpy, neat	Loses glasses	Intelligent	Smart, finds clues
Fred	Confident	Preppy, neat	Saves the day	Matter-of-fact	Handsome, brave
Daphne	Lady-like	Trendy, neat	Disappears or gets caught	Inquisitive	Pretty, kind

NOTES: _____

_____

_____

_____

_____

_____

_____

_____

_____

NAME _____ PERIOD _____ DATE _____

YOU AS A CARTOON CHARACTER

Imagine yourself as a cartoon character. Choose a period of your life to serve as the cartoon. For example, a recent event may be memorable, or you might want to use last school year. It does not matter how long ago the event was, just that you have a good memory of it.

The following is a split character analysis similar to those you will be completing for your scenes in class. There are three columns. The first will give you a trait, and in the second you will analyze one of the cartoon characters you remember. Write the character's name in the box at the top of the middle column. In the third column, you will analyze yourself as though you were a character from a cartoon.

	CARTOON CHARACTER _____	YOU
Describe the character's physical appearance including dress, hair, etc.		
How does the character talk?		
What are some of the character's most outstanding habits?		
Does the character work alone or with a companion? Describe.		
Does the character have a particular enemy or recurring problem? Describe.		
What is the character's best trait?		
What is the character's worst trait?		
What makes the character unique?		

123

CHARACTERIZATION ACTIVITY

As your students work on the *You As a Cartoon Character* worksheet in this chapter, ask them if they've ever noticed that some cartoon characters always wear the same thing. Then share the following bit of cartoon trivia. For a long time, cartoons were created in layers on transparent celluloid (nicknamed "cel"). The background contained everything farthest from the audience, and the foreground held that which was closest. Because they were transparent, cels could be stacked. For example, a nighttime sky cel behind a mountain cel behind a cactus cel behind a Mickey Mouse cel would give the illusion of the character in the desert at night. Replace the starry sky with a cloudy sky, and the scene quickly changes to daylight. The cels were then photographed (twenty-four made one second of film), and the actors' voices and music were added. Want to guess how many photographs made a 75-minute film? 108,000!

NAME _____ PERIOD _____ DATE _____

ROLE SCORING

Answer the following questions in detail. Use any means available to find the answer. When you have exhausted all resources to find the answer, make one up. Explain any answer that you make up.

1. What play is your scene from?

2. Is it a monologue, duet, or a scene containing three or more characters?

3. What is the scene about?

4. What is your character's name? What are they like?

5. To whom is your character talking?

6. What happened just before the start of this scene?

7. What do you think will happen in the play after this scene?

8. When and where does the scene take place?

9. How old is your character? Are they mature or immature for their age? Explain.

CONTINUED ON NEXT PAGE

NOTES: _____

_____

_____

_____

_____

_____

_____

_____

_____

CHAPTER 5 — CHARACTERIZATION

ROLE SCORING, CONT.

10. What do they do for a living?

11. What are their hobbies?

12. How does the title of the play relate to your character?

13. What does your character want in this scene?

14. If your character repeatedly made a gesture in this scene, what would it be and why?

15. What color do you associate with your character and why?

16. What object do you associate with your character and why?

17. What animal do you associate with your character and why?

18. In real life, would you be your character's friend? Why or why not?

CONTINUED ON NEXT PAGE

NOTES: _____

_____

_____

_____

_____

_____

_____

_____

_____

ROLE SCORING, CONT.

19. How is your character like you?

20. How is your character different from you?

21. What is your character's most positive trait?

22. What is your character's status in the world? Do they have money or power?

23. What does your character want from life?

24. What does your character fear and why?

25. Who does your character admire and why?

26. What are/were your character's parents like?

27. If your character had one wish, what would it be and why?

NOTES: _____

_____

_____

_____

_____

_____

_____

_____

_____

CHARACTERIZATION STUDY PROJECTS

Project 1: Character Mask

Using what you know about your character, design and make a mask. The mask should represent your character's fears, dreams, likes, dislikes, obstacles, beliefs, etc. It is only a representation; it is not meant to be worn. You will be graded on the following areas:

- Neatness
- Creativity
- Appeal
- Self-expression
- Half-page written explanation of how your mask represents your character

Project 2: Makeup Morgue

Create a one-page collection of pictures from magazines, newspapers, or other sources of what you think your character might look like or how they might be represented. If you were portraying this character in a play, this collection would be used to apply your makeup, so keep this in mind. You will want to consider age, status, gender, ethnicity, etc. Also, you may use just the individual features you think represent your character. For example, if you find a picture of a person whose eyes have the look you want but the rest of the face does not, cut out just the eyes. Be sure to include your name, the character's name, and the name of the play. You will be graded on the following areas:

- Neatness
- Thoroughness
- Creativity
- Following directions

Project 3: Costume Morgue

Create a one-page collection of pictures from magazines, newspapers, or other sources of what you think your character might dress like. You may also wish to use fabric swatches. If you were portraying this character in a play, this collection might be used to design your costumes, so keep this in mind. You will want to consider age, status, gender, ethnicity, etc. Be sure to include your name, the character's name, and the name of the play. If your character is from a different time period, you may need to make copies from books or research costumes online. You will be graded on the following areas:

- Neatness
- Thoroughness
- Creativity
- Following directions

127

NOTES: _____

_____

_____

_____

_____

_____

_____

_____

_____

SAVING AND STORING SAMPLE PROJECTS

When you assign three-dimensional projects like the character mask suggested on page 127 of the student workbook, hanging on to samples from year to year becomes a challenge. Flat projects like the makeup and costume morgues can be filed away for future use, but what can you do with a handful of masks? You do not want to clutter your room by displaying too many projects on the walls or ceilings because they can become a distraction. However, if you have an adjacent room, like a scene shop or practice rooms, use the masks as decorations. Display them proudly in your trophy case and retrieve them when needed. If none of these options work, then saving samples from past years might not be a good option for you. Instead, ask a reliable student from each class to complete the project in advance so that you will have some samples. Offer extra credit, a chance to go to the library, or a study break on the day the rest of the students make their masks.

MORE CHARACTERIZATION ACTIVITIES

- As your students are learning about characterization, have them create several character morgues. A character morgue is a collage of pictures and words that can be used to define a single character or character type. For example, if you are doing a play about a diverse group of teenagers, each teen would have a page. Students would scour magazines for pictures and words to fit each character and glue them onto that page. Unlike a character collage, the character morgue may actually be used to get realistic ideas for costuming, facial expressions, makeup ideas, and so on. Furthermore, these can be labeled by character type, saved, and filed for future use. Some helpful character types for starting your character morgue are popular girl, troubled boy, caring father, workaholic mother, refugee, 1960s boy, athlete, and soldier. Request that the library and teachers give you their old magazines and catalogs.

- Collect some pictures from magazines that depict "stereotypes" of characters or emotions and glue them onto large, sturdy pieces of paper. Have these laminated and continue to add to your collection. You will need about fifty or more to do this activity with a large class, and some of the pictures can be repeated.

- When students are familiar with their scenes, have them try the *Characterization Study Activity*. Instead of using the labels provided, give each group a handful of the laminated pictures from the activity above. Turning them upside down, students can draw from them and create new characters based on their interpretations. You may even want to include pictures of animals, inanimate objects, and cartoon characters to give the actors a challenging and fun twist to the activity.

- Have other questions you want to encourage students to ask about their characters? Record them for future use.

_____

_____

_____

_____

_____

_____

_____

_____

_____

CHARACTERIZATION STUDY ACTIVITY

Cut out each of the following cards and lay them upside down and a bit spread out. Use a scene from your current performances or use a script—a duet would work best. Each person in your group will select a card, and without sharing its contents, each of you will act out your scene the way the card directs. You may switch at any time or you may try guessing the other person's card. When you have used all of the cards, discuss what you learned and how you could use some of the characterizations in your scene work. Have fun and try new things!

AFRAID	SHY	LOST
ANGRY	OLD	YOUNG
HAPPY	SAD	LONELY
DEFIANT	CALM	EXCITED
LOVING	COURAGEOUS	GUILTY
WHINY	MOTHERLY/FATHERLY	FRUSTRATED
Your idea...	Your idea...	Your idea...

CHAPTER 6
PUBLICITY AND OTHER PRODUCTION BUSINESS

DAILY BELL WORK—FINANCE AND PUBLICITY

DAILY BELL WORK—POSTERS, PROGRAMS, AND MORE

PUBLICITY

Local Media
Creative Publicity
News Release Form
Publicity Checklist
Designing Your Poster

DESIGNING YOUR PROGRAM

Biography Worksheet

DESIGNING FLIERS, TICKETS, AND MORE

Publicity Projects

ADDITIONAL NOTES

Bell Work—Finance and Publicity

Bell Work—Posters, Programs, and More

Creative Publicity Ideas

Posters

The Program

NAME _____ PERIOD _____ DATE _____

DAILY BELL WORK - FINANCE AND PUBLICITY

Answer each question as your teacher assigns it, using the space provided. Be sure to include the date.

1. Date: _____

   After purchasing scripts and paying royalties, you have $1000 left to produce a show. The actors are not paid. You will need to build a set, make a few costumes, purchase makeup, repair some lights, buy some music, and print posters, programs, and tickets. Create a budget for the show and explain how you will get the unbudgeted items.

2. Date: _____

   What traits would you seek in the actor for a lead role if you were the director of an expensive play? Would it be different for an inexpensive show?

3. Date: _____

   There has been a long-standing debate over the amount of money spent on athletics versus fine arts (band, drama, choir, speech, art, dance) in education. Explain your position on the subject as though you were a school board member.

4. Date: _____

   Many directors host design competitions among the students at their schools to create the art for their posters. Others design their own, use what's provided by the publisher, or hire a professional. Which do you think is best and why?

131

BELL WORK 2

The more a director or a producer has invested in the show, the more likely they are to seek out a very disciplined, experienced cast that won't waste time or put the production at risk. Tardiness leaves the rest of the cast waiting, a bad attitude can be contagious or affect morale, and laziness means everyone else must do that much more to complete the job. Directors look for actors with proven track records. If they have been in several successful plays, they probably have what it takes. Directors seek cast members who come to auditions completely prepared and willing to take direction. Another important trait is enthusiasm. An actor who energetically and eagerly attacks their work will probably be much more team-oriented than one who has an "I don't care" attitude. Finally, appearance becomes important at a certain level. Actors must fit the body, style, age, and general appeal of the character.

BELL WORK 1

Directors, cast, and crew can network with fellow teachers, friends, parents, and neighbors to collect items to produce shows, saving precious budget dollars to purchase those items you could not borrow. You—or better yet, your students and/or their parents—can also make items. Some casts minimize their costume needs by adopting a fun and easy uniform for their costume, like overalls with different shirt colors that cast members can purchase themselves, and then each character wears one item—such as a cowboy hat for the sheriff or an apron for the grandma—to suggest characterization. Props can also be representational rather than realistic and can be easy to make. For instance, use foam board to cut out an antique clock, then paint it and put movable hands on it for an easy set piece. Another option is to update your play to more modern times when it won't change the playwright's intent, so that students can wear their own clothes instead of costumes.

INTRODUCTION TO THEATRE ARTS I

NAME _____ PERIOD _____ DATE _____

DAILY BELL WORK - FINANCE AND PUBLICITY

Answer each question as your teacher assigns it, using the space provided. Be sure to include the date.

5. Date: _____

   Many schools with public address systems write "radio commercials" for upcoming plays. Some produce video commercials for in-house TV stations or YouTube. Write a "commercial" for a play at your school.

6. Date: _____

   Do students at your school attend plays? Why or why not? What could be done to improve play attendance?

7. Date: _____

   Should plays be performed as school assemblies? Explain.

8. Date: _____

   Should the publicity reflect the mood of the show? Explain.

BELL WORK 5

Does your school have a public address system? If so, who does the announcements? In many schools, the principal selects those who do announcements from some of the school's more successful students. While this is a nice reward for their hard work, it may not be as closely related to their goals as it is to those of speech and theatre students.

Ask your principal if your students can give the announcements. Not only can they read them, they can also use their writing and acting skills to turn some of the messages into mini-plays and commercials. This is a great way for them to practice what they are learning in class, it adds credibility to your program, and most likely the rest of the student body is more likely to listen to them. Work with students on their professionalism; many school employees become irritated when the announcements take too long or when they are full of errors and giggling.

Also find out if your district has its own closed-circuit TV station. If so, think of all the production possibilities there as well!

NAME _____ PERIOD _____ DATE _____

DAILY BELL WORK - POSTERS, PROGRAMS, AND MORE

Answer each question as your teacher assigns it, using the space provided. Be sure to include the date.

1. Date: _____
    What information do you think needs to appear on the poster? How might a school poster differ from a professional one and why?

2. Date: _____
    Describe "audience etiquette" for a performing arts event.

3. Date: _____
    What information do you think needs to appear in the program? How might a school program differ from a professional one and why?

4. Date: _____
    Imagine you are in a play. The director has asked you to write a paragraph about yourself for the program. What would you say?

133

BELL WORK 1

A poster advertising a middle or high school production should be kept as simple as possible. Unlike professional posters with big-name stars, schools generally avoid crediting students by name on the poster. Instead, the club or organization receives the credit as a whole. Include the club or school name, the play title, the playwright, the dates and times, the location, ticket prices, and the publisher's required statement.

Your poster must contain all the legal information required by the publisher. These requirements are usually printed in the front of the playbook. Here is an example from a play published by Pioneer Drama Service:

On all programs, printing, and advertising, the following information must appear:

*   The full title of the play or musical

*   Writing credit: Playwright, composer, and lyricist

*   Publication notice: "Produced by special arrangement with Pioneer Drama Service, Denver, Colorado"

NAME _____ PERIOD _____ DATE _____

DAILY BELL WORK - POSTERS, PROGRAMS, AND MORE

Answer each question as your teacher assigns it, using the space provided. Be sure to include the date.

5. Date: _____

   The program, poster, and other advertisements are generally created in the same color scheme as the costumes and set. Why is this important?

6. Date: _____

   Create a time line for the poster, program, tickets, and other publicity for a show that has eight weeks of rehearsal. Remember to include time for design, approval, mailing, printing, and distribution.

7. Date: _____

   _____

   _____

8. Date: _____

   _____

   _____

NOTES: _____

_____

_____

_____

_____

_____

_____

_____

PUBLICITY

Publicity is one of the most challenging jobs in theatre. Those helping with publicity for a show have to make sure that the public knows about the performance and that it sounds appealing. Of course, there is no exact formula for getting people to attend, since every school and community is unique.

In small communities where everyone knows everyone else, school-sponsored events may actually be the town's entertainment. Even if not involved with the school, friends and neighbors attend to support the young people involved. In large communities, however, the climate is completely different. Movie theatres and other venues compete with school shows for their audience. The best way to increase attendance is to plan well in advance and to publicize.

In planning your publicity for your show, consider the following:

Dates: Plan around other community events. Do not try to compete with popular sporting events, holidays, or professional theatre.

Price: Check with other entertainment venues in the area to see what they charge, not only for admission, but also for drinks and snacks. Price your tickets and concessions accordingly. If you have a large auditorium, consider giving complimentary tickets to local charities, community leaders, radio stations, newspapers, and your school faculty and administration to create a buzz and level of excitement in town. Besides, people who receive tickets usually bring another person who has to buy a ticket.

Show Selection: The single biggest determinant of your audience size is the cast size of your show, since most of your audience will be comprised of the family and friends of cast members. Choose a large cast show, or if doing a smaller cast show, how can you involve other students? Can you coordinate with the school art department to have an art exhibit in the lobby? Can a group of band or choir students provide pre-show and intermission entertainment? How else can you get more students involved the night of your production without being part of the production itself?

It's also important to choose a show that your community will want to see. Do not produce shows that have been seen recently at other area theatres or whose theme or topic go against the grain of the potential audience. For instance, if you live in a conservative area, *Laramie Project* or *Avenue Q* are not likely to be well-attended. Family-friendly shows don't have to be childish, and they will always bring you the largest audiences since entire families can come.

Form a Publicity Committee: Solicit help from the parent booster club, the drama club, other parents and students, and even other teachers. Can they promote it in their classes? Maybe offer extra credit to students who attend?

Publicize: Leave no stone unturned in your quest for free advertising. Your fellow classmates will make an excellent resource. Start early and get their advice on how to publicize your show.

What are some creative ways to publicize your show for free?

_____

_____

_____

What are some things you can do to increase audience attendance?

_____

_____

_____

135

CREATIVE PUBLICITY IDEAS

Besides posters, there are many other creative ways to bring audience members to your shows. Conventional methods like purchasing ad space in a paper and airtime on the radio are expensive. However, the rewards are generally even greater. There are some less conventional methods too.

- Postcards are fairly inexpensive to print and the postage is reasonable. Print enough cards to send ten or more home with each cast member. They should have the same information as the poster or maybe a fun rehearsal photo. Instruct students to personalize the cards with a short message inviting the recipient to come to their show, address them, and either mail or hand deliver to ten friends or businesses. Parents can pass them out to co-workers, and a stack placed at the cash register of local businesses will catch the eyes of community members as they make purchases. Use left-over cards to send post-show thank-you notes and greetings.

- In addition to advertising your show yourself, become familiar and friendly with your local media. Personalize a note to the staff writer who handles entertainment, announcing your cast and performance dates. Remember to send a thank-you note each time they mention your program. Send a family-pack of free tickets and maybe even leave a gift bag in the seats

LOCAL MEDIA

Of course you will publicize your upcoming show heavily on social media and your school and community's websites. But some people ignore all the advertisements they see online. That is why it is important to diversify your publicity to reach out to your community in a wide variety of ways. Consider these "old school" approaches in the chart below. They can still be very effective! Just make sure you leave yourself plenty of time as many of these will have deadlines several weeks in advance.

Name of Media	Contact	Phone Number	Email Address	Website
School Paper				
Local Paper				
School District Newsletter				
PTA Newsletter				
Local Radio Station				
Public Access TV				
Corporate Sponsors				
Other				

reserved for them. Ask them to be the guest of honor at your end-of-the-year banquet, then ask if they will speak to your classes about how drama prepared them for a career in writing. If this seems like a lot, ask a parent to manage the public relations, but try to personalize your contacts whenever possible. Journalists have the tools to boost a fledgling program to great heights, and they need to be honored.

- Word of mouth and social media are other wonderful and free means of spreading the word. Ask students to encourage their friends to attend the performance.

- Believe it or not, the bathrooms are a great way to win patrons over to the idea of attending the

theatre. School toilets tend to get a bad rap, often for good reason. Adopt the restrooms nearest the theatre. Paint them fun colors (a great job for the technical theatre classes), and keep extra paint for occasional clean-ups and cover-ups. Negotiate the purchase of soft toilet paper and bars of soap that you keep well-stocked. Your bathroom will be the most popular in the school!

Now that you have a captive audience, advertise! When someone is using a stall, the backside of the door has their attention. What better place to advertise shows, club meeting dates, and more? You might even be able to convince your school board to allow you to rent the space to area businesses as a means of raising money for your club when you are

NAME _____ PERIOD _____ DATE _____

CREATIVE PUBLICITY

There are hundreds of ways to publicize in your community. Here are some creative ideas with space for notes plus space at the bottom to add your own ideas.

- Check with the elementary schools. Many send weekly packets home with the children. You may be able to reach a lot of parents and young audience members this way. Remember to use this method only when the show is appropriate for young audiences.

- Hang posters in places where people have time to read them. For example, rather than placing posters near store entrances and exits, ask permission to tape them to the counter at the checkout. The insides of restroom stall doors are also ideal (many businesses rent this space to advertisers). You might also try putting posters on the floor (use clear contact paper instead of tape), or on the ceiling at the dentist office. Remember, always ask permission.

- Ask the local restaurants if you can tape flyers to takeout orders or ask if you can stuff them in the bags at the market. Make bookmarks for the public and school libraries advertising your show. Where are some other places you can employ this type of advertising?

- Ask your friends and family to change the messages on their answering machines and voice mail to advertise the show.

- Offer to exchange ads with fellow schools or local theatres. You will advertise their show in your program, and they will run an ad for yours in their program.

- Other Ideas:

137

not promoting your own shows. What are some other ways to benefit from the idea of space adoption?

- Consider purchasing a vinyl banner from a copy or sign shop. Because these are a little costly and completely recyclable, you may want to keep the message generic, such as "Theatre Show This Week." If you have an artistic group of students, purchase a blank banner and have them paint a large version of your poster on it. Like the posters, you will want to display it about a week or two before the show, so get them started early. Your maintenance crew at school can hang the banner from the roof of the school; it is a big way to advertise your show.

- If the banner is not an option, how about staked signs like real estate agents use? These can also be purchased from sign and copy shops, but at a fraction of the cost of the banner. They can also be generic or customized, and they can be placed just about anywhere. How many neighborhoods would you reach if each cast member put one in their front yard?

- About a week to a week and a half before your opening, you will want to submit a news release to all area media. It should be neatly typed in a normal, easy-to-read font. Include a cover letter, personalized if possible. This would also be a good time to invite the arts editor to have someone come take pictures and do a story on your

INTRODUCTION TO THEATRE ARTS I

NEWS RELEASE FORM

Name of School: _____

Name of Director(s): _____

Title: _____

Playwright: _____

Presented By: _____

Dates and Times: _____

Location: _____

Reserved Tickets? Y   N   Phone: _____

Web Page: _____ Email: _____

Ticket Prices: Adult _____ Children _____ Students _____ Seniors _____

Synopsis or Description of Entertainment:

_____

_____

_____

_____

Event Sponsors:

_____

_____

_____

Other Information:

show. In smaller towns, this is common practice. However, in larger towns and cities, you may have a hard time getting your story ahead of the community theatres and professional companies. If the paper prints your release, follow up with a thank-you note and two complimentary tickets.

- Make commercials advertising your play and publish them to social media. Your school probably has a video production class that would love to help you with this!

- If possible, take a "living commercial" around to perform a scene in various public spaces. Select a two- or three- minute scene with a portable-sized group of actors and plan a way to transport them to busy locations, like a shopping mall, a grocery store, or another performance venue (such as a community or professional theatre). Of course, you will need to clear it with the venue first! Hand out fliers and sell tickets after your commercial.

- Do not forget your most immediate and perhaps most valuable resource when publicizing your show: the faculty, administration, and staff at your school. Provide them each with a single free ticket that says "Staff" so that they do not pass it on to friends or neighbors. Distribute these free tickets along with a cast and crew list so that they can identify which of their students are involved.

CHAPTER 6 — PUBLICITY AND OTHER PRODUCTION BUSINESS

PUBLICITY CHECKLIST

Name of Show: _____ Dates: _____

Publicity Chairperson: _____

Publicity Committee: _____

DUTY	ASSIGNED TO	DEADLINE	COMPLETED?
Announce cast on school PA			
Submit news releases to school papers			
Design program			
Acquire student biographies for program			
Get ads for program			
Print program			
Design poster			
Print posters			
Distribute posters			
Design and print tickets			
Design flier			
Print fliers			
Distribute fliers			
Invite newspapers to rehearsal			
Submit news releases to papers			
Submit news releases to radio			
Make school PA announcement			
Make picture collage for lobby			
Invite administration/board			

139

By passing out these free tickets, not only are you thanking the staff for supporting your theatre program, you are also helping to add to your house numbers. In some places this may not be an issue, but most theatres seat far more people than can be expected at a show, and it's always more fun to play to a full house than a half empty one. In many cases, these individuals will bring along paying family members, and if they like what they see, they will spread the word, which is the best advertising!

DESIGNING YOUR POSTER

Designing your show poster can be a great deal of fun, and the finished products make excellent souvenirs for the cast and crew. This worksheet will help you to design and print your show's poster and can also be used for project posters in class.

Decide on a budget for the posters:

$_____

POSTER CONTENT

Show:_____

Playwright(s): _____

Presented by: _____

Dates: _____ Times:_____

Location:_____

Address:_____

Ticket Prices: Adults_____ Children_____ Students_____ Seniors_____

*How will you credit the publisher (see script):_____

POSTER DESIGN

Who will design the posters?_____

What size will they be?_____

How many colors? Bleed or no bleed?_____

When is the deadline for completing the design?_____

COMPLETING THE PROJECT

How many posters will be printed?_____

Who will print them?_____

When is the deadline for getting them printed?_____

When does the printer need the art to meet the deadline?_____

Who will pick them up from the printer?_____

*Crediting the publisher is a legal and contractual requirement in most cases and is generally specified on the copyright page of the script.

POSTERS

Posters can be an effective form of advertising, especially if they are unique. Try unusual shapes or sizes, like horizontal instead of vertical, or a round poster. The posters should be attractive and well-placed. For some of your shows, a simple 8½x 11" poster printed on the school's color copy machine will suffice. If that will not work, fairly inexpensive posters can be ordered from most local print shops, or if time permits, online. Using black print on colored paper is another inexpensive option. On the other hand, there are some ways, especially with modern technology and a little ingenuity, that you can have handsome, full-color posters for every show without a lot of expense.

- First and foremost, check with the publisher of your play. Are you required to use the trademarked title art or are you allowed to design your own? (For instance, if you're producing *Annie*, many of the poster design elements are already set in stone, whereas publishers such as Pioneer Drama Service encourage you to design your own artwork.) Is color required or is black print on color paper an option? Does the publisher sell posters at a reasonable cost? Or, do they sell a graphics or logo package that includes the title art?

- How many posters do you need? Most color ink cartridges cost about $30; a ream of 500 sheets

NAME _____ PERIOD _____ DATE _____

Create a rough draft of your poster here. Use the space on the side to provide notes about colors, size, etc. Your finished product should be properly scaled and neatly finished.

of heavy pastel paper is only about $10 and will last all year. For $40 you can print very nice full-color posters for your shows.

- Another idea that works wonderfully for children's shows, holiday shows, or any time a child's touch could add to your posters is to print simple black-and-white posters as if they were pages from a coloring book. They should be "black line masters" but should still have all of the necessary information. Ask some primary teachers to have their students color them and return them with the teacher's name/grade, school name, and student's name on the back. Besides being used to publicize your show, it can increase your ticket sales, especially if your cast and crew vote on their favorites and display them at the show in the theatre lobby. You could even use the grand-prize winner on the covers of your programs. Be sure to congratulate the student in the program itself, and thank the winner as well as the teachers who help you with free tickets.

- The posters that won't be posted in the theatre lobby can be hung throughout town to advertise your show. We all love to stop and admire a child's artwork, and the community will appreciate that you involved their youngest artists in the production of your show.

DESIGNING YOUR PROGRAM

The best way to start designing your program is to have a few samples in hand. Many libraries keep programs from both local and Broadway shows in their archives. You may also be able to request these from your cast members who have recently attended shows. Keep in mind that there are professionals who will design your program for you should you choose.

Again, you will need to start with a budget. You may choose to keep your program simple or sell advertisements and make the program a great souvenir and moneymaker. If you have excellent parental support and assistance, you might choose the latter. However, if you find your group completing most tasks without assistance, you may be better off doing a simple, one-page program.

In general, the program should use the same art and same basic color scheme as the posters. Both posters and programs and any additional advertising materials should strive to convey the tone and mood of the show. For example, if your show is a lively, upbeat musical about love in the springtime, your posters, programs, and other publicity should reflect that with bright and lively colors and a whimsical design. On the other hand, a show about political oppression, lack of freedom, and lack of individual expression might employ the use of drab colors, shadowy figures, and a stark, jagged design.

The cover of your program should include your show's logo/title art (check with the publisher if you are required to use their copyrighted art, and if not, if you have permission to use it), who is presenting the program, and the dates, times, and location. Be original when designing your program, especially the cover. Try using a different fold so that the booklet is long and skinny or has an overlap. You may even choose to use a single, unfolded sheet of card stock for your program. This can be very elegant when the information is minimal.

The cast and crew are listed inside. The cast will be listed first with the character name to the left and the actor portraying the character to the right. These are generally listed in order of appearance and can usually be taken from the cast list in the script, which is usually listed the same way. Nonprofit and school shows generally list the crew under the cast in the following order: director, assistant director, stage manager, lights, sound, set, props, costumes, and makeup. Non-performance crew would be listed next, including publicity, ticket sales, house manager, ushers, etc. Like your posters, your program also needs to include the legal "Produced by special arrangement with…" statement that the show's publisher requires.

Some directors like to include a short synopsis of the play for their audience. You may also find it helpful to identify the locations and approximate dates or times of each scene. If your show is a musical, your audience will appreciate a list of musical numbers and who will perform them.

Other items you may wish to include in your program:

- A thank-you section for people and businesses who donated time, money, or supplies
- Pictures and bios of the students in the cast and crew, based on their completed *Biography Worksheet*
- Advertisements
- Pictures of rehearsals
- Advertisements for upcoming shows
- A reminder to turn off cell phones, not to take flash photography, and to tend to crying babies and children in the lobby
- A letter from the director or maybe the department head, principal, or superintendent
- An autograph page

- Finally, a great way to spruce up the color scheme of your poster and your program cover is to use a heavy and brightly colored paper with black ink. You can even stagger two pages together to draw attention to the poster. For example, if your poster is yellow, set it on top of a sheet of blank orange paper the same size, and offset it a bit. The orange will give the yellow poster a shadow effect.

THE PROGRAM

Once you get your audience to the show, you will want to continue to impress them. The program is the one item they will hang on to for the entire time they are at the show, and many will take it home.

You do not have to create your program yourself. Have a parent take on the project or find a copy shop to set it up for you. Take into consideration the first impression it will make. Our first instinct is to take a standard size sheet or two of paper and fold it in half to make an 8½" x 5½" program. This is fine, but is it the best you can do? Here are some options for making your program unique:

1. Fold it to open from top to bottom instead of from the side.

2. Try a different fold to make a long, skinny program.

3. Use a different sized sheet of paper.

BIOGRAPHY WORKSHEET

Complete this form and return it to _____

by _____ for your bio in the program.

Name *(as you want it to appear in the program)*:

_____

Character(s): _____

Crew(s): _____

Number of years in drama: _____ Drama club member: ☐ Yes   ☐ No

Clubs and offices held: _____

_____

_____

Other activities: _____

_____

_____

Out of school activities:_____

_____

_____

Previous roles in plays: _____

Plans for the future: _____

_____

_____

Special thanks *(remember those who lent you props, etc.)*:

_____

_____

_____

_____

143

4. Only fold the paper part way, leaving a flap. Use the flap for the play title or your school's motto.

5. Use shaped paper or colorful, pre-printed paper (clouds, parchment, crayons).

6. Mimic the title or theme of the show in the program. For example, if you are doing a show about the Old West, use a "wanted" poster type of program. If the show is about a restaurant, make your program like a menu.

7. Get creative with punches and die cutters. If you are producing *Arsenic and Old Lace*, buy a lace corner punch and give your program a lacy finish. If you are producing *1984*, use a die cutter to remove a large "1984" from colored card stock.

Print your program on white paper, and fold both so that the white shows through.

Your program should include the play title, the playwright(s), a cast list, a crew list, a synopsis of scenes indicating the time and place for each, and the required information from the publisher. Other optional items may include a list of "special thanks" to those who contributed to the show, student pictures and bios, a note about the production, advertisements (don't forget to advertise your upcoming shows!), rehearsal pictures, and a synopsis of the play. Programs for musicals should also list the musical numbers, the pit band members, and the dancers, if applicable.

DESIGNING FLIERS, TICKETS, AND MORE

FLIERS

Consider creating fliers that can either be sent home with students at all grade levels or distributed to area businesses. These can be designed using the same art as the poster and can even be miniature versions of the poster. However, because these will be mass produced, they should be printed as inexpensively as possible. You may want to have them printed two or four to a page, then cut them for distribution. Consider printing the backside in Spanish or another language common in your area. You may want to include a discount coupon so that people have a greater reason not to discard the flier.

Come up with creative ways to distribute the fliers (see the *Creative Publicity* worksheet earlier in this chapter for ideas). They should start circulating about one to two weeks prior to opening night.

TICKETS

There are two big decisions to make regarding tickets. First, will there be reserved seating or general admission? Then, will you handle ticket sales in-house or sign up with an online ticketing agency that works with schools? There are more and more of these companies every year, and you might find that

the ease and convenience of letting someone else handle ticketing is worth the small fee, especially if your school will be doing multiple performances.

If you are not using an outside company, then you'll need to design the tickets, and, if using reserved seating, figure out if you're writing the seat assignment on each ticket by hand or getting them professionally printed. Either way, the tickets should include the show title, who is presenting the performance, the date and time of the performance that ticket is for, the price of the ticket, and if it's a special category, such as student, child, or senior. You might consider utilizing different colored tickets to distinguish between performances or categories. Two samples are below.

Try adding your own personal flare by cutting the tickets in an unusual shape rather than the typically shaped tickets below. For example, use a die-cutting device to make butterfly-shaped tickets for *Butterflies Are Free* or pine trees for *The Best Christmas Pageant Ever*.

Smallville High School presents

ĦAMLET

By William Shakespeare
April 30, 2020 • 7:30 pm

Sec 2   Row D   Seat 6

ADMIT ONE $10

Smallville High School presents

ĦAMLET

By William Shakespeare
April 25, 26, 27, 28 • 7:30 pm

$6 - Student
General Admission

ADMIT ONE

NOTES: _____

_____

_____

_____

_____

_____

_____

_____

T-SHIRTS

Show t-shirts are like walking billboards advertising your upcoming production if you can get them a few weeks in advance and determine some days that everyone in the cast and crew will wear their shirts. They also make wonderful keepsakes after the show, especially if you print the production dates on the shirts.

Of course, the design on the shirts should tie in with the posters and program. You might be able to order shirts through the play publisher, and some even let you choose the color of your shirt and the color of your ink. Alternatively, if using the publisher's title art, you might be able to purchase a graphics package from them, then have the shirts printed at a local screen printer. Either way, it takes time to gather everyone's size preference, collect their money, and then actually get the shirts from the screen company. Start this process at least two months before opening night, especially if you want your shirts a few weeks in advance to help with advertising. And don't forget to consider parent volunteers, the school principal, and others who might appreciate a shirt!

VIDEO

It's fun to have your parents, the video production class at your school, or a professional company record your performance. However, first you have to find out from the publisher of the play if this is allowed. Some don't allow it, and the ones that do generally require an additional fee to be paid for the video rights. Even if you're not allowed to record the actual performance, you can still create a fun keepsake video that includes rehearsals, interviews with cast members, the makeup applications, and the cast party.

If you are allowed to record your entire performance, you can reach a broader audience by posting the video on your school's website or on a site such as YouTube. That way, even relatives who live far away can watch your production. Again, it is critically important that you first check with the publisher. Many don't allow this, and the ones that do will definitely require additional royalty fees.

145

NOTES: _____

_____

_____

_____

_____

_____

_____

_____

_____

PUBLICITY PROJECTS

Project I: Poster

Select and read a play or use a play with which you are already familiar. Using the information from the plot, the playwright's notes, and your own interpretation, design a poster that communicates the mood and content of the play and publicizes a fictional performance. Your poster must contain all legal information required by the publisher, plus location and address, production dates, times, prices, etc. Write a brief description of your poster explaining all of your choices and attach it to the back of the poster along with your name.

Project 2: Program

Select and read a play or use a play with which you are already familiar. Using the information from the script, the playwright's notes, and your own interpretation, design a program. The program may be any size, and it must contain all legal information required by the publisher, the cast list, plus all pertinent dates, times, etc. Remember that the design, font, and colors should reflect the mood and content of the play. Write a brief description of your program explaining all of your choices and submit it with your completed program.

Project 3: Ticket and Flier

Select and read a play or use a play with which you are already familiar. Using the information from the script, the playwright's notes, and your own interpretation, design a ticket and a flier advertising the performance. Both may be any size and must contain all legal information required by the publisher, plus all other pertinent information. Remember that the design, font, and colors should reflect the mood and content of the play. Write a brief description of your ticket and flier explaining all of your choices and submit it with your completed project.

Project 4: News Releases

Following the format of the *News Release Form* earlier in this chapter, write three news releases for three real events at school. You will need to get the information from the most reliable sources. Events do not have to be theatre-related.

Project 5: Competitive Pricing

Find local printing costs for the following jobs for camera-ready art (no artist pricing needed). Format your findings in a creative but neat way. You must get at least three different price quotes for each item, preferably from the same companies. If you contact local companies, explain that you are doing research for a project and that your teacher may use the information you collect to purchase printing. You may also want to include online options in your research. Be sure to specify variations in paper weights.

Poster: 11" x 17", heavy white paper, full color; 100 pieces

Program: 8 1/2" x 11", one sheet white bond, full color, two-sided, folded; 500 pieces

Tickets: Eight-up on 8½ x 11" white cover stock, one-sided, full color, trimmed out, crop marks provided; 800 pieces (100 sheets)

Fliers: One sheet white bond, two-sided, full color, tri-fold, 100 pieces

T-shirts: Twenty adult large shirts, brand name 50/50 no pocket T's, single color ink printed on front only

NOTES: _____

_____

_____

_____

_____

_____

_____

_____

_____

CHAPTER 7
PLAY PRODUCTION

NAME _____ PERIOD _____ DATE _____

DAILY BELL WORK - PLAY PRODUCTION

Answer each question as your teacher assigns it, using the space provided. Be sure to include the date.

1. Date: _____

    Imagine you are doing a production of *Alice in Wonderland* for which there are many special effects. How might the director have Alice "fall through the rabbit hole" without interrupting the flow of the play?

2. Date: _____

    Directors choose a color scheme for a play based on its mood. This is used in the set, the costumes, and the lighting and is often reflected in the posters and programs too. Why is color such an important part of a production? What effect might this have on the music chosen for the play?

3. Date: _____

    Some actors do not give everything they have in rehearsal, claiming they are saving it for the show. How might this affect everyone else?

4. Date: _____

    There are many jobs to be completed prior to opening night. In most schools, every student in the drama program is expected to pitch in. What kinds of tasks do you think need to be completed and which ones would you volunteer for?

149

BELL WORK 2

Just as your play has a central theme, you will want to come up with a central color scheme. Color is usually based on the play's mood, but it can also be tied to other things like style, or the title might dictate a color scheme, as in *The Ransom of Red Chief*. Playing on the color in the title is an obvious choice, but designers might also choose to omit the color entirely from both the set and costumes. This way, the little rascal with the red hair stands out even more.

Once a color scheme is established, it is often applied to the entire production, from set to costumes and from lighting to publicity. This saturates the play and audience with the mood (such as fierceness in the above play). As for music, it is also closely tied to the color and mood. How about a heavy-handed war drum and battle cries for Red?

BELL WORK 1

Introducing special effects into your shows is a lofty task. A special effect is an illusion that makes the audience believe that they have seen or heard something that they know could not have truly happened. Some are very realistic. For example, lights and sound can be manipulated to produced thunder and lightning that sounds and looks like the real thing. Other effects are more representational and artistic, like using a red scarf tugged at the end of fishing line to make a character bleed.

In the *Alice in Wonderland* example, lights might be flickered as Alice "falls." She might distort her cry so that it sounds like someone moving farther and farther away. Another option is to project images behind her as though she is falling past them. She could arrange a series of cartwheels and flips to make it seem as though she is tumbling through a hole. Dancers running with long scarves on poles, circling around Alice can also create a dramatic effect.

NAME _____ PERIOD _____ DATE _____

DAILY BELL WORK - PLAY PRODUCTION

Answer each question as your teacher assigns it, using the space provided. Be sure to include the date.

5. Date: _____
    Many actors get nervous before a performance. What are some ways this stage fright might be lessened?

6. Date: _____
    Actors should generally avoid being seen by the audience in costume before the show. Why?

7. Date: _____
    What are some realistic unexpected dilemmas that might take place on opening night? How can they be avoided?

8. Date: _____
    What are some things parents could do to aid in the production process?

BELL WORK 7

Whether your show is full of stage combat or a lot of courtly dancing, you will want to be prepared for emergencies. You should always keep one or two first aid kits handy, especially if you have an active technical theatre program. Ask your school nurse to help you stock a full kit or purchase one of the pre-stocked kits.

You will also want to have a "first aid kit" for hurt costumes, set pieces, and props at the stage manager's station. Keep a wide variety of safety pins, a flashlight (cover the end with dark gel), scissors, both electrical and skin tape, bobby pins, note paper and pencil (you never know when you might have to send a note to the director or booth), spare batteries for all headphones and flashlights, and anything specific to your show that you have ever needed during rehearsals. For example, if you are always running to the prop table for coins for an actor who forgets his, keep a few handy.

NAME _____ PERIOD _____ DATE _____

DAILY BELL WORK - PLAY PRODUCTION

Answer each question as your teacher assigns it, using the space provided. Be sure to include the date.

9. Date: _____

    Many actors feel they reach their peak when there is a live audience. Why do you think this is?

10. Date: _____

    After the final show, most directors strike the set immediately, even if there is a cast party. Why is it important for everyone to participate in the strike?

11. Date: _____

    Many directors encourage students to mingle with the audience in costume after the show; others are strongly opposed to this. Explain which you would want and why.

12. Date: _____

    Sometimes the items people lend to the show for props get broken or lost. What are some ways to prevent this, and how should the person be compensated?

151

BELL WORK 8 AND 10

Getting parents involved in the production can help in more ways than many imagine. From the very beginning, parents can help take some of the burden off the director, allowing them to concentrate on the show. For example, one parent can be in charge of the publicity. Another parent might take care of coordinating late rehearsal meals. In many schools, parents are completely in charge of the posters, t-shirts, and programs, tasks that can otherwise take hours of a teacher's time!

Most parents will gladly volunteer their time to assist in their children's school projects. It is a great way to spend quality time together. Parents are great at building set pieces, making costumes, taking measurements, organizing the art gallery that will coincide with the show in the theatre lobby, managing ticket sales, and buying and selling concessions. After closing night, parents can pitch in to strike the set and clean dressing rooms so that everyone can go home together.

INTRODUCTION TO THEATRE ARTS I

NAME _____ PERIOD _____ DATE _____

DAILY BELL WORK - PLAY PRODUCTION

Answer each question as your teacher assigns it, using the space provided. Be sure to include the date.

13. Date: _____

_____

_____

14. Date: _____

_____

_____

15. Date: _____

_____

_____

16. Date: _____

_____

_____

NOTES: _____

_____

_____

_____

_____

_____

_____

_____

_____

WHAT MAKES A PRODUCTION?

When you attend a professional performance—a musical, for example—it is difficult to imagine everything that goes into making it a seamless, spectacular success. The actors are just one part of the production process, though we generally think of them when we hear the words "theatre professional" since they are the ones we see. There are numerous other people involved in a variety of jobs. Each individual performs specific tasks in different areas of the theatre, and only when it all comes together does a performance truly become a production.

At the top of the chain of command are the producers and the director. The producers are mainly concerned with the financial aspects of the show. They decide which shows will make the most money, and then they hire the best people for the job of making sure the money comes in and keeps coming in. Depending on the size of the show, there may be many different producers. In educational theatre, the producer is the theatre teacher's supervisor, principal, or other member of the administrative team responsible for budgets. Not only do they oversee the budget, they also often have final say on which show is produced.

The producers hire the director and sometimes the assistant directors. Because directors and their assistants work so closely together, many are hired as a package deal. The director is the artistic leader of the show and is most concerned with making the show work from an artistic point of view. However, sometimes "art" does not draw audiences, so the director and producers may have a "tug of war" over the final look of the show until they have reached a conclusion that satisfies both of them. In educational theatre, the director is almost always the theatre teacher and/or the choir director for musicals.

The technical director is in charge of the lights, sound, set, props, and maybe even the makeup and costumes. This person hires or assigns a crew chief to each of these areas, and they, in turn, hire teams to work with them. The show's director gives ideas to the technical director, who then creates plans on paper or using models, presents them to the director, and then makes changes to suit the overall goals of the production. Then the teams finalize the technical work, with the technical director making sure that deadlines are met and that the jobs are done to the director's satisfaction. Technical work can be very difficult, especially in settings such as public schools where actors and the tech teams share space. Often the set is built on weekends or late evenings so that rehearsals are not interrupted.

In educational theatre, the technical director is usually a teacher or a properly skilled parent. If your school is lucky enough to have a technical theatre teacher, they will likely serve as tech director on all plays. Many schools have active shop programs, full of students who enjoy the technical aspect of productions. This is great training to become a roadie for musicians, who need the same basic skills.

The stage manager is in charge of the backstage area during both rehearsals and performances. This person coordinates all of the jobs and serves as an information center. Using headsets, they receive cues and relay them to the crews, solve problems as they arise, and ensure that everything runs smoothly behind the curtain. The stage manager is often the one person who knows every aspect of the performance. For that reason, in educational theatre, it is usually a very responsible student or parent. If your program has two theatre teachers, one will often fill in as both tech director and stage manager, since the two jobs

153

HANDLING DISASTERS

If you have produced even one play, you know that the weeks prior to opening night can be very chaotic, especially if your students are younger, dependent, or inexperienced. Prepare them early in the rehearsal process to work through dilemmas without your help; when they ask for your help, ignore the desire to fix it quickly, and instead, tell them they need to figure it out on their own. When they do come up with a solution, compliment their efforts even if not the best and avoid comments like "You should've come to get me." or "That's not how I would have handled it." It takes more time early on, but having students solve their own problems creates an atmosphere of independence and gives them confidence.

Whatever the situation, do not panic and do not allow the students to become upset. Focus on the solution, not the problem, and your cast and crew will follow suit. Remind them that the only time they are allowed to panic—and should immediately come get you—is if someone is ill or hurt or if there is danger.

Tell them that you will expect the same on opening night. If there were one hundred adults standing around backstage waiting to handle disasters, each and every one of them would be busy at every moment. But if you tell your cast and crew that they may not ask an adult for help unless they have first attempted to fix the problem themselves, they will find a way to handle it on their own. The truth is, we are closely related and one is mainly before the production while the other is only during the production.

The house manager ensures that audience members are comfortable and have their needs met from the moment they arrive for a performance. The "house" includes where the audience enters, where they purchase tickets, buy concessions, use the restroom, and sit to see the show, and the house manager is in charge of all these areas. This means they're also responsible for post-performance cleanup.

In educational theatre, this is generally a job best performed by a teacher who has access to the school's Wi-Fi, general hallway lighting, supplies, keys, and so on. Plus, because concessions and/or ticket sales involves money being handled, schools sometimes require teacher oversight anyway.

When you attend a performance and are unaware of any shortcomings, it is because all members of the production staff worked together to make the show a success.

CREATING MOOD

The director reads the play carefully many times before auditions in order to have an idea as to how each role should look and sound. Once the cast is selected and rehearsals begin, the director's mental images solidify as the play comes to life. The performance should also convey a certain mood to the audience. The actors will do their part to create mood with their acting styles and characterizations, but it will also need to be evident in the lighting, sound, costumes, props, set, and even publicity.

Imagine a traditional play based on the story of Count Dracula. Now imagine Dracula's costume. It is probably mostly black with a cape. Now imagine his home. You are probably seeing images of a dark, dank castle with gray walls, dark corners, and grotesquely ornate furniture.

Color is one of the most obvious ways to create mood. Long before psychologists began studying color, society had already begun assigning meanings. For example, white became symbolic of purity, while red was associated with debauchery. Purple became the color of royalty, and brown was symbolic of simplicity. From a theatrical point of view, it is important to establish a color scheme for a play early in the production process so that it can be implemented throughout. A scheme is a selection of several colors that can be used throughout a play to support the message without overpowering it.

Another way to create mood is to manipulate visual lines. Soft, rounded lines come across

as lighthearted, while jagged, edgy lines are perceived as harsh. Repetitive patterns are comfortable, but random, busy patterns are considered chaotic. A set designer can draw the audience's attention to a central place in a room simply by having all lines converge on that spot. Having doorways lean to the side and creating larger-than-life props can signal to the audience that a scene takes place in a dream.

Lighting and sound allow modern technology to play a role in the creation of mood, as does the introduction of special effects, such as fog and smoke machines. Lights can be colored with special sheets of thin plastic called gels. Gels come in thousands of colors, and, combined with special sheets of texture, they wash the set in moonlight, create the appearance of a crackling fire, or create a beautiful sunset. Imagine that sunset. What else does it need? How about the sound of crickets in the distance or a howling coyote, or maybe the sound of a twig snapping under a heavy boot? Add the sound and flash of gunfire, and suddenly the audience is in the middle of an Old West gunfight.

The idea of color and line creating mood can also be used in the selection of costumes and props, in the design and application of stage makeup, and in the publicity. Although color and line will effectively create the tone the director wants, it will lack dimension without texture to further support the director's vision. A polished, glossy finish such as glass, high-gloss paints, or

CONTINUED ON PAGE 156

---

do not teach our children anything by doing for them what they can do on their own. You will have plenty to keep you busy on opening night without worrying about things your students can do for themselves.

PRODUCTION TASK LISTS

Avoid unexpected trouble by planning ahead with production task lists. These are detailed job descriptions that let each crew chief know exactly what they need to do before the show. This is especially important to you, the director, because any discrepancies between what should be done and what gets done will eventually become your business if students cannot handle it. There are no pre-written task lists, because each will differ from show to

show and from theatre to theatre. Wealthy theatre companies can afford a makeup crew chief and several assistants. Community theatres generally require actors to do their own makeup, because there is no room in the budget to hire professionals.

Require each crew chief to type a task list about three weeks before your opening. The lists should include everything they do, even if they think the item is trivial. Remind them that one or two forgotten "trivial" items can add up to disaster. Their list should also include their support crew and each specific job in detail.

After you collect these, have your stage manager create a master list with each person's tasks on a separate page. They will print enough copies of the

NAME _____ PERIOD _____ DATE _____

THE PRODUCTION STAFF

There are many people involved in making any play a success. As a matter of fact, when you see a play, you are only seeing a small percentage of the production staff. Read the job duties at the right and match them with the job descriptions to the left.

Producer - the highest authority in a play. Hires the director and often the director's staff. Also in charge of all the finances.

_____

Director - the artistic mind of the show and the boss. Directs the actors, helping them to become the best they can be. Also advises the technical director.

_____

Assistant Director - bridges the gap between the director and the cast and crew, especially when things get busy. Fills in any time the director is needed in two places at the same time. In school productions, usually the prompter too.

_____

Prompter - the person whose main responsibility is to follow along in the script and give the actors their lines or stage directions when they need them. Also helps keep the director informed of where the actors are or need to be in the script.

_____

Technical Director - in charge of all the technical crew members. Often works together with the director to design the set, lights, and sound if there aren't designers to do so. Makes sure that all technical aspects of the show please the director.

_____

Stage Manager - in charge of the backstage area during rehearsals and performances. Has a script with all the cues and often makes cue sheets for the curtain, scenery changes, props, and even lights and sound. Makes sure that costume changes go smoothly. Prepares for any kind of backstage emergency.

_____

Crew Chiefs - the people in charge of the individual crews. Specialists in their field, such as props, costumes, makeup, set, lights, or sound. Answer to the technical director. May have crew members working with them.

_____

Grips - the backstage crew who fly scenery in and out.

_____

Publicity Manager - promotes the show. Responsible for designing and printing posters and programs, sending out news releases, arranging all advertising.

_____

House Manager - in charge of the "house"—areas where the audience enters, buys their tickets, takes refreshment, uses the restrooms, and sits to watch the show. Makes sure everything is clean, properly stocked, and comfortable. Crew members include ticket sellers, ushers, concessionaires, and even custodians.

_____

If the show is a musical, a **Choreographer** will be in charge of the dance numbers and a **Musical Director** will coordinate the musical numbers.

_____

Match the situation to the production staff member who is best suited to handle the situation (not the person who would tell someone to handle it).

1. An actor forgets a line and needs help.
2. Some of the actors are being loud backstage during a rehearsal.
3. The wig bill is due.
4. An actor needs to be more emotional during a certain scene.
5. The director is sick and cannot attend rehearsal.
6. The stage manager cues a set piece.
7. A costume change is taking too long and the director wants it to run more smoothly.
8. The director is not happy with the way the lights looked in the last scene.
9. It is time to have the posters printed and hung throughout town.
10. One of the chorus members sprained her ankle, and a new girl must be trained in the songs and dances.
11. It is opening night and there are no paper towels in the lobby restrooms.
12. A prop is broken during rehearsal.
13. One of the actors cut his hand during the show and needs a small bandage before he returns to the stage.
14. The technical director has asked that a sound effect be sooner.
15. The director has quit and a new one must be hired.
16. An actor is saying the name of a city wrong.
17. The director needs a design for a small set piece but it is too late to hire a designer.
18. An actress needs an additional costume for the production.
19. A new usher is arriving late for every show.
20. The director thinks one of the actors might be saying a line wrong.
21. There is a production meeting at the same time as a rehearsal; the director must attend the rehearsal.

THE PRODUCTION STAFF KEY

Producer: 3, 15

Director: 4, 16

Assistant Director: 5, 21

Prompter: 1, 20

Tech. Director: 8, 17

Stage Manager: 2, 7, 13

Crew Chiefs: 12, 14, 18

Grips: 6

Publicity Manager: 9

House Manager: 11, 19

Choreographer: 10

155

master document so that each member of the crew will have one, including you and your assistants. In the event that any member of the crew is late or cannot make a performance, no one will have to guess what they were supposed to do; it will be clearly documented. Furthermore, each crew member will know without a doubt what is expected of them.

In the last couple of weeks of rehearsal, you will find yourself assigning little jobs here and there. Be sure that these make it onto the master task list. This should be reprinted and redistributed prior to opening night. After the show, file the master task list away for future use. It may be able to serve as a model for the next show or to introduce students to positions with which they are unfamiliar.

On the next several pages are some highly abbreviated task lists. These will give you a very basic idea as to what you should seek in your students' lists, but theirs should have much more detail.

House Manager

The house manager has an easy job most of the way through unless they are also in charge of ticket pre-sales. Opening night, however, is another story. First, they should make sure that the general maintenance of the house is suitable for a crowd. This includes ensuring that the accessible ramps, entrances, elevator, and lift are usable, restrooms are in good order, the ticket booth is ready and well-stocked, and that the heat or air conditioning will be turned on and working well enough for the expected shiny wood may convey a feeling of cleanliness, while a sandy, uneven, and smudged texture brings to mind filth. Which of the three textures below would you use if you were designing the set for a staged performance of The Grapes of Wrath? If you said C, the straw pattern, you think like a set designer! This texture is most likely to bring to mind images of farm life and drought.

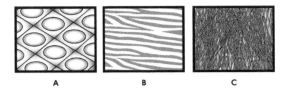

A   B   C

APPLYING STAGE MAKEUP

Stage makeup has several purposes. First, it helps to establish a character, such as adding age or a crooked nose. Also, it helps to define the actors' features so that the audience can see them and make out even subtle facial expressions. Finally, stage makeup can be corrective, evening the skin tone and making it look right under stage lights.

With just a basic knowledge of makeup application, you can supplement your knowledge with a good class, plenty of hands-on experience, plus books, videos, and online tutorials. Most students use the stage makeup provided by their school rather than less expensive street makeup. Theatrical makeup is more expensive, but the coverage is better and it is designed specifically for the stage. No matter the source of the makeup, each student should start by creating their own makeup kit.

Because your kit must move from home to stage and back again, it is important that it is mobile. Tackle boxes make great cases. They are sturdy and they have a convenient handle and several compartments. In the box on page 158 is a list of some items found in a typical student makeup kit.

Always start with a clean face. If you have never worn stage makeup before, do not wait until dress rehearsal to practice. Become familiar with putting on your own makeup long before you must do it with frayed nerves. Not only will you get the needed practice, but you will get to take inventory of your makeup kit, make any necessary purchases, and see how your skin reacts to the makeup.

After your face is clean, apply the foundation using a clean sponge. You will know when your foundation is done right when the entire face and neck are covered thoroughly and evenly and when all excess makeup is blended in. Cover even the lips and around the eyes.

Follow the foundation with facial powder with either a brush or a powder puff. This will set the foundation and give additional coverage.

Next, you will want to define your features. Of course, this will vary depending on your skin tone, your gender, and your character. However, a good rule of thumb is to highlight your existing features without making them appear fake. You will want to use shadow on your eyes, blush on your cheeks, and liner on your brows, eyes, and lips. Fill in your lips with a color that complements your skin tone and fits your character. If you have not yet powdered, do so now. This will tone down some of your

Stage Makeup
Do's and Don'ts

- Learn to apply your own make-up.
- Avoid sharing makeup, and never share mascara.
- Do not use makeup that causes severe skin reactions.
- Be ready to make changes to your application. What looks great in the dressing room may not look right under the stage lights.

CONTINUED ON PAGE 158

number of guests. If your house manager is a student, they may not realize that the temperature that keeps twenty people cool will not be comfortable for two hundred people, especially once the stage lights are on. The house manager instructs the ushers and ticket takers how to do their jobs and makes sure that whoever is passing out programs knows where to get more if needed. If the house manager is also in charge of the box office and concessions area, they must make sure there is enough change for the night. Remember, if your tickets are $6, you will frequently be giving back four singles as change. Be prepared with enough one-dollar bills to handle the demand.

If your production will be accepting credit cards, ensure your school's Wi-Fi remains on through the end of your show. Make sure your house crew knows the Wi-Fi password and the passwords to your devices. Finally, instruct them on how to use the credit card app or software.

Stage Manager

The stage manager should always arrive prior to call time, should have a copy of everyone's task list, and should make sure that each worker backstage is doing their job, including the fly loft, catwalk, props, and booth workers. The stage manager may also be in charge of the makeup and costume crews. The stage manager acts as liaison between all crews and actors and the director and assistant. During the show, they will give cues, handle emergencies, and may serve as prompter.

NAME _____ PERIOD _____ DATE _____

CREATING MOOD PRACTICE

Choose one item from each box and write your choice on the line below the boxes. Once you have finished your selections, create the color, line, and texture schemes to complete the mood for your fictional play.

My play is about...
- a boy and a girl who fall in love but their love is forbidden.
- an evil landlord who is trying to collect on a debt by forcing a young widow to marry him.
- a deaf girl trying to overcome the odds to become a doctor.

It is set in...
- New York City in the wintertime during the Depression.
- the Old West.
- modern day Mexico in a beautiful village rich in heritage and with a bountiful crop.

The ending is...
- a happy one.
- a sad one.
- tragic.

My play is about _____
_____ .

It is set in _____ . **The ending is** _____ .

Choose three colors that will be dominant in your color scheme. You may paint or color them or choose swatches of color from paint chips or magazines. Explain your choices based on what you know about your play and the colors.

COLOR 1	COLOR 2	COLOR 3

Select at least two samples each of texture and line either from actual samples (sand paper, cotton, etc.) or from pictures in magazines. Affix them below and explain your choices based on what you know about your play and the textures and lines. Use additional paper if needed.

TEXTURE 1	TEXTURE 2	LINE PATTERN 1	LINE PATTERN 2

157

If you have a large theatre or complex show, consider having an assistant stage manager.

Makeup Crew Chief

Your makeup crew chief should be sure that the makeup is either evenly divided among the dressing rooms or that each actor has the right items according to their makeup plot. The crew chief should also be sure that there are plenty of consumable supplies like paper towels, sponges, cotton balls, makeup remover, and so on. If the crew chief has a set list of people on whom they will be applying makeup, the list should be in the order they will be applied. Members of the crew should be listed along with the actors to whom they are assigned for makeup application. The list should also note who is in charge of any quick makeup changes during the show, who will do touch-ups during the show and where they will be stationed, and who will clean each station after the show.

Properties Crew Chief

The properties crew chief should have a detailed list of each prop and where it should be placed prior to the curtain opening. It can be arranged in a table with a column for body props, set props, and hand props. A simple check in the appropriate column and a quick note will clarify each prop's exact assigned location for curtain opening. If any props must be moved by a crew member during the show, this should be noted too. Those that must be made fresh makeup, so you may want to reapply lip color and anything that became muted. You can also spritz with a liquid makeup setting spray at this time. Finally, apply mascara after the optional setting spray since the spray will make some mascara run.

Watch stage makeup tutorials on YouTube. If your character is specific, seek videos featuring your character's makeup type as well as your skin tone. For example, search "lion makeup on dark-skinned actor" or "old age makeup for Asian male." This sounds overly specific, but makeup varies greatly from one skin tone to the next and from one ethnicity to another. Your research will be time well-spent. Because most theatres do not hire professional makeup artists, it is important that you learn to apply your own. It is a skill that will benefit you as long as you take the stage!

Various Shades of:	An Assortment of:	For Clean-up:	Other Items:
Foundation	Makeup Brushes	Cleanser	Shaver
Eye Color	Makeup Sponges	Toner	Shaving Cream
Cheek Color	Powder Puffs	Cotton Balls	Hair Brush and Comb
Lip Color	A smock for	Tissue	Hair Spray
Cream Liners	protecting clothes	Wash Cloth	Moisturizer
Pencil Liners	Hair bands or clips	Baby wipes for removing	Nail Polish Remover
Mascara	(even for short hair)	makeup quickly	Deodorant
Powder			Mirror

FINDING, MAKING, AND BUYING PROPS

Props are the things actors use onstage or the items used to dress the set. Hand props are those brought onstage by actors, such as a tray with cups, saucers, and a teapot that a maid carries onstage. Set props are placed on the set prior to the opening of the curtain. They are generally the things that decorate the "room" or the setting, such as a sofa, chair, lamp, and so on, but a set prop may also be a non-decorative item, such as a letter placed in a desk drawer to be found by a character at some point in the play. Body props are placed on an actor's body or costume to be used or referenced at some point during a performance. Say a character is wearing a tuxedo with a red flower in the buttonhole. He enters the scene and hands the flower to a beautiful passerby. The flower is a prop that must be placed onto the costume before each show.

In educational theatre, students in the production often bring props from home. The prop crew should keep record of who provides what props and who is responsible for returning the items. Some schools have well-stocked prop rooms from which many items can be taken. There are theatrical catalogs and specialty stores that sell props, such as realistic-looking rocks made of Styrofoam, swords made especially for stage combat, plastic food, etc. These mail-order companies stock some of the most commonly used items, but they are expensive. There are some companies that rent larger props like wooden foot bridges and Jack-in-the-boxes large enough for a live person. Again, these are expensive but a good option if you have little storage space. If you are doing a period piece (a show from a time period other than modern), you can find props at antique stores and vintage shops. Many of these stores will even lend them to you in trade for an ad in your program. You may also scrounge flea markets and garage and estate sales to cheaply supplement your prop closet.

At some point you will find yourself needing to make props. There are a number of materials that are lightweight, flexible or pliable, and easily available at craft or hobby stores.

- Plaster of paris is a great tool for molding props of detailed shape, such as statues.

- Chicken wire can be shaped into just about any form and covered with a variety of materials like papier-mâché to complete the project. Once dried, the papier-mâché can be painted.

each day, such as food or a break-away, should also be on the list. Finally, note who will be responsible for getting everything back to the prop table after each performance and who will restock the props in storage and return borrowed items after closing night.

Remind the cast that even though there is a prop crew, each actor is equally responsible for checking for their props. This will alleviate stress and confusion.

Costuming Crew Chief

The costuming crew chief should have a large crew, especially for period or costume-focused shows. Before and after each rehearsal and performance, actors should check costumes with the assigned crew member or parent to be sure that all pieces are present. Each actor should be responsible for the care of their costume while it is in their possession, including keeping it on the hanger. Additional costuming crew tasks include ironing, hemming, sewing loose buttons, improvising in case of emergency, taking items to and from the cleaners, freshening stale costumes, and packing, cataloging and returning rented costumes. This crew will work very closely with the makeup crew, and in some cases, they are the same.

- Tulle and netting are lightweight fabrics that are easy to manipulate into various shapes. They can be used to make inexpensive boas, wigs, tutus, petticoats, and more. It can also be used to make foliage, clouds, fog, water, and other set pieces and props with a wispy texture.

- Foam headliner is the padded fabric that lines the interior of the roof of your car. It comes in a variety of colors and can be stiffened with either paint or fabric stiffener.

- Styrofoam can be purchased in just about any size and can be shaped easily. Test your paints on a sample piece since many paints eat away at the foam or do not stick.

- Lightweight woods like balsa, Luan, and some pine are great prop-making materials, but they require special tools for cutting and shaping.

- Cardboard is easy to cut, shape, and paint. Take the two layers of corrugated cardboard apart, exposing the inner layer for a great textured material.

EXTENSION ACTIVITY

Choose one of the props below and tell how you would make it and the approximate cost. Use a clean sheet of paper and include a drawing of your design.

1. A cave large enough for a man to walk in and not be seen by the audience.

2. A floating cloud upon which an adult must sit. It should appear to drift on and offstage without assistance.

3. An elaborate crown that sparkles so much that it is almost luminous.

COSTUMING

The clothes worn by actors onstage are essential in setting the time in which the play takes place. They also help to establish each character's situation.

Imagine the last moments of the Titanic. See the deck of the ship as the last lifeboat is being lowered into the icy water below. It is cold and late at night in the early 1900s. As the great ship sits helpless, those who remain represent the unfortunate hundreds who are sure to perish. They include mostly poor men and members of the crew. Some wives refused to leave their husbands, and so scattered amongst the men are a few women. Life vests are testament that, despite the freezing waters, some still harbor hope of survival.

Now imagine the cast of this play should your theatre produce it. It may include a football player, the short guy with glasses, the blossoming rock star with pink hair, the soccer player who injured her leg and is in a boot, and many others. They are average, modern-day kids, right? How can you convince the audience that this cast of teens is really the heroes and victims of the greatest story of the twentieth century?

Start by underlining every word in the italicized description above that indicates a costume need, then list them in the space below. There are at least seven.

_____

_____

_____

As you can see, you will need costumes that represent the time period (early 1900s), the time of day (evening wear for the crew and wealthy), the temperature (cold), and the situation (many wore several layers both for warmth and because they hoped to save more of their personal belongings).

159

Lighting and Sound Crew Chief

The lighting crew will check all lamps and may choose to run cues. If the spotlights need a warming-up period, they will want to get them turned on in plenty of time. The sound crew will need to pass out microphones, do microphone checks, and check all pre-recorded sound levels.

COSTUME CARE TIPS

- Safety pin loose items such as gloves to your costume between shows.

- When checking out your costumes the first time, make sure you have each item on your card. Keep a list of these for yourself so that you can account for each item every night.

- Keep a bottle of fabric deodorizing spray in your bag for freshening stale-smelling pieces.

Other hints in the description included icy water, poor men, crew members, some wives, and life vests. Think about your school producing *Titanic*. This scene is just one of many that would need costumes! Some shows are much simpler, with just a single costume needed for each character.

Most schools have access to costume closets stocked with various period pieces for both men and women. These costumes are often collected over the years from other shows. If your school is lucky enough to have several sewing machines and a supportive home ec teacher or skilled parent, the school can make any other costumes needed. With the concept of conversion costuming, you rarely have to start from scratch. Rather, find a book that explains how to convert an ordinary pair of men's slacks into knickerbockers or a thrift store blouse into a pirate shirt or peasant top. Of course, after the show, these too can be added to the costume closet.

For contemporary shows, many schools ask each student actor to provide their own costume, especially if they play a student and can just wear everyday street clothes. It is up to the technical director if these clothes will be kept at school as costumes for the run of the show or if the actors will be allowed to just wear them or bring them from home for each performance.

A popular, but very expensive, option for a period show, is to rent the costumes. Most large cities and towns have rental houses, which at least will save some money on shipping. Call in advance to make sure that the company near you has the items you need for the dates you need them. Once that is done, take measurements of each person needing costumes and what looks they require. Send the measurements to the rental company, and about a week before your show, you will receive your shipment of costumes.

Take extra care of every item, because many are vintage and very expensive. As of this date, prices average about $70 per costume, but replacement can be $300 or more.

Old prom dresses like this can be altered slightly, embellished, or remade to create stylish period costumes.

SAMPLE MASTER TASK LIST FOR *THE WIZARD OF OZ*

Westbury High School: Jenn Queen, makeup crew chief; Carter Beck and Jasmine Donnelly, crew

1. Unlock all dressing room doors by 6 PM. Get keys from Ericka and then pass them on to Sarah.

2. Check to make sure there are plenty of paper towels, cold cream, cotton balls, and toner in each dressing room (you are responsible for your own room).

3. Start Wicked Witch makeup (Jenn) by about 6:15, dressing room A at 7, and intermission touchups (DR A only).

4. Carter starts Cowardly Lion makeup at 6:15, begins Tin Man at 7, touchups in dressing room B.

5. Jasmine starts Scarecrow at 6:15, Dorothy at about 7. In charge of dressing room C.

6. After the last character is made up, each crew member is responsible for cleaning, sorting, and putting away makeup (except intermission touch-up makeup). Set out cold cream, cotton balls, and toner.

7. Each will thoroughly clean and lock his or her own room after the last actor is out each night.

8. Closing night: inventory all makeup and lock it in the cabinet. Give Mrs. Denny the inventory or there will not be makeup and supplies for the next show.

DESIGNING THE SET

Behind the set of a play, backstage visitors are often surprised at what they see. Many are surprised that the backside of the scenery is not similar to the front. Because scenery for plays must be lightweight, mobile, and durable while still resembling what it was intended to be, set pieces are built using non-traditional methods of construction.

Most sets are made up of flats (see pictures below), wooden frames with hinged braces on the back to help them stand. The fronts of the flats are often covered with a muslin fabric that is sized to fit and then painted. Sometimes set builders use paneling, Luan (pronounced loo-AHN, which is a thin sheet of plywood), or Masonite (a heavy, thin pressboard) to cover the frames. Once each flat is constructed, it can be painted to look like just about anything. The painted flats are placed together, creating the walls of a room or the exterior of a building. Sometimes the flats are joined together, but if they must be moved in the show, they are left freestanding with sandbags or weights to keep them from tipping over. Still, the backsides of sets are dark and the cast and crew must navigate the treacherous areas in big costumes or with heavy cables or props so sometimes set pieces fall over. Always prepare for the worst and use more sandbags than you think you need!

Many sets include backdrops, which are giant pieces of painted fabric hung from metal bars along the tops of the curtains. These are used for large indoor scenes such as libraries and for outdoor scenes such as a large city or a forest. These can be flown in and out using a system of ropes, pulleys, and weights called a fly rail. Theaters without fly rails rely on ladders and manpower to change the heavy backdrops.

To take the place of backdrops, projected scenery is becoming more and more popular because of its ease and lower cost. Projections can be done from the front onto a scrim, wall, or white sheet. For a different effect, projections onto a scrim can also be done from the back.

There are many other types of scenery, including two- and three-sided pieces on wheels that turn to reveal a new perspective. For example, if a high school was producing a show with three scenes, one in a library, one in a kitchen, and one in a garden, a prism set might be the best bet. Several tall, vertical, triangular pieces could be built and equipped with wheels for mobility. On the three sides of each prism, a piece of the three scenes would be painted. The space between the prisms become the doorways or entrances. With a quick turn of the prisms, the scene would change from a library to a kitchen, and then a garden. Once the basic structure of a scene has been built, the illusion can be completed by adding furniture, set props, and lighting.

The stage at Terrell High School before and after fourteen hours of work on the set.

161

NOTES: _____

_____

_____

_____

_____

_____

_____

_____

_____

LIGHTING AND SOUND

Greg Arp, a high school theatre teacher in Plano, Texas, says that while costumes, makeup, props, and set are all important, perhaps the most essential theatrical elements are lighting and sound. His productions certainly reflect a mastery of these production elements!

If an actor's primary objective is to be heard, then good sound is obviously a high priority. However, good sound is not just about microphones. It includes sound effects, recorded music or tracks if a live orchestra is not being used, and making sure the microphones can be heard over the live orchestra if it is being used. Sound technicians must also know how to operate high-tech equipment with dozens of cables, buttons, knobs, lights, and an infinite number of variables. They must have a very good ear so that they can sense when an actor's microphone needs to be tweaked. A good knowledge of acoustics is also important.

In smaller theaters and in some schools, actors do not use microphones. Instead, they rely on vocal projection to make sure the audience hears their voices. Also, because sound systems can be very expensive, many schools do not own them. Sound systems can be rented, and technicians can even be hired to run them. A less expensive option is to use home stereo equipment for sound cues or to have actors create sound cues offstage using hand-held devices.

What good is sound if the audience struggles to see the characters? The lighting crew must make sure that each lighting instrument is in good working order and that the lights are focused or aimed at the areas that need to be seen. Colored gels can be added or, if LED lighting is being used, a color may be selected from a menu of options to give the scene depth, as well as a time, place, and mood. Lighting is also important to ensure that the audience can see the actors' features and facial expressions and that the overall effect is what the director intended.

Most systems incorporate computerized digital boards, and each show must be programmed independently. Lights need to operate in groups to illuminate areas from several directions at once, and each light cue needs to be assigned a cue number. Once programmed, the light board operator must then follow along with the script at each rehearsal, cuing the light board. The operator also addresses whatever problems may arise during the show. For example, if an actor misses a line and that particular line was a light cue, the operator must adapt and adjust the lighting area to meet the needs of the show. The lamps, or bulbs, inside an instrument may burn out during a show, and the operator must know which instruments to use to illuminate the area in an emergency situation.

The benefits of LED lighting are that the lamps do not burn at a high temperature, they use less electricity, and the life of an LED lamp is significantly longer. The cost and use of LED fixtures have changed dramatically and the quality of light produced has improved. Many schools are transitioning from conventional light fixtures to LED fixtures for cost savings and low maintenance.

One of the great things about lighting is that it can eliminate the need for expensive scenery. Colored lights can be used to create a number of backgrounds such as sunsets, evenings, and just about any surrealistic setting imaginable. By adding a small, metal disk called a gobo to a conventional lighting instrument, stars, clouds, and other shapes can work with the color, creating wonderful effects. Intelligent lighting, or automated instruments that can be programmed to move, can make clouds appear to drift past a sun as it sets and stars begin twinkling on the horizon. Intelligent lighting can often be seen in large-scale productions and concerts and can be rented for school productions to create incredible lighting effects.

If your school is not equipped with the most advanced lighting technology or if you lack any kind of stage lighting, check into renting a portable system. If nothing else, consider making your own "coffee can lights" so that your actors can be seen.

Volumes have been written on lighting and sound, but theatre instructor Greg Arp suggests that the best way to learn is to work with an experienced lighting technician. If you are interested in working in this area of the theatre, Arp suggests seeking a technical internship from your local theatre.

> If you are in need of a student to learn your lighting and sound systems, as well as assisting in set construction, consider a mutually agreeable arrangement with your shop teacher.

NOTES: _____

_____

_____

_____

_____

_____

_____

_____

PRODUCING PLAYS IN NON-TRADITIONAL SETTINGS

A beautifully designed stage is a wonderful gift to the world of theatre. Actors and directors alike relish the idea of having the convenience and ease of the latest technology, the space for large dance numbers or a balcony scene, and a comfortable seating area for the audience. In an ideal stage setting, a workshop located near the stage allows both actors and crew to work simultaneously. When the lights need focusing, many facilities have practice rooms the same size and shape as the stage so that actors may work safely while the heavy equipment is lowered.

Unfortunately, the average school is not ideally equipped. Although many have stages, most were built on tight budgets. Sometimes there is not enough space in the wings for actors to await their cues. Often there is little to no storage space. Without storage, keeping stock set pieces, props, and costumes is difficult. There are a large number of schools with cafetoriums and gymatoriums—clever names for a combined auditorium and cafeteria or gym. Theatre students must juggle their rehearsal and performance schedules around sports, lunches, and gym classes. Regardless of the type of auditorium, most are the largest public gathering places in town, and they are used for a number of community events. All of this means sharing rehearsal and performance space and time slots and sacrificing storage space and technology.

There are also schools without any stage, so they think they cannot produce shows, if they even have a drama program at all. The truth is, a stage can be anywhere. In the Medieval period, actors traveled from town to town in pageant carts, which were wagons with fold-out stages. The wagons could be put together, forming a series of stages, or they could roll in and out in succession while the audience stayed put. When American theatre had its humble beginnings, amateur actors performed in courthouses, barns, and coffeehouses.

Not only is it possible to produce shows without a stage, but it is also a wonderful learning experience and a chance for you to develop your problem-solving skills. Plan on having more performances with fewer audience members due to the small spaces. Call on parents, woodworking classes, and community members to assist you. Here are some more ideas for producing plays in non-traditional settings:

- Host a dinner theatre play in a local restaurant's party room or your school cafeteria. Most publishers have scripts specifically for dinner theatre, where no stage is required beyond perhaps a head table, like at a banquet. Many of these shows are fun murder mysteries and make great fundraisers too!

- Perform in a park to take advantage of natural settings and lighting. You will need to rent cordless microphones so actors can be heard. The audience provides their own seating and admission is usually free. Ask for donations and sell concessions, and have a solid plan for bad weather.

- Ask your community theatre or another school if you can use their stage. Some churches also rent out their social halls or maybe you can even use the sanctuary so that the pulpit becomes the stage.

- Find a play with a setting that works with your present resources. For example, if you have access to a large barn, do a play that takes place at a farm. If your school's library would work, then choose a play with a school setting.

- Build a stage using a series of platforms and walls that can be taken apart and stored. Even if you lack storage, your parents may know of a local business that will store them for you, like a large warehouse or a building that has unused rooms.

163

NOTES: _____

_____

_____

_____

_____

_____

_____

_____

_____

VIRTUAL THEATRE

The term "virtual theatre" means that people are able to watch the performance of your show online. There are many ways this can happen, from livestreaming to posting a pre-recorded video on a website to performing live on a video conferencing site. Taking your theatre production "virtual" means you don't need much room for an audience, and you might not even need a stage at all!

If your performance space has limited room for an audience, you might consider livestreaming your staged performance so that additional people can be watching from home. This is especially nice for relatives who live out of town. However, first you have to find out from the publisher of the play if this is allowed. Some don't allow it, and the ones that do generally require an additional fee to be paid since you're reaching another audience.

You might also post a video of your staged performance on your school's website or on a site such as YouTube. The advantage of this is that people can watch it at their own convenience rather than at a specific time. Again, check the licensing agreement you have with the publisher. Many don't allow this, and the ones that do will definitely require additional royalty fees.

But what if you don't have a stage at all? In 2020, most theatres had to close worldwide because of a pandemic. Instead of cancelling their productions, some groups learned how to perform their show on a video conferencing site such as Zoom. As you can imagine, it's very different to put on a play without any performance space. Each actor is in their own house, yet they're all logged onto the same website at the same time to appear altogether on one screen. Performers can still appear in costume and makeup but there's less emphasis on sets or blocking. This style of performance is quite different and takes much rehearsal. While less than ideal, it is better than nothing when there's no stage available, whether for health or other reasons.

NOTES: _____

_____

_____

_____

_____

_____

_____

_____

CHAPTER 8
THEATRE HISTORY

DAILY BELL WORK—THEATRE HISTORY

THEATRE HISTORY TIME LINE

THE FIRST PERFORMANCES

ANCIENT GREEK THEATRE
Greek Playwrights

ROMAN THEATRE
Early Theatre Review

MEDIEVAL THEATRE
Medieval Plays
Medieval Review

RENAISSANCE THEATRE
The Characters of Commedia dell'Arte
Renaissance Theatre Outside of Italy

ELIZABETHAN THEATRE
The Elizabethan Stage
Elizabethan Playwrights
Renaissance and Elizabethan Theatre Review

THE ENGLISH RESTORATION AND LATER THEATRE

AMERICAN THEATRE
American Playwrights

EASTERN THEATRE
Restoration and Later, American, and Eastern Theatre Review

THEATRE HISTORY REVIEW AND PROJECTS
Theatre History Test Review Crossword Puzzle
Theatre History Projects

NAME _____ PERIOD _____ DATE _____

DAILY BELL WORK - THEATRE HISTORY

Answer each question as your teacher assigns it, using the space provided. Be sure to include the date.

1. Date: _____

    What are some events the prehistoric people may have pantomimed in their early storytelling?

2. Date: _____

    Imagine sitting around a prehistoric campfire listening to a story. What are some of the sounds and lights which may have naturally added to the drama of the story? How can these things be used to enhance drama today?

3. Date: _____

    For the earliest writers, daily life was much harder. Paper and ink were sparse, and politics and religion threatened freedom of speech. Knowing this, write an entry from a fictional writer's diary describing the events of the day.

4. Date: _____

    There was a great deal of disease during the medieval period. How might this have affected the traveling troupes of actors?

NOTES: _____

_____

_____

_____

_____

_____

_____

_____

NAME _____ PERIOD _____ DATE _____

DAILY BELL WORK - THEATRE HISTORY

Answer each question as your teacher assigns it, using the space provided. Be sure to include the date.

5. Date: _____

    Horseplay has long since been a source of enjoyment for audiences. Imagine a medieval performance of a morality play, a play about good and evil. What are some opportunities for the actors to engage in horseplay?

6. Date: _____

    Commedia dell'arte used stock characters. These characters were the same in many plays, but the plot of each play varied. Today, the repetition of a character "type" in a performance is often referred to as a stereotype. List five or six stereotypes that are used in TV and film today.

7. Date: _____

    Many commedia dell'arte plays used a plot in which a young man and woman are in love, but the girl's father is opposed. Can you think of film and TV plots that follow this popular pattern? List them.

8. Date: _____

    Could you imagine a modern world in which people used Shakespeare's language? Why would this work or not work? Write your response in the language of a Shakespearean play.

NOTES: _____

_____

_____

_____

_____

_____

_____

_____

NAME _____ PERIOD _____ DATE _____

DAILY BELL WORK - THEATRE HISTORY

Answer each question as your teacher assigns it, using the space provided. Be sure to include the date.

9.   Date: _____

   Throughout history, literature has been used to voice ideas about politics, religion, ethics, and social consciousness. In recent history, television, music, and movies have been added to the cause. Does the entertainment industry have a responsibility to exercise its power to influence society? Explain your answer.

10. Date: _____

   Theatre has been outlawed several times throughout history, because it was believed to put bad thoughts in people's heads, which would then lead to bad behavior. Compare this theory to modern day beliefs that violence on TV and in video games leads to more violent behavior.

11. Date: _____

   Theatre in the United States lacked its own identity until the early twentieth century when film was introduced and when stage plays began paving the way for American greatness. Write a diary entry from a young actor's actress's point of view as they see more opportunities in acting arise.

12. Date: _____

   Should cartoons be considered art or are they just child's play? Explain.

NOTES: _____

_____

_____

_____

_____

_____

_____

_____

_____

NAME _____ PERIOD _____ DATE _____

DAILY BELL WORK - THEATRE HISTORY

Answer each question as your teacher assigns it, using the space provided. Be sure to include the date.

13. Date: _____

_____

_____

14. Date: _____

_____

_____

15. Date: _____

_____

_____

16. Date: _____

_____

_____

TESTS AND PROJECTS

In this chapter, you will find fewer worksheets. There is a concise review in the form of a crossword puzzle plus two tests. The questions on the two tests cover the exact same materials. However, one is considerably more difficult than the other. The first test has three- or four-answer choices for each question. The second has two. You may want to use the second test for your beginners or as a modified test for special education students.

There is also a page of projects for this chapter; the projects could be used as extra credit, makeup work, in lieu of the theatre history test, or in conjunction with it. The projects are both fun and educational. Requiring one would reinforce the information in this chapter. Try one on your own as an example!

It might be a wise idea to assign these projects at the beginning of your theatre history unit. Projects, like performances, exercise a different part of a student's brain. The student who does not retain information well, but has promise, might learn better by reading a play and reporting on it. Others want to get their hands into a crafty assignment so that they can make full use of their creativity. There is a project for those who are excellent researchers and writers, and one for computer and web enthusiasts. You might even offer each student a choice between completing a project and taking a test.

THEATRE HISTORY TIME LINE
WITH INFLUENTIAL POLITICAL AND SOCIAL WORLD EVENTS

BC

c. 2560 BC: The Great Pyramid of Giza completed in Egypt.

2000 BC: Stone tablet depicting first known performance in Egypt.

c. 1800 BC: World's oldest surviving narrative, *Epic of Gilgamesh*, carved into The Old Babylonian tablets.

1000 BC: Greeks rebuilt their civilization after its collapse in the Late Bronze Age.

776 BC: First documented Olympic Games.

750 BC: Greeks learned the alphabet from Phoenicians; Homer composed *The Iliad* and *The Odyssey* about the Trojan War and the Fall of Troy.

c. 563-400 BC: Buddha born in India.

551-479 BC: Life of Chinese philosopher and politician Confucius.

534 BC: Thespis became the first "actor," stepping from the traditional chorus to act as an individual.

c. 529 BC: Greek thinker Pythagoras developed theories about music, physics, and mathematics, including what became recognized as the Pythagorean Theorem, a fundamental of geometry.

525-456 BC: The life of Aeschylus, Greek playwright, "Father of Tragedy."

509 BC: Roman Republic established.

508 BC: Cleisthenes introduced democratic governance in Greece, ushering in the Classical Period, a high point in culture and the arts that lasted until the death of Alexander the Great in 323 BC.

496-406 BC: The life of Sophocles, Greek playwright, author of *Antigone, Oedipus Rex*, and *Electra*.

490 BC: Greeks repelled Persian invaders at the Battle of Marathon.

480-406 BC: The life of Euripides, Greek playwright, author of *Medea, Hippolytus*, and The *Trojan Women*.

445-385 BC: The life of Aristophanes, Greek playwright, "Father of Comedy."

438 BC: Construction of the Parthenon completed.

431-404 BC: Greek city-states Sparta and Athens fought the Peloponnesian War.

c. 400 BC: Women first allowed to attend the theatre.

342-290 BC: The life of Menander, prolific Greek playwright of comedies. Only *Dyskolos* survives today.

336-323 BC: Macedonian King Phillip II conquered Athens to control Greece. Upon Phillip's assassination, his son Alexander the Great led armies to conquer Persia, Syria, Egypt, and parts of India before dying suddenly in Babylon.

335 BC: Greek philosopher Aristotle penned *Poetics*, the earliest surviving work of dramatic theory. A year later he opened the Lyceum.

254-184 BC: The life of Plautus, Roman playwright, who adapted most of his works from earlier Greek plays.

221-206 BC: China, unified under Emperor Qin Shi Huang. Construction began on The Great Wall.

190-158 BC: The life of Terence, Roman playwright.

146-60 BC: Roman conquest of Greek regions introduced Greek philosophy and theatre to Rome.

146 BC: Rome destroyed Carthage bringing an end to the Third (and final) Punic War, and to the Carthaginians.

44 BC: Assassination of Julius Caesar signaled the end of the Roman Republic and the beginning of the Roman Empire.

3 BC-65 AD: The life of Seneca, Roman philosopher, statesman and playwright, author of *Medea, Thyestes*, and *Phaedra*.

First through Tenth Century AD

33 AD: Crucifixion of Jesus of Nazareth.

43 AD: Romans conquered Britain.

79 AD: Pompeii is buried in twelve feet of volcanic lava and ash.

80 AD: Built amid a nearly 200-year stretch of prosperity and relative peace known as Pax Romana, the Roman Colosseum was completed, allowing for seating of up to 80,000 spectators.

300-645 AD: During the Yamoto period, Japan organized a unified state and established ties to mainland Asia.

c. 350 AD: Indian poet Kālidās composed *Shakuntala*, which would become one of the first Sanskrit works translated into English.

390 AD: Theodosius the Great declared Christianity the official religion of Rome.

410 AD: Visigoths shocked the world by conquering Rome, the "Eternal City."

476 AD: Flavius Odoacer revolted against and replaced Emperor Romulus Augustulus, effectively ending the Western Roman Empire.

500-800: The lotus of Roman power shifted to Constantinople in the East, in what's now known as the Byzantine Empire, and Western Europe fell into disrepair. Since Christians generally opposed theatre, it became virtually non-existent in Western Europe.

574-622: Emulating China, Shōtoku Taishi began to transform Japan, centralizing the government, emphasizing a bureaucracy of merit, and reverence for Buddhism and Confucianism.

630: Mohammed entered Mecca in triumph; two years later the Qu-ran was completed.

171

USING THE TIME LINE

Learning any kind of history—literary history, dance history, theatre history—should be broader than the subject itself. Take the world in which William Shakespeare, Christopher Marlowe, and Ben Jonson lived. Understanding the politics, economy, religion, and social customs of the time makes it easier to know where these writers found inspiration for their plays. In the movie *Shakespeare in Love*, we see young Shakespeare getting his inspiration from the people on the street, his business dealings,

and his own relationship. While this movie took many liberties with reality, scholars say it is an accurate depiction of the living conditions and lifestyles of the time. It serves to show that there is more to theatre history than what took place at the theatre. Plays chronicle the times in which they were written.

The Time Line correlates to the events in this chapter. Use it to engage your students in discussions about the potential inspiration for each playwright's works.

710-794: Japanese court built a new capital in Nara modeled upon Chang-an in China; emperors are Shinto chiefs. They adopted Buddhism hoping that its teachings will bring peace and protection.

711: The Umayyands conquered the Iberian Peninsula spreading Islam to Europe. The Islamic state, or caliphate, would by 750, rule from the Atlantic Ocean in Northern Africa in the west into modern day Afghanistan in the east.

794-1185: In Japan, the Imperial Court moved to Heian-kyō (now Kyoto) to escape domination of Nara's Buddhist establishment.

800: Frankish king Charlemagne crowned the first Holy Roman Emperor.

800-1000: Height of Byzantine Empire, hub of world commerce and industry.

c. 800: Chinese accidentally created gunpowder.

900: The Roman Church resurrected theatre by introducing religious performances to Easter services.

c. 950: Hrosvitha, a member of German nobility, wrote six plays based on Terence's comedies but featuring religious figures. Her work became the first known example of Western dramatic theatre since the Classical Era.

Eleventh Century

1002: Japanese court women produced the best literature of the era; Murasaki Shikibu's *Tale of Genji* is the world's first novel.

1046: Pope Gregory VII took steps to unify the Roman Church and strengthen its rule in Rome.

1066: William I, Duke of Normandy, conquered England.

1095-1271: The Crusades: first of many attempts by the Roman Church to reclaim the Holy Lands from Islamic rule.

Twelfth Century

1100-1220: Troubadour poetry spread throughout France, Spain, and later Italy. Themes mainly concerned chivalry and courtly love.

1100-1300: Origin of universities in Western Europe.

1140-1260: Aristotle's works translated into Latin.

1150-1500: Gothic style in architecture and art.

1192: Shogun Minamoto no Yoritomo overthrew the Taira Emperor, establishing what would become 675 years of military rule in Japan.

Thirteenth Century

1206-1260: Genghis Khan unified tribes of Mongolia and conquered territory throughout China, the Middle East, and as far northwest as Poland. His empire expanded after his death and then contracted after Islamic Mamluks defeated Mongols at the Battle of Ain Jalut.

1212: Spanish victory over Muslims at Las Navas de Tolosac.

1215: King John of England signed the Magna Carta, which would inspire those seeking liberty for hundreds of years hence.

1271-1295: Life of Italian merchant and explorer Marco Polo, whose stories in *The Travels of Marco Polo* inspired Europeans to build trade routes eastward.

1290: Mechanical clock invented.

Fourteenth Century

1314: Italian statesman and poet Albertino Mussato wrote *Ecerinis*, the first tragedy written since Roman Times.

1315-1317: Famine choked Northern Europe.

1337-1453: England and France fought the Hundred Years' War, which helped establish their respective national identities.

1347-1350: The Black Death, a pandemic of the bubonic plague, killed between 75-200 million people in Europe, Asia, and North Africa.

1387-1400: Geoffrey Chaucer penned *The Canterbury Tales*.

Fifteenth Century

1415: Italian inventor Giovanni Fontana wrote *Bellicorum instrumentorum liber* (Book of Instruments of War), an illustrated book about military technology, including a discussion of rockets and torpedoes.

1429: Joan of Arc led French to free Orléans from the English. She was burned at the stake two years later.

1440: Johann Gutenberg invented the printing press. This technological breakthrough allowed the spread of information faster than ever before.

1450-1600: The Renaissance Period: the rediscovery of classical Greek philosophy led to a new, expanded way of thinking, that reverberated through all facets of life.

1453: Ottomans captured Constantinople, leading to the end of the Byzantine Empire. The Ottomans would control Constantinople (later named Istanbul) until the end of the First World War in 1917.

1455-1487: Civil wars, called the Wars of the Roses, were fought between the House of Plantagenet and the House of Lancaster over the English throne.

1467-1477: The ten-year-long Ōnin no Ran (Onin War) brought disintegration of the central government in Japan and led to the beginning of the Sengoku period.

1475-1564: The life of Italian sculptor, painter, and poet Michelangelo di Lodovico Buonarroti Simoni.

1476: Ulrich Han first printed a book containing music, in Rome.

1478: Catholic leaders Ferdinand II of Aragon and Isabella I of Castile implemented the Spanish Inquisition, which would persecute Jews, Muslims, and (so-called) heretics for the next 300 years.

1483-1520: Life of Italian painter and architect Raphael Sanzio de Urbino; his best known work is *The School of Athens* in the Vatican.

1492: Italian explorer Christopher Columbus crossed the Atlantic Ocean and landed in the Bahamas, opening the door for the European colonization of the Americas.

c. 1495: Writing of *Everyman*, a morality play whereupon one's good and evil deeds are tallied by God in a ledger. It has seen many adaptations since.

Sixteenth Century

c. 1500: Transatlantic Slave Trade: Sailing from Europe, merchants kidnapped and enslaved men, women, and children from Western Africa.

1503: Italian painter, scientist, and engineer Leonardo da Vinci began painting the *Mona Lisa*.

1504: Michelangelo completed *David*, a masterpiece in marble.

NOTES: _____

_____

_____

_____

_____

_____

_____

_____

_____

1508-1512: Michelangelo painted the ceiling of the Sistine Chapel in Rome.

1516: In the Venetian Republic, a law limited Jews to San Girolamo Parish, establishing "Ghetto Nuova" as the first ghetto in Europe.

1517: Martin Luther nailed his *Ninety-five Theses* to All Saints' Church in Wittenberg, beginning the Protestant Reformation—and eventually splitting Western Christianity into Catholics and Protestants.

1519: Spanish conquistador Hernán Cortés met Aztec leader Montezuma in one of the world's largest cities Tenochtitlan (modern Mexico). Within two years, the Aztec Empire was destroyed.

1520-1566: Under Suleiman the Magnificent's reign, the Ottoman Empire entered its "Golden Age," expanding to include over 25 million people.

1521: Voyage of Magellan completed with his crew, having circumnavigated the globe.

1524: Italian diplomat and writer, Niccolò Machiavelli published *La Mandragola*, a five-act satire.

1533-1603: Life of Queen Elizabeth, long-reigning ruler of England, patron of the arts.

1542: Pope Paul III established the Roman Inquisition to combat Protestantism.

1543: Firearms introduced in Japan by shipwrecked Portuguese.

1549: Christianity introduced in Japan by Frances Xavier.

1551: Commedia dell'arte gained popularity in Italy and Western Europe.

1562-1589: Catholics and Huguenots Protestants fought the French Wars of Religion.

1564-1593: Life of Christopher Marlowe, English playwright best known for tragedies, wrote *Hero and Leander*, *Tamburlaine the Great*, and *The Tragical History of Doctor Faustus*.

1564-1616: Life of William Shakespeare, English playwright, wrote *Hamlet, Romeo and Juliet, Macbeth, Othello, A Midsummer Night's Dream*, and many more.

1568-1600: Oda Nobunaga started the process of reunifying Japan after a century of civil war, laying the foundation for modern Japan.

1570: The Elizabethan masque, an elaborate combination of dance, music, and costumes performed for aristocrats, debuted.

1572-1637: Life of English poet and playwright Ben Jonson, author of *Every Man in His Humour, The Alchemist*, and *Bartholomew Fair*.

1576: The first Elizabethan playhouse, The Theatre, opened in London.

1581: First ballet performance, "The Comic Ballet of the Queen," staged in Paris.

1582: Pope Gregory XIII instituted the Gregorian Calendar.

1588: English defeated the Spanish Armada.

1590-1600: The Golden Age of Spanish Theatre: Spain produced four times more plays than the English during their theatrical renaissance. Playwrights included the prolific Lope de Vega, soldier and priest-turned-playwright Calderón de la Barca, and former nun Juana Inés de la Cruz.

1594: The foremost Elizabethan theatrical company, Lord Chamberlain's Men, formed with William Shakespeare as its chief playwright and Richard Burbage as its most famous actor.

1598: Edict of Nantes allowed Protestants in France to practice their religion in peace.

Seventeenth Century

1600: The Globe Theatre staged its first production, *Julius Caesar*.

1600-1750: Baroque Period: encouraged by the Catholic Church to counter the simplicity of Protestant art, Baroque art used color, detail, and movement to create works that would create a sense of awe in the viewer. Later baroque works, known as rococo, became even more extreme and ornamental.

1605: Spanish writer Miguel de Cervantes published *Don Quixote, Part I*, considered among the most important novels ever written.

1607: Englishman John Smith founded the first colony of Virginia at Jamestown.

1609: Italian inventor and scientist Galileo Galilei published *The Starry Messenger*, a compilation of his astronomical discoveries.

1611: The King James Bible was published.

1613: Fire destroyed the Globe Theatre.

1620: Pilgrims sailed to America on the Mayflower.

1622-1673: Life of French writer and actor Molière (born Jean-Baptiste Poquelin), author of *Tartuffe, The Misanthrope*, and *The Learned Women*.

1631-1700: Life of critic, poet, and playwright John Dryden, England's first Poet Laureate.

1631: Mt. Vesuvius erupted, destroying everything around the volcano and killing between 3000 and 6000 people.

1636: Harvard College founded in Cambridge, Massachusetts.

1637: The first public opera house, the Teatro San Cassiano, opened in Venice.

1639-1699: Life of French playwright Jean Racine, a tragedian, who wrote *Andromaque, Phèdre*, and *Athalie*.

1640-1689: Life of Aphra Behn, one of the first English women to make her living as a writer.

1641-1716: Life of English dramatist William Wycherley, writer of *The Country Wife* and *The Plain Dealer*.

1642-1660: English Civil War: Tensions between King Charles I and Parliament erupted in armed hostilities. Throughout the war, the Puritan majority ruled, and Parliament closed all theatres in England.

1643: Molière founded Illustre Theatre in Paris.

1651: First public comedy house opened in Vienna, Austria.

1653-1725: Life of Japanese dramatist Chikamatsu Monzaemon, innovator in bunraku and kabuki, writer of *The Courier for Hell*, and *The Love Suicides at Amijima*.

1660-1710: The Restoration Period: The reopening of English theatres led to a theatre boom that welcomed women to the stage, diversity to the audiences, and popularized comedy.

1661: Lincoln's Inn Fields, London's largest public square, opened.

NOTES:

1662: The English Royal Patent mandated that women perform female theatrical roles.

1663: The Theatre Royal, Drury Lane, London, opened.

1665: *Ye Bare and Ye Cubb*, on record as the first English-language play presented in the colonies in the colony of Virginia.

1665-1666: Bubonic plague killed an estimated 100,000 people, nearly a quarter of all Londoners.

1673-1841: Golden age of kabuki theatre: Japan starts to flourish with kabuki and bunraku theatre and broader access to education and books.

1681: Professional female dancers appeared in Paris for the first time.

1687: English physicist, theologian, and astronomer Isaac Newton published *Mathematical Principles of Natural Philosophy.*

Eighteenth Century

c. 1700: Italian Bartolomeo Cristofori invented the first modern piano.

1705: The Queen's Theatre opened in London.

1707-1793: Life of Italian playwright Carlo Goldoni, founder of modern Italian comedy, author of *Servant of Two Masters* and *The Mistress of the Inn.*

1711-1785: Life of Kitty Clive, English actress.

1714: Italian composer Antonio Vivaldi (1678-1741) became the impresario of the Teatro Sant' Angelo, helping popularize opera throughout Europe.

1720-1860: Life of Italian playwright Carlo Gozzi, revitalized commedia dell'arte by bringing an intense satirical edge to it.

1728-1774: Life of Irish writer Oliver Goldsmith, author of the plays *The Good-Natur'd Man* and *She Stoops to Conquer.*

1730: *Romeo and Juliet,* performed in New York, is the first play by Shakespeare to be presented in America.

1737: One of the largest theatres in Europe, Teatro di San Carlo, connected to the Royal Palace, opened in Naples.

1737: English Parliament passed the Stage Licensing Act, which required all public performances to be examined and, if necessary, censored by the government. It would exist in some form until 1968.

1748: The excavation of Pompeii, buried by a volcano eruption 1700 years earlier, inspired what will become known as the Neoclassical Period (1750-1815), an embrace of Greeco-Roman ideals, of simplicity and grace. In theatre that meant decorous plays, acted very broadly, with meticulous costumes and sets.

1749-1803: Life of Italian dramatist and poet Vittorio Alfieri, the founder of Italian tragedy.

1750: First resident theatre company established in New York City.

1751-1816: Life of English playwright, poet and politician Richard Brinsley Sheridan, author of *The Rivals, The School for Scandal, The Duenna,* and *A Trip to Scarborough.*

1751: The Virginia Company of Comedians, the colonies' first professional theatre company, opened a temporary playhouse in Williamsburg, Virginia.

1766: The first permanent American theatre building, Philadelphia's Southwark Theatre, was built.

1766-1839: Life of American playwright, actor and historian William Dunlap, author of over 60 plays and the encyclopedia *History of the Rise and Progress of the Arts of Design in the United States.*

1768: Italian naturalist Lazzaro Spallanzani proved that boiling and sealing food products will keep them free of microorganisms, thus creating modern-day canning.

1775-1783: The American Revolution, prompted by Americans drafting the Declaration of Independence, declaring their intent to secede from Great Britain.

1784: Pierre Beaumarchais' comic play, *Marriage of Figaro,* premiered. It was later developed into an opera composed by Mozart and a libretto written by Lorenzo Da Ponte.

1788: United States ratified The Constitution. The next year, George Washington became the first US president.

1789-1815: The French Revolution and Napoleonic Wars: Inspired by the ideals of liberty, equality, and fraternity, civilian insurgents stormed the Bastille, a symbol of monarchy rule in Paris. Political struggle, wars with other European nations, the beheading of King Louis XVI, and the abolishment and reestablishment of the Catholic Church culminated in dictatorial rule by a council known as the Directorate—which was subsequently commandeered by Napoleon Bonaparte. Napoleon and the *Grande Armée* engaged nearly every other European power in battle until his ultimate defeat at the Battle of Waterloo. The peace, negotiated at the Congress of Vienna, re-drew the borders of Europe, and established the British Empire as the world's foremost power.

1791-1861: Life of French playwright Eugène Scribe, who developed the "well-made play," a popular, though criticized genre that emphasized rigid plot structure and entertainment over didactic-ism.

Nineteenth Century

1800s: Using simple characterization and exaggerated emotions, melodrama—as written by August von Kotzebue and René Charles Guilbert de Pixérécourt—dominated French theatre.

1800-1890: Born from Germany's sturm und drang movement, Romanticism offered artists and thinkers an opportunity to focus on emotion and individualism instead of the encroaching modernity and industrialization.

1808: German writer Johann Wolfgang von Goethe published *Faust, Part I.*

1816: Philadelphia's Chestnut Street Theatre became the earliest gas-lit playhouse in the world.

1821-1881: Life of Russian writer Aleksey Pisemky, who introduced psychological realism to playwriting, authored *A Bitter Fate* about serfdom.

1828-1910: Life of Russian author Leo Tolstoy, author of the novels *War and Peace, Anna Karenina,* and the play *The Power of Darkness.*

1837: A London theatre first used Thomas Drummond's limelight, similar to today's spotlight.

1848: Germans Karl Marx and Friedrich Engels published *The Communist Manifesto*, a political document describing society through the lens of class struggle.

NOTES: _____

_____

_____

_____

_____

_____

_____

_____

1854-1900: Life of Irish poet and playwright Oscar Wilde, author of *The Importance of Being Earnest*.

1856-1950: Life of British/Irish playwright George Bernard Shaw, writer of *Man and Superman, Pygmalion,* and *Saint Joan*.

1859: English naturalist Charles Darwin published *On the Origin of Species*, founding the science of evolutionary biology.

1861-1865: American Civil War: After the election of President Abraham Lincoln and fearing the abolition of slavery, seven southern states seceded from the United States and formed the Confederate States of America. During the war, Lincoln issued The Emancipation Proclamation, freeing slaves in rebel territory. Shortly before the war's end, John Wilkes Booth assassinated Lincoln.

1861: The transcontinental telegraph linked the east and west coasts of the United States.

1868-1912: Emperor Meiji transformed Japan from a feudal island nation into an industrialized world power.

1869: The Transcontinental Railroad was completed at Promontory Point, Utah.

c. 1870s: Realism: Following the trend of French painters, dramatists sought to represent life as it appeared. In realistic plays, characters spoke without verse or meter, sets were dressed as if they were actual locations, and psychological considerations motivated characters' decisions.

1871: To create *Thespis*, English producer John Hollingshead introduced librettist W.S. Gilbert to the composer Arthur Sullivan. Gilbert and Sullivan would write 14 comedic operas, including *H.M.S. Pinafore, The Pirates of Penzance,* and *The Mikado*.

1879: Eadweard Muybridge invented the zoöpraxiscope, forerunner to the motion picture projector.

1879: *A Doll's House*, Henrik Ibsen's drama about the repression of women, premiered at the Royal Theatre in Copenhagen.

1881: The first building lit entirely by electric light, The Savoy Theatre, opened in London's West End. The West End and New York City's Broadway would become the pinnacles of professional theatre in the English-speaking world.

1884: European leaders divided Africa into imperial colonies at the Berlin Conference.

1884: First elevator stage constructed at the Budapest Opera House.

1888-1953: Life of American playwright Eugene O'Neill, whose *Long Day's Journey into Night* is considered one of the best American plays of the 20th century.

1891: First public demonstration of a working motion picture at Thomas Edison's lab.

1896: First US movie theaters opened in Buffalo, NY and New Orleans, LA.

1897-1975: Life of American playwright Thornton Wilder, who authored *Our Town* and *Skin of Our Teeth*.

1898: Spanish-American War: The United States conquered Cuba, destroyed the Spanish navy in the Pacific and decisively ended the Spanish Empire.

Twentieth Century

1900: At Broadway's Casino Theatre, *Floradora* opened, introducing the Floradora sextet, a forerunner to the modern day chorus line.

1902: Los Angeles built its first movie theatre.

1904: Anton Chekhov's play of modern realism, *The Cherry Orchard*, premiered at the Moscow Art Theatre.

1904-1905: The Russo-Japanese War pitted Japan and Russia against one another for competing colonial claims in Korea. Japan surprised the world with their resounding victory.

1905-1984: Life of American dramatist Lillian Hellman, who wrote *Foxes* and *Toys in the Attic*.

1907: Broadway producer Florenz Ziegfeld Jr. introduced his legendary theatrical revue Ziegfeld Follies.

1908-1981: Life of novelist and playwright William Saroyan, who authored *The Time of Your Life, My Name Is Aram,* and *My Heart's in the Highlands*.

1909: Russian theatre actor and director, Konstantin Stanislavsky, introduced "method acting," whereupon a character's internal decisions influence their external action.

1911-1983: Life of American playwright Tennessee Williams, writer of *The Glass Menagerie, A Streetcar Named Desire, Cat on a Hot Tin Roof, Sweet Bird of Youth,* and *The Night of the Iguana*.

1913: Featuring an all-black cast, the large scale musical *Darktown Follies* helped launch Harlem as an African-American cultural center.

1914-1918: World War I: Ultimately, the war resulted in nearly thirty million casualties, the end of all empires in Europe (Germany, Russia, Austria-Hungary, Ottoman), and ongoing political upheaval.

1915-2005: Life of American playwright Arthur Miller, writer of *All My Sons, Death of a Salesman, The Crucible,* and *A View from the Bridge*.

1917: Russian Revolution: The March and October Revolutions in Russia deposed Emperor Nicholas II and instigated the Russian Civil War that would end in 1922 with the founding of the USSR, led by Vladimir Lenin.

1920: *Beyond the Horizon*, Eugene O'Neill's first full-length play, won the Pulitzer Prize, marking the beginning of modern American drama.

1920: The African-American migration to northern cities ignited the Harlem Renaissance.

1921: America's first resident professional theatre, The Cleveland Playhouse, opened.

1927-2018: Life of American play- and screenwriter Neil Simon, author of *Biloxi Blues, Come Blow Your Horn,* and *The Odd Couple*.

1927: Jerome Kern and Oscar Hammerstein's musical *Show Boat* debuts on Broadway. Despite heavy themes involving race and tragic love, *Show Boat* is chock-full of song, dance, and spectacle, marking Broadway and musical theatre as a distinctly American art form.

1927-1949: Chinese Civil War: The Chinese Nationalist Party (CNP) and Communist Party (CPC) of China vied for control of the largest country on Earth, suspending hostilities during Japan's invasion from 1937-1945. Ultimately CPC, led by Mao Zedong gained control of mainland China, while CNP took residence in Taiwan.

NOTES: _____

_____

_____

_____

_____

_____

_____

_____

_____

1929: The New York Stock Market crashed and the Great Depression followed.

1930: American Jean Rosenthal pioneered stage lighting and the idea of it as a career.

1930-1965: Life of Lorraine Hansberry, whose *A Raisin in the Sun* tells of an African American family's experience in Chicago.

1932: Radio City Music Hall opened in New York City. The "Showplace of the Nation" is home to the leggy dance company, The Rockettes.

1935: Opening in Boston, George Gershwin's *Porgy and Bess* featured a cast of classically trained African-American actors.

1937-1945: World War II: The war and its consequences ultimately killed up to 85 million people, including 6 million Jews and 5 million others killed in the Holocaust. It also led to the formation of the United Nations, established the United States and the Soviet Union as the world's only superpowers, and kicked off a nuclear standoff between them, called the Cold War, that would last until 1991.

1950: Frank Loesser, Joe Swerling, and Abe Burrows's *Guys and Dolls* debuted on Broadway.

1952 - : Life of American playwright Beth Henley, winner of the Pulitzer Prize for her play *Crimes of the Heart.*

1954: In Brown v. Board of Education, the US Supreme Court declared that segregated schools were unconstitutional per the 14th Amendment.

1955-1975: Vietnam War: In one of the Cold War's proxy wars, the US and the USSR took opposing sides in a civil war in Vietnam. In the US, where the government conscripted young men to fight, the war became a cultural flashpoint.

1957: Leonard Bernstein, Stephen Sondheim, and Arthur Laurents brought *West Side Story* to Broadway. Its complex and enduring music, societal themes, and extended dance numbers still influence Broadway theatre.

1957: Both the Tony Award and the Pulitzer Prize are awarded to Eugene O'Neill's *A Long Day's Journey into Night.*

1957: The Soviet Union launched Sputnik 1 into Earth's orbit.

1963: Civil rights leader Martin Luther King Jr. delivered the "I Have a Dream" speech in Washington DC, a call for racial equality. Five years later he was assassinated.

1968: The controversial rock musical, *Hair,* opened on Broadway. *Hair* dealt frankly with profanity, drug use, and sexuality and notoriously included a nude scene.

1969: The United States landed astronauts Neil Armstrong and Buzz Aldrin on the moon with pilot Michael Collins delivering them back to Earth.

1982: Andrew Lloyd Webber's *Cats* opened. It became Broadway's longest running play until it was surpassed by Webber's own *Phantom of the Opera.*

1989: The Fall of the Berlin Wall led to the reunification of Germany (which had been split since 1945) and symbolized the end of the Cold War. The USSR dissolved two years later.

1989: English engineer Tim Berners-Lee wrote the code for the World Wide Web, the first web browser, allowing what had started as an U.S. Department of Defense project, ARPANET, to develop into a global network serving 3.2 billion people and counting.

1991: In the Gulf War, America forced Iraqi dictator Saddam Hussein's armies out of Kuwait.

1998: Osama Bin Laden and his Al-Qaeda terrorist network destroyed two American embassies in eastern Africa.

Twenty-First Century

2001: Al-Qaeda terrorists hijacked four planes and used three of them to bring down the World Trade Center Buildings in New York City and to attack the Pentagon; the fourth plane, which is thought to have been heading for the White House, crashed in an empty field.

2003: US invaded Iraq a second time to eject tyrannical leader, Saddam Hussein, and to install a democratic system of government.

2008: Barack Obama became the first African-American President of the United States.

2012: Simon Stephens' play, *The Curious Incident of the Dog in the Night-Time,* premiered on Broadway, showcasing an autistic main character.

2013: Scientists successfully cloned human stem cells.

2015: Lin Manuel Miranda's musical *Hamilton* debuted on Broadway featuring an ethnically diverse cast portraying America's founding fathers and music drawn from hip hop and R&B.

2020 - : A worldwide pandemic shut down countries around the globe. In the US, state-at-home orders forced businesses, schools, and theatres to close. Broadway shows and national tours were cancelled, as schools and amateur theatres scramble to create Virtual Theatre.

NOTES: _____

THE FIRST PERFORMANCES

The history of theatre is closely tied to that of the world. When a writer sat down with his quill and paper, he looked around him for inspiration. He may have written about the wars, the politicians, the attitudes of the day, or some young couple he heard about from the friend of a friend. Even if what he wrote about was fantasy, in most cases it was still based on those things to which he had been exposed. Years later, we read these old plays and stories, and we get a glimmer of an idea as to what life must have been like for the people in that place and time.

Before the written word, stories were told around campfires. Imagine a darkened hillside with tall trees rustling in the wind. The golden glow of a campfire sends shadows creeping up the sides of the cliffs. The cool wind carries the howl of a distant wolf pack barely heard over the crackling of the fire. You are a tribal person sitting in the dirt, dressed in skins, waiting for the day's hunt to come off the fire. While you wait with the rest of the tribe, the huntsmen act out the pursuit of the hunt while the youngest in the group, costumed in the skin of the kill, plays the role of the prey.

The story starts low; the group has come upon a bison grazing in a small enclosed valley. Quietly they surround it, spears propped and ready. Someone steps on a stick, alerting the beast to the danger. He darts, and the chase begins. One of the young huntsmen finds himself cornered by the frightened animal, who has lowered his head in preparation for the attack. He snorts and paws the dusty ground, then hurls his huge body at the hunter. With no place to go, the man thrusts his spear, hitting right between the shoulder blades, but it is not enough to stop the charging beast. He braces himself for certain death, when out of the brush a barrage of spears and bodies bring the giant animal down.

It is possible that many stories like the one above were enacted for thousands and thousands of years. Topics probably included great hunts, the harvest, feats of heroism and bravery, and perhaps even some love stories. Eventually, music may have been added, such as the beat of a drum. Dancing would almost certainly accompany that. However, we have no written records of these performances, just speculation.

The first record of a theatrical performance was found on a stone tablet in Egypt dating back to about 2000 BC. It describes a three-day performance arranged by and starring I-Kher-Wofret of Abydos. Proving that violence is not a new theatrical device, this performance used realistic battles and high ceremony to reenact the murder, dismemberment, and resurrection of the god Osiris.

177

TEACHING THEATRE HISTORY

Just as the history of the world is vast, so is the history of theatre. It would be difficult, in any volume of work, to recount every significant event of the stage and its players, but there are some that stand out.

In this chapter, you will find a concise history of theatre. Each part represents a period or piece of a period. Students with no interest in theatre will complain that theatre history is not fun. Remind them that each playwright's works represent the real-life events and ideas of the day and that by understanding theatre history, students are improving their understanding of world history.

If you strive to keep the theatre history unit short, try gathering some of the works mentioned in the chapter and have students read from the plays. They will get a better sense of the language and the structure of the piece. However, you can really impact their learning by approaching each section as follows:

1. Introduce the period by discussing this section's corresponding pages with the class.

2. Assign students to do a scene from the period; if you plan to do this with each period, make memorization optional. During the days or weeks to follow, periodically introduce new information

ANCIENT GREEK THEATRE

Despite the Egyptian performance, the Greeks are generally credited with giving theatre its start. About 1,400 years after the reenactment of Osiris's demise, Greeks were paying tribute to their gods as well. In honor of Dionysus, the god of wine and fertility, and to commemorate his death, the Greek chorus danced around an altar, upon which a sacrificed goat was placed. They sang a song called a "goat song," or tragos. It is from this word that we get the word "tragedy."

The chorus played an important role in Greek theatre, keeping the audience informed as to what was happening onstage. However, in 534 BC, a man named Thespis did something no one had done before. He broke away from the chorus and held dialogue with them onstage. This action made him history's first actor. Today, actors are called thespians, named after this trendsetter.

The development of the stage was one of the greatest contributions the Greeks gave to the theatre. Originally held with semicircular hillside seating, the addition of wooden and eventually stone seats added a sense of sophistication for the all-male spectators. By the time women attended the theatre around 400 BC, the theatre could seat over 15,000 people. It was large enough that those seated at the back had a hard time hearing and seeing. The large masks worn by the actors helped with this.

Elaborately decorated with exaggerated characteristics, these masks added size to the characters, making them easier to see. There were about thirty different types of masks worn by Greek actors onstage. Believed to be introduced by Thespis, the masks were made of lightweight wood, cork, or linen and served many purposes. Because the plays had few actors (one early on and three later), the masks allowed one actor to play several roles. Also, because women did not act, these devices allowed men to play women's roles. Unfortunately, the masks prevented the actor's own facial expressions from being seen, so he had to rely on his voice to make his characters real and interesting.

The area where the chorus danced was called the orchestra. Behind the acting area was a small hut-like building called a skene (pronounced SKEE-nee). This served as the actors' dressing rooms. Eventually, several stories and wings were added to the building, the front of which was used to paint scenery. The roof was used as an acting area for the gods. If the gods needed to fly, a crane-like device called a machina (MAH-kee-nah) would hoist them into the air. The term "deus ex machina" refers to the plot device originating in the Greek theatre in which a problem was resolved quite unexpectedly when a god would appear from nowhere and save the day.

GREEK PLAYWRIGHTS

We still have many of the plays that were written by ancient Greeks, but because of the passage of time, many are fragments with the remainder of the play lost. It is believed that many great works are gone altogether. Despite their age, these classic plays remain popular, many based on universal and timeless themes that never seem to lose popularity.

There were many playwriting competitions held in ancient Greece in which playwrights competed for prizes and public favor. The playwright of the competing play not only wrote the text itself, but he composed the music, choreographed the dances, directed, and often held the lead role. The entries were divided into two categories: tragedies and comedies. It was not uncommon for the great playwriting competitions to require writers to submit four plays in the tragic category—three

about the period using videos, pages from websites, PowerPoint presentations, or guest speakers.

3. Pair up with a history teacher or the entire department. Plan to trade scene work for videos or guest speakers. Cross-curriculum learning can be a powerful tool!

4. Also, your art and music teachers could provide sights and sounds from the period so that the learning is multisensory. Can you find recipes from the eras? Yum, turkey legs!

5. Create a time line scroll and use different highlighters to distinguish between political,

economic, religious, and cultural events. Invite students to find other relevant dates to add. When finished, display the scroll where all students can appreciate it.

6. Have students present their scenes with scripts in hand, then advance to the next period in theatre history.

Also, encourage students to interject their own ideas, opinions, and stories related to each period. For example, ask them how they feel about women not being allowed to act on the Elizabethan stage because their presence was thought to encourage immorality. Or, do they see any similarities between what people look for in entertainment today and tragedies and a satyr play or a trilogy and a satyr play—all related in theme. However, to compete for the comedy prize, a writer only had to submit one play. Hidden within these two types of Greek plays was a third type—the tragicomedy or satyr play. This was a tragic story with comic undertones.

Aeschylus: Aeschylus (ES-kil-us) is the earliest known Greek playwright. Born in about 525 BC, he is believed to have written around Ninety plays. Of those, only seven survive in their entirety. He is also credited with having the only surviving trilogy—the *Oresteia*, three closely connected tragedies, first performed in 458 BC. Because of his long career and the influence of his writings, we

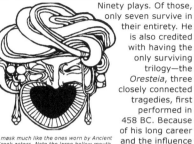

A mask much like the ones worn by Ancient Greek actors. Note the large hollow mouth which allowed actors to project their voices.

can see the development of Greek theatre in his works. His earlier plays have choruses of fifty and only one actor, but his later works show the trend of his contemporaries toward the smaller chorus and several actors. He died in 456 BC; his tombstone did not mention his career as a writer.

- His most famous plays are *Agamemnon, The Libation Bearers*, and *The Eumenides*.

- He is often referred to as the "Father of Tragedy."

- He wrote about the choices men make and the consequences that follow.

Sophocles: During Aeschylus's lifetime, the younger playwright Sophocles (SOF-uh-clees) began his career. He wrote between 90 and 110 plays, but only seven survive today. He is said to have won the playwriting prize eighteen times! He compared the power of the gods to the importance of humanity, believing that humans possess god-like qualities that make them want to change fate. In a time when it was considered impious to doubt fate, Sophocles armed his characters with the power to challenge the paths the gods set before them. Many believe that this was what made his characters some of the greatest to take the stage.

- His most famous plays are *Oedipus* (EH-di-pus) *the King, Oedipus at Colonus, Electra*, and *Antigone* (an-TI-guh-nee).

- He was born in 497 BC and died in 406 BC.

- Along with Shakespeare, he is considered one of the greatest playwright of all time.

Euripides: The last great writer of Greek tragedy, Euripides (yoo-RIP-eh-dees) was born in 484 BC and died in 406 BC, the same year as Sophocles. He wrote about ninety plays, eighteen of which survive. Winning the prize only five times, it wasn't until after his death that his plays truly earned public appreciation. His exploration into the psychology of the individual, especially women, as opposed to the larger public issues taken on by his predecessors, seemed to be a bit too modern for his time.

- His most famous plays are *The Trojan Women, Medea*, and *Hippolytus*.

- His *Cyclops* is the only complete satyr play known to exist.

- He originated the use of the prologue to summarize the play for the audience before the action.

Aristophanes: Born in 448 BC, Aristophanes (air-uh-STAH-fuh-nees) is the only writer of ancient Greek comedy whose works still exist in whole today. However, it is believed that like his tragic counterparts, three-fourths of his works are missing or incomplete. Furthermore, because his comedy is based on a type of wit that gets lost in translation, modern audiences have less appreciation than those of his day. He died in 380 BC.

- His most famous plays are *The Birds, The Clouds*, and *The Frogs*.

- His plays made fun of the leaders of Athens, the gods, and even his playwright counterparts.

what they sought historically? Most importantly, draw parallels between the information they are learning about the stage and what they have already learned about the history of the world during the time period they are studying.

At the end of each period, have a fun review, such as "trashcan basketball." Face it, theatre history can be hard and unrewarding compared to improvising and acting, but there are ways to add some fun.

ROMAN THEATRE

Unfortunately, theatre did not flourish in Rome as it did in Greece. Instead, it veered sharply into a bawdy and decadent form of base entertainment that appealed to the audience's sense of vulgarity, sensuality, and violence. Featuring obscene mimes, drunken horseplay, and dancers in meager bikinis, the performances rarely had plots that dealt with challenging issues. With plays based on the lowest aspects of human nature, it is not surprising that actors' reputations suffered. This set a trend that would take centuries to change.

The Romans had great impact on the architecture of the theatre, bringing it closer to the stages of today. The theatres were built in a flat area instead of on a hillside, as had been done in neighboring Greece. The once-open space was replaced with an elaborately decorated wall that surrounded the seats and the stage. Because the chorus was no longer being used, the orchestra became obsolete, making the stage the central focus. The stage was positioned high off the ground with tiers of benches at the front and the scaenae frons (an elaborately decorated wall) at the rear. Later stages even featured curtains that could be closed at the end of a scene, awnings for the audience, concessions, and even perfumed water mists to cool and deodorize the audience on hot days.

There were two great writers of Roman comedy, Plautus and Terence. During their time, Rome lacked the elaborate stages that were yet to come (as were the large audiences). Later, Seneca, a writer of larger-than-life dramas, wrote plays that are better read than produced. Consequently and ironically, none of Rome's esteemed playwrights benefited much from the great architecture of the period.

Plautus: Twenty of this writer's plays are still in existence today, all written between 205 BC and 184 BC. Because they were not published in his lifetime but left in the hands of actors, it is believed that a great deal of Plautus's work has been modified. Regardless, at a time when the audience seemed indifferent to political issues, his plays found popularity and longevity. Like Terence and Seneca, he borrowed his plots from the Greeks, but he added a personal touch to them that made them uniquely his. He used poetic devices (which would get lost in translation), proving that he was an artist, and the subsequent imitation of his plots by later writers like Shakespeare and Molière, prove that he had a profound historical impact.

- His most famous plays are *Menaechmi (The Twin Brothers)* and *Amphitryon.*
- Despite his borrowed plots, his plays paint an accurate picture of life in his times.

Terence: Born an African slave to a Roman senator, Terence exhibited brilliance early in life, winning for himself an uncommon education and his subsequent freedom. Using applicable plots and a universal dialogue, he had less popularity with the Roman audiences who craved buffoonery and vulgarity. Born in 195 BC, he wrote all six of his plays by the age of twenty-five. He left Rome under suspicion of plagiarism, never to return. He died in 159 BC.

- His most famous plays are *Andria* and *The Eunuch.*
- He was paid 8,000 sesterces for *The Eunuch*, which was the greatest sum ever paid for a comedy at that time.

Seneca: A native of Cordoba in Spain, Seneca was born in 4 BC with fragile health. As a result of this and the fact that his father was a great speaker, he devoted himself to the spoken word and to the study of philosophy. He was banished in AD 41 by Claudius, but recalled by the Empress Agrippina eight years later and employed as her son Nero's tutor. Seneca was devoted to the family for many years, but when mother and son broke apart, he sided with Nero, drawing up all of his state papers and defending him in his mother's murder. After falling out of favor with the new ruler, Seneca committed suicide in AD 65 rather than be subjected to a more humiliating death.

- His most famous plays are *Octavia, The Phoenician Women*, and *Hercules.*
- His plays are generally considered closet dramas, plays that are meant to be read rather than acted.

NOTES: _____

_____

_____

_____

_____

_____

_____

_____

NAME _____ PERIOD _____ DATE _____

EARLY THEATRE REVIEW

1. How did the earliest performances probably originate?

2. A stone tablet is the first record of a theatrical performance in _____ ,
    dating back to about _____ BC. It describes a _____ -day performance by
    _____ of Abydos.

3. Describe the Egyptian performance.

4. The _____ are credited with the origins of theatre, despite the earlier Egyptian
    performance. They were honoring their god of wine and fertility, _____.

5. The word tragedy comes from the Greek word _____ which means _____ _____.

6. The _____ played an important role in Greek theatre, keeping the audience
    informed of the action onstage. In 534 BC, _____ stepped from the chorus and
    engaged in dialogue with them, making him the first actor. It is from him that we get the word
    "thespian," a term used today which means actor.

7. What was the purpose of the Greek mask?

8. Define:
    a. Orchestra

    b. Skene

    c. Machina

9. _____ is the earliest recorded Greek playwright. His trilogy, _____, is the
    only one known to have survived. He is often referred to as _____ _____
    of _____. His plays include _____, the _____
    _____, and the _____.

10. _____ is often referred to alongside Shakespeare as the greatest writer
    of all time. He took a great risk when he gave his characters the power to change the
    _____ the _____ had put before them. He wrote _____ the King,
    _____ at Colonus, _____, and _____.

11. _____ earned public appreciation for his writings only after his death. While
    other playwrights of the time dealt with larger _____ _____, he explored the
    psychology of _____, especially women. His _____ is the only
    complete satyr play known to exist.

12. _____ is the only writer of Greek comedies whose plays are
    still known to exist today. His plays, which included _____, _____, and
    _____, poked fun at Athenian leaders and the gods at a time when free speech was
    not well accepted.

13. Roman performances included a great deal of mime, dancing, and _____.

14. Roman playwrights included ex-slave _____, _____, and the
    Spanish-born _____.

181

EARLY THEATRE REVIEW KEY

1. It is likely that hunters told their tribesmen about the drama of their hunts, adding movement, sounds, and taking advantage of the flickering campfire for dramatic lighting.

2. Egypt, 2000, three, I-Kher-Wofret

3. This performance used realistic battles and high ceremony to reenact the murder, dismemberment, and resurrection of the god Osiris.

4. Greeks, Dionysis

5. tragos, goat song

6. chorus, Thespis

7. The masks added size to the characters, which made them easier to see, allowed one actor to play several roles, and allowed men to play women's roles.

8. a. The area where the chorus danced
    b. A small hut-like building behind the acting area that served as the actors' dressing rooms
    c. A crane-like device used to hoist the actors playing gods into the air

9. Aeschylus, the *Orestia*, the father of tragedy, *Agamemnon, Liberation Bearers, Euminides*

10. Sophocles, fates, gods, *Oedipus, Oedipus, Electra, Antigone*

11. Euripedes, social issues, individual, *Cyclops*

12. Aristophanes, *Birds, Clouds, Frogs*

13. horseplay

14. Terence, Plautus, Seneca

MEDIEVAL THEATRE

The period from about AD 500 to AD 1500 is known as the medieval period in theatre history. Following the decline in popularity of the theatre in Rome and the demise of respect for actors, the period to follow was a difficult one for the theatre. Traces of performances such as mimes, acrobatics, and singing can be found, but anything structured like a play remained difficult to find until later. Like the Greeks who used plays to worship Dionysus, Christians would introduce theatrical performance to the church and its mostly illiterate congregation as a means of worship and teaching the gospel.

Initially, priests used liturgical chants during the Mass to teach those who could not read about the events in the Bible. Eventually these chants grew into more elaborate productions that, because of the limited space within the church, had to be moved outdoors. Because of the content and probably due to the texts being in Latin, the players were priests, nuns, and choirboys. However, at some point the plays were translated from Latin, which opened the doors for commoners to participate.

Medieval drama has a language all its own. The following are some terms from the period:

Miracle and mystery plays—plays based on the saints' lives and Bible stories.

Passion plays—plays based on the last week in the life of Christ.

Mansion—a series of acting stations in a line, including heaven, Pilate's house, Jerusalem, and hell's mouth.

Guilds—groups of tradesmen with a common trade (bakers, goldsmiths, etc.). Each guild would be responsible for part of a Bible story that, when combined with other guilds' performances, made a cycle. Each guild competed with the others to see who could produce the most elaborate story.

Cycle—the combined stories produced by the guilds.

Morality play—similar in theme to miracle and mystery plays, yet more concerned with the principles taught by Christianity rather than stories from the Bible.

Masque—a spectacular play glorifying the nobility.

Pageant cart—a two-storied cart that doubled as a stage (with the underside being a dressing room). During a cycle, the carts would move from place to place, each producing the same story over and over again for different segments of the audience, which would remain stationary and enjoy each performance as it moved through.

Some groups not associated with the church began performing miracle and mystery plays, but they drew criticism from those with church ties, and it was not long before their performances were repressed. However, these pioneers do represent the first acting companies and were later recognized and patronized by the nobles.

Despite the seriousness of the message and the religious content of medieval theatre, the performances continued to appeal to the audience's sense of horseplay. Any opportunity for silliness and buffoonery was seized. Noah's wife became a nag, and the Tower of Babel lent itself to unlimited comic dialogue. However, the audience's favorite figure to take comic pokes and humorous stabs at was Satan. The gleeful attitude with which he and his assistants handled hell's business gave the viewers a frighteningly enjoyable incentive to be good. Even after the scenes in which Satan was a part of the story, his assistants, adorned in horrific masks, continued to pop into the story for no apparent reason other than to keep the audience amused with feats of acrobatics and farcical miming. Perhaps this is why even today one of the most prolific symbols of the medieval period continues to be the jester.

NOTES: _____

_____

_____

_____

_____

_____

_____

_____

Other aspects of the medieval stage that helped to draw in large audiences were the complicated technical devices and special effects. For example, trap doors were hidden in the raised stages so that characters could appear from nowhere or disappear. Some troupes had cranes to fly angels in. However, one of the most fascinating devices had to be the contraption known as hell's mouth. With a moving jaw, real flames, and smoke bellowing from its bowels, the device would consume those characters who were too evil for heaven. It took seventeen men to operate one such device.

MEDIEVAL PLAYS

- *The Second Shepherd's Play*—a secular play about a clever scoundrel named Mak who steals a sheep, hides it in a crib, and passes it off as his son.

- *Everyman*—an allegorical (utilizing strong symbolism) morality play in which Everyman is summoned to meet Death, appear before God, and seek salvation. Other characters include Five Wits, Fellowship, Kindred, Discretion, Beauty, Strength, Knowledge, and Good Deeds.

Christians would introduce theatrical performance to the church and its mostly illiterate congregation as a means of worship and teaching the gospel.

MEDIEVAL REVIEW

1. Medieval plays were based mainly on stories from the _____ and the lives of saints. They were called _____ and _____ plays.

2. Plays based on the last week of Christ's life, called _____ plays, are still performed today.

3. Similar to the above were _____ plays, only these taught the difference between right and wrong rather than about Christianity itself.

4. A _____ was a glorious spectacle performed for the benefit of the nobility.

5. Despite the seriousness of the message, medieval plays still had a lot of _____ _____.

6. Name two medieval plays: _____

MEDIEVAL REVIEW KEY

1. Bible, Miracle, Mystery

2. passion

3. morality

4. masque

5. horseplay

6. *The Second Shepherd's Play, Everyman*

183

NOTES: _____

_____

_____

_____

_____

_____

_____

_____

_____

RENAISSANCE THEATRE

Perhaps the busiest period in theatre history was the Renaissance era, which began early in the fourteenth century and continued until the start of the seventeenth century. Renaissance means "rebirth," which is fitting since this is the time when theatre sought new life after being almost non-existent for many centuries following the Roman period and then forbidden for all but clergy during the medieval period.

The Renaissance in theatre had its first sparks of life in Italy with a rediscovery of the classics. The pageant carts that had been the medieval standard were not suited for more modern plays, so new playhouses were constructed. Ancient Roman theatres became the model from which the newer facilities were built. New theatres, however, progressed even further with the addition of a proscenium arch—the arched wall above the stage opening. Furthermore, the Italians began using fabulously painted scenery that reflected the development of the visual artistry flourishing in southern Europe at that time. Despite the new designs, the revived classics, which were suited to a more educated audience, lacked mass appeal.

The most famous contribution of the Italian Renaissance was a style of theatre called commedia dell'arte. Although it has its roots in the classical styles of the Greek and Roman plays and even in the burlesque style of the medieval period, this new development was unique unto itself. Aside from a basic plot and subplot and stock characters, the entire performance was improvised, including brief comedic moments called "lazzi" and longer comedic scenes called "burle" that often involved practical jokes. The actors experienced a freedom—or responsibility—previously unheard of. The necessity for dancing and singing, acrobatics, mime, juggling, and quick wit meant that actors had to be skilled as well as intelligent and talented.

The plays were performed by traveling companies, which were groups of performers who worked together continually as an organization. Because of the mobile nature of the new style, portable stages again became a necessity.

THE CHARACTERS OF COMMEDIA DELL'ARTE

The colorful characters of commedia dell'arte may be its most outstanding legacy. Each was based on a stock personality, a lot like modern-day typecasting. As a matter of fact, many of the stock characters used during this period are still used today. During the Italian Renaissance, the actors who played each of these roles were specialized and would play the same character from one play to the next and even throughout their lifetime. Unless there was a major change in appearance due to age, actors did not change characters.

The Innamorati, a pair of young lovers, generally provided the main plot. In most cases, they wanted to marry, but the heroine's father or guardian opposed it. The heroine was referred to as the "inamorata" and her lover as the "inamorato." They were attractive characters, beautifully dressed, and they did not wear masks. Today, when a boy and girl are in love, they are said to be "enamored," which derives from the same root word.

The heroine's maidservant, Columbina, was the Fontesca or shrewd female servant. She

NOTES: _____

_____

_____

_____

_____

_____

_____

_____

_____

was flirtatious and witty. She and the various comic menservants and nagging housekeepers, called Zanni, were responsible for keeping the action dynamic yet always returning to the plot. They were often paired similarly to Laurel and Hardy—one bright and mischievous and the other fumbling and foolish. Some familiar stock servants were Arlecchino, Pulcinella, and Pedrolino. Brighella, who often played the female counterpart to the manservant, was brash, rude, and could make men blush.

The heroine's father or guardian, Pantalone, was a worldly lover and contrary parent who struggled against a rebellious child. He was overbearing and a bit sneaky.

Il Capitano was a braggart soldier who acted like a brave hero, but eventually the audience learned that he lived in constant fear of his own shadow.

Although commedia dell'arte eventually died out, its influences remain strong and undeniable. Even today, characters similar to those stock characters of the period are still seen in plays, movies, and TV shows, as is the typical plot. Can you think of some modern-day characters from TV, movies, or plays that might have been influenced by commedia dell'arte?

With the exception of The Innamorati, commedia dell'arte actors often wore masks to designate their character. These half masks were often made of leather and included exaggerated features.

RENAISSANCE THEATRE OUTSIDE OF ITALY

Besides the Renaissance in Italy, theatre continued to develop elsewhere in Europe. Traveling troupes and players went from town to town performing smaller plays, while more well-known companies were invited to play in the great castles.

In Spain, Miguel de Cervantes was busy writing the famous novel *Don Quixote*, which over the centuries became the inspiration for many plays, including the musical *Man of La Mancha*. Lope de Vega and Pedro Calderon de la Barca are famous Spanish playwrights from the Renaissance period.

With the support of the government, theatre flourished in France. Some famous plays include Pierre Corneilles' *Le Cid* and Jean Racine's *Phaedra*. Perhaps France's most famous playwright of the late Renaissance period was Molière, who lived from 1622 to 1673. Several of his comedic plays, such as *The Miser, Tartuffe, The Misanthrope,* and *The Imaginary Invalid* are still performed and enjoyed today.

185

NOTES: _____

_____

_____

_____

_____

_____

_____

_____

_____

ELIZABETHAN THEATRE

The Renaissance spread through Europe to England and brought about a new type of theatre there, Elizabethan theatre. Named after Queen Elizabeth I, whose reign started in 1558, she was a patron of the arts. The Elizabethan era produced many great plays and playwrights, three of whom stand above the rest: Christopher Marlowe, Ben Jonson, and William Shakespeare.

Elizabethan drama flourished after England conquered the Spanish Armada in 1588, resulting in a burst of patriotic confidence and national identity. At this time in history, performers sought the patronage of wealthy noblemen. This protected their reputations while providing funding and stability. In the eyes of their fellow actors, those with noble endorsement were considered "legitimate." Any actors who failed to secure this royal support were considered rogues. That's why the idea of "legitimate" theatre has its roots in the Elizabethan era.

During the Elizabethan period, women were not permitted to act because the stage was considered unladylike and unsuitable for women. Instead, young boys who possessed smaller frames and higher voices played the women's parts. While we might consider this practice odd today, it was all that the players of the time knew, so it was considered quite normal and acceptable.

The plays of Shakespeare, Marlowe, and Jonson drew large, boisterous crowds seeking out bawdy entertainment, especially in the lower levels where admission was the cheapest. However, in the early 1600s, theatre started to veer off in a new direction, and a different kind of play started to emerge. This new form of entertainment, called court plays, was geared to a more intellectual audience—royalty and nobility. Unlike the raucous plays of Shakespeare and Jonson, the newer works by Francis Beaumont and John Fletcher were subtle and sophisticated.

Civil war erupted in 1642, and the theatre again went into hibernation. Banned by the Puritans, most of the stages were destroyed or allowed to deteriorate. England would not see a new theatre until 1660.

THE ELIZABETHAN STAGE

Playhouses in the Elizabethan period were round or octagonal with three levels or galleries of seating, with the best seats reserved for those who could afford the highest fee. Those with little money stood in the pit, the bare dirt floor in front of the stage; thus, they were called groundlings. Those willing to pay the greatest fee could sit on the stage.

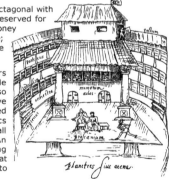

The actors performed on a platform stage with trap doors throughout, but because the theatre itself was open, little scenery was used. Likewise, there was no stage lighting, so plays were performed in the daylight. The stage did have a partial roof, however, and it was elaborately decorated to resemble the nighttime sky with stars and the zodiacs surrounding the sun, thus its name—the heavens. The wall behind the actors resembled the exterior of a building. An area above the stage could be used as an additional acting area, but more often it housed the musicians. Above that was storage, and at the top of the building was a flag to inform the public of an impending performance.

186

NOTES: _____

_____

_____

_____

_____

_____

_____

_____

ELIZABETHAN PLAYWRIGHTS

Christopher Marlowe: Born in 1564 in Canterbury and dying when he was just 29 years old, Marlowe is credited with the introduction of blank verse. He acted and wrote under the patronage of Lord Admiral. He was hailed as the greatest English dramatist until Shakespeare began to make his mark. This comparison and eventual dethroning led to a fierce rivalry between Marlowe and Shakespeare. His unfortunate death after being stabbed in a tavern brawl may have robbed history of a literary genius before his prime.

- His most famous plays are *Tamburlaine the Great*, *The Jew of Malta*, *Edward II*, and *The Tragical History of the Life and Death of Doctor Faustus*, commonly called *Doctor Faustus*.

- Although born the same year as Shakespeare, Marlowe began his theatre career at an earlier age.

Ben Jonson: Jonson (1572-1637) is considered the first real English comic. He was born the son of a clergyman and educated at Westminster School by William Camden, the great classical scholar. However, he was deprived a university education by a domineering stepfather who made him an apprentice bricklayer. Eventually he joined the army, serving in Flanders, and returned to England in 1592, marrying Anne Lewis.

Painfully aware of his lack of higher learning, Jonson became bitter and often found himself in trouble. His rebellious nature was also evident in his work, as he wrote and spoke with little self-censoring.

- His most famous plays are *Volpone*, *The Alchemist*, and *Every Man in His Humour*.

- He was imprisoned several times.

William Shakespeare: The Bard (1564-1616) has almost undisputedly been granted the title of the greatest playwright ever. He produced a huge and diverse collection of works—154 sonnets and 37 comedic, tragic, and historical plays. The popularity of his historical plays was likely fueled by the patriotic sentiment in England at the time.

Shakespeare was born in Stratford-on-Avon and moved to London in 1594 in order to act. Shakespeare's acting company built The Globe Theatre in 1599, and many of Shakespeare's most famous plays were performed there. In 1613, a theatrical cannon in a production of *Henry VIII* misfired, starting a fire that caused the entire structure to burn down. It was rebuilt the following year.

- His most famous plays are *Romeo and Juliet*, *Hamlet*, *Macbeth*, *Othello*, *A Midsummer Night's Dream*, *King Lear*, *The Taming of the Shrew,* and *The Tempest*.

- None of his plays was published until after his death; consequently, many dispute the purity of the plays, arguing that they were altered by the playhouses that kept them over the years.

NOTES: _____

_____

_____

_____

_____

_____

_____

_____

_____

_____

RENAISSANCE AND ELIZABETHAN THEATRE REVIEW KEY

1. rebirth

2. companies

3. stock

4. inamorata, inamorato, Pantalone, fontesca, Il Capitano

5. Today characters similar to those stock characters of the period are still seen in plays, movies, and TV as is the typical plot

6. Elizabeth, noblemen

7. groundlings, stage

8. Jonson, *Valpone, The Alchemist, Every Man in His Humor*

9. blank verse, Shakespeare's, *Tamburlaine the Great, The Jew of Malta, Edward II, The Tragical History of Doctor Faustus*

10. 37, 154, after his death

11. *Romeo and Juliet, Hamlet, Macbeth, Othello, Midsummer Night's Dream, King Lear, The Taming of the Shrew, The Tempest*

12. women, young boys

NAME _____ PERIOD _____ DATE _____

RENAISSANCE & ELIZABETHAN THEATRE REVIEW

1. Renaissance means _____. This applies to the theatre, because it was almost non-existent after it was forbidden to all but clergy in the medieval period.

2. Commedia dell'arte plays were performed by traveling _____, or groups that worked together as organizations.

3. Commedia dell'arte characters were _____ characters, meaning the actors played the same ones from play to play despite the changing plots.

4. The young female character, the heroine, was called the _____ and her young male lover the _____. Her father was called _____, and her maidservant was the _____. The braggart soldier was named _____.

5. Describe the influence of commedia dell'arte on modern-day entertainment:

6. Queen _____ was the ruler during the period of English theatre that produced greats like Shakespeare, Marlowe, and Jonson. To be considered a part of legitimate theatre, actors and writers sought the patronage of wealthy _____.

7. During this period, wealthy spectators sat in the galleries while the poor, or _____, stood in the pit. The wealthiest were seated on the _____.

8. _____ was the most rebellious of the three great Elizabethan playwrights. He wrote _____, _____, and _____.

9. Marlowe is credited with the introduction of _____ _____. He was considered the greatest English playwright until _____ plays became more popular, dethroning Marlowe. Marlowe wrote _____, _____, _____, and _____.

10. William Shakespeare has almost undisputedly been dubbed the greatest playwright of all time. He wrote _____ plays and _____ sonnets. None of his plays were published until _____, creating a theory that they may have been written by others or perhaps altered by those who had been charged with their keeping.

11. List five of Shakespeare's plays:

12. During the Elizabethan Period, _____ were not allowed to act. Their roles were played by _____.

NOTES: _____

_____

_____

_____

_____

_____

_____

_____

_____

THE ENGLISH RESTORATION AND LATER THEATRE

In 1642, the Puritans closed all theatres in England, and for eighteen years, theatre stayed shuttered under the rule of the Puritan leaders. The Restoration started when Charles II was "restored" to the throne in 1660. Theatre was again made legal, and with it came many important innovations. The old theatres had fallen into ruin, and the old plays did not fit the mood of the times and the people. There was an opportunity for a fresh start, and two men were assigned to supervise the task: Thomas Killigrew and William Davenant. They were both experienced playwrights, and Davenant was rumored to be Shakespeare's son by a mistress. He is even attributed with what could be called the first English opera.

The major tool used to restore theatre was the English Royal Patent of 1662, which mandated that women perform female roles. It also endorsed the theatre as "useful and instructive." Only two theatres, the Drury Lane and the Covent Garden, received official sanction, but this was still a huge improvement from the past two decades. Other small theatres popped up, but only those with official sanction were considered legitimate.

During this time, the architecture of the playhouse also saw important changes. For one, they had complete roofs for the first time, which allowed for more elaborate scenery and stage mechanics. They also added lighting by elaborate chandeliers, and the orchestra moved to the front of the stage. The back wall was replaced with shutters that rolled back and forth in grooves in the stage. This allowed for multiple scene changes. The audience sat on level floors, and to help them see the actors, the stage was tilted slightly toward them. Because the actors were performing on an incline, they had to move "up" and "down" the stage. Consequently, we now use the terms upstage and downstage despite most modern theatres being level. Like the slant of these Restoration theatres, upstage is furthest from the audience; downstage is closest.

There were several famous writers from the period: William Wycherley (1641-1716), who wrote *The Country Wife* and is known for being a comic trendsetter; William Congreve (1670-1729), who is considered a master of comedy and wrote *Love for Love* and *The Way of the World*; and George Farquhar (1678-1707), who wrote *The Beaux' Stratagem*.

The greatest actor of the Restoration was David Garrick. Unlike many who specialized in either comedy or drama, Garrick was equally good at both, and his natural movement and line delivery set him apart from the previously stiff style. Besides acting, he wrote plays, and he made an important innovation in stage lighting when he blocked the lighting instruments from the audience's view. One of the most famous actresses of the period, Peg Woffington, was Garrick's mistress for many years. She rebelled against the gender-biased Elizabethans by effectively portraying men's roles.

Within five months of each other in 1808 and 1809, both the Drury Lane and the Covent Garden burned to the ground. This symbolized the end of an era, and as new buildings were built to replace them, a new period of theatre emerged.

Teetering between the Restoration and the period to follow were Richard Brinsley Sheridan and Oliver Goldsmith. Sheridan (1751-1816) wrote *The School for Scandal* and *The Rivals*. Goldsmith (1728-1774) was a "one-hit wonder" with his play *She Stoops to Conquer*.

189

NOTES: _____

_____

_____

_____

_____

_____

_____

_____

_____

Starting in the 1870s, W.S. Gilbert and Arthur Sullivan produced fourteen operas, the most famous being *H.M.S. Pinafore, The Pirates of Penzance*, and *The Mikado*, which are all still extremely popular. Oscar Wilde gave us the delightful *The Importance of Being Earnest.* However, it is George Bernard Shaw (1856-1950) who dominated the late nineteenth and early twentieth centuries. Many rank him next to Shakespeare as one of England's greatest playwrights. A philosopher of sorts, Shaw used his writings as vehicles to voice his theories on humanity and intellect. His most famous plays are *Arms and the Man, Saint Joan*, and *Pygmalion*, from which the musical *My Fair Lady* was fashioned.

NOTES: _____

_____

_____

_____

_____

_____

_____

_____

AMERICAN THEATRE

The American colonies were under strict puritanical control in the 1600s, and theatrical performances were outlawed. Viewing dramatic or comic plays was thought to negatively influence the behavior of the young and lead to maliciousness. Laws were passed prohibiting any such entertainment, and when the actors persisted, the audience was targeted with fines for viewing the "devilish acts." We know that amateur companies produced plays, but due to the lack of newspapers and public records, little is known about them. There is even some documentation of professional actors touring with amateur groups, but due to laws prohibiting these performances, there is little physical evidence.

In the early to mid-1700s, ideas began to change. Elegant balls became popular recreation for the wealthy. Tantalizing stories of the glamour of the English stage arrived with each docking ship. The settlers began to feel the void impressed upon them by a government fearful of self-expression. As rebellious attitudes grew, so did the acceptance of new ideas. Subsequently, many plays were produced, probably by amateurs, but it is impossible to say when or where the first professional American performance took place. Many were performed in courtrooms or coffeehouses, anywhere the actors could find room. At times the overcrowding led to fighting or even riots. New laws sought to keep stage plays out, but the people won their freedom, and American theatre was born.

There were few American-written plays at that time. Whether amateur or professional, the tried and true works of Shakespeare and other British writers became the staple of the local actors. The first American theatre was built in Williamsburg, Virginia in 1716, but its existence was a short one when its mortgage was foreclosed in 1723. It was later used to produce amateur college performances.

Theatrical families were not uncommon overseas, and in the mid-1700s they began appearing in the colonies. It was easier and less expensive to travel and produce plays as a family; all resources were readily available. Each family member had a special trade and several stock roles. Of course, there had to be some actors from outside the family, but where the company branched, another family often developed as actors married actors. Their children, who were exposed at an early age, naturally gravitated to acting careers. One of the most prevalent of these families was the Hallams. Young Lewis Hallam Jr. made his debut at the age of twelve with a single line, but he became so overcome by stage fright that he ran from the stage in tears before he could utter a single word. His stage fright in check, his reign on the American stage spanned fifty years until his death in 1808.

Another American theatrical family, the Barrymores, bridged the gap between early American theatre and modern film. Irish actor John Drew traveled to the states in 1846 and married actress Louise Lane. They had three children, and their daughter, Georgiana, married Irish actor, Maurice Barrymore. Their famous children—Lionel, Ethel, and John Barrymore—became some of the stage's first "household names." John was arguably one of the most acclaimed American actors of his generation and the grandfather of Drew Barrymore, a favorite current movie star both in the United States and around the world. What do you think her great-great-grandparents would say if they could see one of her movies?

Even as it grew and strengthened, American theatre lacked its own identity. Companies capitalized on European plays until the early twentieth century when writers like Eugene O'Neill, Thornton Wilder, and Tennessee Williams emerged. At the same time, however, Hollywood was becoming the center of the film industry for the world, somewhat overshadowing the development of the American stage.

NOTES: _____

_____

_____

_____

_____

_____

_____

_____

_____

AMERICAN PLAYWRIGHTS

The twentieth century brought an explosion of American playwrights, truly defining theatre in the United States both on and off-Broadway. The Pulitzer Prize in Drama started in 1917 and recognizes annually the best play or musical dealing with American life.

The plays listed below are just a sampling of some American playwrights' more recognizable titles. Plays that have won the Pulitzer Prize are indicated with an asterisk.

Eugene O'Neill**	1888-1953	Beyond the Horizon* Mourning Becomes Electra	The Iceman Cometh Long Day's Journey into Night*
Oscar Hammerstein II	1895-1960	Oklahoma South Pacific*	The King and I The Sound of Music
Thornton Wilder	1897-1975	Our Town* The Skin of Our Teeth*	The Matchmaker
Lillian Hellman	1905-1984	The Little Foxes Watch on the Rhine	The Searching Wind
William Saroyan	1908-1981	The Time of Your Life*	
Arthur Miller	1915-2005	All My Sons Death of a Salesman*	The Crucible After the Fall
Tennessee Williams	1911-1983	The Glass Menagerie A Streetcar Named Desire*	Cat on a Hot Tin Roof* The Night of the Iguana
Neil Simon	1927-2018	Barefoot in the Park The Odd Couple	Brighton Beach Memoirs Lost in Yonkers*
Edward Albee	1928-2016	Who's Afraid of Virginia Woolf? A Delicate Balance*	Three Tall Women*
Lorraine Hansberry	1930-1965	A Raisin in the Sun Les Blancs	Fences* The Piano Lesson*
Sam Shepard	1943-2017	Buried Child* A Lie of the Mind	
August Wilson	1945-2005	Ma Rainey's Black Bottom Jo Turner's Come and Gone	
David Mamet	1947-	Glengarry Rose* Speed-the-Plow	
Christopher Durang	1949-	Sister Mary Ignatius Explains It All For You Vanya and Sonia and Masha and Spike	
Wendy Wasserstein	1950-2006	The Sisters Rosenweig The Heidi Chronicles*	
Beth Henley	1952-	Crimes of the Heart* The Miss Firecracker Contest	
Tony Kushner	1956-	Angels in America*	
Tracy Letts	1965-	August: Osage County	
Lin-Manuel Miranda	1980-	In the Heights Hamilton*	

**Not only has Eugene O'Neill received more Pulitzer Prizes than any other playwright, he was also awarded the Nobel Prize in Literature in 1936, the only American playwright to ever receive this international honor as of 2020.

NOTES: _____

_____

_____

_____

_____

_____

_____

_____

EASTERN THEATRE

One of the immediately visible appeals of any form of theatre is the lure of sound and color. Eastern theatre seems to have perfected this with larger-than-life costumes, expressive masks, life-like puppets, and a contagious, rhythmic beat.

Noh, the oldest form of Eastern theatre dating back to the fourteenth century, is deeply rooted in religion and ceremony. It is a combination of acting, dance, and music, rhythmically entwined in a strict form that has been passed to each new generation in a rigid training, which starts in an actor's childhood. The short plots generally deal with myths and legends, and the characters, like those of commedia dell'arte, are stock roles symbolized onstage by masks. Each Noh also has a kyogen, or comic interlude (remember the Greek satyr play?). The performance combines actors' gliding movements, chanting, and stomping in unison with a flute and drum accompaniment. The ultimate strength of the performance is in the fluid beauty of the combined movement, sound, and speech. It is the oldest form of theatre still performed today.

Noh Masks

Bunraku is a form of Japanese theatre that uses intricately hinged wooden puppets. Each elaborately costumed puppet stands four feet tall, and with moving fingers and facial expressions, it is no surprise that it takes three puppeteers for each figure. The puppeteers are masked in all black but are visible to the audience. However, once the elaborate story begins, they seem to disappear. This traditional Japanese puppet theatre first became popular in the seventeenth century.

The most influential of the Asian theatres is the Kabuki, which employs singing, dancing, and acting, just as its name would imply (ka = singing, bu = dancing, ki = acting). Originally produced by women, the newest of the three Eastern forms was an imitation of the Noh and the Bunraku. The plots are based on historical tales or stories about everyday life. Unlike the Noh, Kabuki actors do not wear masks. Instead, each is characterized by dramatic face paint, stylized movement, and elaborate costumes. Today, only men act in the plays. These men spend most of their lives studying their art, starting as children and remaining loyal actors until their deaths.

The Kabuki stage is a raised wooden platform, but because rhythmic stomping is such a prevalent part of the style, amplifying wooden sections are often laid on top of the stage. The hanamichi (flower path) is a raised passageway that extends from one corner of the stage through the audience. Here the actors make entrances and exits, often pausing midway for a pose or bit of dialogue. Like the Greeks, the Kabuki audience will hear narration and dialogue from a chorus of twelve to eighteen members. Each chorus member is uniformly dressed and carries a fan, adding to the beauty of the performance. The orchestra sits at the rear of the stage. They use drums, a flute, and a stringed instrument called a samisen. Dressed like the chorus, they add an almost burlesque quality to the performance, punctuating actors' entrances, exits, or emotional moments by clacking two wooden blocks together.

The kimono, the traditional, floor-length robe with draping sleeves, is worn by both male and female characters, each distinguished by a variance in color, fabric, or accessories. Stylized wigs are worn to add size and color, and unrealistic makeup is painted with brightly colored, sharply contrasting lines meant to show expression. At no point do the actors ever try to

193

NOTES: _____

_____

_____

_____

_____

_____

_____

_____

_____

achieve realism, nor is that what the audience wants. Kabuki is fantasy storytelling. The actors' movements look more like dancing than acting, and their props are brought onstage by crew members dressed in all black with netting over their faces. Speeches are told with rhythmic musical accompaniment, or they may be told by several actors in unison or speaking in turn. It is theatre at its most ceremonial.

China boasts the Peking opera, a harmonious blend of song, dance, dialogue, and acrobatics. The subjects of the operas come from fiction, legend, and history. The superb costumes serve to enhance the performance, so they lack historical accuracy. Color is used to indicate rank and temperament. Originally acted by men, women were later introduced to the Chinese stage. After the establishment of the People's Republic in 1949, new plays were saturated with military propaganda. Only occasionally do new playwrights surface now.

NOTES: _____

_____

_____

_____

_____

_____

_____

_____

NAME _____ PERIOD _____ DATE _____

RESTORATION AND LATER, AMERICAN, AND EASTERN THEATRE REVIEW

1. Where does the term "Restoration" come from?

2. What did the English Royal Patent do to change theatre?

3. _____ wrote *The Country Wife* and is known for being a comic trendsetter, but _____ is considered the master of comedy. The greatest actor of the Restoration was _____, who also wrote plays and made innovative changes to lighting. His former girlfriend, _____, was a feminist of sorts who was known for effectively playing women's and men's roles.

4. List the plays for which each of the following playwrights is famous:
   a. Richard Brinsley Sheridan
   b. Oliver Goldsmith
   c. Gilbert and Sullivan
   d. Oscar Wilde
   e. George Bernard Shaw

5. Theatre in America was outlawed until the mid 1700s when attitudes began to change. Early American theatres either produced plays from the _____ stage or borrowed plots from their plays to produce new ones. Americans wrote few plays of literary merit, and the introduction of _____ in the early twentieth century may have overshadowed the emergence of such greats as O'Neill and Wilder.

6. List three great American playwrights and some of their most outstanding works:

7. The oldest form of Japanese theatre is the _____, which is deeply rooted in religion and ceremony. _____, a form of Japanese puppet theatre with Korean roots, uses large wooden puppets rather than live actors.

8. The newest and most influential form of Japanese theatre is the _____, which combines singing (_____), dancing (_____), and acting (_____), as its name implies. It was originally produced by _____ and was an imitation of the older two forms. It is characterized by _____, _____, and _____. Today, only _____ perform in this form, and they dedicate their lives to the art.

9. Define kimono:

10. Define samisen:

195

RESTORATION AND LATER, AMERICAN, AND EASTERN THEATRE REVIEW KEY

1. Charles II was *restored* to the throne

2. It was mandated that women perform female roles, and it endorsed the theatre as "useful and instructive." It officially endorsed the Drury Lane and the Covent Garden theatres.

3. William Wycherly, William Congreve, David Garrick, Peg Woffington

4. a. *The School for Scandal, The Rivals*
   b. *She Stoops to Conquer*
   c. *The Mikado, The Pirates of Penzance, H.M.S. Pinafore*
   d. *The Importance of Being Earnest*
   e. *Arms and the Man, Saint Joan, Pygmalion*

5. British, film

6. Eugene O'Neill—*The Iceman Cometh, Mourning Becomes Electra, A Long Day's Journey Into Night*
   Thornton Wilder—*Our Town, The Matchmaker*
   Lillian Hellman—*The Little Foxes, Watch on the Rhine, The Searching Wind*
   William Saroyan—*The Time of Your Life, After the Fall*
   Arthur Miller—*Death of a Salesman, The Crucible, All My Sons*
   Tennessee Williams—*Cat on a Hot Tin Roof, Night of the Iguana, A Streetcar Named Desire*
   Neil Simon—*The Odd Couple, Brighton Beach Memoirs, Barefoot in the Park, Star-Spangled Girl*
   Lorraine Hansberry—*A Raisin in the Son, Les Blancs*
   Beth Henley—*Crimes of the Heart, The Miss Firecracker Contest*

7. Noh, Bunraku

8. Kabuki (k, bu, ki), women, dramatic face paint, stylized movement, elaborate costumes, men

9. The traditional, floor-length robe with draping sleeves; it is worn by both male and female characters; each distinguished by a variance in color, fabric, or accessories.

10. A stringed instrument used in Kabuki theatre

THEATRE HISTORY TEST REVIEW CROSSWORD CLUES KEY

ACROSS

1. Bunraku
4. Companies
9. Improvised
13. Noblemen
15. Pit
16. Miracle
18. Shaw
20. Men
21. Passion
22. Jonson
23. Shakespeare
24. Thespis
26. Tragos
28. Marlowe
31. Iceman
34. Sophocles
35. Elizabeth
36. Miller

DOWN

2. Kabuki
3. Williams
5. Masque
6. Legitimized
7. Dionysis
8. Film
10. Pantalone
11. Women
12. Euripides
14. Horseplay
17. Fontesca
25. Congreve
26. Terence
27. British
29. Aeschylus
30. Hansberry
32. Egypt
33. Comedy

THEATRE HISTORY TEST REVIEW CROSSWORD CLUES

ACROSS

1. Japanese "puppet" theatre
4. Commedia dell'arte performers travelled in _____
9. Commedia dell'arte plays were basically _____
13. Financed writers and actors and gave them credibility
15. Where "groundlings" viewed the plays
16. _____ plays were based on stories from the Bible and saints' lives
18. Philosophical author of *Arms and the Man*
19. Greek actors
20. _____ plays were based on Christ's final week
21. Rebellious Elizabethan writer
22. Marlowe's and Jonson's biggest rival
23. The first actor to step from the chorus
25. Means "goat song"_____
27. Wrote *The Tragical History of Doctor Faustus*
30. O'Neill's *The _____ Cometh*
33. Wrote *Antigone* and *Oedipus the King*
34. Shakespeare's patron queen
35. *The Crucible* playwright

DOWN

2. Japanese "singing, dancing, and acting" theatre
3. Twentieth century writer of cats, streetcars, and iguanas
5. A play of noble extravagance
6. The English Royal Patent _____ theatre
7. Greeks honored this god with theatre
8. American _____ almost overshadowed American stage
10. Commedia dell'arte ingenue's father
11. Elizabethans feared their presence onstage would cause immorality
12. Wrote *Medea*
14. Roman plays consisted of mimes, dancing, and _____
17. Commedia dell'arte maidservant, the _____
24. Wrote *Love for Love*
25. Ex-slave and Roman writer
26. Early American theatre plots were borrowed from the _____
28. Greek "father of tragedy"
29. Penned *A Raisin in the Sun*
31. Place of performance recorded on stone tablet
32. Aristophanes wrote Greek _____

NAME _____ PERIOD _____ DATE _____

THEATRE HISTORY TEST REVIEW
CROSSWORD PUZZLE

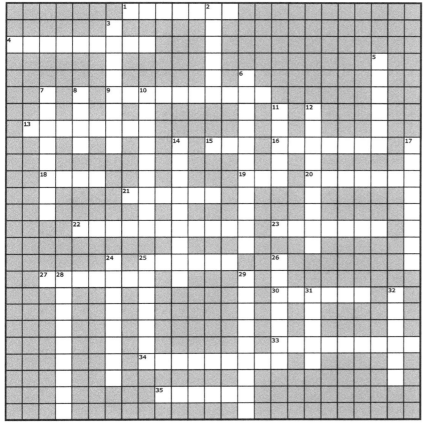

				B	U	N	R	A	K	U							
			W				A										
C	O	M	P	A	N	I	E	S		B						M	
			L					K		U						A	
			L						L							A	
	D	F	I	M	P	R	O	V	I	S	E	D				S	
	I	I	A		A					G		W		E		Q	
N	O	B	L	E	M	E	N			I		O		U		U	
	N	M	S		T		H		P	I	T		M	I	R	A	C	L	E		F
	Y			A		O				A		E		I			O
	S	H	A	W			L		R			M	E	N		P	A	S	S	I	O	N
	I			J	O	N	S	O	N		I				I			T
	S				N		E				Z				D			E
			S	H	A	K	E	S	P	E	A	R	E		T	H	E	S	P	I	S	S
					L					D				S				C
			C		T	R	A	G	O	S				B				A
	M	A	R	L	O	W	E		Y				H		R	
		E		N		R						A		I	C	E	M	A	N		C
		S		G		E						N		T		G			O
		C		R		N						S		I		Y			M
		H		E		C						B		S	O	P	H	O	C	L	E	S
		Y		V		E	L	I	Z	A	B	E	T	H		T			D
		L		E								R							Y
		U			M	I	L	L	E	R							
		S									Y						

THEATRE HISTORY PROJECTS

Project 1: Performance

Select a play from any period other than modern. Read the play and then select a scene from the play to perform (monologue, duet, or group of three). Study the acting style of the period, the resources, the acting area, costumes, etc., and prepare your scene accordingly. Remember, in many periods women were not allowed to act. How will you deal with this without "getting into trouble with the law"? Be creative. Ask your teacher about time limits.

Project 2: Research Paper

Select one of the time periods or theatrical regions mentioned in this section and research it in greater detail than was included in this unit. Write a research paper on your findings. Even though this is a theatre class, your research will need to include non-theatre information, too, and explain why these are relevant.

Project 3: Play Reports

Read two of the plays mentioned in this unit and fill out a play report for each. Be prepared to discuss the plays with the class.

Project 4: Website Poster

Create a poster advertising ten websites that would be helpful to students who want to learn more about theatre history. Be neat and creative. Ask you teacher about requirements.

Project 5: Costume Poster

Create a poster that clearly depicts two costumes and the makeup styles of a particular time period, one male and one female. Include fabric swatches. If the costumes are from a particular play, note the title, author, and character. Be neat and creative. Ask your teacher about size requirements.

Project 6: Theatre

Create a poster or model of a theatre house or stage area from one of the regions or time periods in this unit. Be neat and creative. Ask your teacher about size requirements.

Project 7: Biography

Research any playwright of your choosing. Write a research paper on them and be prepared to present it to the class. Ask your teacher about length and other requirements.

NOTES: _____

_____

_____

_____

_____

_____

_____

_____

CHAPTER 9
GAMES AND IMPROVISATION

DAILY BELL WORK—GAMES AND IMPROVISATION

IMPROVISATION

> *Understanding Improvisation*
> *Improvisation Projects*

ADDITIONAL NOTES

Using Games

Why Use Improvisation?

> *Understanding*
> *Improvisation Key*
>
> *Improv Suggestions*

Games and Activities

> *Discovery and*
> *Concentration Games*
>
> *Action Games*
>
> *Improvisation Games*

On the More Serious Side

NAME _____ PERIOD _____ DATE _____

DAILY BELL WORK - GAMES AND IMPROVISATION

Answer each question as your teacher assigns it, using the space provided. Be sure to include the date.

1. Date: _____
What is your favorite theatre game and why?

2. Date: _____
What is your least favorite theatre game and why?

3. Date: _____
Which game has provided you with the greatest theatrical insight and why?

4. Date: _____
Why is it important for actors to play these games?

201

USING GAMES

Games can be a very useful and fun tool for teaching any subject, but perhaps more than anywhere else, they are a natural for the expressive and spirited actor! There are any number of places to fit theatre games into your drama program. Use games as a reward for students' hard work or to break up the monotony of a difficult lesson. Use them on shortened school days when there is not enough time to have a regular lecture. Use them on those days when part of your class is away on a field trip. Use them in drama club to get members to participate in the acting process after the business portion of the meeting. Use theatre games or activities to reinforce specific lessons, such as characterization or non-verbal communication. They can even be used as fundraisers, as when some schools and professional acting companies host an "Improv Night."

After your class has successfully played any game, make it a habit to discuss what they learned and how they can use that particular game to

NAME _____ PERIOD _____ DATE _____

DAILY BELL WORK - GAMES AND IMPROVISATION

Answer each question as your teacher assigns it, using the space provided. Be sure to include the date.

5. Date: _____

    How might theatre games benefit non-actors or other groups?

6. Date: _____

    Why do young people sometimes clam up when it comes to playing the games, acting, or expressing themselves?

7. Date: _____

    Actors are told to be uninhibited. That means they are to totally "let go" of their fears about how others may perceive them. Why is this important?

8. Date: _____

    Tell how to play a game you know but that has not been played in this class. How might it help a young actor sharpen their skills?

202   Photocopying this page violates federal copyright law.

broaden their theatrical horizons. Have them record their thoughts and experiences in their daily journal or use the *Game/Activity Evaluation* form in Section 2. This encourages them to think from a theatrical point of view and give you additional activities to share with your students. You may want to offer extra credit to students who complete the evaluation form with their own exercises (such as those they learned at camp or in other classes).

NAME _____ PERIOD _____ DATE _____

DAILY BELL WORK - GAMES AND IMPROVISATION

Answer each question as your teacher assigns it, using the space provided. Be sure to include the date.

9. Date: _____

   Create a plan for using improvisation or theatre games as a fundraiser. Include specific information such as the audience, the price of admission, and so on.

10. Date: _____

    List as many "places" as you can for improvisation settings.

11. Date: _____

    List a variety of stock characters for improvisations.

12. Date: _____

    Can improvisation be practiced? Can someone learn to be an improvisational actor? Explain.

203

NOTES: _____

_____

_____

_____

_____

_____

_____

_____

_____

_____

NAME _____ PERIOD _____ DATE _____

DAILY BELL WORK - GAMES AND IMPROVISATION

Answer each question as your teacher assigns it, using the space provided. Be sure to include the date.

13. Date: _____

Paying attention to the instructions, listening to the other actors, and taking turns are vital to good improvisation. Explain.

14. Date: _____

List some "situations" two characters might find themselves in for humorous improvisation.

15. Date: _____

_____

_____

16. Date: _____

_____

_____

NOTES: _____

_____

_____

_____

_____

_____

_____

_____

_____

IMPROVISATION

Improvisation, or improv, is a type of acting done without a script or rehearsal. An actor or group of actors is given a situation and sometimes characters, and they act it out spontaneously, making up the dialogue and action as they work their way to a solid conclusion. Part of what makes improvisation enjoyable to the audience is that they know and appreciate that the performance they are enjoying is being created especially for them.

There are several different types of improvisational games and activities actors can practice to improve their skills, and the number of scenes and types of characters is infinite. However, before you start, you need to know some of the basic ideas that make spontaneous scenes successful.

- **Define your character.** Take the director's prompt and do a quick character analysis before taking the stage: How do I walk and talk? How old am I? Do I have any odd habits?

- **Be a good listener.** Listen to the other actors onstage, because their lines are your cue lines, and if the scene lacks good teamwork, it will not be a success.

- **Know where you are.** Is your character at the mall, the zoo, the beach, or any other place that would enhance the scene? If there is not enough time to establish the location before beginning, work it into the skit as close to the beginning as possible. Then the imaginary location can become a part of the scene, giving you and the other actors more to go on.

- **Know the conflict.** Almost all scenes, improvisational or scripted, revolve around a conflict, and if improvisational actors are not clear on what it is, the scene will be confusing to the audience.

- **Identify the focus.** Sometimes beginning improv actors think their idea is better than what's happening in the main part of the scene, so they try to redirect the scene, which is the same as upstaging or stealing focus. Rather than upstaging, lend your energy to the area of main focus and help build the storyline.

- **Pay attention.** Whether playing a game or improvising a scene, remember the instructions: If there is a goal—and there almost always is—keep the goal in sight.

- **Establish relationships.** If relationships are not established by the teacher or director, clarify them early in the scene. This will help to clear the path for the conclusion.

- **Include plenty of action.** With no scenery or props, the actor has it within his power to "pretend" to possess anything he wishes! Good actors can use pantomime to make the audience believe they see a light saber or giant clown shoes.

- **Never say "no"** to wherever the scene is going. Saying "no" brings the scene to a sudden halt. If your scene partner says the grass just turned purple, then it did and you need to work with that instead of going against your partner. It keeps the scene moving toward the goal and tends to be funnier.

- **Find a conclusion.** Every scene needs to have a sense of completion, though when you are on the spot, this can be hard to do. Many improv troupes use bells and buzzers to end scenes that actors cannot seem to end on their own. You do not want to be buzzed out every time, so practice ending your own scenes.

205

WHY USE IMPROVISATION?

There is a common misconception that acting requires a script, but that is not true. Some of the most notable moments in comedy have taken place when the cast strays from the original content. Of course, that does not work with stage plays, but with comic sketches, there can be some room for flexibility and artistic flare. Teaching your students to improvise is like arming them with a quick wit, instant problem-solving abilities, and a sense of timing that cannot be taught from a book.

At auditions for film and television, many directors look for the talented individuals who can make them laugh. They want real people who can take a moment outside the lines (such as introducing one's self or handling an unexpected situation) and make it work the way the character would. People with strong improvisation skills are often the most impressive and best equipped actors at auditions.

Many of the games that you will play in class require you to be able to quickly generate ideas for character types, settings, and situations. The first few come easily, but after a while, it is harder to come up with fresh ideas. On the following few pages, you will get some help. Mix and match characteristics to come up with interesting jumbles of characters. For example, instead of using a cheerleader in a scene, assign a student to be a slow-motion cheerleader. By adding this extra element, the character becomes

UNDERSTANDING IMPROVISATION KEY

1. Scripts, rehearsal

2. Dialog, action, conclusion

3. How he walks, talks, his age, odd habits, and any other defining traits

4. Listeners

5. Location

6. Conflict

7. Goal

8. Clear the path for the conclusion

9. Action

10. "Positive rather than the negative"

11. Conclusion

NAME _____ PERIOD _____ DATE _____

UNDERSTANDING IMPROVISATION

Do you understand improvisation or improv?
Check your understanding by filling in the blanks on the following questions.

1. *Improvisation* or *improv* is a type of impromptu acting done without a _____ or _____.

2. The actors are given a situation to act spontaneously, making up the _____ and _____ as they work their way to a solid _____.

3. It is important to quickly define one's character when doing improvisation. What are some things you might decide about characterization before taking the stage?

   _____

   _____

   _____

4. Improvisational actors must be good _____. What others say onstage is important to each actor, because it may prompt them to say something useful to the outcome of the scene.

5. If there is not time to work it out before taking the stage, establish the _____ of the scene as close to the beginning as possible, then the "surroundings" can be worked into the scene.

6. Know the _____. Almost all scenes revolve around some struggle, and if you and your partners are not clear on exactly what it is, your scene will be confusing.

7. Pay attention. Whether playing a game or improvising a scene, remember the director's instructions: if there is a _____, keep it in sight.

8. Establish relationships. If relationships are not established by the teacher or director, clarify them early in the scene. This will help to _____.

9. Include plenty of _____. With no scenery or props, the actor has it within their power to "pretend" to possess anything they wish! Good actors can use pantomime to make the audience believe they see anything.

10. Try to keep the scene in the _____ rather than the _____. Work with your partners instead of *against* them.

11. Every improvisation must have a _____ that wraps up the events in the scene.

206   Photocopying this page violates federal copyright law.

---

more defined and interesting. Also, the actor playing the cheerleader will have the opportunity to explore a facet of movement that can be both fun and entertaining.

Add you own ideas to the lists and encourage students to concoct their own characters; jot these down for future reference.

In most games, you will only need to provide one or two suggestions—maybe just a character or a character and a setting. Rarely will you need a characteristic, character, situation, and setting. For best results, make your selections from each group random. For example, you may end up with an exaggerating hillbilly asking the other for her hand in marriage in an operating room. Imagine a scene in which your "hillbilly" student is asking the air-headed cheerleader doctor to marry him while she tries to operate on him!

Here are some more examples of how the characteristics, characters, situations, and settings can be randomly pieced together. Can you see how they can benefit your improvisation?

- A body-building, hypochondriac TV talk show host is seeking advice from a psychic in a math class.

- A religious Southern belle cannot stop talking while asking for directions while escaping from prison.

IMPROVISATION PROJECTS

Select one of the following projects to be completed and presented to the class on _____. Each project must be neat and show strong effort. See your teacher for details or questions.

Project 1: Instructional Video

Make an instructional video with several other people to teach the class how to play a particular improvisational game or activity. The video should be well organized and cleanly pieced together.

Include:
- The title of the activity
- The source for the activity (where you found it)
- How many can play
- Materials needed
- Instructions and/or rules
- A successful sample of the activity
- How this particular activity is useful to theatre
- Credits

Project 2: Improvisation Notebook

Create an improvisation notebook that clearly instructs the reader how to play ten improvisation games or activities. The notebook should be neat and well organized. All of the material must be in the student's own words and format.

Each activity must include:
- The title of the activity
- The source for the activity (where you found it)
- How many can play
- Materials needed
- Instructions and/or rules
- How this particular activity is useful to theatre

Project 3: Fifty Famous Lines

Create a list of fifty famous lines, sayings, slogans, or lyrics for the "Whose Line Is Next?" game. The lines must be neatly typed and triple spaced on clean paper. Make sure the lines are appropriate for class.

Project 4: Fifty Pictures

Gather fifty pictures of people, animals, and items to be used in "The Picture Game." Cut them out neatly and mount each to a clean piece of paper slightly larger than the picture. Make sure the pictures are appropriate for class.

207

You may wish to make a poster out of the game pages to laminate and place in your classroom. Be sure to add students' ideas to the poster!

- An air-headed crocodile hunter cannot stop snorting while conducting busy intersection traffic and making his three wishes.

- A loud-mouthed policeman is a double agent, spying on a child pretending to be a superhero at the playground.

- A slow-motion psychiatrist cannot stop crying in an elevator, much to the discomfort of the rodeo clown who's also in the elevator.

- A joyful, country teacher in a windstorm is meeting his fiancée's/her fiancé's whining parents for the first time.

- A tired, fast-talking, over-caffeinated person is awarding a sneezing fireman with a sweepstakes grand prize.

Because improvisation is "off-the-cuff" and can be quite challenging, you may want to start students with just a characteristic and setting. As they become more comfortable with this, add the character and then the situation. They will learn to hone their skills without becoming overwhelmed with details. You might also want to write the suggestions on individual slips of paper and place those from each category in a separate box. Allow your students to draw one from each of the four categories so that luck has a hand in your games.

IMPROV SUGGESTIONS

CHARACTERISTIC:

Aging	In slow motion	Fast-talking	Cannot stop laughing
Tired	Air-headed	Hyperactive	Cannot stop crying
Joyful	Country	Religious	Cannot stop snorting
Childish	Hot-headed	Complimentary	Cannot stop staring
Flirtatious	Exaggerating	Bad-breathed	Cannot stop lying
Bossy	Mind-changing	Negotiating	Cannot stop hiccupping
Timid	Shoplifting	Whining	Cannot stay awake
Cold	Sneezing	Evesdropping	Cannot see clearly
Queasy	Concerned	Apologetic	Cannot hear clearly
Body-building	Loudmouthed	Cannot stop talking	

CHARACTER:

Lawyer	Aerobics instructor	Astronaut
Policeman	Sorority sister	Angel
Teacher	Surfer dude	Over-caffeinated person
Auctioneer	Hillbilly	Kindergarten teacher
Ballerina	Actor	Southern belle
Investigator	Mime	Bride/groom late for wedding
Salesman	Psychiatrist	Special agent on a mission
Psychic	Doctor	Someone hearing voices
Snob	Child	Tightrope walker
Pirate	Old man/woman	Action film movie star
Hypochondriac	Witch doctor	Compulsive list maker
Crocodile hunter	Superhero	Broadway dancer
TV talk show host	Rodeo clown	
Dentist	Preacher	

SITUATION: One of the characters...

Is locked out of the car	Is asking the other for directions	(dance, sing)
Wakes from sleep walking	Is seeking advice from a psychic	Is robbing the other
Is applying for a job	Is awarding the other a sweepstakes grand prize	Is always changing the subject
Is about to bungee jump		Is extremely forgetful
Is doing research at the library	Is kidnapping the other	Has a very annoying habit
Is meeting the fiancé's parents	Thinks they are really (attractive, smart, etc.)	Cannot bring him/herself to say something
Is asking for the other's hand in marriage	Is trying to teach the other how to	Is a double agent, spying on the other

SETTING:

Has three wishes	Tunnel of Love	At one character's wedding
Beach	In an airplane	Between takes on a movie set
Mall	In a beauty parlor	While attempting to play in the symphony
Elevator	In math class	While conducting busy intersection traffic
Playground	In a wind storm	While escaping from prison
Car	In the operating room	While posing for a big fashion layout
Front porch	In the nursery	While trying not to be noticed
Library	In yoga class	While fighting off a wild beast
Police station	While playing video games	At a pie eating contest
Roller coaster	In the middle of a robbery	In the middle of a Wild West shootout
		While onstage during opening night of a play

GAMES AND ACTIVITIES

 GETTING TO KNOW ONE ANOTHER

 FOCUS & CONCENTRATION

 DISCOVERY

 CREATIVITY

 AGILITY

 EYE CONTACT

 LISTENING

 SMALL GROUPS

 MEDIUM GROUPS

 LARGE GROUPS

 LOW ENERGY (CALMING)

 HIGH ENERGY (EXCITING)

 TIMING

DISCOVERY AND CONCENTRATION GAMES

PASS THE PASTRAMI, PLEASE

Have the class make a standing circle with one person in the middle. The person in the middle approaches someone in the circle and says, "I'd like to share my pastrami sandwich with you. If you would like that, smile." The approached actor must respond, "I would like that, but I just can't smile." If that person can say this without smiling, the person in the middle finds someone else and repeats the process. However, if the approached actor does smile, the two actors switch places and the game continues. The objective of this game is to stay focused and avoid smiling so as to never end up in the middle. The sentence can be anything as long as it does not embarrass anyone. The person in the middle can choose any emotion or voice but cannot touch the other person.

IN THE MIDDLE

Three players participate at a time. Place the three players in a triangle facing each other. Assign one person to be the listener and the other two to be talkers. Each of the two talkers will speak to the listener as though they are the only other person in the triangle, ignoring the other talker. The talkers must continue their parts of the conversation even if the listener gets confused. The listener must try to participate actively in both conversations.

GUESS WHO?

Start by pairing students off. Have the pairs stand together with their eyes closed and give each a minute to feel the other's hands. No talking! Then, keeping their eyes closed, have them mix up and get in a circle holding hands; you may have to corral some strays. Pick one student to go to the middle, keeping their eyes closed; the rest may now open their eyes. Have the one in the middle feel their way around the hands in the circle until they have found their partner's hands. Once they have successfully done this, mix the students up again, picking a new student for the middle. Continue doing this until everyone has had a chance to find their partner.

ACTION GAMES

I NEVER

Everyone plays, but limit each group to about twelve to fifteen. Have the class get in a circle with one player in the middle. That player says "I never" and then adds something they have never done. Those in the circle who have done it try to change places quickly while the person in the middle tries to beat one of them to their new spot. The last one to a spot then goes to the middle and says something they have never done, and the game continues.

KITTY WANTS A CORNER

Have the class stand in a circle with one player in the middle. They go around the circle saying, "Kitty wants a corner," to the others, who reply, "Go see my neighbor." While the "kitty's" back is to the others, they will make eye contact with others communicating a desire to change spots with them. The kitty has to try to beat one of them to their spot, putting that person in the middle.

LINE TAG

A large open space is required. One person starts by trying to tag another. When anyone else is tagged, they link up to the original tagger, forming a short chain, and they try to tag more. Eventually, the linked taggers will form a long chain and can encircle their prey. The last person to be tagged wins, but they start the next game as the tagger. For a variation on the game, have the tagger close their eyes (be sure to move furniture and other hazards out of the way). Each additional tagger must also close their eyes.

IMPROVISATION GAMES

THE BUZZER GAME

You will need a bell or buzzer for this game, or allow students in the class to "bzzz" with their mouths. Two players act out a scene based on a prompt. At any time during the scene, the teacher or designated class member can buzz the actors, who must then back up the scene and change the last line, changing how the scene will proceed. After five or six buzzes, the actors wrap it up.

KEYWORDS

Three players participate at a time. The audience picks a situation such as "haggling at a fruit stand." Each player is assigned a unique keyword that somehow relates to the situation, maybe apple, money, and rain. The three will then act out a scene, but whenever an actor's keyword is said, they must then leave the scene, clearly justifying his exit. When they hear the word again, they must re-enter, again justifying their entrance. The actors may conclude the scene at any time.

SWITCH

Two players participate at a time. The audience picks a scene, including a situation and a setting, and the actors begin acting it out. At any time, the teacher may call "switch" and the actors will switch places and characters with each other, picking up exactly where their scene partner left off.

PICTURE GAME

Assign students to each bring in two or three small newspaper or magazine pictures of people, famous or not, of any gender, age, or ethnicity. You may want to mount and laminate them, because this is an excellent resource for character study and other games. Choose eight to ten students to start and have each draw from the stack of pictures. Give them a couple of minutes to study their picture, using it to develop characters. Then bring them together for a party in the center of the room. Each will mingle as their character. For an extra challenge, you may even include pictures of animals, insects, or inanimate objects in the stack. After about five minutes, select a new group to pick new pictures.

ZAP

Students sit in a circle with two actors in the middle. The teacher will give the two a scene and they will act it out. At some point, someone from the outer circle will call "zap" and the two in the middle will freeze. The one who called "zap" will trade places with one of the actors in the scene and will then start a new scene from exactly the same physical posture. If no one calls "zap," then the teacher can call it and send anyone into the circle. The objective is to make sure each "zap" takes the scene in a completely different direction.

DUBBING

Using any video of two or more people talking, the teacher will assign students to fill-in for each actor in the scene. As the movie plays without any sound, each student playing a character will "dub" the voices, creating their own dialogue for the scene on the video. The dubbed dialogue should match the emotions and actions of the video as much as possible. It is best for the students to know nothing about the actual movie plot or even the title. Once the students have finished creating dialogue, watch the scene with the sound turned up to see how you did.

TOUCH ON (OR TOUCH OFF)

Four to six players participate at a time. Decide if you will play Touch On or Touch Off. The class will define the situation, and the actors will then act out the scene. All touching must be motivated. In the first version, players can only talk when two or more are touching. In the second version, players must continue to talk unless they are touching another player. The scene is over when all players are touching and a justifiable conclusion is made.

In another version of the game, each initiated touch turns the player either on or off, so a player will be "on" until she is touched again, at which point she will be unable to speak. The fun is in justifying the change using more than just "I lost my voice." Reward creativity!

SIT, STAND, BEND

Three players participate at a time, and there should be one chair onstage. The teacher gives the three players a scene to improvise, and at all times during the scene, one player must be sitting down, one player must be standing, and one player must be bending over. Each must effectively express their reason for the movement. For example, the bending player might be picking something up or have a crick in his back. The standing player might be waving at someone off in the distance. When a player changes to one of the other positions, the others must adjust as well. This is a difficult scene, and wrap-up is even harder, so praise those who come up with effective conclusions!

PARTY CRASHERS

Four players participate at a time, and one of them, the party host, leaves the room. They should not be able to hear what happens next. The audience assigns the remaining three players odd characters, such as a rabid dog, Goldilocks, and a timid football player. They then move to the side and the host returns. He prepares for his party when the doorbell rings. The first guest, the rabid dog, enters in character, and the two interact. The guest should be giving clues as to his character (barking, acting rabid, etc.). After a short exchange, the next player rings and enters, and the three interact. The fourth player then enters, and the party is in full swing. When the host thinks he has deciphered a character, he must use the character's name (or description) in dialogue. For example, "Goldilocks, will you go in the kitchen and get the rabid dog a snack?" If he is correct, the characters may then find motivation for leaving the party. Each character must remain at the party until his character is identified. The final character or characters are responsible for the ending.

DATING GAME

Four players participate; three are the contestants and the fourth is the one they hope to date. The latter will leave the room while the audience, like in Party Crashers, assigns characters to the other three. There should be a chair for each player with the single player to one side and the three characters lined up at the opposite side. When the single player returns, they will then ask Dating Game-style questions to the others, who will answer in character, giving hints without giving away who they are. After two rounds of questions, the single player may choose a date, but his dialogue must attempt to correctly name all three characters.

WHOSE LINE IS NEXT?

Before the game, write random lines of dialogue, slogans, sayings, or lyrics on small pieces of paper. Two actors will take the stage. Each will draw three slips and put them in their pockets without looking at them. The class will then give them a scene including a situation and a setting. During the improvisation, each player must pull out a slip of paper and use that line in the improvisation until all of the mystery lines are used.

MOVIE STYLES

Start by discussing the "styles" of acting or film (such as melodrama, cartoon, action, horror, Western, etc.) and what makes each different. Two players will take the stage. The class will give them a simple scene to improvise, such as a boy trying to break up with a girl at the library. During the course of the scene, cue the students to change styles by calling out a new one. They should pick up exactly where they left off, only with the newly introduced style. Actors should not stop to think, back up in the scene, or discuss what to do.

GEORGE IS LATE AGAIN!

Three to five players act out a scene onstage while "George" sits on the side of the stage taking mental notes. The players onstage use George's lateness to talk about him, giving him peculiar characteristics during their dialogue. For example, one might say that George is probably late because he is seeing a doctor about his chronic hiccups, and another might say that he has never heard anyone hiccup a musical scale. "George" notes that his character hiccups the musical scale chronically. Allow the gossipers to talk about George for about two to three minutes, then have "George" enter in character. Each gossiper must find and clearly improvise their reason to leave until only "George" and one other player remain. The remaining two must find a clever end to the scene.

WORLD'S WORST

A quick-thinking game! Four or five players take the stage, standing to the side. Someone offers a "World's Worst" category such as "worst thing to say at a wedding," or "worst thing to say when pulled over for speeding." (Because this game goes so quickly, it might be a good idea to have the students list their categories and submit them before the game starts.) As actors quickly think of responses, they step to the center and say them, then step out of the center. After two to three responses or when responses no longer seem to be coming, introduce a new "World's Worst."

NEWS REPORT

Four players participate at a time. Two are opposing characters from the same fairy tale (such as Cinderella and her evil stepmother) and the other two are news reporters on the scene. The four must conduct an interview in character with a solid conclusion.

OLD JOB, NEW JOB

List as many occupations as you can on separate squares of paper. Put them in a hat. Three players participate at a time. Let's say Bob is player one and draws a job from the hat. This is his old job, which he keeps a secret. He then draws another, which is his new job that he announces to the class. The class gives the trio a scene that must somehow include Bob's new job. As the three act out the scene, Bob must allow traces of his old job to interfere with his new one until players two and three can guess his old job. For example, a waiter trying to serve a meal can't help but check his customers' pulse and temperature. What is his old job? A nurse! Rotate parts so all three get to have a chance with old and new jobs.

EXPERT OLYMPICS

Three players participate at a time. One player is a sportscaster, and the other two are competitors in an odd Olympic sport. (Have fun with this! Maybe dishwashing or the getting-ready-for-school triathlon, consisting of dressing, eating, and catching the bus.) The sportscaster has control of the scene and can use prompts such as fast forward, rewind, instant replay, and slow motion. The sportscaster can also call fouls or any other creative means of enhancing the scene, including pre- or post-competition interviews. All three players must contribute to the creative conclusion of the scene.

THE WAITING ROOM

Gather all of the items you might have with you in a waiting room, such as bottles of water, a telephone, a magazine, candy or chips, pencil and paper, lipstick, a comb or brush, etc. You will also need two chairs with a table between them that holds these props. Four players will take the stage, two in the chairs and two kneeling behind them. The two in the chairs may

not use their hands; instead, their arms are behind them and the two kneeling players will wrap their arms around from behind to be the sitters' hands. The sitters will engage in dialogue while the kneelers attempt to follow the sitters' verbal cues with their hands. For example, one sitter may say, "is that your phone ringing?" The "hands" actor must then find the phone, answer it, and get it to the sitter's ear.

SUPERHEROES

Three players participate, but only one starts. While the other two stand to the side, the audience gives the player #1 a superhero name, a super power, and a situation. This superhero will start the scene, basically talking to himself or the audience about the situation. Suddenly, superhero #2 appears from the wings, and #1 must name them spontaneously, at which point #2 instantly begins acting according to this new name. When #3 comes in, #2 calls them by name. Once all three heroes are in, they will solve the problem introduced by the situation, and each must announce how they will use their special superhero power to help. As each does so, they may then leave in character. The last one onstage must wrap up the scene.

ABC GAME

The teacher assigns two players, a scene, and a random letter from the alphabet. The first line of the scene will start with that letter, and each player's next line must always advance one letter in the alphabet from the previous player's line. After Z, go back to A. The scene must wrap up precisely 27 lines later, on exactly the same letter as it started.

THE QUESTION GAME

The teacher assigns a scene to two players, but every line must be phrased as a question. A member of the audience can buzz out and replace a player who waits too long or makes a statement instead of a question.

BUS STOP

The entire class can play. Set up three chairs like a bench. In this game, two to three people must be onstage at all times waiting for the bus. As a bus arrives, some will leave the scene and others will enter it. Each actor takes a very specific character and interacts with the others. Dialogue is random, but a scene or two will inevitably develop and carry over into new characters' arrivals. Because this scene keeps going, there will not be an ending until the teacher assigns a player to end it.

DEAD BODIES

Four players participate, two to do the acting and two others to control their movements. The class gives the two actors a scene, and they act it out; however, they cannot move anything other than their faces and heads without the help of their movers. The movers must help the actors by moving and positioning their arms and legs, including for walking. The actors and the movers will inspire one another based on what the other says or does. For example, if the actor Nicole says, "What's that sound?" her mover should place Nicole's hand to her ear as though she is listening. Conversely, if the mover puts Nicole's hand on her hip, Nicole might respond by saying something like, "Do these jeans make me look fat?"

TAXI

You will need four chairs; two for the front seat and two for the back seat, leaving the back passenger seat empty. Everyone plays this game, so line up all of the players and have three get into the car, two in front and one behind the driver. The driver starts driving, and when at a stop, a player from the line gets in. This player will have an unusual personality, an odd habit, or will be doing something physically or vocally. The others in the car may adopt the trait, play off it, or use it as a reason to stop the car. The front passenger then finds a reason to stop and get out, at which point everyone will shift clockwise, and a new character will get in. Continue repeating this process until everyone has been in the taxi.

ON THE MORE SERIOUS SIDE

Improvisation also gives young people the chance to practice some social role playing. One reason kids smoke when their friends pressure them is that they are not comfortable saying "no." Perhaps they want to refuse, but the word just gets caught in their throats. Or maybe under the scrutiny of his friends' smoky glare, a boy is not sure how his "no" will sound. No one wants to sound scared or weak. Allow your students to practice some of these social situations in your class. Teach them to say, "No. My parents would ground me for a year!" Ask your students to write those things they would like to practice saying on paper and pass them to you anonymously. You can help them put words to their thoughts, practice saying them, find avenues for compromise, or come up with a Plan B if the pressure does not let up. Your counselor might be able to offer you a list of common concerns that they handle each day in their office or use the ones below. Your students, their parents, and the community will all thank you.

1. How can I talk to my parents about something I really believe is unfair? I love them and don't want to be disrespectful, but I would like to voice my feelings on this issue.

2. One of my friends is doing something very destructive to herself. How can I talk to her without seeming like I am not her friend or that she can never trust me again?

3. Someone in one of my classes continually makes comments about the teacher that are rude and might even be considered harassing. I don't want to get this person in trouble, but they won't stop. I think the teacher should know. How can I tell the teacher without getting this person in trouble?

4. I lied to my friend about something really stupid because he was making me mad. It's no big deal, but now I have to keep lying about it. How can I handle this?

5. I told my best friend a secret and now everyone knows. Should I address this with my best friend?

6. Someone I trusted has physically abused me. I would like to get help, but I am scared. Who should I talk to and what should I say?

7. My best friend is going out with a girl who has bragged to her friends about "using him for his money." He really likes her, but I hate to see him get hurt. What should I say?

8. My best friend is always bossing me around and cutting me down. She thinks it's a joke, but it really gets under my skin. I like her and don't want to lose her as a friend, but I am wondering if being friendless would be a healthier option.

CHAPTER 10
PLANNING FOR THE FUTURE

DAILY BELL WORK— PLANNING FOR THE FUTURE

WHY DO DRAMA?

WORKING AS AN ACTOR

ADDITIONAL NOTES

NAME _____ PERIOD _____ DATE _____

DAILY BELL WORK - PLANNING FOR THE FUTURE

Answer each question as your teacher assigns it, using the space provided. Be sure to include the date.

1.   Date: _____

List as many jobs as you can think of in the field of theatre. Don't forget the ones backstage and in offices.

2.   Date: _____

What are some non-theatre jobs that involve acting or good speaking skills?

3.   Date: _____

What are some jobs that involve the skills learned in technical theatre?

4.   Date: _____

Who do you know whose job is theatre related or uses theatre skills? Explain how they could benefit from using what you learned in this class.

211

NOTES: _____

_____

_____

_____

_____

_____

_____

_____

_____

NAME _____ PERIOD _____ DATE _____

DAILY BELL WORK - PLANNING FOR THE FUTURE

Answer each question as your teacher assigns it, using the space provided. Be sure to include the date.

5. Date: _____

    Explain some of the things directors might look for on an actor's resume.

6. Date: _____

    What might a director seek in an actor's headshot?

7. Date: _____

    What are some ways an actor can get acting jobs?

8. Date: _____

    Most actors have other jobs to pay bills while they try to find their big break. Which jobs would best accommodate actors' audition and rehearsal schedule?

NOTES: _____

_____

_____

_____

_____

_____

_____

_____

NAME _____ PERIOD _____ DATE _____

DAILY BELL WORK - PLANNING FOR THE FUTURE

Answer each question as your teacher assigns it, using the space provided. Be sure to include the date.

9. Date: _____

   Agents rarely represent actors without experience, and it is hard to get experience without an agent. What would be a reasonable solution to this problem?

10. Date: _____

    Often, good training can take the place of a lot of experience. What kinds of classes should actors seek?

11. Date: _____

    List places actors can look to find information on agents.

12. Date: _____

    Write an entry from an actor's journal on a typical day before getting their big break.

213

NOTES: _____

_____

_____

_____

_____

_____

_____

_____

_____

INTRODUCTION TO THEATRE ARTS I

NAME _____ PERIOD _____ DATE _____

DAILY BELL WORK - PLANNING FOR THE FUTURE

Answer each question as your teacher assigns it, using the space provided. Be sure to include the date.

13. Date: _____

    Write an entry from the same actor's journal on a typical day after getting their big break.

14. Date: _____

    Athletes, musicians, and models often "break into acting" after building a name for themselves. Actors occasionally break into modeling and music, but rarely sports. What does this say about acting? What do you think of this practice?

15. Date: _____

16. Date: _____

NOTES: _____

_____

_____

_____

_____

_____

_____

_____

_____

WHY DO DRAMA?

Most students who take drama classes have no intention of becoming professional actors. Many are interested in acting because it is fun. They know they have a creative side and they wish to have an outlet to express themselves, but they do not dream of being on the red carpet someday. There are also those who do not really care for acting, but they must have a fine arts credit, and drama seems like the best solution. Many of these students eventually find that not only do they actually like the class, but also that they are talented. And yes, in our class there are also students with stars in their eyes who hope to act for a living one day. They are eager to learn all they can, be discovered, and become famous.

Whether you are one of the above students or somewhere in between, it is important to understand just why your theatre teacher asked you to do some activities. Believe it or not, acting like you are brushing your teeth in slow motion does serve a purpose. On a broader scale, it is also necessary to know and appreciate the reasons behind learning good articulation, speaking confidently and energetically, and using pauses effectively. Everything you have learned in this class translates to valuable life skills, regardless of your chosen career.

Think back on the various activities and lessons in this theatre class. In one column, list the activities for which you have a clear understanding of how they will one day benefit you. In the other, list those activities that remain unclear as to how they will impact your future. Discuss them in your class. Your fellow theatre students or your teacher may have a perspective on a particular activity that had not occurred to you.

I *understand* the potential future impact of these activities and lessons:	I *do not understand* the potential future impact of these activities and lessons:

215

Let's be realistic. Not every student enrolled in our wonderful theatre classes will go on to be an actor. Most take the class because they need the fine arts credit. Many enjoy "showing off." Some are genuinely interested in theatre but not acting. And then there are those who love acting and know exactly what they want. There is something to be gained from this curriculum for each and every individual enrolled, whatever their goals.

The objective of this chapter is not to create future stage or movie stars. Rather, it seeks to enlighten students on the many careers for which theatre training can be beneficial. The greatest benefit of this topic will be gained from discussion in your classroom. Encourage students to talk about their goals and what they have in common with theatre. Invite counselors to speak with students about the importance of good communication skills and thinking on your feet whether in school, at scholarship interviews, and when seeking employment. You may also want to explore the significance of a diverse high school experience on a student's college application. Theatre is generally considered a perfect balance to a resume that is heavy in athletics and academics because of the broad spectrum of both thinking skills and physical demands.

NAME _____ PERIOD _____ DATE _____

THEATRE JOBS

There are many jobs one can do in the entertainment industry. Some are theatre jobs, such as acting, makeup, and technical work. Others are in the film, TV, and commercial industries. The following is a small sampling of the jobs one might seek.

STAGE CREW: There are many jobs within the stage crew. For example, grips move the scenery around during the show. The props manager buys or creates the many props used in the show and makes sure that they are always placed where they are needed. Sometimes the members of the stage crew even build and paint the set, but some theatres have construction crews who do this. All of these jobs and many more are overseen by the technical director, who runs all of the technical aspects of the show and works in the interest of the director and the stage manager, who handles the show from backstage.

Imagine you are on the crew for a children's comedy about Aladdin. Explain how your show's set and props would differ from an adult drama about the same character.

_____

_____

_____

LIGHTING: There are many people on the lighting team. A designer designs the lights, including where to hang which instruments, what gel color to put in the instrument frame, when to bring lights up and down during the show, and what intensity and effects to use. Light technicians hang and gel the instruments and take care of them throughout the show. The light board operator runs the lights during the show. Spotlight operators maneuver the lights used to follow actors during certain scenes.

How can lighting be used to establish the mood of a play? Give examples.

_____

_____

_____

SOUND: The sound crew has quite a few responsibilities. Depending on the show's requirements, there may be as few as a single sound crew member or as many as ten. The sound crew is responsible for all of the microphones, the crew's headsets used to communicate during the show, and all of the sound effects used during the show. They are also responsible for any background music that might be used. Most importantly, they monitor the sound levels during the show to make sure that the quality stays good.

How could sound effects add realism to a scene about a campfire on a starry night?

_____

_____

_____

_____

MAKING THEATRE ARTS RELEVANT

Do you remember being in school and, as the teacher thoroughly covered the complex lesson, you just knew you would never catch on? Everyone else seemed to get it. All around you, heads nodded their understanding, but it went over your head! How could you raise your hand for clarification? The rest of the bright, knowing students would surely think you were a dunce, right? It was not until the walk home that you realized that the nodding heads were probably equally confused, but class was over and it was too late for help.

What about when you were told you had to learn something, but for the life of you, you could not imagine its real-life application? Adding and subtracting seemed awfully important, because people use math several times a day. But when will we ever need to know how to act like a baby duck who has lost its mother? At what point will "Peter Piper picked a peck of peppers" pay off?

Students deserve to know the impact of each lesson. No one wants to invest time and valuable brain cells if there is no goal. Fortunately, drama is really quite useful, and once students understand its functionality, they are more eager to learn and to participate. Talk to your students about the curriculum. Do not get angry when they ask why they need to know something. Instead, use it as an opportunity to prove that your subject is worthy of their efforts.

NAME _____ PERIOD _____ DATE _____

COSTUMES AND MAKEUP: The costumers and makeup artists work very closely with the director and the technical director to provide a style, theme, and overall look that is congruent with the rest of the production. Larger theatres have a designer and a seamstress (and sometimes several of each). Smaller theatres rely on costume rental houses to provide them with appropriate costumes. In the world of professional theatre, talented artisans create complex designs, which can truly complete the actor's characterization.

Color is a very important part of any show's overall design, but especially when it comes to costuming. Explain how color can be symbolic within the costume design of a show.

_____

_____

_____

PUBLICITY: The person or crew responsible for the promotion of a show has a huge job. They must coordinate news releases and advertisements. They must create a schedule in which pictures can be taken in costume for publicity and programs but without disturbing the most important phase of the rehearsal process—the technical rehearsals. Posters must be designed and printed and visibly hung in appropriate places and tickets must be printed and sold. Programs have to be designed and printed, and often advertisers purchase ad space in these. Many theatres have a phone line to be maintained and a mailing list for sending out flyers. Finally, theatres often have reserved seating or special offers on season tickets. All of this is maintained by the publicity crew.

Discuss the pros and cons of general admission seating at a lower rate versus reserved seating at a higher rate.

_____

_____

_____

CHOREOGRAPHER: Makes up the dance routines for any show that involves dancing.

SPECIAL EFFECTS MANAGER: Creates and monitors special effects for shows and is responsible for the safety of the actors and the audience.

HOUSE MANAGER: Takes charge of the audience area of the theatre before, during, and after performances, including managing the ushers and concessions and attending to the general comfort of the audience.

WRITER: Creates the script.

MUSICAL DIRECTOR: In musical theatre, this person is in charge of bringing all of the musical elements together to support the goals of the director.

STAGE COMBAT DIRECTOR: Choreographs the more physical part of the show and monitors actors for safety. Stage combat can include fist fighting, wrestling, swordplay, or simply a trip or kick. It is very complex and requires extensive training.

STUNTPERSON: Used mainly in film and TV, the stuntperson, who has received special training, doubles for an actor to perform physically challenging or dangerous tasks.

CAMERAPERSON: Operates the camera for film and video.

217

USING THE WORKSHEETS

The student worksheets in this chapter are informative, but due to the nature of the topic, they lack a great deal of new vocabulary. However, each discussion-centered page encourages students to compare theatre to their individual career choices while considering a wide range of occupations.

Planning for the Future recognizes that most students do not want to become professional actors. If they did, the need for theatre skills would be obvious. Despite their careers of choice, though, the knowledge is still completely applicable and the skills beneficial. Allow students to question the activities and skills and take the time to address their concerns. Your answers will create more eager and understanding learners.

Theatre Jobs is a two-page worksheet that discusses the careers students could explore backstage and includes mention of some television careers. The discussion questions try to motivate students to think as though they are "on the job."

For the performers in your classroom, *Acting Opportunities* gives a sampling of the jobs and opportunities in which acting or speaking skills are used. Many of these are often overlooked as "acting" jobs, and often students' interests are renewed at

NAME _____ PERIOD _____ DATE _____

ACTING OPPORTUNITIES

There are many careers that involve acting or acting skills that offer reasonable incomes. Granted, most actors would like to "hit the big time" and become stars. However, many take on more stable jobs to pay bills while seeking their big break on the side. Others who love acting but decide to keep it a hobby while building another career altogether.

The following list of careers are typical jobs many actors will do at one time or another. Some offer lucrative salaries; some do not. Discuss the jobs as a class. Do you know what is meant by each? If not, take a moment to find out. Which jobs appeal to you? Which seem more like fun than work? Which seem more like work than fun? Which are easy and which are difficult? Can you see yourself doing any of these? After you have discussed the acting alternatives, answer the questions below.

_____TV Commercial Actor	_____Dinner Theatre Actor	_____Voice-over Talent
_____Movie Actor	_____Murder Mystery Actor	_____Cartoon Voice
_____Newscaster	_____Play Actor	_____Audio Book Voice
_____Disc Jockey	_____Children's Theatre Actor	_____Educational Video Actor
_____Model	_____Public Speaker	_____Community Theatre Actor
_____Movie Extra	_____Master of Ceremonies	_____Stand-up Comedian
_____Industrial Video Actor	_____Improv Player	_____Motivational Speaker

1. In the spaces to the left of the job, rank them in the order of preference with 1 being the most preferred and 21 being the least preferred. Then think about your ranking. What motivated your choices? Was it ability, salary, or personal enjoyment? Maybe it was something else. Explain your reasoning below.

2. Can you think of other jobs that involve acting that are not on the list?

3. Which jobs do you think are hardest to get into? Why?

4. Which jobs do you think would offer a part-time actor the most flexibility to attend auditions and rehearsals? Why?

the prospect of pursuing one of these less obvious fields.

Non-Theatre Jobs reminds the reluctant student who is there only for the credit of the importance of the curriculum. Furthermore, it forces the actors in your class to think about alternative career choices. Remind them about the passionate speeches given in a closing argument at a trial, during political meetings, or at church. Encourage them to think about uncomfortable meetings and interviews and how the confidence gained from performing can make these meetings successful. Help them realize the amount of public speaking and improvisation a teacher does every day. By including some of your own personal insights, students will soon understand that performing can be a boost to many good careers.

You can also assign one or more of the assignments on the *Career Projects* worksheet to reinforce the message in this chapter. These diversions from the daily lesson will give students a break from the norm.

CHAPTER 10 — PLANNING FOR THE FUTURE

NAME _____ PERIOD _____ DATE _____

NON-THEATRE JOBS

There are many jobs that involve the skills you learn in this class but have nothing or very little to do with theatre. Many involve being in front of large groups of people on a daily basis. Some involve being "a character" or being emotional. Others require the ability to move or speak as actors do. In small groups, discuss the following questions and write your answers in the space provided.

1. What are some of the primary skills students learn in this class? Be specific.

_____ _____ _____

_____ _____ _____

_____ _____ _____

2. List as many jobs as you can think of that involve any of these skills.

_____ _____ _____

_____ _____ _____

_____ _____ _____

_____ _____ _____

3. Pick one of the jobs listed above and explain specifically how theatre skills might help someone in this particular career.

4. Can you think of some jobs that do not involve any theatre skills?

5. Write an advertisement for this theatre class explaining the benefits for people interested in all types of careers. Be creative!

219

COMPETITIONS

Many teachers agree that some of the most rewarding experiences for both themselves and their students are the competitions. The best thing about contests is that students will experience the same competitiveness that is at the root of many careers like marketing, advertising, law, finance, sales, and entertainment.

If you have a Thespian or Junior Thespian Troupe, then you'll certainly want to look into the International Thespian Society's competitions. But you don't need to limit your students to just those competitions. For example, some colleges offer yearly playwriting contests as a means of recruiting. This gives you the platform for conducting a playwriting unit and gives your students a great learning opportunity and a chance to win some cash or a scholarship. There are also many public speaking contests in events like prose, poetry, oral interpretation, and others. Drama and speech are very closely related, and many drama teachers use speeches as a way of teaching articulation and diction and to help ease stage fright.

NETWORKING

Networking is a valuable skill to learn as you begin to plan your future. Whether you're working on skills to start a career or enrolling in a college or trade school, the people you meet along the way are good resources to help you move forward. Working to stay in touch with your contacts and developing a solid base of other resources will help you succeed. Keep a contact list of people, businesses, and places that could benefit your future. You never know what kind of contacts you might need in the future, so think broadly and develop a place where you keep information for a broad range of resources.

WHO	WHAT
Accompanists	Accessories
Acting teachers	Alterations
Advertising Agents	Backdrops
Animal trainers	Construction (scenery)
Casting directors	Drapery maintenance
Choral directors	Ear pieces and microphones
Choreographers	Floor maintenance
Combat trainers	General maintenance
Costumers	House maintenance
Dance instructors	Karaoke rentals
Dialect instructor	Lighting maintenance
Gymnasts	Lighting rentals
Hair stylists	Makeup supplies
Headshot photographers	Masks
Headshot printers	Program/poster
Jugglers	Recording (voice over)
Magicians	Scenery
Makeup artists	Scripts
Marketing firms	Sound effects
Mimes	Sound systems
Musicians	Tickets
News agencies	
Painters/artists	**WHERE**
Photographers	Amateur theatres
Printers	Children's theatre
Production companies	Colleges/universities
Public relations companies	Comedy clubs
Public speaking organizations	Convention center
Resume companies	Festivals
Sound companies	Opera production studios
Speech teachers	Professional theatres
Voice teachers	Radio stations
	Theatre camps

NETWORKING AND EVENT PLANNING

Besides acting and communication skills, it is always wise to teach students to network. Those hoping to get jobs or to improve their standings in their careers can use networking to stay in touch with others in their field. As in so many careers, it is not what you know but also who you know that matters.

Show students how to make contacts and develop them to network professionally. Demonstrate by showing them yours. You can explain how you communicate with teachers at other schools, outside coaches, principals, and theatre professionals. Make a list of the resources within a thirty- to fifty-mile radius of your school. These would include acting teachers, colleges with theatre programs, voice teachers, camps, photographers, accompanists, talent agents, dance teachers and choreographers, musical organizations who "rent" themselves out for musicals, and public speaking organizations. Even better are the companies, individuals, and organizations that may be able to employ your young students:

- Playwrights need to see their plays staged before submitting them to publishers.

- Production companies, production studios, marketing firms, radio stations, recording studios for voice-over, public relations companies, and

WORKING AS AN ACTOR

Anyone wishing to work seriously and make a living as an actor needs to know exactly what tools are required for the job. Just as an artist needs canvas and paints, there are many things an actor needs to get the job done.

The first preparation anyone needs for any career is education. For actors, education means training. Many colleges and universities offer degrees in theatre or musical theatre. One benefit of attending college is that one can select both a major and a minor. Many theatre majors select a minor in the career with which they will "pay bills." Also, attending college gives actors excellent training in a working environment. Theatre majors must participate in the shows, the greatest hands-on training available.

Versatile actors train for the broadest of possibilities, covering all of their bases. They take voice and dance lessons to prepare for musical theatre. Even those who have no faith in their own musical and dance abilities should consider this, as they will learn to grasp voice and movement concepts not always taught in acting classes. Many realize that they are better than they thought and are quite trainable. Others simply take the classes hoping to network with other actors, learn their limitations, or have skills to put on their resumes.

There are several types of acting classes as well. There are classes that specifically deal with commercial acting and others that deal with movie acting. Many classes have beginner, intermediate, and advanced levels. Some are taught privately and some in groups. At the college level, acting classes are more specifically focused. Voice and diction classes teach actors proper speaking techniques. Movement classes deal with the actor's body and how it relates to the character, the environment, and the situation. There are even classes that deal specifically with classical acting.

Beyond training, actors must obtain the physical tools of the trade: the professional headshot and resume. A headshot is an 8 x 10" "head and shoulders" photo of the actor with their name along the top or bottom. Some still require this in black and white; others now prefer color. Just like fashion, the trend of these photos changes with each passing year, the specific acting industry being sought, and even geographical location. For example, some jobs seek a glamorous look, while others seek a more relaxed look. It may be wise to consult a few professional actors and photographers in your area before making an investment. The actor will also need a resume that tells as much as possible about the actor without being cumbersome. While an actor gets fifty or a hundred headshots printed at a time, they might only print ten resumes, as they will want to update it after each job. The resume is generally attached back-to-back with the headshot. At auditions, this allows the casting director to either separate the two pieces or easily flip one over to view the other.

Now the actor has the tools necessary to seek an agent. Talent agents are people who work for the actor to get auditions. Once the actor auditions for the job, the agent negotiates the contract and acts as liaison between the actor and the producer or director. The agent works for a percentage of the actor's pay, so it is in their best interest to negotiate the highest possible pay. Some actors never get agents, but because many directors will not hire a non-represented actor, most seek professional representation. A good agent can turn a part-time actor into a full-time professional.

221

news agencies are sometimes responsible for hiring their own actors and models.

- Companies with film apprenticeships can teach young people the ropes, though there is no pay.

- Besides networking, become an expert on the events that may impact your program. You have a blank black-line weekly calendar in Section 1. Make enough copies of this weekly calendar for the entire school year and hole-punch them. Then begin planning. Note all of the school holidays and the exam schedules, assemblies, and so on. This will help you to plan lessons and performances so that disruptions do not affect

them. Most importantly, research events online and through your networking. Jot down plays, contests, speaking engagements, volunteer opportunities at area theatres, auditions, scholarship deadlines, and so on. All of these are excellent ways for students to learn and engage in theatre.

RESUMES AND HEADSHOTS

Resumes and headshots are the actor's calling card. Without impressive credentials, it is unlikely that they will ever get their foot in the door of an audition. As with any other profession, the acting industry has standards, but those standards vary depending on the market. The market may include the geographic region, the type of acting job, and the job's physical requirements.

The sample resume in this section is for an Austin, Texas, actor seeking commercial and film work. That is why commercials are listed first. Stage actors would list their stage experience first. Do not be discouraged if you cannot write something for every category. Many actors spend years building their resumes. Some wonderful books and online resources are available to help you format yours so that it looks professional and fits your market. There are also many professionals who create resumes for a living. While they charge for this service, the results are worth the investment, especially if you hire someone with experience formatting entertainment resumes.

Name—Use the name you want people to remember. For example, if you are Jonathan Smith but you only go by John Smith, then use the latter name. Many actors use their nicknames, and some choose stage names. While stage names are fun, they are becoming less common. The most recent trend is wholesome and natural, and that even applies to one's name. Names that sound pretend have no real theatrical appeal.

Some actors will use easy versions of difficult names. For example, Mikaela Ricardini might choose to go by Miki Richards, simply because it is easier for casting directors to pronounce. Androgynous names help actors get extra work if they can easily pull off gender non-specific roles. Pricilla might choose to go by Presley, or Coby James might go by CJ. And names with a strong cultural tilt might not work as well as culturally generic ones. One young actor was getting called to auditions for Russian characters because of her Russian name. But she wasn't being hired because she didn't look the part and couldn't speak the language or even fake the accent. She experimented with a more generic name, and suddenly, she was being called for a larger variety of auditions, and she began booking roles.

Actors should never feel pressured to adopt stage names. It's a personal choice, and it should be one you consider carefully. If you choose to use a name other than your own, check with your bank before your first paying job to determine if you need to do anything special to deposit checks!

Address, Phone, and Email—If you do not have an agent, you will use your own contact information on all printed and electronic materials. After securing an agent, you will use your name but your agent's contact information on your headshot and resume.

Hair and Eyes—Generally you will include some information about your appearance, such as hair and eye color. You may also need to include sizes or measurements, height and weight, and any unusual physical characteristics of particular interest, such as "professional bodybuilder." However, until you have an agent and for safety reasons, include only your hair and eye color.

Training, Special Skills, and Professional Organizations—List each class and workshop individually. If the class is school-related, do not include the name of the school until the college level, but always include the teachers' names. Training is generally considered as important as experience and is easy to get. Special skills are those things you can do that many others cannot, such as sports (be specific) and tricks. They may include ballroom dancing, volleyball, martial arts, juggling, and speaking Japanese. Professional organizations may include any organization related to your particular fields of interest as they are relevant to your career. For example, Screen Actors Guild is certainly worthy of being included in your resume, but chess club is not.

RESUMES AND HEADSHOTS

One of the most beneficial and enjoyable things you will do with your students, especially those in your advanced classes, is developing their resume and headshot. In this chapter you will find a *Resume Form*, ideas for taking students' photos for headshots, and a sample resume and headshot. Almost everyone will need a resume at one time or another regardless of their career choice. While the resume template in this book is for actors, it will give each student the opportunity to learn to format a professional-looking self-marketing tool. Furthermore, the finished product will give you more insight into your students and give you everything you need for future show programs!

Find out which of your students would like to apply for acting jobs outside of school at the types of companies and organizations listed on page 220 of the student workbook. They will need several copies of both their headshot and resume, either stapled or printed back-to-back. Stapling, while it may look messier, is often preferred because many of the recipients separate them into two stacks. Your students will need to research the trends for your area, which can vary from city to city, and also the specific requirements of the job, the director, and so on. It is a lot to track, but the actor who knows that a certain director prefers large print or color headshots has an advantage over the actor who does not.

Headshots are a bit more difficult to manufacture. You may go to a professional headshot photographer. While this is the most expensive option, it's likely to be the best if you are in a competitive market. One way to reduce the cost is to hire a professional who will give you a better rate by coming to the school and taking a dozen pictures of each serious acting student.

Another budget-friendly option is to find a friend who is a good photographer and create homemade headshots. Find an indoor location with good lighting and a solid background and pose naturally in portrait mode. Do basic editing to enhance the quality of the photo; however, do not change the person in the photo. Do not use filters, and do not try to make the person look better, thinner, younger, or with a clearer complexion. The only exception would be to erase something temporary, like a bruise, blemish, or hair out of place. But making someone with severe acne look like they have a clear complexion is unacceptable because it is not the truth. Now, add your name to the top or bottom so that it is easy to read. Keep the font simple. A busy font will frustrate casting directors and agents!

The best way for students to get decent-looking headshots is to have a headshot photographer take professional pictures in a natural style. If they are not a headshot photographer, they need to be told that the pictures cannot be copyright protected. Otherwise, getting copies will be difficult, and students need to be able to make unlimited copies in both color and black and white.

The sample headshot in this chapter is for a specific market. This actor will be considered for jobs in commercial, film, and industrial work in the Dallas area. In other markets she might need a more glamorous or athletic look, but for the area in which she lives and works, her picture is perfect.

Note that the photo is from the shoulders up, and she is looking straight at the camera. She has a nice, natural, happy smile that shows her teeth. There is no distracting background, and her clothing is a solid color, not a print. When you look at the picture, you notice only the actor and what she can bring to a job, as far as looks and personality are concerned.

A casting director can look at both the headshot and resume and know immediately if the actor is a candidate for the job. That is what these tools do; they help actors to get their foot in the door of the audition.

INTRODUCTION TO THEATRE ARTS I

RESUME FORM

Name: _____

Address: _____

Phone: _____ Email: _____

Hair color: _____ Eye Color: _____

COMMERCIALS

Role	Title or Product	Product/Production Company

FILM/TELEVISION

Role	Title	Production Company/Director

PLAYS

Role	Title	Theatre or Company

MUSICALS

Role	Title	Theatre or Company

MISCELLANEOUS EXPERIENCE

Role or Job	Event Title	Company

TRAINING

_____

SPECIAL SKILLS

_____

PROFESSIONAL ORGANIZATIONS

_____

NOTES: _____

_____

_____

_____

_____

_____

_____

_____

CHAPTER 10 — PLANNING FOR THE FUTURE

SAMPLE HEADSHOT

A sample headshot for a female commercial actor in the 14-22 year age range in Dallas.

Rachel DeRouen

Photo credit: Arthur Bryan Marroquin, ABM Photography.

225

You may want to compile your class's headshots and resumes in a packet to send to an area agent. Explain that you are looking for a professional critique of the materials. Invite a classroom visit from the agent or one of their associates. Some might be interested in this free marketing opportunity for them as long as it is not during their busy season.

INTRODUCTION TO THEATRE ARTS I

SAMPLE FICTIONAL RESUME

Rachel DeRouen
Studio Talent, Inc.
123 Main • Dallas, Texas 75555
972-555-1234
Studiotalent@fiction.com
Blue eyes • Blonde hair

COMMERCIALS

Principal non-speaking	Visionmart	PLQ & Associates
Student	Republican Promotional	GH Productions
Principal speaking	Burger Hut	TRU Productions

FILM/TELEVISION

Witness	Police Academy Instructional	Bradore College Police Association
Extra/Diner	*Case of the Missing Piano*	Robert Boyce, director
Extra/Cheerleader	*The Special Game*	Clueless Productions
Debbie Charles	*A Walk in the Rain*	Gifford Productions

THEATRE

Stella Kowalski	*A Streetcar Named Desire*	Lake Bend High School
Doreen	*Tartuffe*	Bradore College Junior Camp
Tansy	*The Nerd*	Theatre Off the Wall
Florence Unger	*The Odd Couple, Female Version*	Lakeside Teens
Katherine	*Taming of the Shrew*	Spotlight Productions

MUSICALS

Auntie Mame	*Mame*	Spotlight Productions
Assistant Director	*Annie Get Your Gun*	Spotlight Productions
Wicked Witch	*The Wizard of Oz*	Bradore College Junior Camp

MISCELLANEOUS EXPERIENCE
Three years of experience singing telegrams, Blue Bunny Singers
Two seasons as "Genie," State Fair
One season as "ballerina," Children's Tent, State Fair

TRAINING
In second year of Associate of Fine Arts degree program, Bradore College, acting scholarship. Receiving specialized training in acting (Jim Caldwell) and stage makeup (Brodie Ballard).
Voice-over training by QZP Productions (Hugh Lory and Betty Simmons).
Seven years ballet with Dallas Children's Ballet and Dallas Choral Ballet.

SPECIAL SKILLS
Voice-over, various dialects/accents, fluent in French and Spanish, experienced ballet dancer, can juggle and do illusions, softball, ice hockey, karate, dirt bike riding, various forms of stunt work. Member SAG, AFTRA, Actors Equity.

226

GUEST SPEAKERS

Another way to reach both the future actors and the non-actors in your group is to bring in some non-traditional guest speakers. Parents are excellent choices, as students will instantly relate to them. Prepare a list of questions in advance, and ask several parents to come in for twenty-minute time slots throughout the day. Classes can ask them how acting and public speaking may have helped them to get where they are and how they use these skills in their day-to-day activities. Again, students become more eager learners when they earnestly believe that the activities and skills have real-life importance.

Sample questions for guest speakers may include:

- What kind of speech and theatre classes did you take in middle school, high school, and college?

- In what speech and drama competitions did you participate?

- As an adult, how do you find yourself using the skills in your day-to-day activities? What about at work?

- What goes through your mind when you deal with someone at work who is a confident and effective speaker?

- Have you encountered incompetent speakers? How did that affect job performance and your impression of the worker's abilities?

CAREER PROJECTS

Project 1: Interview

Select someone who is either in the field of theatre or uses theatre skills on the job. Ask them as many questions as you like, but for this project, you must ask at least ten theatre-related questions. Prepare your questions before you go in for the interview and be as professional as possible. You may record the interview and present it to the class or write the results in essay form.

Project 2: Research Paper

Select one of the careers mentioned in this section and research it. Write a research paper on your findings as the career relates to theatre.

Project 3: Guest Speaker

Arrange a guest speaker for the class for a twenty-minute question-and-answer session about their career and how it either relates to theatre or uses theatre skills. Be sure to prepare a complimentary introduction of your guest to the class. Have the class prepare questions in advance, and make sure that the speaking engagement is cleared through both your teacher and the school first.

Project 4: Website Poster

Create a poster advertising ten websites that would be helpful to students who may be trying to find jobs in theatre or alternative acting careers. Be neat and creative, and make sure everything is visible. Use caution about the appropriateness of the websites you advertise.

227

- Other than your job and day-to-day life, do you still participate in public speaking or theatre? Explain.

- What advice would you have for a young person who is interested in either theatre or public speaking as a career?

- What would you say to someone who thinks this class is not important for their career of choice?

Ask your students for their questions too, especially as they relate to the individual speakers. It is polite to provide guest speakers with a list of questions in advance, and students should never appear confrontational in their line of questioning. It is also polite to present guest speakers with a token of appreciation upon their departure and to follow up with a thank-you note from a class representative in the week to follow.

If getting guest speakers from outside of school proves too difficult, consider your in-school resources. Use a short questionnaire to find out which adults on your campus were in theatre, who may have studied theatre in college, and who is still active in some form of the art. Even if they do not volunteer to speak to your classes, you may find that you have a valuable theatre resource right under your nose. Forge a bond with this person. In the event of an emergency, they might be able to help with rehearsals, shows, or public relations.

INTRODUCTION TO THEATRE ARTS I

NAME _____ PERIOD _____ DATE _____

YOUR FUTURE IN THEATRE CROSSWORD PUZZLE

Complete the crossword puzzle about theatre as a part of your future. The answers to the clues come from the worksheets in this section. Eliminate spaces, hyphens, and apostrophes from your puzzle answers.

ACROSS

1. The group of people responsible for music, microphones, and sound effects during a show
4. The 8 x 10" photo of the actor
7. The person who takes care of the show from backstage
9. Stagehands who move scenery during a show
10. The stage crew member who is responsible for props
12. The light _____ operator runs lights during the show
14. The person who is in charge of the "artistry" of the lights
15. Takes the actors' places for dangerous or difficult tasks

DOWN

2. Creates the dance routines for a musical or dance
3. _____ may be created by a seamstress or rented
5. In most high schools, students apply their own _____ rather than hiring an artist
6. The _____ manager takes care of the audience's needs
8. The first thing an actor must obtain before starting a career
11. The document that "sells" the actor, explaining education, experience, and skills
13. The person who gets the professional actor auditions and negotiates contracts

YOUR FUTURE IN THEATRE CROSSWORD KEY

ACROSS	DOWN
1. Soundcrew	2. Choreographer
4. Headshot	3. Costumes
7. Stage manager	5. Makeup
9. Grips	6. House
10. Props manager	8. Training
12. Board	11. Resume
14. Designer	13. Agent
15. Stuntman	

BIBLIOGRAPHY

Blanchard, Laura V. and Carolyn Schriber. *ORB: The Online Reference Book for Medieval Studies*. Rhodes College and Western Michigan University. 1995-2002. Kalamazoo, Michigan.

Brater, Enoch and Phyllis Hartnoll. *The Theatre: A Concise History*. Third Edition. Thames and Hudson. 1998. London, Great Britain.

Carr, Dr. Karen E. *History for Kids*. Portland State University. 2002, 2003. Portland, Oregon.

Dollinger, André. *Introduction to the History and Culture of Pharaonic Egypt*. www.reshafim.org.il. 2000.

Gascoigne, Bamber. *History of Theatre*. HistoryWorld. From 2001, ongoing. http://www.historyworld.net

Pettengill, R. *Theatre Art in Action*. Lisa Abel (editor). NTC/Contemporary Publishing Company. 2001. Chicago, Illinois.

Schanker, Harry H. and Katharine Anne Ommanney. *The Stage and the School*. Eighth Edition. Glencoe/MacMillan McGraw Hill. 1998. New York, New York.

Theatre History.com. http://www.theatrehistory.com. 2002. Burlington, Massachusetts.

Van Heldon, Albert. *Galileo Timeline*. Rice University. 1995. Houston, Texas.

ABOUT THE AUTHOR

Suzi Zimmerman was the youngest of three children and, admittedly, a bit of a troublemaker. Her siblings were good at sports and music, but she seemed to be flailing. She knew she was creative and loved to perform, but her community focused mainly on sports and music. Those who lacked a place tended to become bored, which led to unacceptable behavior.

She finally discovered theatre, but only because it was offered at the high school level. It was then that she vowed to fight for more accessible performance opportunities for all levels. After college, she founded a local theatre troupe, which eventually became a community theatre, fulfilling her dream of bringing performance opportunities to all. After twenty years in public education, she is now a full-time writer, artist, and businessperson.

Zimmerman has acted professionally in film and on the stage. She is the spokesperson for and director of New Hope Foundation, a nonprofit in northern Texas working to improve the lives of underprivileged families. She is married with five children, two of whom are successful in the film industry.